REVITALIZATION IN ASIA

REVITALIZATION IN ASIA

ADAPTIVE REUSE in MACAO, MUMBAI, and PENANG

Edited by Lavina Ahuja and Lynne D. DiStefano

Hong Kong University Press
The University of Hong Kong
Pok Fu Lam Road
Hong Kong
https://hkupress.hku.hk

ISBN 978-988-8842-97-1 (*Paperback*)

British Library Cataloguing-in-Publication Data
A catalogue record for this book is available from the British Library.

Digitally printed

This book is dedicated to the legacy of the Architectural Conservation Programmes (ACP) at The University of Hong Kong (2000–2022), which brought the book's authors together and contributed to the conservation movement in Asia.

Contents

Acknowledgments

Continued thanks to Ester van Steekelenburg (director, Urban Discovery) for first suggesting the topic some ten years ago. *Asian Revitalization: Adaptive Reuse in Hong Kong, Shanghai, and Singapore* was the result, sparking the interest of many, pushing us to pursue this book.

We express our deep appreciation to the individuals who contributed to this publication through essays, timelines, case studies, photographs, and drawings. We thank each of you for your dedication to the project and for responding to our innumerable comments and questions with patience and understanding. Our many thanks to the Faculty of Architecture at The University of Hong Kong for its financial support and to the Division of Architectural Conservation Programmes (ACP) for its assistance and encouragement. With special thanks to Shams Sharif Imon and Lee Hoyin, who provided important information about adaptive reuse initiatives in Macao, and to Dorothy Lau, who provided comprehensive indexes for both books—*Asian Revitalization* and *Revitalization in Asia*. And, of course, we must thank the staff at Hong Kong University Press.

Through the journey of writing this book, the world has faced many hardships—the COVID-19 pandemic being the most devastating. We hope that these events have served as wake-up calls emphasizing that it is no longer an option but a necessity to make choices that protect and strengthen our environment. The theme of sustainability followed through from *Asian Revitalization* to this book is a continuing reminder that every individual action contributes to our common future. It is our sincere hope that this book will continue to help promote adaptive reuse as one of the means to meet the United Nations' Sustainable Development Goals.

Finally, we express heartfelt appreciation to our families for their ongoing support throughout this project.

Lavina Ahuja and Lynne D. DiStefano
January 2024

Contributors

Lavina Ahuja

Author and Editor

Lavina was trained in architecture and cultural heritage conservation at Mumbai University and The University of Hong Kong (HKU), respectively. She has been a lecturer for the Division of Architectural Conservation Programmes, Faculty of Architecture, The University of Hong Kong. She has collaborated with organizations such as UNESCO, ICOMOS, and HKICON to work on initiatives related to cultural heritage conservation and sustainable development, including research and publications. She is a registered architect with the Council of Architecture, India, an individual member of the Indian National Committee of the International Council on Monuments and Sites (ICOMOS India), and a professional member of the Hong Kong Institute of Architectural Conservationists (HKICON).

Adelina Chan

Author

Adelina Chan is an assistant lecturer in the Faculty of Architecture, The University of Hong Kong. She has a BA (Architecture) from the University of California, Berkeley and an AA Diploma from the Architectural Association School of Architecture. After practicing in architectural firms in San Francisco and Hong Kong, she returned to university, earning an MSc (Conservation) from The University of Hong Kong. Her current research is chronologizing material palettes of buildings in Macao.

Hui Lai Chick, Katie

Author

Katie is the assistant director of the Centre for Civil Society and Governance at The University of Hong Kong. Her academic expertise covers both cultural and nature conservation. She has over eighteen years of experience in cultural landscape management and has been the person in charge of Lai Chi Wo revitalization projects since 2014. She received an MSc (Conservation) from The University of Hong Kong.

Lynne D. DiStefano

Author and Editor

Lynne DiStefano, who holds a PhD from the University of Pennsylvania, is a founder and past director of the first graduate program in architectural conservation at The University of Hong Kong. She serves currently as an adjunct professor in the Department of Real Estate and Construction. She is also a faculty associate at Willowbank School of Restoration Arts (Canada) and was previously an associate professor at Brescia University College, Western University (Canada), as well as chief curator at Museum London (Canada).

Lynne has been involved in activities related to World Heritage. Since 2006, she has been appointed by the International Council on Monuments and Sites (ICOMOS) as a technical evaluator for nominated World Heritage Sites in China, Japan, and South Korea, as well as an expert for reactive monitoring missions in China, Laos, and the Philippines. She has authored and coauthored a number of publications and served as a consultant to local and regional governments, especially in Asia. She is a member of ICOMOS Canada.

Rupali Gupte

Author

Rupali is an architect, urbanist, and an artist based in Mumbai. She is one of the founding members of the School of Environment and Architecture (sea.edu.in) and a professor at the institute. She is a partner at the Bard Studio, Mumbai (bardstudio.in), and she is one of the cofounders of the urban research network CRIT. She has studied architecture (BArch, Mumbai University) and urban design (MArch, Cornell University), and recently she was a senior research fellow at the University of Brighton.

Rupali's work includes research on South Asian architecture and urbanism with a focus on urban culture, urban form, housing, tactical practices, and gender and space. It crosses disciplinary boundaries and takes different forms—drawings, mixed-media works, storytelling, spatial interventions, teaching, walks, and writing. Her works have been shown at several places including the 56th Venice Biennale, X Sao Paulo Biennale of Architecture, 1st Seoul Biennale of Architecture and Urbanism, MACBA, Barcelona, MAAT Museum, Lisbon, Project 88, Devi Art Foundation, and Mumbai Art Room, among others.

Sharif Shams Imon

Author

Imon holds a PhD in urban conservation from The University of Hong Kong. He specializes in heritage management and heritage tourism. His teaching, research, and professional experience spans more than twenty-six years, including extensive consultancy work for international organizations, United Nations bodies, and governments across sixteen countries. He has also authored over forty articles on topics such as heritage interpretation, managing historic cities, sustainable tourism, and more. He taught in the Cultural and Heritage Management program at the Macao Institute for Tourism Studies for over seventeen years. Currently, he is a professor in the Department of Architecture, North South University, Bangladesh. He is also the president of ICOMOS Bangladesh.

Jennifer Lang

Author

Jennifer holds a PhD in architectural conservation from The University of Hong Kong. She is an architectural historian and a conservationist with over thirty years of combined professional and academic experience in conservation and cultural heritage in Asia and the United States, including academia, built heritage conservation, environmental review, and sustainable development. From 2017 to 2022, she was an adjunct associate professor and the director of the MSc (Conservation) at The University of Hong Kong, where she led the graduate program in architectural conservation with an emphasis on values-based conservation, management, and sustainability. She was the president of the Hong Kong Institute of Architectural Conservationists (HKICON) from 2017 to 2019.

Jennifer is a member of the United States National Committee of the International Council on Monuments and Sites (ICOMOS US), a member of the ICOMOS International Scientific Committee for Twentieth Century Heritage (ISC20), a member of Docomomo in the United States, and a board member of Docomomo New England. Currently, she is a senior architectural historian with Tetra Tech carrying out environmental review for green energy projects throughout the United States.

Hoyin Lee

Author

Hoyin, who holds a PhD from The University of Hong Kong (HKU), cofounded the postgraduate and undergraduate programs in architectural conservation at HKU. In 2015, he established the Division of Architectural Conservation Programmes (ACP) in the Faculty of Architecture at HKU and became the founding head of the division. Before joining HKU in 2000, he was an associate director of an architectural practice and was involved in architectural projects in Hong Kong, Indonesia, mainland China, and Singapore.

As a well-published academic and an experienced practitioner in built heritage conservation, Hoyin has been appointed by government agencies in Hong Kong, mainland China, and overseas as an expert adviser or a consultant for conservation projects and the designation and monitoring of UNESCO World Heritage Sites. He has been appointed to a number of heritage conservation statutory boards and committees, including the Hong Kong government's Antiquities Advisory Board, Tai Kwun Advisory Committee, Tai Kwun Heritage Working Group (as chairman), and the Urban Renewal Authority Board of Directors (as a nonexecutive director).

Laurence Loh

Author

Laurence, who holds an AA Diploma from the Architectural Association School of Architecture, is an adjunct professor at The University of Hong Kong. He has been conserving and sustaining cultural heritage through management and design for the past thirty-five years. His practice, Arkitek LLA Sdn. Bhd., consistently creates conservation best-practice exemplars through a process of cultural mapping, consensus building, and design ideation. He positions heritage conservation as a critical activity for maintaining the spirit of place, the preservation of knowledge, and the continuity of artistic expressions. He is a recipient of the 2019 PAM Gold Medal Award for his lifelong contribution to the advancement of architecture in Malaysia as well as several UNESCO Asia-Pacific Awards for Cultural Heritage Conservation.

Laurence has lectured about cultural heritage management in the first Architectural Conservation Programme (ACP) at The University of Hong Kong and has lectured in the Getty Conservation Institute Urban Conservation Planning Course for ASEAN countries. He collaborates with UNESCO to develop and deepen its outreach through new programs and with the World Heritage Center through ICOMOS to undertake site evaluation missions and technical reviews.

He is a director of ThinkCity, a social purpose organization driven by impact that promotes cross-fertilization of ideas and knowledge sharing to deliver sustainable urban solutions developed through an iterative data-driven visioning approach to city-making. He is presently engaged in promoting culture-based local economic development programs.

Lin Lee Loh-Lim

Author

Lin Lee holds an MPhil from the London School of Economics and was a Duncan Sandys–PATA scholarship awardee with the Conservation Foundation of Britain and the University of York. She has been a senior council member of the Penang Heritage Trust since 1990, a consultant for UNESCO Beijing for the World Heritage Site of Mount Lushan in Jiangxi Province, and a trainer for the UNESCO Certification Programme for Cultural Heritage Guides. Lin Lee is co-conservator of Cheong Fatt Tze (Blue Mansion), which received the Most Excellent Award at the 2000 UNESCO Asia-Pacific Awards for Cultural Heritage Conservation, and she is the author of the associated book *The Blue Mansion*.

Lin Lee is a consultant for the interpretation of cultural heritage sites, and she has been the convenor of Penang Heritage Trust projects, particularly those related to Intangible Cultural Heritage, such as the Living Heritage Treasures Awards of Penang and the Penang Apprenticeship Programme for Artisans. She was also the initiator and prime mover of the Historic Street Names Blue Plaques in the George Town World Heritage Site and the author of the book by the same name.

Fergus T. Maclaren

Author

Fergus holds a master of environmental design from the University of Calgary and is the president emeritus of the ICOMOS International Cultural Tourism Committee. He is a Canadian sustainable tourism and cultural heritage management professional with twenty-five years of experience in Africa, Asia, Europe, and North America, with much of his current professional focus involving tourism to World Heritage Sites and the implementation of the 2030 United Nations' Sustainable Development Goals.

Fergus has a background in tourism planning, destination management, and development expertise. His professional experience includes coordinating international meetings and input as the director of the UN-funded International Year of Ecotourism (IYE), teaching sustainable tourism at Canada's McGill University, and lecturing on the subject at postsecondary institutions internationally. He currently works in expert and professional capacities for the Economic Innovation Institute for Africa, the Heritage and Cultural Society for Africa, the Organization of World Heritage Cities, UNESCO, UNWTO, and the World Monuments Fund. He also has his own private consulting firm, MAC-DUFF Tourism | Heritage | Planning.

Bee Eu Tan

Author

Bee Eu has twenty years of architectural experience and a diversified portfolio, which includes design, master planning, and project management. After working for a number of firms, she founded BETA Architects to pursue her belief in honest architecture. She believes good architecture is possible regardless of budget, complexity, and scale. In 2019, her firm became the youngest firm to win the PAM Gold Medal. In 2021, her work for the Penang Harmony Centre won the Edge-PAM Green Excellence Award for exemplary excellence in Passive Design Strategies within a small budget.

In 2019, BETA Architects was featured in *Architecture Malaysia* as an emerging practice in Malaysia. In December 2021, Bee Eu was recognized as one of *Tatler Asia*'s most influential people shaping Asia. She is the current Penang organizer of Pecha Kucha Penang, a global network event originating in Tokyo.

Shih Thoe Tan

Author

Shih Thoe graduated from Monash University, Melbourne, in industrial engineering and returned to Penang in 1995. He worked as an engineer in one of the multinational companies in the early years and subsequently joined the family business dealing in industrial materials supply. He is one of the co-owners tasked with managing the Hin Company bus depot that was repurposed into a creative arts space in Penang in 2013. Hin Bus Depot has since been supporting progressive and upcoming artists, artworks, events, and art forms of all kinds. In 2017, it was named one of the ten best contemporary art spaces in Southeast Asia by *The Guardian*, and recently it won the Placemaker awards ASEAN 2021 in the category Best Placemaker: Private Organisation (Private-Public Space).

Montira Horayangura Unakul

Author

Montira is a culture programme officer at UNESCO Bangkok. She has managed various UNESCO programs within the Asia-Pacific region related to the safeguarding and sustainable development of cultural heritage, with a focus on World Heritage. She has developed capacity-building programs such as reviving traditional knowledge for conserving built heritage, sustainable heritage tourism, and collections management. She has a BA in economics and East Asian studies from Harvard University, MCP and MArch from the University of California, Berkeley in architecture and in city planning, and a PhD in urban planning from Chulalongkorn University.

Elizabeth Vines

Author

Elizabeth, an adjunct professor at The University of Hong Kong (HKU), is an award-winning conservation architect and author. She is a past president of Australia ICOMOS, visiting professor at HKU, adjunct professor at Deakin University, Melbourne, and partner in the Adelaide-based firm McDougall & Vines. She studied architecture at Melbourne University and Carleton University, Ottawa, Canada. She has built up extensive experience in conservation architecture and heritage town rejuvenation throughout Australia and the Asia-Pacific. She consults to a wide range of agencies throughout the region, including the European Union, UNESCO, and the World Bank. Her recent role as a core teacher in the 2021 Getty Conservation Institute/ThinkCity (Malaysia) "Old Cities New Challenges" has continued her decade-long teaching role with this organization. She is committed to the practical reuse, improvement, and rejuvenation of historic towns and city centers and is a passionate and vocal advocate for heritage conservation issues.

ESSAYS

Cultural Heritage | Revitalization | Sustainability

Introduction

Lynne D. DiStefano and Lavina Ahuja

Background

This book is a continuation of *Asian Revitalization: Adaptive Reuse in Hong Kong, Shanghai, and Singapore* (hereon *Asian Revitalization*), published in January 2021 by Hong Kong University Press. *Asian Revitalization* filled a research gap by providing an overview of adaptive reuse in three urban centers in Asia through city-specific essays, timelines, and a range of case studies based on five shared building typologies (industrial, institutional, military, mixed use, and residential). Centers were chosen based on access to experts who understood adaptive reuse within the places. The introduction offered a detailed understanding of the term "adaptive reuse." Opening essays considered adaptive reuse as a heritage conservation approach, touching on dimensions of sustainability ranging from understanding the economic impact of adaptive reuse to recognizing heritage as a driver for sustainable development. City-specific essays considered adaptive reuse within the local context of heritage conservation and urban planning; detailed case studies looked at aspects of sustainability, especially economic sustainability. Concluding comments argued for more research on the topic—and more Asian examples. *Revitalization in Asia: Adaptive Reuse in Macao, Mumbai, and Penang* (hereon *Revitalization in Asia*) is a response to this challenge.

Revitalization in Asia

Urban Centers

Envisioned as a continuation of *Asian Revitalization*, this book considers the shared and unique aspects of adaptive reuse in Asia through the lens of three "new" urban centers, which are also World Heritage Sites—Macao, Mumbai, and Penang. The centers are chosen for their distinctive histories of conservation and adaptive reuse, both within their countries (Macao SAR, India, and Malaysia) and within Asia. They are also chosen based on access to experts with firsthand knowledge of adaptive reuse within these places. Interestingly, these three centers have a commonality: a shared colonial past.

Following the format of *Asian Revitalization*, a series of essays on aspects of sustainability complement center-specific essays and timelines that provide a heritage conservation and urban planning framework for adaptive reuse in each place. For the case studies, even though the building typology approach worked well for *Asian Revitalization*, the editors decided it was instructive to show the evolution of conservation (specifically, adaptive reuse) practice in this book. Accordingly, case studies were selected for each urban center that are not only impactful projects within themselves but also provide an implicit narrative of development in adaptive reuse practice for each center when read as a series. The selection of case study projects is also based on a vision to bring variety and diversity in terms of accessibility (public/private), heritage recognition (listed or not listed), scale of project (building size as well as funding available), user profile (government/official use as well as community use), and so forth. The rationale for selection is mentioned in the opening few sentences for each case study.

There is much to learn from the adaptive reuse journeys of these three centers, which set the context for understanding the case study projects that have been recognized locally (and some regionally) as exemplars of best practice in conservation.

Sustainability

The past few decades have seen a wider understanding of cultural heritage. Recognition has expanded from a narrow focus on archaeological sites and buildings/structures per se to acknowledging the inextricable linkage of places to their intangible attributes and the interconnectedness of culture and nature, the nature-culture link. Also, there has been an expansion of stakeholders; an increasing number of "actors" are taking ownership of their cultural heritage, thus devolving the responsibility from the hands of government or "experts" to the community and civil society.

In this book, the interrelationship of cultural heritage conservation and sustainable development is further explored and aligned to the three dimensions (pillars) of sustainability as well as the United Nations' Sustainable Development Goals (SDGs) as benchmarks for sustainability initiatives. As mentioned in *Asia Conserved Volume III*,

> Heritage is no longer viewed as the preserve of experts focusing solely on technical conservation matters, or as a real estate proposition to add value to a historic property. Rather, heritage is increasingly seen as an integral pillar for sustainable development in all its dimensions, and therefore deeply relevant to everyone. Indeed, the 2030 Agenda for Sustainable Development recognizes heritage, both cultural and natural, as a fundamental part of the global development agenda.[1]

With the increased awareness of the importance of sustainability, there is also more understanding of the underlying role of culture *as an enabler* for implementation of the SDGs. Although heritage considerations play a role in adaptive reuse, this should be seen as an added incentive for reuse. So-called ordinary or nondescript buildings and structures are as important as those deemed heritage in the context of sustainability. In fact, one of the Mumbai case studies speaks explicitly to this.

Revitalization in Asia posits adaptive reuse as a conservation approach that can help achieve the SDGs and contribute to broader well-being—economically, environmentally, and socially, the three dimensions or pillars of sustainability. It recognizes that tenable actions can ensure sustainability for a heritage place and, in turn, can generate positive impacts beyond site boundaries in the long term. It can, for example, create economic opportunities that adapt to local realities and needs,

1. UNESCO, *Asia Conserved Volume III: Lessons Learned from the UNESCO Asia-Pacific Awards for Cultural Heritage Conservation (2010–2014)*, ed. William Chapman (Bangkok: UNESCO, 2019), 324.

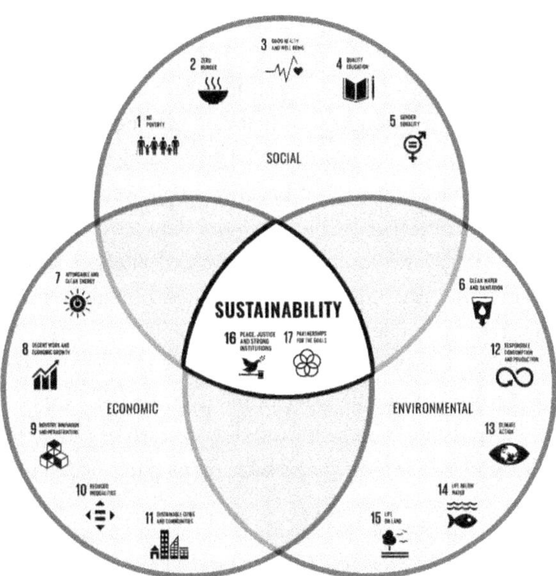

Figure 1.1: The diagram shows the interrelationship of the three dimensions of sustainability and the seventeen SDGs, illustrating the commonalities between individual goals and the economic, environmental, and social dimensions. However, and more important, the seventeen SDGs are theoretically applicable to all dimensions of sustainability. (Source: Drawn by Lavina Ahuja based on icons of the United Nations' SDGs.)

contribute to strengthening the nature-culture link, and help establish a resilient community network.

Revitalization in Asia discusses the adaptive reuse of existing buildings, structures, and spaces demonstrating how such projects—at either the micro or macro level—can exhibit the pillars of sustainability and meet multiple SDGs. The end result, when successful, transforms a physical asset into a viable community asset or, when at the macro level, a viable community. The following quotation from Carl Elefante's article "The Greenest Building Is . . . One that Is Already Built" is especially relevant in this context:

> Taking into account the massive investment of materials and energy in existing buildings, it is both obvious and profound that extending the useful service life of the building stock is common sense, good business, and sound resource management.[2]

Adaptive Reuse

The meaning of adaptive reuse can be as simple as identifying a new use or reverting to an original use for a building or structure (not a façade!) that is vacant or as complex as finding new uses for buildings, structures, and spaces within an entire community. Professionals argue as to what constitutes an appropriate new use. Should it be close to the original use, or is it a straightforward matter of linking a vacant or underused building, structure, or space with a new use? This is a "matchmaking" exercise that has existed for centuries but has become more formalized and seen as part of a larger discourse—revitalization and ultimately sustainability. But no matter how formal or informal, physical interventions and changes in use can be subtle, and arguably, such subtlety, especially at the community level, can contribute to sustainability. (*Asian Revitalization* explores the meaning of adaptive reuse in greater detail and provides references to relevant conservation documents.)

2. Carl Elefante, "The Greenest Building Is . . . One that Is Already Built," *Forum Journal: The Journal of the National Trust for Historic Preservation* 21, no. 4 (Summer 2007): 32.

A Dilemma

One of the dilemmas faced in adapted reuse is how to evaluate the success of a project in terms of sustainability. Economic sustainability may be the easiest to determine, although a simple "bottom line" approach can be misleading—that is, critical products or services may have been eliminated to produce a balanced budget. Environmental sustainability is harder to measure, although more data are available now to "defend" the retention of buildings and structures (embodied energy) instead of replacing them. Social sustainability is complex and sometimes difficult to measure. What are the indicators? Are there adequate baseline data?

A note of caution. "Checklists" for sustainability actions can be misleading or seductive. Although the Sustainable Development Goals (SDGs) have performance targets and a range of indicators, to be useful, they need to be modified to reflect local capabilities—a daunting but important task for many parts of Asia.

Book Format

Essays

Revitalization in Asia is organized into two sections. The first section features six essays that focus on the relationship between cultural heritage, including the nature-culture link, and sustainable development and the implementation of the Sustainable Development Goals (SDGs) in adaptive reuse projects. They offer new insight and understanding about what sustainability means and how it is (and can be) applied in the field of conservation, both natural and cultural.

The first essay, "Patrick Geddes: The Conservative Surgeon" by Ken Nicolson, considers the work of Patrick Geddes, an early city planner, who coined the expression "destructive impatience" to describe the needless demolition of structurally sound buildings. He was an advocate of sustainability well before the post–World War II "rush" to acknowledge the need for sustainable actions. Montira Unakul's essay, "Heritage, Urban Revitalization, and a New Sustainability Mindset," which follows that of Nicolson, leads the reader through international sustainability documents and initiatives, some of which echo Geddes's early work and provide a framework for revitalization in general and adaptive reuse in particular.

In the third essay, "Adaptive Reuse from an Urban Planning Perspective," Elizabeth Vines looks at the environmental dimension of sustainability from an architectural and urban planning perspective. Katie H. L. Chick, in the fourth essay, "Transforming a Dilapidated Rural Village into a Nature-Culture Interface for Social-Ecological Sustainability: Lai Chi Wo, Hong Kong," focuses on the social dimension using an important nature-culture example, while Sharif Shams Imon, in the fifth essay, "Nizamuddin Urban Renewal Initiative: Socio-economic Sustainability through Conservation," considers all three dimensions in a standard-setting example.

Last, Fergus T. Maclaren, in "Creating Sustainable Urban Visitor Economies: Adaptive Reuse of Asian Cultural Heritage Places for Tourism," considers tourism from the lens of socioeconomic sustainability and its impact on communities and built heritage resources, especially those adapted for tourism purposes. For readers with a specific interest in the economic dimension, Donovan Rypkema's essay, "Measuring the Impacts: Making a Case for the Adaptive Reuse of Heritage Buildings," in *Asian Revitalization* offers a succinct analysis of the financial benefits of adaptive reuse.

Urban Center Essays, Timelines, and Case Studies

The second section includes an essay, timeline, and case studies for each of the three urban centers—Macao, Mumbai, and Penang. The essays and timelines set out the heritage conservation and urban planning frameworks for each place, providing a context for the adaptive reuse projects mentioned in the essay or explored as case studies. The case studies (fifteen, five for each place) are considered milestones in the development of adaptive reuse practice in each of the urban centers. The case studies address all three pillars or dimensions of sustainability.

For ease of comparison, each case study is presented using a set framework, which includes the following categories: Project Information (basic facts) and Project Description, Site History and Project History, Development Environment, Intervention (conservation approach[es]), Key Challenges, Keeping Heritage Alive (continuity), Long-Term Viability, and Impact (using the dimensions of sustainability as indicators). Plans and photographs accompany each case study.

Case studies are an art in the best of times, but in the time of COVID-19 there have been unique challenges, especially having easy access to individuals for interviews and to facilities for research. Access to projects for interior photography proved to be challenging, too.

Conclusion

The conclusion summarizes the understanding and applicability of the Sustainable Development Goals (SDGs). It considers and compares evolving practices in adaptive reuse in the three urban centers, particularly in regard to revitalization and sustainability. Concluding remarks are made, noting the similarities and differences between the urban centers. Reflections on the future role of adaptive reuse in Asia draw the book to a close.

A Note for the Reader

This book is intended for classroom use and professional readership, including government decision-makers. It is not a book to be read from cover to cover. Each essay is intended to be valuable and complete in itself. Although this does create some repetition of key principles, it allows for essays to be extracted as individual readings for classroom or workshop use. The case studies in particular are of considerable value in Asia and elsewhere, as few such materials exist for discussion and instructional purposes. Through this book, we hope to provoke practitioners and students to question their own practice. The examples included in the publication are not perfect but are real and show the way to navigating challenges in heritage conservation practice.

Bibliography

Cummer, Katie, and Lynne D. DiStefano, eds. *Asian Revitalization: Adaptive Reuse in Hong Kong, Shanghai, and Singapore*. Hong Kong: Hong Kong University Press, 2021.

Elefante, Carl. "The Greenest Building Is . . . One that Is Already Built." *Forum Journal: The Journal of the National Trust for Historic Preservation* 21, no. 4 (Summer 2007): 32.

UNESCO. *Asia Conserved Volume III: Lessons Learned from the UNESCO Asia-Pacific Awards for Cultural Heritage Conservation (2010–2014)*. Edited by William Chapman. Bangkok: UNESCO, 2019.

United Nations. "SDG Moment 2020." Accessed May 3, 2023. https://www.un.org/sustainabledevelopment/sdg-moment/.

Patrick Geddes: The Conservative Surgeon

Ken Nicolson

> **Conservative surgery:** "Surgery in which as much as possible of a part or structure is retained. It is often an equally effective alternative to radical surgery."[1]

Introduction

In 1886, Patrick Geddes, an up-and-coming teacher of sociology, moved with his wife into a tenement flat in James Court, off the Royal Mile, in Edinburgh's Old Town. Today, the neighborhood is part of the city's prestigious World Heritage Site. In 1886, it was a slum. The street, flats, and courtyards were dank, dark, and insanitary. The wealthy residents had moved out long ago to more fashionable properties in the New Town, and the city council had earmarked the area for wholesale clearance to facilitate housing renewal programs. What, then, had compelled Geddes to make a home here for his family? The earnest young sociologist had a motto—*Vivendo discimus* (By living we learn)[2]—and was preparing to test his theory about urban and social revitalization with a practical and very personal experiment.

Geddes's first task was to don an old shirt as an overall, roll up the sleeves, and start cleaning and repairing his dilapidated flat. Next, he moved outside to tackle the tenement close and back courtyard. Week after week, he spent his spare time clearing the rubbish and scrubbing the accumulated grime off the walls before transforming them with whitewash. Gradually, curious neighbors offered to lend a hand. With Geddes's guidance and encouragement, they helped him remove the derelict structures and a ruinous building that cluttered the courtyard. This was Geddes's first act of what he called "conservative surgery."[3] Apart from letting in more light and fresh air to the courtyard, the selective demolition also improved the outlook of the historical buildings. Inspired by Geddes's boundless energy and vision, the motley team of neighborhood volunteers made the most of the small plot that they had created by leveling the ground and planting shrubs and a tree.

1. "Conservative Surgery," *Medical Dictionary*, accessed August 16, 2021, https://medical-dictionary.thefreedictionary.com/conservative+surgery.
2. Patrick Geddes, *Cities in Evolution: An Introduction to the Town Planning Movement and to the Study of Civics* (London: Williams & Norgate, 1915), 317.
3. David Lock, "Patrick Geddes: The Conservative Surgeon," *Built Environment Quarterly* 3, no. 4 (1977): 325.

Apart from the obvious revitalization of the living conditions, Geddes's experiment in self-improvement had also succeeded in creating and sustaining a new spirit of optimism, hope, and camaraderie among the inhabitants, replacing the mood of despair and isolation that had previously hung over the slum community. Geddes made sure the work did not go unnoticed by the city council who appreciated his hands-on initiatives and acknowledged the benefits of his conservative surgery approach to revitalization. The community experienced minimal disruption and it was significantly cheaper to implement. As a result, the council reviewed its 1867 Major Redevelopment Plans and replaced them with the 1893 Old Town Improvement Scheme, which endorsed Geddes's methods and implementation of numerous similar revitalization projects.[4]

This was a major vindication for Geddes whose unconventional theories were often misunderstood and criticized by his peers. At the time, Britain was emerging from the Industrial Revolution. Urbanists and social reformers were calling for a more coherent and inclusive approach to resolving the pressing cultural and environmental problems of industrial cities. In the following years, Geddes became one of the most influential voices and is now widely regarded as the father of modern town planning. Understanding how Geddes's theories evolved from these early social experiments to shape Britain's planning profession has important lessons for us today in tackling revitalization projects and achieving sustainable development.

The Cultural-Ecological Approach

Born in Ballater, Aberdeenshire, in 1854, Geddes grew up in a rural setting that influenced his interest in the natural world. Geology was his first field of study. However, unimpressed with the formal teaching method that he encountered, he soon turned to biology instead. While carrying out fieldwork in Mexico, Geddes suffered temporary blindness brought about by the use of microscopes. The risk of causing permanent damage to his sight forced him to change his field once again and focus instead on social science.[5]

Geddes never obtained a degree but continued to expand his knowledge in diverse topics and seek inspiration from contemporary writers and teachers. He combined his interests in geology, biology, ecology, art, and sociology in the study of what he termed "civics," or the cultural-ecological characteristics of cities.[6] He corresponded regularly with Thomas Henry Huxley, Charles Darwin's pupil. It is said that Darwin was impressed by Geddes and held him in high regard. Another important influence was John Ruskin, the art critic, philosopher, and philanthropist who had a similarly broad range of interests and whose writing emphasized the connections between nature, art, and society.[7]

Geddes's quest was to encourage city planners to take time to understand how the complex interrelationship between nature and culture shapes the city physically and influences the evolution of society. A recurring theme in his teaching was that to achieve and maintain a healthy standard of living for city dwellers, the unique characteristics of each culture and natural environment should be understood, protected,

4. Institute of Historic Building Conservation, "Conservative Surgery in Edinburgh," accessed July 2, 2021, https://www.designingbuildings.co.uk/wiki/Conservative_surgery_in_Edinburgh.
5. Mairi McFadyen, "The Cultural-Ecological Imagination of Patrick Geddes (1854–1932)," *Northlight* (blog), 2019, http://www.mairimcfadyen.scot/blog/2015/8/2/patrick-geddes.
6. McFadyen, "Cultural-Ecological Imagination."
7. McFadyen, "Cultural-Ecological Imagination."

and nurtured.[8] In other words, Geddes was advocating a new "sustainable" approach to planning. Today, sustainability is a household word, but a century ago, when models of economic sustainability drove industrialization and urbanization, the notion of applying the concept to culture and the environment was not widely held.

Geddes first recognized the connectivity between the natural environment, the human activities in response to that environment, and the culture that evolves as a result in the work of French sociologist Frédéric Le Play, who described this process as "*Lieu, Travail, Famille*," translated by Geddes in his writings as "Place, Work, Folk."[9] He then developed an engaging graphic he called the Valley Section to illustrate this concept.[10]

Briefly, the Valley Section is a transect drawn through a city, from its center to the outer limit of its hinterland, to identify and interpret the Place, Work, and Folk elements. The natural environment that supports the city will provide the basics for survival—water, food, and shelter. Water may be sourced from rivers, springs, and lakes in upland areas. Forests and quarries will provide materials for building. Agriculture will make use of lower slopes with more fertile soils and grazing pastures to produce food. As the rural hinterland merges with the urban development, human activities change from primary to secondary and tertiary, becoming focused around homes, parks, places of worship, and recreation.

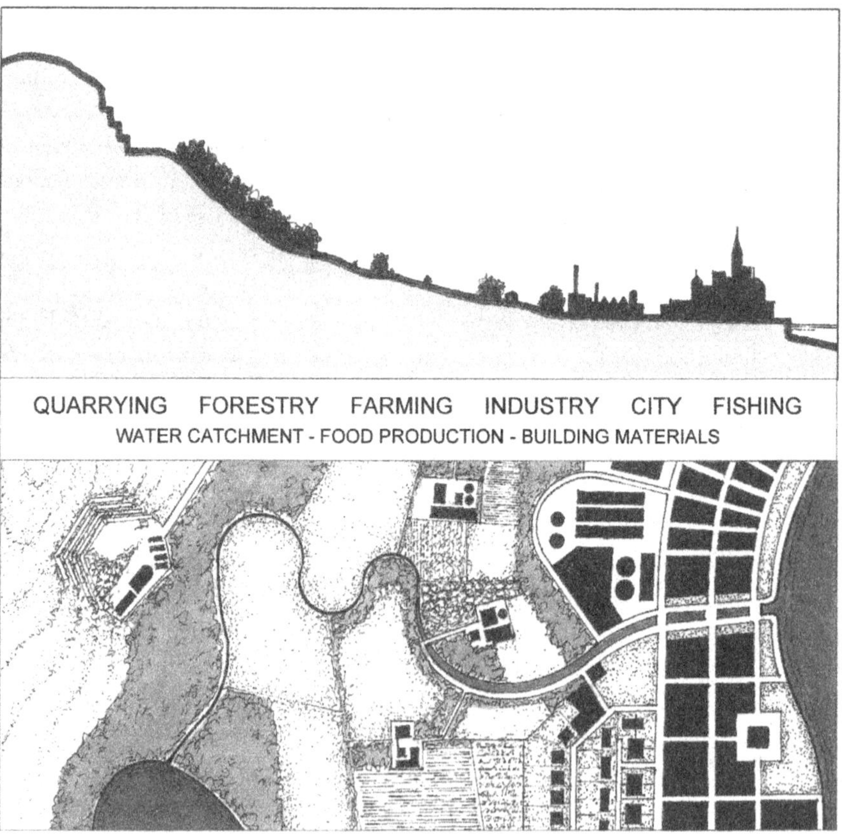

Figure 2.1: Valley Section. (Source: Adapted by Ken Nicolson from the original by Geddes, published in 1909, and reproduced in Welter, 2003, 60.)

8. Geddes, *Cities in Evolution*, 397.
9. Murdo MacDonald, "The Outlook Tower: Patrick Geddes in Context: Glossing Lewis Mumford in the Light of John Hewitt," *Irish Review (Cork)*, no. 16 (1994): 53–73, https://doi.org/10.2307/29735756.
10. MacDonald, "The Outlook Tower," 68.

Old Wine in a New Bottle

If this discussion of Geddes's sustainable planning theory and Place, Work, Folk concept sounds familiar, it may be because the current United Nations agenda to establish Sustainable Development Goals (SDGs) is underpinned by three elements: environmental (place), economic (work), and social (folk). Geddes's unique insight contributed many other words to the planning lexicon. For example, he predicted that the opportunities, real and imaginary, for a better life in the city would continue to attract migrants from the countryside. The logical extrapolation of this sustained expansion would, in some cases, result in cities merging to form what he termed "conurbations."[11] Geddes witnessed the role that key cities played in powering the Industrial Revolution and expanding trade regionally as well as globally. However, he also understood the importance for cities and their urban communities not to lose their identity in the stampede for a share of global markets. His advice for city planners was yet another surprisingly familiar concept that we have come to call "Think Global, Act Local."[12]

Why are these terms not commonly credited to Geddes? After all, they have been cherry-picked by academics and planners in the guise of a "fresh" approach to urban studies ever since. One of his students, the American planner Lewis Mumford, helped to explain this apparent oversight by recording some personal observations about Geddes's character. Mumford wrote that he was the "most fully alive person" he had ever met;[13] "Geddes was a teacher [who] relied upon direct intercourse rather than the printed word. He gave himself tirelessly in conversation with anyone who was willing to listen to him";[14] "Tidying up after Patrick Geddes was like putting the contents back into a volcano after an eruption."[15] Although Geddes was clearly an engaging and inspiring teacher, his books and papers are very challenging to read, particularly the publication that is widely regarded as his seminal work, *Cities in Evolution*, published in 1915. In his efforts to illustrate the complex interconnections between economics, ecology, and sociology, the narrative is convoluted with tortuous sentences and qualifying subclauses that often obscure the text's nuggets of wisdom.

In addition, Geddes's maverick character and controversial theories did not endear him to the mainstream academia of the time. He criticized the prevailing learn-by-rote mode of teaching and had a profound distrust of what he called the "modern habit of verbalistic empaperment"[16] by which he meant the relentless pursuit of academics to have their research published. Not surprisingly, he seldom committed his thoughts and words to paper, and those published works that he did complete do not do justice to his innovative research. As a result, his vision of a cultural-ecological evolution of cities did not gain broad support. Instead, city authorities focused on clearing slums, providing affordable housing, and paid more attention to other planning theories, such as the garden city movement, in an attempt to reverse or at least slow down the relentless rural to urban migration.

11. Geddes, *Cities in Evolution*, 34.
12. Geddes, *Cities in Evolution*, 397.
13. McFadyen, "Cultural-Ecological Imagination."
14. Lewis Mumford, introduction to *Patrick Geddes, Maker of the Future*, ed. Philip Boardman (Chapel Hill: University of North Carolina Press, 1944).
15. Quote attributed to Lewis Mumford ("Rediscovering Patrick Geddes," Patrick Geddes Centre, accessed April 16, 2020, https://www.patrickgeddescentre.org.uk/patrick-geddes/).
16. McFadyen, "Cultural-Ecological Imagination."

Geddes was not anti-urban. He did not advocate a return to rural life as the solution to urban problems.[17] His vision was that the city was the natural evolution of human development and that a sustainable city would be one that managed to balance economic growth without neglecting its environmental roots or losing its unique cultural "fingerprint." Just as nature evolved, so too should the urban community. Putting social needs first and applying sociological analysis could guide practical planning decisions to counter the damage caused by the economic models of the Industrial Revolution and create more satisfying forms of social life within the context of the modern city.

This required an understanding of the city on both a macro and micro scale. On the macro scale, Geddes recommended the use of a regional survey that would focus on geographic and historical elements.[18] The topographical nature of the region had a major influence on the form and growth of the city. The history of people's responses to the opportunities and constraints of the topography established cultural landscapes colored with cultural traditions and community structures. He urged planners to identify and nurture this dynamic interrelationship between the city and its surrounding environment instead of using arbitrary political/economic boundaries to define cities and regions. This is a key principle in sustainable resource management practiced around the world today.

On the micro scale, Geddes stressed the need to take time to understand and respect the historical development and sociology of the different communities that make up the city. This requires detailed inquiry into the origins and growth of the settlement as well as the people who were drawn to the place, put down roots, and called it home. By doing so, planners would appreciate the phases of evolutionary influences on society and be better informed on how to direct future growth most appropriate to the community's needs and aspirations. Geddes's "conservative surgery"[19] is an example of a more sensitive approach to redevelopment and revitalization of city neighborhoods. His Edinburgh experiment illustrated how a small-scale local refurbishment of the urban fabric could encourage and empower bottom-up, community-led projects better than heavy-handed, top-down initiatives by city authorities to carry out wholesale clearance that would uproot and disperse established communities.

Geddes in India

Unfortunately, it is true that a prophet is rarely recognized in his own land, and Geddes was only able to apply his theories on a larger scale overseas, most notably in India. His work in the slums of Edinburgh caught the attention of the governor of Madras, and he was invited to come to India to advise on urban planning problems. In particular, he was charged with advising how to carry out necessary urban renewal and resettlement schemes while respecting local cultural standards and traditions. Between 1915 and 1919, Geddes, now in his sixties, prepared a series of exhaustive town planning reports for at least eighteen Indian cities.

Unfortunately, he was unable to remain in India to oversee implementation of the plans, and in the following years, his schemes were altered and their innovations undone by city planners, engineers, and bureaucrats. Fortunately, copies of his

17. H. E. Meller, "Patrick Geddes; An Analysis of His Theory of Civics, 1880–1904," *Victorian Studies* 16, no. 3 (1973): 298.
18. Meller, "Patrick Geddes," 310.
19. Lewis Mumford, introduction to *Patrick Geddes in India*, ed. Jaqueline Tyrwhitt (London: Lund Humphries, 1947), 11.

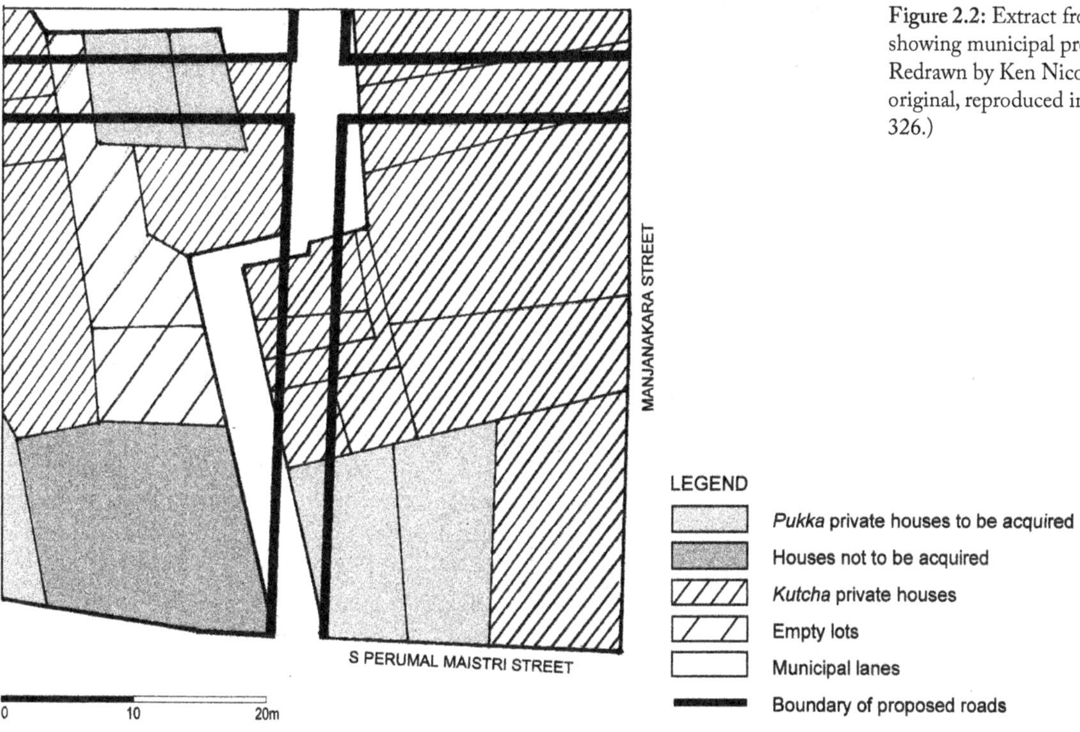

Figure 2.2: Extract from Madura Plan showing municipal proposals. (Source: Redrawn by Ken Nicolson from the original, reproduced in Lock, 1977, 326.)

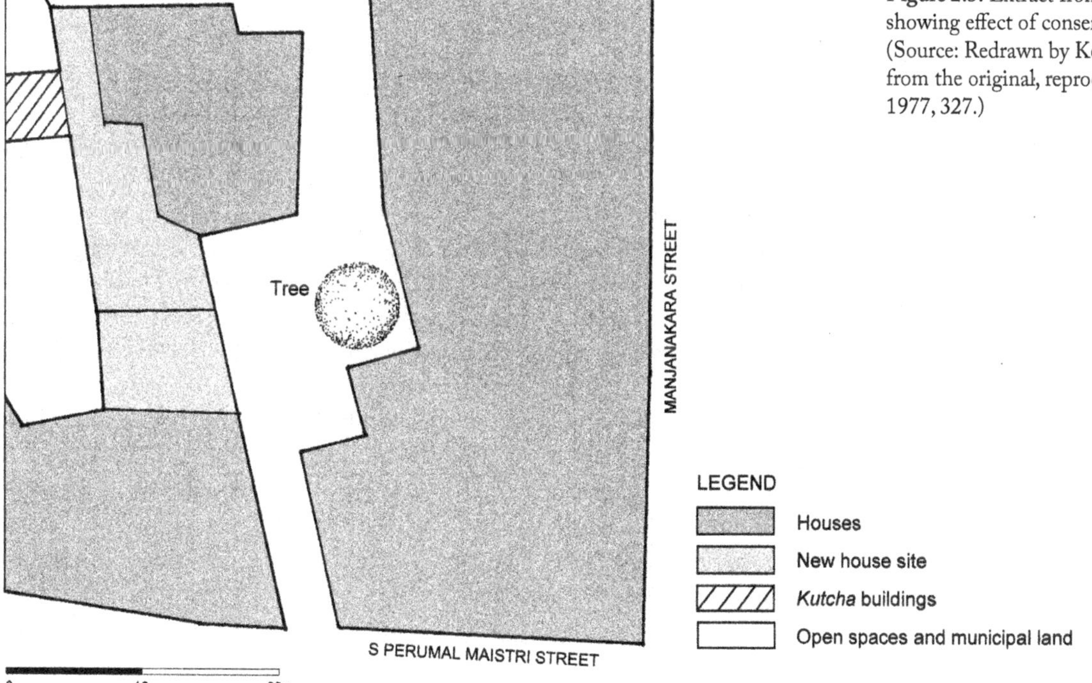

Figure 2.3: Extract from Madura Plan showing effect of conservative surgery. (Source: Redrawn by Ken Nicolson from the original, reproduced in Lock, 1977, 327.)

plans did survive, and in 1947, illustrative extracts, compiled by H. V. Lancaster and Geddes's son Arthur, who assisted in the original work, were published in the book *Patrick Geddes in India*, edited by Jacqueline Tyrwhitt. These extracts provide valuable insight into Geddes's methods and application of conservative surgery in India, thirty years after his first Edinburgh experiment.

Upon his arrival, Geddes quickly identified that the main challenge was the colonial government's approach to the problems of poor sanitation, inefficient road systems, and overcrowding in rapidly expanding Indian cities. Regrettably, the government officers were not adequately trained to deal with the local circumstances and were proposing standardized Western engineering solutions which, if implemented, would drive an overdesigned gridiron of streets through congested neighborhoods, resulting in expulsion of large numbers of residents. Geddes was highly critical of this kind of treatment, saying that it "should be recognised for what I believe it is; one of the most disastrous and pernicious blunders in the chequered history of sanitation."[20] Furthermore, he noted, it was usually the poorer residents who were first to be displaced by such schemes and who were least able to afford either relocation to other neighborhoods or new homes in the redeveloped area.[21]

Madura Plan

When Geddes started his detailed surveys, he found that in many cases, the street plans provided by the city authorities did not have sufficient detail or were hopelessly out of date. The older, congested neighborhoods that were earmarked for redevelopment had grown incrementally through the years, resulting in an organic and chaotic urban form. Resisting the temptation to make an expedient, broad-brush assessment, Geddes patiently walked down every street and back alley, recording the character and condition of the buildings as well as cultural and commercial activities within each community. An extract from his 1915 Madura report illustrates how he went about this.

Figure 2.2 shows part of a typical street block and the superimposed municipal proposals for new roads intended to relieve congestion and improve sanitation. The arbitrary new development plan did not take the alignment of the existing lane or the relative condition of the houses into consideration. However, when Geddes walked through the lane, he noted that the first residence scheduled for demolition (keyed as *pukka*, meaning "well built") was "as substantial, decent, and even pleasing, as one could wish to see."[22] By comparison, he noted that the smaller mud-brick shacks to the rear (keyed as *kutcha*, meaning "unfinished" or "crude") were in a very dilapidated state and, if removed, would present an opportunity to widen the lane into a small courtyard large enough to plant a tree. On the other side of the lane were two vacant plots. Geddes suggested that the money saved by not demolishing the first house could be used to purchase these plots. This would provide a valuable resource to build new houses to compensate residents whose homes may have to be cleared in other parts of the neighborhood. Figure 2.3 shows how this arrangement would look. Geddes continued in this way, hour after hour, day after day, eventually compiling an alternative plan for the Madura report, writing that,

20. Tyrwhitt, *Geddes in India*, 45.
21. Tyrwhitt, *Geddes in India*, 41.
22. Tyrwhitt, *Geddes in India*, 53.

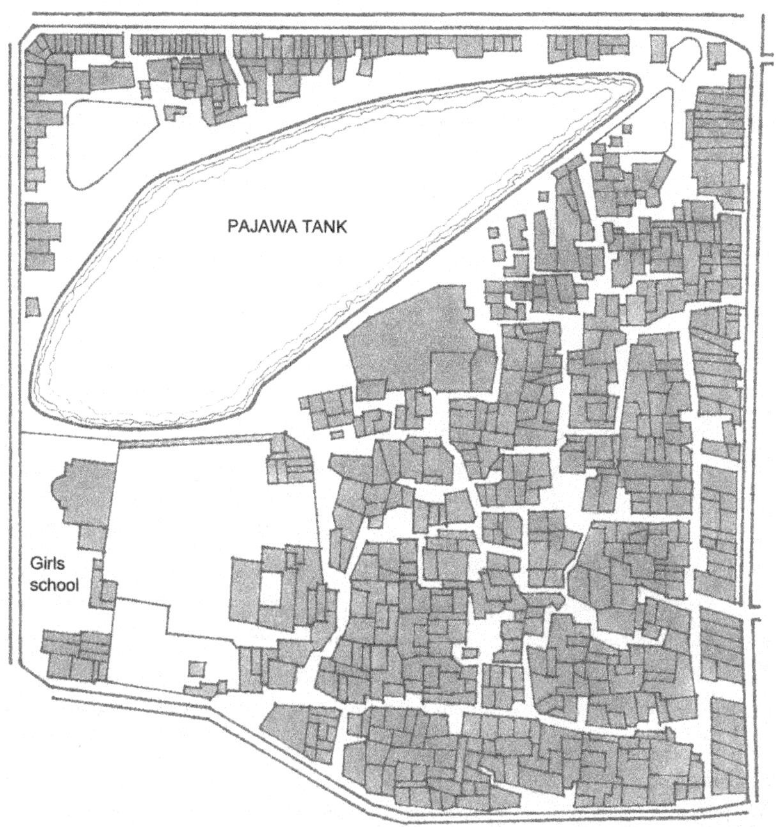

Figure 2.4: Extract from Balrampur Municipal Plan. (Source: Redrawn by Ken Nicolson from the original, reproduced in Lock, 1977, 326.)

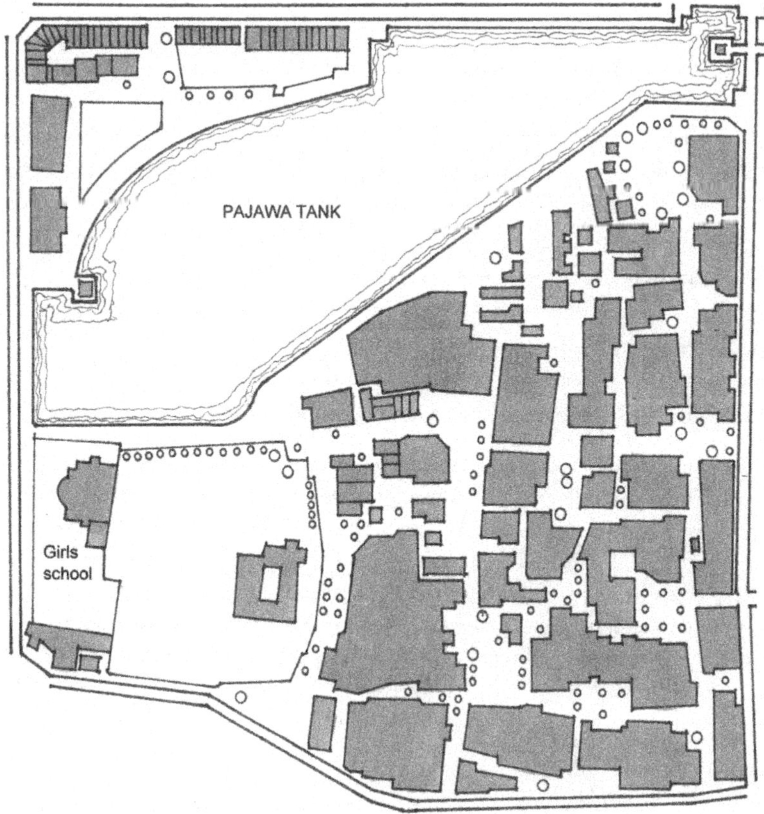

Figure 2.5: Extract from Balrampur Plan showing Geddes's scheme. (Source: Redrawn by Ken Nicolson from the original, reproduced in Lock, 1977, 327.)

> True, even upon this conservative plan, we find a number of families will have to be evicted. In this particular case it comes to eight families instead of 20 times that number. It should, however, be comparatively easy to compensate these few families sufficiently to find, or to build, homes that are better than those they have left and that are still at no great distance. . . . This small amount of disturbance can be faced by the common sense of the community and even the evicted can be expected to accept the situation with good will.[23]

Balrampur Plan

A further illustration of Geddes's "conservative surgery" is his plan for a part of Balrampur. Figure 2.4 shows an area of congested housing beside the Pajawa Tank, a reservoir that was scheduled to be filled in to prevent mosquito breeding and help combat malaria. Once again, Geddes surveyed the neighborhood in detail, house by house, lane by lane, to identify the derelict and vacant sites that could be cleared for new housing or converted into communal open spaces. Figure 2.5 shows Geddes's proposed plan with subtle but effective improvements to circulation by selective widening of lanes and creation of tree-planted courtyards. During his survey, he noticed that the reservoir played an important role in cooling the air in the surrounding streets and was a focal point for local people to meet and socialize. So instead of losing such an important local amenity by filling it in, Geddes proposed that the mosquito problem be solved by stocking it with larva-eating fish that could also be a source of food.[24]

In both examples, Geddes was able to demonstrate that the brutal scale and rigid geometry of the road schemes were unnecessary. The "conservative surgery" approach, using a keen-edged "scalpel" instead of a "blunt instrument," would have significantly less impact on the local community, cost considerably less than the municipal schemes, and achieve an acceptable improvement to local circulation and sanitation. In fairness, he also acknowledged the conservative method has its difficulties: "It requires long and patient study. The work cannot be done in the office with ruler and parallels, for the plan must be sketched out on the spot, after wearying hours of perambulations."[25] However, the alternative was to succumb to the temptation of what he termed the "destructive impatience"[26] of the municipal schemes that did not spend the time to undertake such detailed surveys and opted instead for the more administratively convenient but less community-sensitive choice of wholesale redevelopment.

Geddes's empathy with the communities that he encountered in the slums of Bombay and other cities that were under the threat of redevelopment is neatly summed up in one of his most celebrated quotes, found in the 1915 Madura report:

> Town planning is not mere place-planning, nor even work planning. If it is to be successful it must be folk planning. This means that its task is not to coerce people into new places against their associations, wishes, and interest, as we find bad schemes trying to do. Instead, its task is to find the right places for each sort of people; places where they will really flourish. To give people, in fact, the same care that we give when transplanting flowers, instead of harsh evictions and arbitrary instructions to "move on," delivered in the manner of an officious policeman.[27]

23. Lock, "Patrick Geddes," 328.
24. Lock, "Patrick Geddes," 328.
25. Tyrwhitt, *Geddes in India*, 44.
26. Tyrwhitt, *Geddes in India*, 45.
27. Tyrwhitt, *Geddes in India*, 22.

Conclusion

When communities emerged from the Industrial Revolution, battered, bruised, and somewhat shell-shocked by the experience, urbanists and social reformers called for a more holistic and sustainable approach to planning cities. Geddes's legacy is a treasure trove of insight and principles for sustainable planning by integrating environmental, economic, and cultural values and using "conservative surgery" to protect communities and their built heritage.

Above all, Geddes is remembered and admired for his ability to relate, without prejudice, to the needs of each urban community he encountered, from the tenements of Edinburgh to the slums of Bombay. His folk-centered approach is reflected in his personal emblem of three doves. In addition to symbolizing peace, he referred to them as the three S's: Sympathy (empathy) for the people and their environment, Synthesis of all the relevant factors affecting the plan, and Synergy of the combined cooperation of all stakeholders.[28]

Today, communities around the world are gradually emerging from the sobering lockdowns of the COVID-19 pandemic. This anthropause has provided a rare, once-in-a-century opportunity for individuals and society as a whole to take stock and establish new priorities. With an uncanny sense of déjà vu, there are calls to do things differently and adopt more sustainable development goals to protect our cultural and natural heritage. Geddes showed us the way before with a masterclass in folk-centered planning. It now falls on this generation of conservation surgeons to roll up our sleeves and lead by example.

Bibliography

Boardman, Philip. *Patrick Geddes, Maker of the Future*. Chapel Hill: University of North Carolina Press, 1944.

"Conservative Surgery." *Medical Dictionary*. Accessed August 16, 2021. https://medical-dictionary.thefreedictionary.com/conservative+surgery.

Geddes, Patrick. *Cities in Evolution: An Introduction to the Town Planning Movement and to the Study of Civics*. London: Williams & Norgate, 1915.

Institute of Historic Building Conservation. "Conservative Surgery in Edinburgh." Last modified March 30, 2021. https://www.designingbuildings.co.uk/wiki/Conservative_surgery_in_Edinburgh.

Lock, David. "Patrick Geddes: The Conservative Surgeon." *Built Environment Quarterly* 3, no. 4 (1977): 325–28.

MacDonald, Murdo. "The Outlook Tower: Patrick Geddes in Context: Glossing Lewis Mumford in the Light of John Hewitt." *Irish Review (Cork)*, no. 16 (1994): 53–73. https://doi.org/10.2307/29735756.

McFadyen, Mairi. "The Cultural-Ecological Imagination of Patrick Geddes (1854–1932)." *Northlight* (blog), 2019. http://www.mairimcfadyen.scot/blog/2015/8/2/patrick-geddes.

Meller, H. E. "Patrick Geddes; An Analysis of His Theory of Civics, 1880–1904." *Victorian Studies* 16, no. 3 (1973): 291–315.

Patrick Geddes Centre. "Rediscovering Patrick Geddes." Accessed April 16, 2020. https://www.patrickgeddescentre.org.uk/patrick-geddes/.

Tyrwhitt, Jaqueline. *Patrick Geddes in India*. London: Lund Humphries, 1947.

Welter, Volker M. *Biopolis: Patrick Geddes and the City of Life*. Cambridge, MA: MIT Press, 2003.

28. McFadyen, "Cultural-Ecological Imagination."

Heritage, Urban Revitalization, and a New Sustainability Mindset

Montira Horayangura Unakul

Heritage and Sustainability: An Overview

A paradigm shift faces heritage management. On the one hand, the inclusion of heritage as a part of the Sustainable Development Goals (SDGs) is a long-overdue acknowledgment of the role of heritage within the larger development agenda. On the other hand, growing pressures from a host of unprecedented challenges to heritage—sometimes at a transboundary or even global scale—underscore the futility of managing heritage within a narrow conservation perspective and within isolated conceptual and sectoral silos.[1]

What are the implications for heritage management? How does heritage management engage with sustainable development at a policy or operational level? In this context, how have the goalposts shifted in defining and then assessing the outcomes of heritage management, particularly for marquee sites like World Heritage properties?

Within the heritage profession, embedded within the new rhetoric about sustainable development is the core kernel of conservation. What Gustavo Araoz, during his tenure as president of the International Council on Monuments and Sites (ICOMOS), ostensibly calls a paradigm shift still revolves around preservation in his directive for "Preserving Heritage Places under a New Paradigm."[2] This enduring focus on sustaining the heritage place itself versus the contributions of heritage toward larger goals of sustainable development has led to a bifurcation in the debate about heritage and sustainable development.[3] On the one hand, ensuring the sustainability of heritage places has led to more reflexive considerations of how heritage practices need to be rethought, such as the recognition of the role of local stewards as custodians of their heritage sites. On the other hand, there is growing awareness that heritage should contribute to all dimensions of sustainability.

Logan and Larsen offer a more nuanced approach to understanding this relationship beyond a binary approach, stating "sustainable development may be identified as

1. Montira Unakul, "Heritage Management and Sustainable Development," in *Enhancing Our Heritage Toolkit 2.0* (Paris: UNESCO, 2021), 35.
2. Gustavo F. Araoz, "Preserving Heritage Places under a New Paradigm," *Journal of Cultural Heritage Management and Sustainable Development* 1, no. 1 (2011): 55–60, https://doi.org/10.1108/2044 1261111129933.
3. Peter Bille Larsen and William Logan, eds., *World Heritage and Sustainable Development: New Directions in World Heritage Management* (Abingdon: Routledge, 2018).

a need, a threat, a solution or even an objective of heritage."[4] Reflecting these permutations, they propose four possible interfaces between heritage and sustainable development:[5]

i. Sustainable heritage (which seeks to sustain the heritage resources)
ii. Heritage versus sustainable development (where the two are seen in opposition to each other)
iii. Sustainable development for heritage (where development should be aligned with conserving heritage)
iv. Heritage for sustainable development (where heritage is seen as an important contributor to overcoming a range of development challenges)

Target 11.4 of the SDGs focuses on sustaining the heritage resources themselves (corresponding directly with the first scenario and implied in the second scenario above). It calls for member states to "strengthen efforts to protect and safeguard the world's cultural and natural heritage," which aligns with the intentions of the 1972 *Convention Concerning the Protection of the World Cultural and Natural Heritage*. For the first time, the protection of heritage has been identified as an integral part of sustainable development, and conversely, the loss of heritage is seen as detrimental to sustainable development—from an economic, environmental, or social perspective.

In the first and second scenarios, prevalent in many places, the task of heritage management is still seen as the primary responsibility of the heritage sector. A conventional heritage management approach focused on safeguarding the heritage assets as the primary task is still carried out, largely by heritage professionals and practitioners. When the inevitable conflicts arise—by residents seeking expanded livelihood opportunities or investors seeking economic gains through new projects—these are seen as being either outside the remit of heritage policies and plans (per the first scenario) or else being detrimental to the primary goal of heritage protection (per the second scenario). In both these scenarios, the indicators of effective management measure the well-being of heritage assets; indicators of economic or social well-being are an external consideration. At a higher policy level, the indicators for SDG 11, target 11.4 in fact only measure the budgetary investment that countries make in heritage safeguarding efforts. Indeed, where economic or social activities are perceived as undercutting the effectiveness of heritage management efforts, they can be seen to have an undesirable effect on heritage management indicators.

In the third and fourth scenarios, an alignment of heritage objectives and development aims is called for, albeit with different ultimate aims: either development at the service of heritage or vice versa. In either case, a fundamental reconsideration of heritage management is required. In this expanded worldview, it is not only ineffective but maybe impossible to carry out the task of heritage protection by itself. Heritage protection can only be effective if intertwined with efforts to improve well-being in various dimensions. For example, instead of relying on punitive measures to crack down on poaching, employing ex-poachers in monitoring operations could yield win-win solutions. In so doing, the management approach is designed to acknowledge existing socioeconomic realities and political contexts using strategies, which rely as much on conservation know-how as good development practices. Within this multidimensional approach, assessing outcomes purely on the basis of heritage assets is no longer meaningful; it may be necessary to also consider indicators that link the impacts of heritage work to larger measures of development impact as well. In so

4. Larsen and Logan, *World Heritage and Sustainable Development*, 8.
5. Larsen and Logan, *World Heritage and Sustainable Development*, 7.

doing, the fundamental definition and framework for assessing management effectiveness also broadens into the development realm as well.

In this spirit, the *Policy for the Integration of a Sustainable Development Perspective into the Processes of the World Heritage Convention* (*World Heritage Sustainable Development Policy*) was adopted in 2015.[6] The policy reflects the earlier 2002 *Budapest Declaration on World Heritage* calling for appropriate and equitable balance between conservation, sustainability, and development. It seeks to harness the potential of heritage, particularly World Heritage, to contribute to sustainable development and to ensure that conservation and management strategies are appropriately aligned with sustainable development objectives. That said, it notes that the primary objective of the *World Heritage Convention*, to protect the world cultural and natural heritage, should not be compromised. The policy identifies four core dimensions, which correspond to the 5Ps of the *2030 Agenda for Sustainable Development* (*2030 Agenda*)—People, Planet, Prosperity, Peace, and Partnerships:

i. Inclusive social development (championing human rights, gender equality, and Indigenous peoples and local communities)
ii. Environmental sustainability (including resilience to disasters and climate change)
iii. Inclusive economic development
iv. Peace and security[7]

This more expansive approach to embedding heritage within a larger agenda for sustainable development is reflected in the range of other SDGs. UNESCO has mapped the intersection of heritage and culture more broadly in the implementation of the *2030 Agenda* by various member states, as reported in their Voluntary National Reviews. This analysis demonstrates how countries have made progress in improving the well-being of people. For instance, local and Indigenous knowledge has been mobilized to promote sustainable agricultural practices and thus contributes to food security under SDG 2. Of particular resonance in the pandemic era, a culturally nuanced approach to communication supports disease prevention under SDG 3. An appreciation for cultural diversity, as manifested in heritage, contributes to attaining quality education under SDG 4.

Meanwhile, in terms of contributing to economic sustainability, heritage resources have proven to be a valuable asset for creating decent jobs and powering economic growth under SDG 8. Harnessing heritage can thus contribute to eradicating poverty under SDG 1. Fairly low barriers to entry and the ubiquity of heritage assets encourage entrepreneurship among women and youth, leading to the reduction of inequalities under SDG 10.

Finally, heritage is fundamental to environmental protection both on land and in water, per SDG 15 and SDG 14, respectively. Participatory efforts to safeguard cultural and natural heritage contribute to the management of water-related ecosystems under SDG 6. Adapting heritage know-how, particularly in the design or adaptation of buildings and infrastructure, can contribute to more sustainable energy consumption under SDG 7. Traditional knowledge can also contribute to climate change adaptation under SDG 13.

This seemingly newfound ubiquity of heritage across the various goals of sustainable development can actually be traced back to the landmark World Conference

---

6. UNESCO, *Policy for the Integration of a Sustainable Development Perspective into the Processes of the World Heritage Convention* (Paris: UNESCO, 2015).
7. UNESCO, *Policy for Sustainable Development.*

on Cultural Policies held in Mexico City in 1982, which already tabled the links between culture and development. The follow-up to this milestone event, hosted again by Mexico City in 2022, offers an opportunity to reflect on the progress that has been made in the intervening four decades.

While the encouraging reports back from member states regarding the role of culture and heritage in implementing the SDGs point to the promise of mobilizing heritage to contribute to the sustainable development agenda, many challenges remain. This turn toward sustainable development through a heritage lens requires a new mindset both among those who are within the heritage world as well as those in other sectors. Existing frameworks for heritage management need to be reevaluated and better alignments with development policy are more urgently needed than ever, especially in face of the urgent crises that face us today. At an operational level, sweeping changes in our approach to designing management objectives and mechanisms at heritage sites also need to occur. The governance of heritage, within the larger landscape of development governance, also needs to be reoriented toward building better partnerships across different silos.

Heritage, Sustainability, and Urban Revitalization

All three dimensions linking heritage to sustainability have particular resonance when it comes to the issue of urban revitalization. Even before the COVID-19 pandemic, the health, dynamism, and integrity of human settlements have been long intertwined with sustaining natural and cultural heritage. Reflecting this point of view, the Global Network of Cities, Local and Regional Governments (UCLG) issued in 2010 (presaging the adoption of the Sustainable Development Goals [SDGs] in 2015) a policy statement, *Culture Is the Fourth Pillar of Sustainable Development*, at its Third World Congress in Mexico City. It regards culture as a dimension that is on equal footing and fully interconnected with the existing three pillars related to economy, environment, and society.

The *New Urban Agenda* (*NUA*), adopted at Habitat III in Quito in 2016, explicitly notes the role of heritage in various aspects of urban development. It highlights both dimensions of linking heritage and sustainability (sustaining heritage itself as an integral pillar of sustainable development and mobilizing heritage for larger sustainability goals). From a protection point of view, Article 38 commits to

> the sustainable leveraging of natural and cultural heritage, both tangible and intangible, in cities and human settlements, as appropriate, through integrated urban and territorial policies and adequate investments at the national, subnational and local levels, to safeguard and promote cultural infrastructures and sites, museums, indigenous cultures and languages, as well as traditional knowledge and the arts, highlighting the role that these play in rehabilitating and revitalizing urban areas and in strengthening social participation and the exercise of citizenship.[8]

From a future-oriented point of view, Article 45 mines the potential of heritage as a driver for urban growth through

> developing vibrant, sustainable and inclusive urban economies, building on endogenous potential, competitive advantages, cultural heritage and local resources, as well as resource-efficient and resilient infrastructure, promoting sustainable

8. United Nations Habitat, *New Urban Agenda*, A/RES/71/256 (October 2016), http://habitat3.org/the-new-urban-agenda/.

and inclusive industrial development and sustainable consumption and production patterns and fostering an enabling environment for businesses and innovation, as well as livelihoods.[9]

With regard to adaptive use, the *NUA* notes the importance of promoting the "innovative and sustainable use of architectural monuments and sites, with the intention of value creation, through respectful restoration and adaptation" in Article 125.[10] Whereas this article is focused on the somewhat outdated scope of heritage as monuments and sites, other parts of the *NUA* adopts a more expansive understanding of what constitutes cultural heritage, spanning various forms of tangible and intangible heritage, including those of value to Indigenous peoples and local communities.

The 2010 *Recommendation on the Historic Urban Landscape* (*HUL Recommendation*) adopts an even more multilayered and multidimensional approach to understanding and valuing urban ensembles and settlements. Beyond discrete attributes of either cultural or natural heritage in a static manner, it uses the rubric of the "historic urban landscape," which is the "result of the layering and intertwining of cultural and natural values over time." In this way, a dynamic quality to urban resources is captured in a holistic manner, encompassing everything from the built heritage to open spaces, infrastructure, as well as cultural practices, economic processes, and social values.

The *HUL Recommendation* takes the built environment as being fundamentally and inextricably connected to its underlying geomorphology, topography, and ecological systems. From a geographic standpoint, it emphasizes that "beyond the notion of 'historic centre,' it includes the broader urban context and its geographical setting. The *Policy for the Integration of a Sustainable Development Perspective into the Processes of the World Heritage Convention* similarly emphasizes the need to operate as a larger planning scale, noting that "for many World Heritage properties, achieving sustainable development will require acting at a scale that is much larger than the property itself. . . . Thus, States Parties should integrate conservation and management approaches for World Heritage properties within their larger regional planning frameworks, giving consideration in particular to the integrity of socio-ecological systems."[11]

Together, this comprehensive notion of what constitutes the historic urban landscape and the interlinked nature of achieving sustainable development across the 5Ps drives a new connotation for urban revitalization as well. Urban revitalization is therefore not confined to rehabilitating run-down buildings or urban ensembles. It also necessitates bringing on board an economic agenda, an environmental agenda, as well as a social agenda.

Indeed, from an urban development perspective, these three agendas are not new in an urban context. Advocates and scholars of inclusive social development have long championed the need to deliver housing and access to urban services to all residents. Similarly, policymakers and practitioners have worked at the intersection of spatial planning and urban ecology in response to both anthropogenic as well as biodiversity concerns. Finally, finding the economic value of heritage and using that as a motivator for decision-makers to support urban preservation has been a primary strategy for managing urban heritage assets.

From an implementation point of view, two challenges remain at the intersection of these three agendas in linking heritage with the sustainable development agenda. First, how can heritage management policies, plans, and operations straddle these

9. United Nations Habitat, *New Urban Agenda*.
10. United Nations Habitat, *New Urban Agenda*.
11. UNESCO, *Policy for Sustainable Development*.

disciplinary and sectoral silos to ensure that the multilayered historical urban landscape is managed in a holistic, interdisciplinary, and intersectoral manner? In this way, the underlying ecological systems or the social fabric of an urban settlement are well mapped and well understood as the basis for interventions that do not focus only on the built environment.

Second, from an economic point of view, the intrinsic "heritage value" of urban settlements should be used as the basis for creating new value propositions as well in the business sense of the term "value." This leads to the fabrication of new products and services that make use of available cultural and heritage assets in a way that is creative and contemporary in their outlook. The economics of heritage has been well studied, and the act of conservation itself has been documented to generate significant economic value in terms of job creation, new revenue streams, property value, and municipal tax revenue.[12]

Beyond finding meaningful and productive new value for historic properties from rent or other income streams, using them to anchor urban hubs of creativity provides an expanded possibility for adding value. UNESCO and the World Bank have documented that cities both benefit from and enable culture and creativity—with these industries generating some US$2.25 trillion globally in 2013.[13] As these industries operate as agglomeration economies—with talent and capital attracting other talent and capital—municipal and national planners have leveraged (historical) urban centers by transforming them into hubs for cultural and creative ecosystems. This includes investing to regenerate urban neighborhoods in a manner that enables creative activities—by having the requisite amenities, infrastructure, resources, and support systems in place to attract creative entrepreneurs. In a World Heritage context, the *World Heritage Sustainable Development Policy* emphasizes strengthening capacity building, innovation, and local entrepreneurship as part of inclusive economic development. It emphasizes the need to support entrepreneurship at "small/medium/micro scale levels, to promote sustainable economic benefits for local communities" and promote "public and private investment in sustainable development projects that foster local cultural and creative industries and safeguard intangible heritage associated with World Heritage properties."[14]

These two implementation issues challenge the exercise of urban revitalization to go beyond the adaptive reuse of single monuments, the upgrades of streetscapes, or the improvement of neighborhoods. By bringing environmental sustainability into the picture, it prepares us to deal with challenges, such as climate change, by focusing on strengthening urban resilience in a systemic, landscape-scale manner. Such interventions would need to be conceived, for instance, in terms of managing entire systems. So, responding to urban flooding in a historic city would entail dealing not only with adapting individual buildings to be disaster resilient but reviving historical waterway systems that have broken down or been obstructed by poorly designed modern infrastructure and, if necessary, even improving the management of the related floodplains. It would also require putting in place the necessary operating "software," including sustainable financing mechanisms as well as meaningful

12. Donovan D. Rypkema, *The Economics of Historic Preservation: A Community Leader's Guide* (Washington, DC: National Trust for Historic Preservation, 2005); Christian Ost and Nathalie van Drooghenbroeck, *Report on Economics of Conservation: An Appraisal of Theories, Principles and Methods* (Brussels: International Economics Committee, ICOMOS, 1998).
13. UNESCO, *Cities, Culture, Creativity Leveraging Culture and Creativity for Sustainable Urban Development and Inclusive Growth* (Paris: UNESCO, 2021), http://elibrary.worldbank.org/doi/book/10.1596/35621.
14. UNESCO, *Policy for Sustainable Development.*

community involvement, to ensure that such interventions can continue to be implemented in the long run. Such approaches echo nature-based solutions to restoring both natural and modified ecosystems in rural and urban settings that ecologists have been advocating since the 1970s and that have gained greater credence through the advocacy and technical efforts of global organizations, such as the International Union for Conservation of Nature (IUCN).

In a similar vein, the revitalization of an urban district would ring hollow if only built heritage was restored. To be truly sustainable, such a program would require a sound economic development scheme and a strategy to improve human well-being in terms of better social services or social cohesion as well. That said, an economic-driven approach to urban revitalization, perhaps the conversion of historic shophouses into luxury boutiques, may contribute to the financial bottom line but neglect the social dimensions that give cities their character and soul. The key message is that achieving the SDGs requires pushing forward all three development agendas at once, and this holds true in the context of urban revitalization as well.

Figure 3.1: Damage in the historical town of Kesennuma following the 2011 earthquake and tsunami. (Source: Christopher Johnson.)

Defining New Benchmarks for "Heritage × Sustainable Development" through the UNESCO Heritage Awards

Multidimensional approaches to sustainable development in the heritage sphere are beginning to become more prevalent in practice with exemplary projects setting new standards in policy and practice. To recognize such efforts and identify them as new benchmarks for future endeavors, UNESCO introduced the Special Recognition for Sustainable Development (Special Recognition) as a new category to its long-running Asia-Pacific Awards for Cultural Heritage Conservation program in 2020. The Special Recognition can apply to either heritage conservation or new design in heritage contexts.

In its inaugural year, UNESCO awarded the Special Recognition to two projects: Lai Chi Wo Rural Landscape in Hong Kong SAR, China and Sunder Nursery in India. Both of the heritage conservation projects demonstrated a masterly achievement of sustainable development across its three pillars, in two very different contexts. The Lai Chi Wo project undertook the holistic revival of an abandoned village on the rural fringe of the New Territories, Hong Kong SAR, while the Sunder Nursery accomplished the renewal of a derelict mausoleum complex into an urban hotspot for biodiversity and cultural heritage in a crowded district of New Delhi, India.

The Lai Chi Wo project is one of a series of rural revitalization projects that have been initiated in Hong Kong SAR, in line with a growing recognition of the vulnerability of rural settlements and increasing interest from the policy sector and urban society. The four-hundred-year-old Hakka village declined with the out-migration of its residents in search of better economic opportunities starting in the 1950s. The terraced farmlands, the managed woodlands, and the housing fell into disrepair. The project restored the agroecosystem in a holistic manner from the seaside mangroves up to the hillside forest, along with the revival of the community life of the village by attracting residents to form a new rural community. The restoration of houses and communal buildings in the village provided a physical anchor for the initiative but was only one component of the overall scheme.

The project carried out a total of twenty-eight actions in four different streams that reflect a whole-of-place sensibility to heritage revitalization: community, socioeconomy, landscape ecology, and agriculture. In this way, the natural landscape was restored alongside the cultivated landscape, starting with baseline surveys of biodiversity indicators, the reintroduction of selected key species, and ongoing biodiversity monitoring by citizen scientists. The restoration of the ecological function provided the necessary conditions for reinstating the agro-forestry production, terraced farming, and rice farming. On the socioeconomic front, the collection of local Indigenous knowledge through oral histories and training for urban dwellers, who were attracted to move to Lai Chi Wo, formed the basis to design and then implement efforts to repopulate the village, revive lost foodways that used both produce as well as local customs and link these to a market economy through cultural events, ecotourism, and a farmers' market. Taking a biocultural systems approach allowed the project to restore both the cultural diversity and biodiversity of Lai Chi Wo in a sustainable manner.

The UNESCO Heritage Awards jury lauded the Lai Chi Wo project for,

> its pioneering approach to reviving a once-abandoned rural cultural landscape. The project upholds the key dimensions of sustainable development—economic, social, and environmental—in undertaking the holistic rejuvenation of the historic Hakka agricultural settlement using nature-based solutions. The reinstatement of the farmland, woodlands, and coastal eco-system; the light-handed restoration of various historic buildings; the repopulation of the village; the renewal of rural lifeways; and the flourishing of new social enterprises herald a new era for Lai Chi Wo. Through its multi-pronged strategy, the project transforms notions of heritage practice from its conventional focus on material conservation to encompass living heritage in all its manifestations. Drawing upon indigenous know-how, geomancy principles, and conservation science, the project demonstrates the importance of interweaving nature and cultural heritage in setting a new urban-rural sustainability agenda for Hong Kong SAR and beyond.[15]

15. UNESCO Bangkok, "2020 UNESCO Asia-Pacific Awards for Cultural Heritage Conservation—Winners Announced," December 16, 2020, https://bangkok.unesco.org/index.php/content/2020-unesco-asia-pacific-awards-cultural-heritage-conservation-winners-announced.

Figure 3.2: Sunder Nursery, a project that transformed a barren historical site into an urban oasis. (Source: Aga Khan Trust for Culture.)

The Sunder Nursery scheme shares a similarly expansive vision for the revival of this site, which prior to the project had been considered an urban wasteland. In the vicinity of the famed Humayun's Tomb World Heritage Site, the ensemble of Sufi tombs, once set in a designed Mughal garden landscape, had been neglected, gradually encroached upon, and grown over with vegetation. Part of the complex served as a waste disposal site. The world-class conservation work on the monuments was nested within a larger landscape approach to the site (Figure 3.2). The project was able to take an eco-friendly approach to relandscaping the site, bearing in mind both the Mughal landscape in the designed sections surrounding the monuments and the native ecology of this area in the more natural zone. Now touted as "Delhi's Heritage Park," the Sunder Nursery has become a popular green space for city dwellers and a much-needed amenity for local residents. The Sunder Nursery project is part of a larger suite of projects encompassing not only the World Heritage Site but also the nearby Nizamuddin Urban Renewal Initiative (NURI). This project, which subsequently garnered another Special Recognition in its own right in 2021, brought about substantial improvements for local people, particularly women and youth, in terms of education, public space, livelihoods, and various social services. It was notable that these development efforts were given priority and executed first, before any of the historic buildings were restored.

The UNESCO Heritage Awards jury praised the Sunder Nursery project for,

> its transformative impact in turning a barren site into an urban oasis in the heart of New Delhi. The historic ensemble of Mughal garden tombs and their associated sacred landscape was restored with native plantings and an extensive rainwater harvesting system. Meanwhile, a former dumpsite was converted into the city's only arboretum, which was planned as a designed wilderness and has become a local biodiversity hotspot for birds and other species. The project showcases technical excellence in built-heritage restoration alongside a commitment to socio-

economic development, long a hallmark of the Aga Khan Trust for Culture. At the same time, it pays equal attention to ecological restoration, thus underscoring the message that heritage conservation is beyond monuments and is only truly sustainable when essential linkages between nature and culture are profoundly understood and nurtured.[16]

These projects demonstrated exemplary achievement of the UNESCO Heritage Awards criteria related to "sustainability and impact." Concomitant with the launch of this new category, UNESCO revamped the awards criteria with substantial expansions in this set of criteria to reflect the organization's leading-edge efforts to advocate for the intersection of culture and heritage with the *2030 Agenda for Sustainable Development* (*2030 Agenda*). The expanded UNESCO Heritage Awards criteria related to sustainability and impact can provide a useful benchmark in evaluating conservation outcomes or to plan for new heritage initiatives within a sustainability mindset.

These criteria assess how well a heritage project deals with the following:

- The **engagement of the local community** in the conservation process.
- **Sustainable use and preservation of heritage place** through appropriate use, adaptation, maintenance, and strategic and financial planning.
- How well the project contributes to **environmental sustainability and resilience** of the heritage place.
- How well the project contributes to the **local community's socio-economic well-being, cultural continuum, and development needs.**
- How well the project fosters **local knowledge and living heritage.**
- How well the project contributes to enhancing the **quality of the urban, rural, natural setting and spaces.**
- The **influence of the project** on conservation practice and policy locally, nationally, regionally or internationally.[17]

Subsequent awardees of the Special Recognition illustrate how these criteria can be applied to a range of urban contexts and development objectives, with a different approach to sustainability in each case. In addition to the NURI project, three others were also recognized in 2021. The Shajing Ancient Fair initiative in Shenzhen, China (Figure 3.3) applied an "urban acupuncture" approach to insert a series of interventions in the historic city fabric that aimed to improve the socioeconomic well-being of the local residents. The Kesennuma project in Miyagi, Japan undertook the revival of key buildings in a seaside town devasted by the 2011 Tohoku earthquake and tsunami, demonstrating a new model for urban resilience where heritage revival becomes the key to postdisaster recovery in a historical community (Figure 3.1). Last, the new carpenter woodshop at Mrigadayavan Palace in Phetchaburi, Thailand, using recycled timber and a passive ventilation system, showcases how contemporary design with a heritage conservation sensibility and green design ethos can allow a new building to fit in seamlessly as part of a notable architectural ensemble and a sensitive coastal setting.

16. UNESCO Bangkok, "2020 UNESCO Asia-Pacific Awards for Cultural Heritage Conservation."
17. UNESCO Bangkok, "Apply for the Awards: Awards Regulations," March 1, 2022, https://bangkok.unesco.org/content/apply-awards.

Figure 3.3: Shajing Ancient Fair initiative in Shenzhen, China. (Source: Rejuvenation of Shajing Ancient Fair.)

Implications for Applying the New Sustainability Mindset in the Heritage Context

From being confined in its own disciplinary silo with a bunker mentality in trying to defend monuments and sites to a later stage of encompassing more voices in a living heritage approach, the future of heritage is now seen as being inextricably linked with larger realms of sustainability. Thompson and Wijesuriya flag this broader perspective for heritage that is finally infusing into both heritage and development discourse and, to a certain extent, practice, as the third stage in the evolution of heritage conceptualization since the 1960s.[18] In the context of World Heritage, the 2012 *Kyoto Vision* drafted on the occasion of the fortieth anniversary of the convention states,

> Only through strengthened relationships between people and heritage, based on respect for cultural and biological diversity as a whole, integrating tangible and intangible aspects and geared toward sustainable development will the "future we want" become attainable.[19]

However, the stark reality is that many heritage governance models have traditional mandates in conservation rooted in the *Venice Charter* era and struggle to take on an expanded worldview linked to sustainable development, even though the deeper roots of many of the daily management challenges they face are actually related to various aspects of economic, environmental, or social sustainability. The sluggishness of change at many sites suggests that the systemic transformation of the current heritage system will be difficult to carry out. Nonetheless, with the growing urgency to deal with big-picture development issues, such as climate change or postpandemic recovery, essential reforms need to be carried out with regard to (i) governance models, (ii) capacities, and (iii) metrics for assessing progress and outcomes. These can be identified as key prerequisites in the exercise of "expanding

18. Jane Thompson and Gamini Wijesuriya, "From 'Sustaining Heritage' to 'Heritage Sustaining Broader Societal Wellbeing and Benefits': An ICCROM Perspective," in *World Heritage and Sustainable Development: New Directions in World Heritage Management*, ed. Peter Bille Larsen and William Logan (Abingdon: Routledge, 2018).
19. UNESCO, *The Kyoto Vision*, November 8, 2012.

boundaries of practice" related to heritage within a new global context and fundamentally changed realities.[20]

To allow the practice of heritage and sustainable development to align at both a policy level and at an operational level, governance models need to be revisited. This includes updating legislative and regulatory frameworks to allow more strategic crossovers between heritage and development strategies. As seen with the *Policy for the Integration of a Sustainable Development Perspective into the Processes of the World Heritage Convention* or like-minded efforts to provide a "sustainable development toolbox" for the 2003 *Convention for the Safeguarding of the Intangible Cultural Heritage*, international statutory frameworks are now moving toward the intersection between heritage and sustainable development. At the national level, newer versions of heritage laws also promote the use of heritage as development assets. For instance, the *Law of the People's Republic of China on Intangible Cultural Heritage* (2011) does not just promote safeguarding. It also, in Article 37, "encourages and supports the leveraging of the special advantages of intangible cultural heritage resources and the reasonable utilization of the representative items of intangible cultural heritage to develop cultural products and cultural services with local and ethnical features and market potential on the basis of effective protection of those items."[21]

In terms of institutions, heritage organizations should be supported to move beyond conventional heritage conservation to deal with the greater complexity associated with sustainable development issues. Certain issues can be dealt with within the confines of their sites and their institutional mandates. Other issues may require cooperation with other agencies and stakeholders in a way that tries to use a partnership approach to achieve common heritage and development objectives. To do so, fundamental shifts in cognitive frameworks need to be triggered and learning should be supported, especially in the acquisition of new knowledge and skills pertaining to sustainable development. Current investments in institutional capacity building are still too narrowly focused on technical conservation issues or stand-alone management issues and are not well matched to the challenges of economic, environmental, and social sustainability.[22]

With this sustainability mindset as the starting point, UNESCO has developed a new professional competence framework for cultural heritage management.[23] This framework defines "core competencies" to cover the ability to uphold laws and regulations; apply heritage policy, principles, process, and ethics; deal with community, rights, and knowledge; undertake heritage education and interpretation; and orient practice toward sustainable development. In addition to the core competencies, managerial competencies were also defined related to various aspects of organizational management, such as financial and human resource management. Surveys of professional heritage management bodies and educational institutions revealed that many heritage personnel were lacking mastery in a number of these competences. "Sustainable development" in particular was acknowledged as being of high relevance but still an area where many people and organizations faced gaps. To overcome these gaps, further education and training are needed or organizations need to be reformed.[24]

20. Unakul, "Heritage Management," 32.
21. "Intangible Cultural Heritage Law," China CN179, accessed June 14, 2022, https://wipolex.wipo.int/en/text/336567.
22. Unakul, "Heritage Management," 35.
23. UNESCO, *Competence Framework for Cultural Heritage Management: A Guide to the Essential Skills and Knowledge for Heritage Practitioners* (Bangkok: UNESCO, 2021).
24. Unakul, "Heritage Management," 32.

As an alternative to expanding organizations to take on new sustainability competences, new alliances could be encouraged as a way of addressing a growing range of issues in a more agile manner, bringing together actors from different backgrounds and specializations.[25] These alliances could include organizations that may not have a statutory mandate or a heritage remit, including civil society organizations and organizations dealing with livelihoods, environment, and other issues mirroring the gamut of the Sustainable Development Goals (SDGs). Local governments with their broader view of development issues may provide an alternative institutional base for dealing with heritage in a more holistic way, provided they are inculcated with commitment and capacity related to heritage.

Finally, new metrics need to be applied to capture progress toward joint heritage and sustainable development objectives. These metrics must be more expansive than the conservation outputs and outcomes which form the bulk of heritage monitoring regimes today that have a narrow focus on technical matters. They do not capture the development issues related to local livelihoods and economy, access to social services and environmental integrity which also need to be considered and monitored. Such holistic monitoring will be a barometer for measuring and then advocating for proactive change. As an example, the World Heritage Periodic Monitoring exercise now includes dimensions related to sustainable development. In a broader way, UNESCO has also formulated a suite of indicators for assessing the role of culture in the *2030 Agenda for Sustainable Development (2030 Agenda)*, which is popularly known as the *UNESCO Culture 2030 Indicators*. The framework covers four thematic areas echoing the 5Ps: environment and resilience, prosperity and livelihoods, knowledge and skills, and inclusion and participation. Together, they help to paint a picture of how culture contributes both as a sector of activity and transversally across other sectors, such as education, healthcare, and others. In addition to these official sets of indicators, new tools and methodologies should also be applied to better characterize heritage and sustainable development. For instance, methods such as "social return on investment" can be used to understand impacts in terms of social dimensions of sustainability and can complement other tools used to measure economic impact, environmental outcomes, or conservation outcomes.

In the context of urban revitalization, with the multilayered complexities of cities and their heritage significance, having enhanced governance, strengthened capacities, and more well-rounded metrics will allow heritage actors to move beyond current technobureaucratic limitations to embrace larger concerns, particularly those related to sustainable development.

Bibliography

Araoz, Gustavo F. "Preserving Heritage Places under a New Paradigm." *Journal of Cultural Heritage Management and Sustainable Development* 1, no. 1 (2011): 55–60. https://doi.org/10.1108/20441261111129933.

Larsen, Peter Bille, and William Logan, eds. *World Heritage and Sustainable Development: New Directions in World Heritage Management*. Abingdon: Routledge, 2018.

Ost, Christian, and Nathalie van Drooghenbroeck. *Report on Economics of Conservation: An Appraisal of Theories, Principles and Methods*. Brussels: ICOMOS, International Economics Committee, 1998.

Rypkema, Donovan D. *The Economics of Historic Preservation: A Community Leader's Guide*. Washington, DC: National Trust for Historic Preservation, 2005.

25. Unakul, "Heritage Management," 35.

Unakul, Montira. "Expanding Boundaries of Practice in (World) Heritage Management: From Conservation to Sustainable Development." *Najua: Architecture, Design and Built Environment* 34, no. 2 (2019): A1-A-18. https://so04.tci-thaijo.org/index.php/NAJUA-Arch/article/view/225911.

Unakul, Montira. "Heritage Management and Sustainable Development." In *Enhancing Our Heritage Toolkit 2.0*, 32–35. Paris: UNESCO, 2021.

UNESCO. *Cities, Culture, Creativity Leveraging Culture and Creativity for Sustainable Urban Development and Inclusive Growth*. Paris: UNESCO, 2021. http://elibrary.worldbank.org/doi/book/10.1596/35621.

UNESCO. *Competence Framework for Cultural Heritage Management: A Guide to the Essential Skills and Knowledge for Heritage Practitioners*. Bangkok: UNESCO, 2021. https://bangkok.unesco.org/content/competence-framework-cultural-heritage-management-user-guide-essential-skills-and-knowledge.

UNESCO. *Culture for the 2030 Agenda*. Paris: UNESCO, 2018. https://unesdoc.unesco.org/ark:/48223/pf0000264687.

UNESCO. Policy for the Integration of a Sustainable Development Perspective into the Processes of the World Heritage Convention. Resolution 20 GA 13, 2015.

UNESCO. *Recommendation on the Historic Urban Landscape*. Paris: UNESCO, November 2011. https://whc.unesco.org/uploads/activities/documents/activity-638-98.pdf.

UNESCO. *The Kyoto Vision*. November 8, 2012.

UNESCO Bangkok. "2020 UNESCO Asia-Pacific Awards for Cultural Heritage Conservation—Winners Announced." December 16, 2020. https://bangkok.unesco.org/index.php/content/2020-unesco-asia-pacific-awards-cultural-heritage-conservation-winners-announced.

UNESCO Bangkok. "Apply for the Awards: Awards Regulations." March 1, 2022. https://bangkok.unesco.org/content/apply-awards.

United Nations. "Transforming Our World: The 2030 Agenda for Sustainable Development." 2015. https://sdgs.un.org/sites/default/files/publications/21252030%20Agenda%20for%20Sustainable%20Development%20web.pdf.

United Nations Habitat. *New Urban Agenda*. A/RES/71/256. October 2016. http://habitat3.org/the-new-urban-agenda/.

Adaptive Reuse from an Urban Planning Perspective

Elizabeth Vines

Sustainable Development Goals and COP26

The United Nations' Sustainable Development Goals (SDGs) are a set of global principles to guide action for making the world a more sustainable place.[1] Seventeen goals sit atop 169 detailed global targets and a corresponding set of indicators. Adopted in 2015, the SDGs were designed with national governments in mind and are a voluntary agreement among the United Nations' 193 member states. All member states agree on the intent behind the goals to address common global issues. However, since 2015, and particularly recently, there has been growing concern that actions are not meeting the intent of these goals.

The SDGs are meant to be practical and helpful for cities and urban areas. Many local governments and nongovernmental organizations are now using them as benchmarks to measure progress on the seventeen goals.[2] While there are global targets sitting underneath each goal, the SDGs are best made practical when they address specific issues that are relevant in a local context. In this way, local efforts can collectively contribute to the global effort. There are no mandatory requirements from member states to publicly state a level of commitment—the SDGs serve as a guide and can be used as a framework by local organizations to align contextual issues to one or more goals (a process now called localization).

However, the November 2021 United Nations Climate Change Conference (more commonly referred to as Conference of the Parties, COP26), held in Glasgow six years after the 2015 SDGs were adopted, was seen as a reporting opportunity for Conference of the Parties (COP) on progress made specifically in relation to SDG 13—Climate Action.[3] (COP26 had been delayed for a year due to the COVID-19 pandemic.) The conference was the third meeting of the parties to the 2015 Paris Agreement. More enhanced commitments were anticipated, but owing to late interventions from India and China, which weakened a move to end coal power and fossil fuel subsidies, and Australia's reluctance to declare emission reduction commitments for 2030, the conference ended with disappointment and less stringent resolutions

1. "The 17 Goals," accessed March 23, 2022, https://sdgs.un.org/goals.
2. For example, the of Melbourne in Australia. See City of Melbourne (Government), "City of Melbourne Desktop SDG Assessment," Sustainable Development Goals, accessed March 23, 2022, https://sdgs.org.au/project/city-of-melbourne-desktop-sdg-assessment/.
3. "COP26," accessed March 23, 2022, https://ukcop26.org.

Figure 4.1: The seventeen Sustainable Development Goals (SDGs). (Source: United Nations, Department of Economic and Social Affairs, Sustainable Development.)

than hoped for.[4] However, the pact was to explicitly commit to reducing the use of coal, a key contributor to greenhouse gas emissions and climate change. Such reduced emissions will contribute to achieving a better urban environment—less pollution and better control of rising temperatures in urban centers.

> The Sustainable Development Goals show that the World has a common vision of sustainability and a shared understanding of the tools—including heritage—that make that vision achievable. Now it's up to all of us to build and re-build that future together. . . . The new SDGs reflect a hard-learned global realization that heritage is a necessary enabler and a powerful driver of sustainable development.[5]
>
> —Gustavo Araoz, President, International Council on Monuments and Sites (ICOMOS), 2015

It is heartening to see that in the Australian federal election of May 21, 2022, the incumbent Liberal government was defeated "ending almost a decade of conservative rule and electing a raft of Greens and new independents. There were many issues in play, but it was undeniably a climate change election, one that many Australians had been waiting for."[6]

Culture and Heritage in Sustainable Development

In 2015, the important role of culture and heritage in sustainable development was recognized more fully for the first time in the newly adopted Sustainable Development Goals (SDGs). Cultural heritage appears most prominently under SDG 11—Sustainable Cities and Communities as target 11.4: "[Aims to] strengthen

4. The Australian government's policy response to the climate crisis was ranked last in an assessment of countries released at the global climate summit in Glasgow. See "COP26 Ends with Stark Warning: Step Up on Emission Cuts This Decade AUS, or Pay the Price," November 14, 2021, https://www.climatecouncil.org.au/resources/cop26-ends-with-stark-warning-step-up-on-emission-cuts-this-decade-aus-or-pay-the-price/.
5. "Statement by ICOMOS on the Adoption of the UN Sustainable Development Goals," October 5, 2015, https://www.icomos.org/en/focus/un-sustainable-development-goals/4372-statement-by-icomos-on-the-adoption-of-the-un-sustainable-development-goals.
6. "In April, more 60% (of 10,000) Nominated Climate Change as Their Top Issue, Followed by the Environment with 28% and the Cost of Living with 20%" *The Conservation*, May 22, 2022.

efforts to protect the world's cultural and natural heritage." Here, culture is specifically referenced, and heritage has now been given prominence as a key part in achieving sustainable urban growth.

It is evident to many experts and practitioners that culture in general and heritage in particular have much wider applications beyond SDG 11. Most of the SDGs affect all aspects of our lives.[7] The global disruption caused by the outbreak of COVID-19 in late 2019, and that continues at the time of writing, has tested the resilience of communities, governments, and world leaders at a global scale and increased the challenges and inequalities of living standards and human opportunities, especially in urban environments. It has also caused significant negative impacts to the heritage sector, with pressure to sweep away "old buildings" and build new. The economic opportunities in the construction of new infrastructure and new (often out-of-scale) high-rise buildings is seen as the overriding economic indicator. Even demolition and replacement of like with like (e.g., buildings of similar scale) is seen as an important economic generator, ignoring the equivalent but more specialized employment generation of conservation projects. This has a dramatic impact on the unique character of cities and neighborhoods.

The post-pandemic recovery period provides an opportunity for heritage practice to adapt rather than destroy, ensuring a resilient and sustainable future. This reality makes the SDGs, and the contributions that heritage can make in attaining them, more urgent and relevant than ever. Accordingly, a number of cities around the world have started mapping local initiatives against relevant SDGs, including indicators, on which their national government will report their implementation progress. The United States has made considerable progress through the development of the US Cities SDG Index.[8]

City Livability and Neighborhood Connections in the Urban Context

Healthy communities feel attached to their neighborhoods, and consequently, city dwellers and workers value many parts (sometimes all) of their urban environment. There is a desire to preserve places of attachment. Livable cities are creative in the way they approach economic development, recognizing that retention of heritage buildings and consistent streetscapes, landscapes, pocket parks, avenues of trees, plazas, and meeting places all establish and contribute to improved well-being for residents and workers.[9] Heritage conservation presents a wide spectrum of opportunities for action—not only keeping and passing on what is valued but also harnessing and enhancing heritage resources to support the goal of sustaining life on earth. All the Sustainable Development Goals (SDGs) are related to city livability.

7. There are many SDGs that apply specifically to the urban context in other goals, such as SDG 1—No Poverty, SDG 3—Good Health and Well-Being, SDG 4—Quality Education, SDG 6—Clean Water and Sanitation, SDG 8—Decent Work and Economic Growth, SDG 9—Industry, Innovation and Infrastructure, SDG 12—Responsible Consumption and Production, and SDG 13—Climate Action.
8. "Achieving a Sustainable Urban America: SDSN's U.S. Cities SDG Index," August 10, 2017, https://resources.unsdsn.org/achieving-a-sustainable-urban-america-sdsns-first-u-s-cities-sdg-index.
9. The Livable City, Mission and Goals outlines the five fundamental aspects of livable cities: robust and complete neighborhoods, accessibility and sustainable mobility, a diverse and resilient local economy, vibrant public spaces, and affordability. See "Mission and Goals," accessed March 23, 2022, https://www.livablecity.org/missiongoals/.

What Are the Characteristics of Sustainable Cities? How Does Heritage Retention Support Sustainability Goals?

We now live in an "urban century," where the sustainability and resilience of cities has become urgent. Sustainable cities are those that have short- and long-term strategies that integrate cultural, economic, environmental, and social objectives to meet the needs of the present generation while planning for future generations to also meet their needs. While cities can become places of economic and social mobility with a focus on livability, they can also become environmentally degraded and places of inequality and social injustice. Urban sustainability is a key issue, and it needs to be incorporated into urban management systems that are well organized and maintained.

> The sustainability of urban areas circles around healthy people, a healthy environment, and healthy human-environment interactions. For a city to thrive, human well-being and health are of utmost importance. However, maintaining human health at the cost of natural urban ecosystems will not only degrade the livability but also undermine urban sustainability of a city.[10]

For a city to be sustainable, it must provide a safe place for inhabitants to live and work and manage energy consumption and waste. Sustainable cities employ all their resources, including their unique cultural heritage, to promote healthy environments for investment and community connections. Historical city cores, which retain and celebrate their cultural assets, differentiate themselves from their competitors with improved livability and urban vitality. Heritage assets are an important component requiring good management within our urban environments.

What Is Sustainable Development? How Does It Relate to the Adaptive Reuse of Heritage Buildings?

The *Practice Note, Heritage and Sustainability 1: Built Heritage* by Australia ICOMOS is part of a series of practice notes and relates to the conservation of existing buildings and improvements to their environmental performance. This section references the excellent work of this document.

Sustainable development aims to reduce carbon emissions and utilize increasingly scarce resources in a responsible way. The conservation of existing cultural and natural heritage assets reduces environmental impacts by the following:[11]

- **Retaining the embodied energy of existing structures and landscapes, recognizing the environmental cost already paid.** Embodied energy refers to the energy and resources already expended in the construction of an existing building or years of growth in a natural landscape. For the built environment, it is the energy consumed by all the processes associated with the production

10. Meghna Patnaik, "What re the Principles of Urban Sustainability," Rethinking the Future, accessed March 23, 2022, https://www.re-thinkingthefuture.com/sustainable-architecture/a4249-what-are-the-principles-of-urban-sustainability/.
11. The *2021 Policy Guidance* document prepared by ICOMOS in 2021 provides a good summary of how impacts can be reduced. See ICOMOS, *Heritage and the Sustainable Development Goals: Policy Guidance for Heritage and Development Actors* (Paris: Sustainable Development Goals Working Group, March 2021), https://www.icomos.org/images/DOCUMENTS/Secretariat/2021/SDG/ICOMOS_SDGs_Policy_Guidance_2021.pdf; and Australia ICOMOS, *Practice Note, Heritage and Sustainability 1: Built Heritage* (Burra: Australia ICOMOS, August 2019), https://australia.icomos.org/wp-content/uploads/Practice-Note_Heritage-and-Sustainability-1-Built-Heritage.pdf.

Figure 4.2: Well-constructed masonry buildings retain embodied energy and provide opportunities for adaptive reuse (Yangon, Myanmar). (Source: Elizabeth Vines.)

of a place. Demolition and replacement with equivalent new construction no matter how energy efficient requires considerably more energy to equal the energy savings of rehabilitating an existing building. Building retention reduces carbon emissions by minimizing the energy needed to demolish and build new (SDG 11—Sustainable Cities and Communities, SDG 12—Responsible Consumption and Production).

- **Minimizing construction waste by reducing the demolition cycle, ensuring places are adapted and retained until the end of their useful life.** In addition, recycling material that results from demolition on the same site is an efficient and appropriate response (SDG 11—Sustainable Cities and Communities, SDG 12—Responsible Consumption and Production).
- **Continuing the life of building materials that can no longer be sustainably sourced.** High-quality building materials, such as stone and aged timber, are often found in heritage buildings and are now rare, and skilled tradesmen who built these buildings are also far less available. Adaptively reusing buildings lessens the need for new materials and retains existing materials to the end of their life cycle. In addition, the continuation of traditional building skills and practices ensures the ongoing use of renewable, local, and sustainable natural materials (SDG 8—Decent Work and Economic Growth, SDG 9—Industry, Innovation and Infrastructure, SDG 11—Sustainable Cities and Communities, SDG 12—Responsible Consumption and Production).
- **Continuing to utilize buildings that have been designed to respond to local climatic conditions and operate using passive environmental control.** The choice of forms and materials has evolved over time to suit the climate of a

particular area. Natural ventilation and careful choice of building orientation for daylight access (either to let sunlight in or exclude heat) provide long-term benefits in terms of lower energy usage. Heritage buildings in temperate climates are often constructed with high masonry content and have better qualities for insultation against external temperature fluctuations. Timber-framed heritage buildings in the tropics employ well-known methods of preventing cumulative heat buildup, such as cross-ventilation and high ceilings (SDG 3—Good Health and Well-Being, SDG 7—Affordable and Clean Energy, SDG 13—Climate Action).

- **Providing an alternative model to replacement with one that retains and adapts an existing building or place.** New buildings are constructed in materials that require energy for their production, and current sustainable design measuring criteria (such as green star rating) underestimate and do not measure embodied energy or costs of demolition, including landfill waste disposal impacts. At present, there is no single environmental rating tool that includes the environmental or embodied energy benefits of conserving and adapting heritage buildings. The existing rating tools fail to recognize the broader environmental benefits of retrofitting existing buildings and therefore encourage a constant cycle of demolition and rebuilding over retention and adaptation of existing buildings. The full environmental cost of new construction needs to be considered as there is a current bias that favors constant demolition and rebuilding (with arguments of employment generation) over retention and adaptive reuse that can create a similar number of jobs (SDG 8—Decent Work and Economic Growth, SDG 11—Sustainable Cities and Communities, SDG 12—Responsible Consumption and Production).
- **Contributing toward maintaining a community's sense of place in a rapidly changing world.** Cultural heritage is an inheritance to be passed on to the next generation. Conserving the built environment and adaptively reusing existing places, where identified and assessed as contributors to the city's identity, allows heritage values and meaning to be passed on to the next generation, contributing toward an emotionally sustainable future. Conservation of heritage places helps maintain livable places that communities identify with and provides positive and continuing cultural, economic, and social benefits for communities (SDG 3—Good Health and Well-Being, SDG 8—Decent Work and Economic Growth, SDG 11—Sustainable Cities and Communities).

Benefits of Adaptive Reuse

The benefits of keeping and adapting heritage buildings extend beyond reducing environmental impacts.

- **Adaptive reuse of heritage assets helps ensure the protection of a city or neighborhood's cultural heritage.** Visionary heritage strategies, prepared with community consultation and input, ensure that detailed heritage surveys and inventories outline the values of a place and what should be protected. An inventory of heritage places (which includes both tangible and intangible heritage assets and characteristics) then requires legal protection to ensure clarity of intent for neighborhood/city protection. This needs to be carefully considered in relation to other development parameters in the planning system. For example, if consistent streetscapes of two to four

Figure 4.3: Inner Melbourne changed its planning laws in the early 1980s to protect extensive inner-city conservation areas. These include residential and industrial areas and commercial streetscapes (as seen in this photo). It was a bold move by a newly elected planning minister (who was an architect) at the time of a change of state government (Clarendon Street, South Melbourne, Australia). (Source: Elizabeth Vines.)

stories of traditional development are identified as significant, yet there are no height restrictions for the area, development opportunities and pressure will ensure that places are not retained and demolition will be a constant threat. Identification and protection of heritage areas or precincts ensures fair and equitable rules across multiple properties, and height controls are critical. For example, it has been found in inner-city areas of Australia that such controls have served to increase property values more than those in areas outside of defined conservation areas. There is certainty about expectations and what happens to the land around heritage properties.

However, heritage protection often has low government priority, which is reflected in weak protection and outmoded planning frameworks. Unclear legal structures and inadequate financial resources for protection of local character can prevent community aspirations for adaptive reuse rather than redevelopment.

- **Heritage protection creates opportunities for community education.** Adapted heritage places can provide both place-based tangible and intangible learning opportunities that engage all ages, providing opportunities to discover the past and strengthen connections and local identity. The repair, adaptation, and management of heritage buildings involves many skills. These can go beyond building construction skills to include crafts associated with tangible heritage (i.e., fabrics, furnishings, and appropriate interior fit outs), and skills associated with intangible heritage, such as rituals that can introduce school and tertiary students to a wide range of cultural opportunities. Students can become actively engaged in understanding their cultural heritage with programs that pass on skills and information from the past.

  For example, a Gabaldon School in the Philippines was proposed for demolition and replacement with a concrete structure. For the same financial investment, the existing school building was retained, conserved, and adapted to new education needs. Supported strongly by the school headmaster, students became involved in the initiative, learning about the importance of heritage and adaptive reuse.

Figure 4.4: Proposed type of replacement school building with no environmental design considerations and no air-conditioning (Camiguin, the Philippines). (Source: Elizabeth Vines.)

Figure 4.5: Alternative conserved school building project, which retained an important heritage place and engaged students in the conservation process, leading to an understanding of the heritage values of the place. Project was undertaken in 2010 at Kuguita Elementary School, Mambajao, Camiguin, the Philippines. (Source: Elizabeth Vines.)

- **Linkages between heritage assets and layers of history are reinforced.** There is an opportunity to respect the layers of history of cities when it is understood that these layers contribute to their cultural heritage, are valuable, and need to be retained. Urban areas are comprised of the contributions of different inhabitants and cultures, resulting in urban expressions that are mixtures of tangible and intangible heritage. In the Asia-Pacific region and elsewhere, Eurocentric colonial building typologies were introduced (or sometimes laid over existing Indigenous designs), and imported architecture soon adapted to local conditions. Immense economic growth has now changed how cities have evolved as seen in the introduction of new architecture, including commercial towers and housing developments that are often side by side with historical quarters and districts. Planning frameworks need to respect historical layering, and this is well articulated in UNESCO's *Recommendation on the Historic Urban Landscape*, 2011 (HUL Recommendation).[12]

  "The key to understanding and managing any historic urban environment is the recognition that the city is not a static monument or group of buildings, but subject to dynamic forces in the economic, social and cultural spheres that shaped it and keep shaping it. . . . Historic context and new development can interact and mutually reinforce their role and meaning."[13]

12. UNESCO, *Recommendation on the Historic Urban Landscape* (Paris: UNESCO, November 2011), https://whc.unesco.org/uploads/activities/documents/activity-638-98.pdf.
13. UNESCO, *New Life for Historic Cities: The Historic Urban Landscape Approach Explained* (Paris: UNESCO, 2013), http://whc.unesco.org/en/activities/727/.

Figure 4.6: Example of a development that has overlaid the traditional historical streetscape (central building) with an out-of-scale (too-high) and inconsistent design approach, negatively impacting the values of this once-consistent urban shophouse environment (Penang, Malaysia). (Source: Elizabeth Vines.)

Historically, buildings have always been adapted, repaired, extended, and reused, and in the past, new additions frequently imitated their "host buildings," with extensions following traditional lines. Alternatively, quite different "fashions or periods" of design were introduced, sometimes rather discordantly as evidenced in altered façades and extensions. In all cases, whatever planning framework guides the decisions for a place, it is critical to understand the significance and values of the place.[14] The decisions made for a place must reflect its significance so that any new layers are appropriate, and the earlier layers, where important, should be expressed and understood.

UNESCO's World Heritage City Lab, commenced in June 2020, has facilitated international discussion on the implementation of the HUL Recommendation, reflecting on the practical problems and challenges of World Heritage properties.[15] The COVID-19 global health crisis has highlighted the vulnerability of cities, and the City Lab has offered a forum to reestablish thriving urban centers using "heritage-based strategies to build back the cities to be stronger, more sustainable, more resilient, and more deeply connected to their histories and landscape."[16] The City Lab has reinforced the knowledge base on how best to apply the HUL Recommendation as well as promoted urban regeneration and adaptive reuse in historic urban centers, including ways to finance heritage-related projects.

- **Reuse of heritage assets and creativity are complementary.** Cultural identity, which finds expression in layers of history and human creativity are

14. The Australia ICOMOS *Burra Charter* provides a framework for assessing values and managing change according to a logical process and is used in many countries.
15. UNESCO's World Heritage City Lab commenced in June 2020 in collaboration with the Advisory Bodies to the World Heritage Convention namely the International Council on Monuments and Sites (ICOMOS), International Union for the Conservation of Nature (IUCN), and the International Centre for the Study of the Preservation and Restoration of Cultural Property (ICCROM).
16. UNESCO, World Heritage Centre, *World Heritage City Lab, Summary Outcomes, 2020* (Paris: UNESCO, World Heritage Cities Programme, 2021), https://whc.unesco.org/en/news/2130.

Figure 4.7: Public art enlivening the walls of retained heritage buildings creates a vibrant townscape (Boston, USA). (Source: Elizabeth Vines.)

essential components of a vibrant and economically viable city. Heritage embodies centuries of history, innovation, and creativity. Both tangible assets (e.g., traditionally built vernacular architecture, urban plazas, and established landscaping in the physical realm) and intangible assets (e.g., rituals, social practices, and support systems) enhance the adaptability and resilience of communities. Adaptively reusing existing heritage places provides an ideal framework for creative enterprises. The UNESCO Creative Cities Network (UCCN) was created in 2004 to promote cooperation with and among cities that have identified creativity as a strategic factor for sustainable urban development. The cities in this network work together toward a common objective: placing creativity and cultural industries at the heart of their development plans at the local level and cooperating actively at the international level through this network. Cities are now engaged in making creativity an essential component of urban development, notably through partnerships involving the public and private sectors.

- **Heritage is part of well-being.** Heritage neighborhoods can play a fundamental role in ensuring healthy lives and promoting well-being for all ages, and they can include cultural landscapes, public spaces, and historic urban areas centered on pedestrian movement and bicycle paths with lessened impact of intrusive traffic. Neighborhood heritage character, an identified sense of place, established urban planting, pocket parks, and community gardens can all help to address mental health issues and can assist in reducing loneliness. Social connection is facilitated with small-scale interactions resulting from a strong sense of community. An identified sense of place and connection to that place creates opportunities that enhance the meaning and value of life.
- **Heritage and cultural tourism.** Cultural tourism has been severely impacted by the COVID-19 pandemic. Sustainable cultural tourism is closely linked with the targets of SDG 12—Responsible Consumption and Production. Prepandemic tourist numbers were high in many historic city centers or

Figure 4.8: Prepandemic visitation to historical sites and urban areas had, in many cases, become unsustainable, damaging the fabric of places (courtyard in Qiao family compound, Qi County, Shanxi Province, China). (Source: Elizabeth Vines.)

individual World Heritage Sites, placing heavy pressure on the environments and communities that were the focus of tourism. The physical impact and damage on significant urban cultural sites and the displacement of traditional activities to make way for new tourist-based activities and products critically endangered the authenticity of sites. Although businesses related to tourism are essential for local economies, it is hoped that greater attention will be placed on the management of sites and their carrying capacities. Practices grounded in traditional wisdom can help ensure that sustainable development tourism programs are culturally appropriate and effective as well as able to safeguard diversity. The process of conserving and adaptively reusing buildings is by nature an act of sustainable consumption and production. Traditional customs and lifestyles can also help to create the behavioral change needed to mitigate modern wasteful tourism practices.

Conclusion

It is evident that the contribution of heritage to the entire range of Sustainable Development Goals (SDGs) deserves recognition in the development process. Attention also needs to be paid by urban planners and the more-focused heritage sector in strengthening the dimensions of sustainable development as in the SDGs. The excellent *2021 Policy Guidance* document prepared by ICOMOS in 2021, which is referred to earlier, provides an invaluable resource for discussing practical application of the SDGs.[17] Each of the seventeen SDGs are examined, a specific goal formulated, current context (i.e., threats and potentials) identified, and a policy statement prepared. The report outlines "specific recommendations for the integration of

17. ICOMOS, *Heritage and the Sustainable Development Goals: Policy Guidance for Heritage and Development Actors* (Paris: Sustainable Development Goals Working Group, March 2021), https://www.icomos.org/images/DOCUMENTS/Secretariat/2021/SDG/ICOMOS_SDGs_Policy_Guidance_2021.pdf.

heritage as a positive contributor to development, the protection of heritage from harm during development processes, and the improvement of heritage practice for a better alignment with sustainable development objectives." The inclusion of case studies for each of the seventeen SDGs provides a helpful and practical reference document. While some SDGs may seem more relevant to heritage than others, it is important to examine them all consistently, as heritage practices can contribute to sustainable development in more ways than conventionally assumed.

Another helpful resource is the UNESCO Asia-Pacific Heritage Awards for Cultural Heritage Conservation program and the four associated publications—the *Asia Conserved* series.[18] Using the case study format, this illustrated series focuses on award-winning projects that exhibit best conservation practices during the twenty years of the awards program (2000–2020), providing encouragement to communities, and important recognition for the projects. *Asia Conserved Volume III* is of particular relevance as it links projects with the SDGs framework. The series as a whole outlines the importance of strong public-private partnerships and innovative grassroots initiatives and includes technical information that provides in-depth solutions to distinct conservation problems.

Conserving and adaptively reusing our urban heritage makes a very positive contribution to achieving the aims and implementation of the SDGs. An approach of sustainable development, as opposed to demolition and building new structures, retains the embodied energy of an existing place, minimizing the use of new resources, and sustainably recycling existing materials. It is important in the urban planning context to ensure that heritage regulations clearly outline what should be retained in a traditional townscape context and not allow out-of-scale high-rise development that actively encourages demolition and replacement. Well-considered conservation of our important urban cultural heritage, through well-considered adaptive reuse, will contribute to the well-being of urban inhabitants. Focusing on sustainable development will ensure that future generations will be able to enjoy places of meaning and significance, both built heritage and the natural environment. It is urgent to ensure that the SDGs are used as benchmarks in our cities and that goals are seriously pursued and implemented.

Bibliography

Australia ICOMOS. *The Burra Charter: The Australia ICOMOS Charter for Places of Cultural Significance*. Burra: Australia ICOMOS, 2013.

Australia ICOMOS. *Practice Note Heritage and Sustainability 1: Built Heritage*. Burra: Australia ICOMOS, August 2019.

Australian National University. *Implications of Climate Change for Australia's World Heritage Properties: A Preliminary Assessment*. Canberra: Department of Climate Change and the Department of the Environment, Water, Heritage and the Arts, 2009. http://ccsl.iccip.net/worldheritage-climatechange.pdf.

18. UNESCO, *Asia Conserved: Lessons Learned from the UNESCO Asia-Pacific Awards for Cultural Heritage Conservation (2000–2004)*, ed. Richard A. Engelhardt (Bangkok: UNESCO, 2007); UNESCO, *Asia Conserved II: Lessons Learned from the UNESCO Asia-Pacific Awards for Cultural Heritage Conservation (2005–2009)*, ed. Montira Unakul (Bangkok: UNESCO and iGroup Press, 2014); UNESCO, *Asia Conserved III: Lessons Learned from the UNESCO Asia-Pacific Awards for Cultural Heritage Conservation (2010–2014)*, ed. William Chapman (Bangkok: UNESCO, 2019); UNESCO, *Asia Conserved IV: Lessons Learned from the UNESCO Asia-Pacific Awards for Cultural Heritage Conservation (2015–2019)*, ed. William Chapman (Bangkok: UNESCO and iGroup Press, 2020).

City of Melbourne (Government). "City of Melbourne Desktop SDG Assessment." *Sustainable Development Goals*. Accessed March 23, 2022. https://sdgs.org.au/project/city-of-melbourne-desktop-sdg-assessment/.

City of Melbourne (Government). *Opportunities and Recommendations Report 2017 Annual Plan Initiative 1.13 Complete a Desktop Assessment of How City of Melbourne's Strategies and Plans Deliver the UN's Sustainable Development Goals (SDGs)*. Melbourne: City of Melbourne, 2017. https://www.melbourne.vic.gov.au/sitecollectiondocuments/sustainable-development-goals.pdf.

City of Melbourne (Government). *Urban Forest Strategy: Making a Great City Greener 2012–2032*. Melbourne: City of Melbourne, 2014. http://www.melbourne.vic.gov.au/SiteCollectionDocuments/urban-forest-strategy.pdf.

City of Melbourne (Government). *Walking Plan 2014–17*. Melbourne: City of Melbourne, 2014. http://www.melbourne.vic.gov.au/SiteCollectionDocuments/walking-plan-2014-17.pdf.

Climate Council. "COP26 Ends with Stark Warning: Step Up on Emission Cuts This Decade AUS, or Pay the Price." November 14, 2021. Accessed March 23, 2022. https://www.climatecouncil.org.au/resources/cop26-ends-with-stark-warning-step-up-on-emission-cuts-this-decade-aus-or-pay-the-price/.

International Council on Monuments and Sites (ICOMOS). "Statement by ICOMOS on the Adoption of the UN Sustainable Development Goals." October 5, 2015. Accessed March 23, 2022. https://www.icomos.org/en/focus/un-sustainable-development-goals/4372-statement-by-icomos-on-the-adoption-of-the-un-sustainable-development-goals.

Labadi, Sophia, Francesca Giliberto, Ilaria Rosetti, Linda Shetabi, and Ege Yildirim. *Heritage and the Sustainable Development Goals: Policy Guidance for Heritage and Development Actors*. Paris: ICOMOS, International Council on Monuments and Sites, 2021. https://www.icomos.org/images/DOCUMENTS/Secretariat/2021/SDG/ICOMOS_SDGs_Policy_Guidance_2021.pdf.

Livable City. "Mission and Goals." Accessed March 23, 2022. https://www.livablecity.org/missiongoals/.

Patnaik, Meghna. "What Are the Principles of Urban Sustainability." *Rethinking the Future*. Accessed March 23, 2022. https://www.re-thinkingthefuture.com/sustainable-architecture/a4249-what-are-the-principles-of-urban-sustainability/.

Sustainable Development Solutions Network. "Achieving a Sustainable Urban America: SDSN's U.S. Cities SDG Index." August 10, 2017. https://resources.unsdsn.org/achieving-a-sustainable-urban-america-sdsns-first-u-s-cities-sdg-index.

UN Climate Change Conference, UK 2021. "COP26." Accessed March 23, 2022. https://ukcop26.org.

UNESCO. *Asia Conserved: Lessons Learned from the UNESCO Asia-Pacific Awards for Cultural Heritage Conservation (2000–2004)*. Edited by Richard A. Engelhardt. Bangkok: UNESCO, 2007.

UNESCO. *Asia Conserved II: Lessons Learned from the UNESCO Asia-Pacific Awards for Cultural Heritage Conservation (2005–2009)*. Edited by Montira Unakul. Bangkok: UNESCO and iGroup Press, 2014.

UNESCO. *Asia Conserved III: Lessons Learned from the UNESCO Asia-Pacific Awards for Cultural Heritage Conservation (2010–2014)*. Edited by William Chapman. Bangkok: UNESCO, 2019.

UNESCO. *Asia Conserved IV: Lessons Learned from the UNESCO Asia-Pacific Awards for Cultural Heritage Conservation (2015–2019)*. Edited by William Chapman. Bangkok: UNESCO, 2020.

UNESCO. "Creative Cities Network." 2016. Accessed April 1, 2022. http://en.unesco.org/creative-cities.

UNESCO. *New Life for Historic Cities: The Historic Urban Landscape Approach Explained*. Paris: UNESCO, 2013. http://whc.unesco.org/en/activities/727/.

UNESCO. *Recommendation on the Historic Urban Landscape*. Paris: UNESCO, November 2011. https://whc.unesco.org/uploads/activities/documents/activity-638-98.pdf.

UNESCO World Heritage Centre. *World Heritage City Lab, Summary Outcomes, 2020*. Paris: World Heritage Cities Programme, 2021. https://whc.unesco.org/en/news/2130.

United Nations, Department of Economic and Social Affairs, Sustainable Development. "The 17 Goals." Accessed March 23, 2022. https://sdgs.un.org/goals.

Transforming a Dilapidated Rural Village into a Nature-Culture Interface for Social-Ecological Sustainability: Lai Chi Wo, Hong Kong

Hiu Lai Chick, Katie

Introduction

Frequently, humankind is considered as a separate entity from nature and is situated in a hierarchical relationship of dominance.[1] Such a nature-culture alienation, rooted in modern Western beliefs, manifests itself in different and increasingly adverse ways, such as pollution, depletion of natural resources, and destruction of ecosystems, among others.[2] There is a much-needed reflection on the importance of safeguarding the nature-culture relationship.

In the 1960s, there was growing awareness about the impact of rapid development on natural systems. This became a global concern, prompting the emergence of formalized sustainable development as an approach to address conflicts between economic growth and environmental protection (and later, social development).[3] Humankind's impact on the environment continues to be one of the most important and discussed issues today. This is reflected in the United Nations' *2030 Agenda for Sustainable Development* (*2030 Agenda*), which includes the Sustainable Development Goals (SDGs). In the preamble to the *2030 Agenda*, world leaders affirmed that they are "determined to protect the planet from degradation, including through sustainable consumption and production, sustainably managing its natural resources and taking urgent action on climate change, so that it can support the needs of the present and future generations."[4] With its seventeen goals and 169 targets, the SDGs set out the most ambitious but urgent objectives to guide the path of a sustainable future.[5] It is notable that the *2030 Agenda* gives explicit recognition to the interrelationship

1. Augustin Berque, *Thinking through Landscape* (Abingdon: Routledge, 2013); Yrjö Haila, "Beyond the Nature-Culture Dualism," *Biology & Philosophy* 15, no. 2 (2000): 155–75.
2. Sally Brockwell, Sue O'Connor, and Denis Byrne, "Introduction: Engaging Culture and Nature," in *Transcending the Culture-Nature Divide in Cultural Heritage: Views from the Asia–Pacific Region*, ed. Sally Brockwell, Sue O'Connor, and Denis Byrne (Canberra: ANU Press, 2013), 1–11.
3. J. A. Du Pisani, "Sustainable Development—Historical Roots of the Concept," *Environmental Sciences* 3, no. 2 (2006): 83–96.
4. United Nations, "Transforming Our World: The 2030 Agenda for Sustainable Development," 2015, https://sdgs.un.org/sites/default/files/publications/21252030%20Agenda%20for%20Sustainable%20Development%20web.pdf.
5. Andrew Potts, "An Urgent Journey: Realizing the Potential of Integrated Nature-Culture Approaches to Create a Sustainable World," *George Wright Forum* 34, no. 2 (2017): 229–37.

of natural and cultural systems, and the fundamental role of heritage in sustainable development.[6]

In particular, SDG 11—Sustainable Cities and Communities, which aims "to protect the world's culture and natural heritage" (target 11.4), recalls the UNESCO *World Heritage Convention* (*The Convention*), the leading international instrument for heritage conservation that brings together nature and culture.[7] *The Convention* was the first international legal instrument to recognize "cultural landscapes" as a representation of the "combined works of nature and man," where natural and cultural values are not only inextricably related, but also the interaction between the natural environment and humankind is emphasized and acknowledged for its heritage significance.[8] The *Policy Guidance for Heritage and Development Actors* (*Policy Guidance*) was produced by the International Council on Monuments and Sites (ICOMOS) in 2021 for helping heritage and development actors to "harness the power of heritage to accelerate the achievement of the SDGs."[9] This *Policy Guidance* suggests adopting a "culture-nature" approach and "landscape-based" solutions to achieve well-being of the planet. It gives a hint of the potential role that cultural landscapes can play in promoting sustainability, especially under a fast-changing urban context.

In all these international documents, the term "heritage" covers both natural and cultural as well as tangible and intangible aspects. It is used in place of either "natural heritage" or "cultural heritage" to emphasize their inherently connected and inseparable character.[10] However, a division between natural and cultural sectors is often observed, influencing policymaking at local, regional, and international levels as well as rural and urban development.[11] Abandoning this dichotomy to embrace a more integrated system for effective protection of both natural and cultural heritage resources remains a challenge.

Revitalizing Hong Kong's Cultural Landscape

In the case of Hong Kong, the consequences of urbanization have created unsustainable living conditions for the majority of the population. The urban-biased development mode has threatened the survival of the city's fragile cultural landscapes, thus weakening Hong Kong's resilience to climate change and other disasters, both man-made and natural, such as the COVID-19 pandemic. The award-winning sustainable rural revitalization project of the Lai Chi Wo cultural landscape, which is examined in this essay, aims to reestablish the rural-urban and nature-culture linkages in Hong Kong through a collaborative, integrative, and interdisciplinary approach. In the essay, the evolution of Lai Chi Wo as a historical agricultural village landscape in Hong Kong is presented, including the threats it faces due to the inhabitants' desire for an urban lifestyle. This is followed by a discussion of the practical implementation strategies for revitalization that engaged a broad cross section of stakeholders. The

6. United Nations, "2030 Agenda."
7. UNESCO, *Operational Guidelines for the Implementation of the World Heritage Convention* (Paris: UNESCO, 2021).
8. Mechtild Rössler, "World Heritage Cultural Landscapes: A UNESCO Flagship Programme 1992–2006," *Landscape Research* 31, no. 4 (2006): 333–53.
9. Sophia Labadi, Francesca Giliberto, Ilaria Rosetti, Linda Shetabi, and Ege Yildirim, *Heritage and the Sustainable Development Goals: Policy Guidance for Heritage and Development Actors* (Paris: ICOMOS, 2021).
10. Kurmo Konsa, "Natural and Cultural Heritage: Framing Meanings and Practices," *International Journal of Sustainability in Economic, Social, and Cultural Context* 12, no. 4 (2016): 9–18.
11. Maya Ishizawa, "Cultural Landscapes Link to Nature: Learning from Satoyama and Satoumi," *Built Heritage* 2 (2018): 7–19.

"nature-culture bond" and "living-heritage approach" are highlighted as strategies for tackling contemporary environmental challenges and sustaining long-term stewardship of the Lai Chi Wo cultural landscape, thus highlighting the role of heritage in achieving the Sustainable Development Goals (SDGs).

Hong Kong's Historical Hakka Village Landscape

Around three-quarters of Hong Kong's territory is countryside, much of which was once occupied by self-sustaining rural villages. These traditional villages are the main constituents of Hong Kong's rich cultural landscapes. Although rapid urbanization over the past decades has brought economic prosperity to the city's urban areas, it has threatened, and in some cases eradicated, Hong Kong's rural villages and communities. Lai Chi Wo is an example of a traditional agricultural rural village that was at brink of disappearance.

Lai Chi Wo is a rural village in the northeastern part of Hong Kong. Although its location is technically not remote, access to the village makes it feel as such (one can reach the village only by boat or an informal hiking trail; there is no direct drop-off via car/bus). It is situated in a natural valley embraced by mountains and occupies an area of more than one square kilometer. This rural village landscape is rooted in Hakka culture and shaped by generations of inhabitants over the past four hundred years. In Hong Kong, Hakkas are recognized as one of the four major Indigenous ethnic groups. They are a subgroup of the Han Chinese that originated in north China and migrated to south China after the repeal of the Coastal Evacuation Order in 1669.[12] As the fertile lowland areas in south China were already intensively occupied by earlier settlers, Hakkas generally built their homes in less-desirable, rugged, and remote areas with limited resources, like Lai Chi Wo.[13]

The existing Lai Chi Wo village was set up by two Hakka clans, the Tsangs and Wongs, that migrated from Dongguan in mainland China in the seventeenth century.[14] They brought their Hakka culture to Lai Chi Wo, including agricultural and traditional skills as well as feng shui beliefs. They tamed the harsh hilly landscape, cultivated a large forest at the back of the village near the hillside, and planted a woodland at the fringe of the estuary based on feng shui principles. They transformed the hilly slopes into terraces for paddy farming and built over two hundred village houses, creating an extensive village landscape (Figure 5.1). Living off the land and surrounded by the sea, the Hakka Indigenous community in Lai Chi Wo was self-sufficient for hundreds of years. By the 1950–1960s, the Hakka population of Lai Chi Wo reached hundreds of villagers.

Lai Chi Wo's secluded location has shielded it from urban development. Unlike many other rural villages in Hong Kong, its village ecosystem is in a better condition. Although the village is small in size, it is rich in ecological resources.[15] It has been recognized, both locally and internationally, for its unique ecological and geological

12. Patrick H. Hase, "Eastern Peace: Sha Tau Kok Market in 1925," *Journal of the Hong Kong Branch of the Royal Asiatic Society* 33 (1993): 147–202.
13. R. H. Liu, *Xinjie Jianshi* (A brief history of the New Territories) (Hong Kong: Joint Publishing, 1999).
14. Hiu Lai Chick, "The Significance, Conservation Potential and Challenges of a Traditional Farming Landscape in an Asian Metropolis: A Case Study of Lai Chi Wo, Hong Kong," *Journal of World Heritage Studies*, Special Issue (2017): 17–23.
15. Billy Chi Hang Hau, K. W. F. Lo, and K. Y. K. So, *Living Water and Community Revitalization—An Agricultural-Led Action, Engagement and Incubation Programme at Lai Chi Wo: Biodiversity Baseline and Management Plan of Freshwater and Terrestrial Habitats of Lai Chi Wo* (Hong Kong: Policy for Sustainability Lab, The University of Hong Kong, 2018).

Figure 5.1: Aerial photo showing the village landscape features of Lai Chi Wo in 1956. 1. Cluster of village houses; 2. Feng shui forest at the back of the village near the hillside; 3. Feng shui woodland at the fringe of the estuary; 4. Paddy fields; 5. Streams; 6. Nearby Mui Tsz Lam village; 7. Nearby Siu Tan village; and 8. Polder fields for paddy farming at Siu Tan. (Source: Lands Department, Hong Kong SAR Government.)

features. The site is considered as the most intact "seaweed bed–mangroves–forest" ecosystem remaining in south China.[16]

Spirit of Place: The Nature-Culture Bond

"Spirit of place is defined as the tangible (buildings, sites, landscapes, routes, objects) and the intangible elements (memories, narratives, written documents, rituals, festivals, traditional knowledge, values, textures, colors, odors, etc.), that is to say the physical and the spiritual elements that give meaning, value, emotion and mystery to place."[17] The Lai Chi Wo village landscape illustrates an authentic, intact, and rare organically evolved and associative cultural landscape shaped by the local Hakka community.[18] It embodies a harmonious relationship between nature and human settlement, giving the village landscape a unique spirit of place.

Lai Chi Wo exemplifies the Chinese philosophy of tranquil coexistence between nature and culture through the expression of ancient feng shui principles, which represent Chinese Indigenous notions of environmental design that nurture the delicate

16. Brian Morton, "Hong Kong's Mangrove Biodiversity and Its Conservation within the Context of a Southern Chinese Megalopolis. A Review and a Proposal for Lai Chi Wo to Be Designated as a World Heritage Site," *Regional Studies in Marine Science* 8 (2016): 382–99.
17. ICOMOS, *Québec Declaration on the Preservation of the Spirit of Place* (Quebec: ICOMOS, 2008).
18. Chick, "Significance, Conservation Potential and Challenges."

nature-culture balance.[19] The village sits at the foot of the hill shielded by a mountain ridge at the back. A species-rich mature feng shui forest blankets the village forming a protective arc. The woodland near the estuary and mangrove lies near the seashore and is maintained by the villagers. In front of the village is a winding stream that nourishes the farmlands (Figure 5.2). In Lai Chi Wo, feng shui principles guide the living practices and all forms of construction work, such as the layout and orientation of village houses. The village houses are neatly arranged along three vertical and nine horizontal lanes facing the same direction (southeast) and enclosed by a village wall. This spatial setting is well preserved today with minimal modern intervention. The principles of feng shui, together with other spiritual beliefs, have not only protected the site's integrity as a self-sufficient village but also established a tradition of worshipping nature through earth gods, sacred trees, and temples (Figure 5.3).

Lai Chi Wo is a four-hundred-year-old living testimony of Hakka stewardship. The Hakka ancestors overcame the geographic limitations of the site, adapting to the rugged topography as they developed their terraced agriculture and irrigation system. The agricultural practice was developed on the basis of traditional knowledge, which emphasizes mutual-aid collaboration networks, a resource management system, and

Figure 5.2: Lai Chi Wo sits at the foot of the hill shielded by a mountain ridge at the back and blanketed by a forest that forms a protective arc around the village. (Source: Centre for Civil Society and Governance, The University of Hong Kong.)

19. David R. Kinsley, *Ecology and Religion: Ecological Spirituality in Cross-Cultural Perspective* (Englewood Cliffs, NJ: Prentice Hall, 1994); S. Y. Li, "Community-Based Forestry and the Functions of Institutions: A Case Study of Fung Shui Forests in Hong Kong," *International Forestry Review* 20, no. 3 (2018): 362–74.

Figure 5.3: An example of the tradition of worshipping nature through earth gods, sacred trees, and temples in Lai Chi Wo. (Source: Centre for Civil Society and Governance, The University of Hong Kong.)

a sustainable land-use pattern.[20] Adaptation was also reflected in the extensive use of local natural resources, such as earth, masonry, and wood, in the construction of village buildings and structures. Since similar landscapes in south China have been seriously damaged in the process of rapid urbanization, Lai Chi Wo remains the most intact and unique traditional agricultural village landscapes in the region.[21]

Threats to the Village Landscape and Its Vitality

Although Lai Chi Wo demonstrates high levels of cultural authenticity, ecological uniqueness, and spatial integrity, attributes that are rarely found elsewhere in Hong Kong and south China, the continuity of the rural village landscape as well as its heritage value, in particular traditional Hakka culture and traditions, were under serious threat due to the decline of its Indigenous community.[22] Similar to other villages in the region, Lai Chi Wo was affected by sociopolitical changes during the urbanization process. Beginning in the 1960s, many villagers chose to leave Lai Chi Wo and emigrate to the United Kingdom or other European countries, or move to urban areas in Hong Kong, seeking better living conditions and employment opportunities. Large-scale emigration continued through the 1970s–1990s. After the last villager left Lai Chi Wo in the 1990s, most village houses and cultivated land were left unattended and abandoned.[23]

Land in Lai Chi Wo was traditionally owned by the Hakka community, but during the British colonial period, land ownership was compartmentalized by the Block Crown Lease in 1898, which complicated the management issues and weakened the community's role in protecting the significance of an Indigenous cultural landscape.[24] Although most of the premises and terraced areas within the village are

20. Jessica M. William, V. Chu, W. F. Lam, and W. W. Y. Law, *Springer Briefs on Case Studies of Sustainable Development: Revitalising Rural Communities* (Singapore: Springer, 2021).
21. Chick, "Significance, Conservation Potential and Challenges."
22. Chick, "Significance, Conservation Potential and Challenges."
23. Winnie Wai Yee Law, S. I. S. Yiu, and H. L. Chick, *Vivifying Lai Chi Wo: Sustainable Lai Chi Wo Programme Four Year Review and Outlook* (Hong Kong: Policy for Sustainability Lab, The University of Hong Kong, 2018).
24. Roger Nissim, *Land Administration and Practice in Hong Kong*, rev. ed. (Hong Kong: Hong Kong University Press, 2012).

still under Indigenous community ownership, the hilly and coastal areas of the village that were once used as forage areas and orchards were designated as the Plover Cove Country Park and Yan Chau Tong (Double Haven) Marine Park in 1978 and 1996, respectively (Figure 5.4).[25] The woodland as well as the estuary, which were once owned and managed by the villagers, became public assets under the protection of what is now the Hong Kong SAR government. A large area of the village landscape in Lai Chi Wo is designated as a Site of Archaeological Interest and two temple buildings are officially recognized as graded historical buildings. Four Old and Valuable Trees in the village, which were maintained by the villagers, are now on government land and officially managed by different government departments.

It is noteworthy that much of the undeveloped natural and rural landscape in Hong Kong remains protected under the Country Parks and Marine Parks Ordinance, but villages and agricultural lands have been mostly excluded from this designation, creating remote pockets of land such as Lai Chi Wo.[26] Although the Country Parks and Marine Parks designation is effective in protecting sites from urbanization and major landscape change, at the same time it limits the accessibility and development options of Hong Kong's rural villages.[27] Furthermore, the dismissal of community management rights over natural resources leads to the loss of some traditional practices, such as manual siltation of the stream and selective pruning of the mangrove forest, even though these practices are essential for maintaining the ecosystem's functions.

While the environmental designation acknowledges and protects Lai Chi Wo's ecological significance, it is based on the "classic" nature-culture separation, which ignores the fact that human activities have long been part of the rural ecosystem.[28] Conserving the heritage of rural village landscapes in Hong Kong challenges the existing development policy and heritage protection laws and practices. The existing policy and regulatory regime are designed for an urban-centered development and management mode. For instance, the current heritage grading system only recognizes buildings but not landscapes. Although a nature conservation policy exists for the management of rural natural resources in Hong Kong, an integrated policy for the recognition of biocultural value and the sustainable development of cultural landscapes is generally lacking.[29] The urban-biased development and monument-based heritage system simply do not protect the multilayered heritage significance of Hong Kong's cultural landscapes.

---

25. Agriculture, Fisheries and Conservation Department, Hong Kong SAR Government, "Plover Cove Country Park and Plover Cove (Extension) Country Park," accessed June 5, 2022, https://www.afcd.gov.hk/english/country/cou_vis/cou_vis_cou/cou_vis_cou_pc/cou_vis_cou_pc.html; Agriculture, Fisheries and Conservation Department, Hong Kong SAR Government, "Yan Chau Tong Marine Park," accessed June 5, 2022, https://www.afcd.gov.hk/english/country/cou_vis/cou_vis_mar/cou_vis_mar_des/cou_vis_mar_des_yan.html.
26. Agriculture, Fisheries and Conservation Department, Hong Kong SAR Government, "Hong Kong: The Facts—Country Parks and Special Areas," accessed June 5, 2022, https://www.afcd.gov.hk/english/country/cou_lea/the_facts.html.
27. When designating certain sites as country parks in the past, the Hong Kong SAR government has excluded villages and agricultural lands as well as some adjacent government lands as the buffer area from the boundaries of country parks. There are currently seventy-seven such country park enclaves in Hong Kong. Legislative Council Archives of Hong Kong Special Administrative Region, "Press Release. Lcq15: Conservation of Country Park Enclaves,"" November 18, 2015, https://www.info.gov.hk/gia/general/201511/18/P201511180710.htm; William et al., *Springer Briefs*.
28. Ishizawa, "Cultural Landscapes Link to Nature."
29. Erika Kraus, "Book Review: Gloria Pungetti, Gonzalo Oviedo, and Della Hooke (Eds.), *Sacred Species and Sites: Advances in Biocultural Conservation*," *Landscape Ecology* 29 (2014): 1461–62.

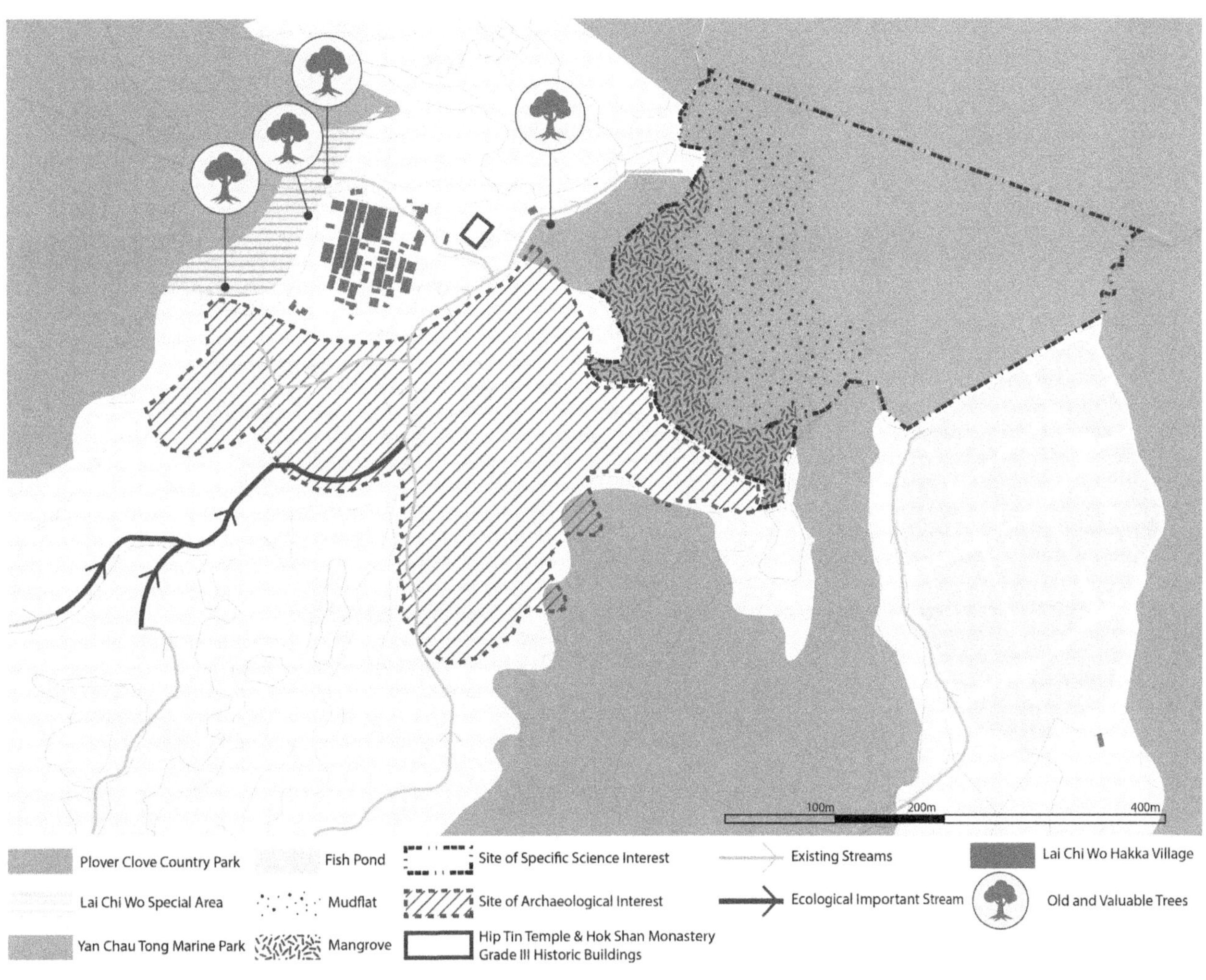

Figure 5.4: Areas and features under protection in Lai Chi Wo. (Source: Jessica M. William, V. Chu, W. F. Lam, and W. W. Y. Law, *Springer Briefs on Case Studies of Sustainable Development: Revitalising Rural Communities* [Singapore: Springer, 2021].)

A Living Heritage Approach to Revitalization

Understanding and addressing the complexities of a cultural landscape are crucial steps for appropriate conservation and revitalization.[30] The Lai Chi Wo revitalization project is built on the understanding that a traditional rural village landscape is a dynamic and living system in which nature and culture continuously interact. The long-term nature-culture coevolution is woven into both the tangible and intangible fabric—from spatial organization and land use to agriculture, architecture, biodiversity, customs, language, local knowledge systems, and religion. A sustainable revitalization model, which recognizes these living dimensions as key attributes contributing to the vibrancy of the place, was developed to reactivate the village landscape and its nature-culture bond. Since 2013, a cross-sectoral collaborative initiative has been launched to revive and sustain the vitality of the cultural, natural, and social capital of Lai Chi Wo. The project combines a series of conservation actions that are categorized into five major strategies (Figure 5.5):

30. Mechtild Rössler and Roland Chih-Hung Lin, "Cultural Landscape in World Heritage Conservation and Cultural Landscape Conservation Challenges in Asia," *Built Heritage* 2 (2018): 3–26.

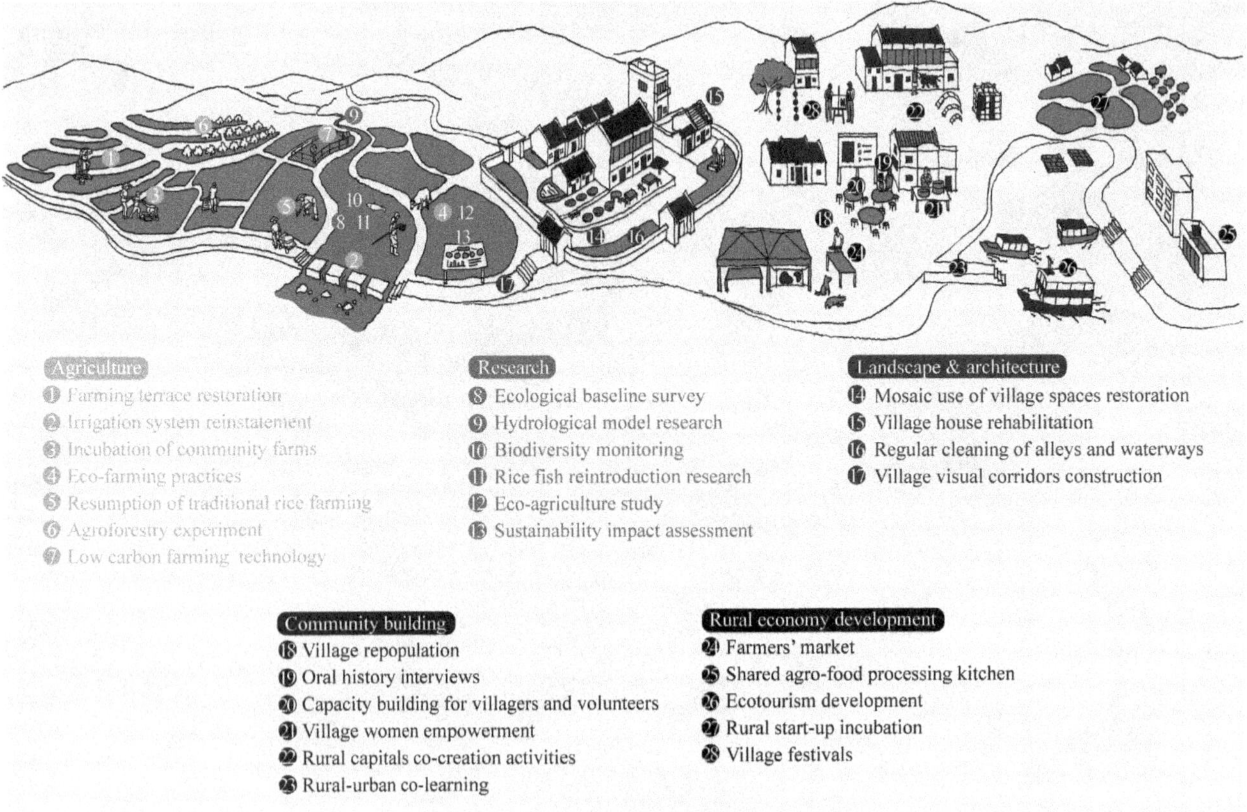

Figure 5.5: Illustration showing twenty-eight major actions, categorized into five major strategies, carried out under the Lai Chi Wo revitalization project. (Source: Hiu Lai Chick and S. I. Yiu, *A Nine-Year Journey of HSBC Rural Sustainability*, ed. W. F. Lam and W. W. Y. Law [Hong Kong: Centre for Civil Society and Governance, The University of Hong Kong, 2023], 20–21.)

1. Rehabilitating the comanagement practices of the agricultural landscape.
2. Reviving the rural community through network development and capacity building.
3. Strengthening the village governance and management structures for cultural inheritance.
4. Building a creative and self-sustaining community economy.
5. Rebranding rural landscape heritage.

These actions are helping to conserve the integrity and functionality of a rural cultural landscape, rejuvenate the local community, and enhance the natural environment. The project uses the living heritage approach as a conceptual framework to do the following:

- Guide the conservation design to embrace change and allow for spontaneous but continuous evolution of the landscape, while protecting the landscape's integrity and authenticity.
- Frame the project as an ongoing process to sustain the community stewardship and foster the cocreation of values.
- Emphasize the recognition and relevance of cultural landscapes in contemporary society and provide incentives for long-term care of the site.[31]

31. Gamani Wijesuriya, *Living Heritage: A Summary* (Rome: ICCROM, 2015).

Figure 5.6: Village cleanup is organized annually since the commencement of the revitalization project to engage Indigenous villagers, new settlers, volunteers, and the project team, who work collaboratively for the Lai Chi Wo environment. (Source: Centre for Civil Society and Governance, The University of Hong Kong.)

Multidisciplinary Collaboration to Maintain Rural Structure and Institutions

With strong funding support from a private corporation, the Lai Chi Wo project was the first civil society–led cultural landscape revitalization project codesigned and comanaged by the local community and a conservation team of multidisciplinary professionals and scientists from a local university and nonprofit organizations. The project identified multiple stakeholders, which included not only the local Indigenous community but also various communities of interest—government, private sector, and public sector, all of whom were invited to join the endeavor.[32] This approach created a problem-focused and participatory process to cope with the social-ecological complexity of a living community, generating enough momentum to undertake the monumental task of revitalizing Lai Chi Wo.[33]

The project fully recognizes the Indigenous Hakka community's role as hosts and knowledge holders of the place. Given that the overseas-born younger generations of the Indigenous community do not plan to return to Hong Kong, it was unrealistic to rely on the remaining senior villagers to sustain the community and the larger village landscape. With the support and endorsement of the Indigenous community, the project has brought new life to the village by encouraging city dwellers to settle in the village. The new settlers share a similar vision of safeguarding rural heritage and are willing to contribute to the revitalization initiative.[34] They have been engaged to co-live, co-learn, and co-create with the Indigenous villagers of Lai Chi Wo through different networking and capacity-building programs.[35] The initiative has not only supplemented the original clan-based community structure, which was no longer

32. William et al., *Springer Briefs*.
33. Cora J. van Oosten and Wouter Leen Hijweege, "Governing Biocultural Diversity in Mosaic Landscapes," in *Forest-People Interfaces*, ed. B. Arts, S. van Bommel, M. Ros-Tonen, and G. Verschoor (Wageningen: Wageningen Academic Publishers, 2012), 211–22.
34. Law, Yiu, and Chick, *Vivifying Lai Chi Wo*.
35. Centre for Civil Society and Governance, The University of Hong Kong, "HSBC Rural Sustainability Programme," 2022, https://ccsg.hku.hk/ruralsd.

sustainable, but has provided necessary manpower for maintenance of the village infrastructure and the revival of agricultural practice in Lai Chi Wo. The strengthened local community has created new social capital to support active management of communal resources (Figure 5.6).[36] Through new social ties and interactions, a sense of belonging, a set of collective beliefs and values, and a shared identity have gradually emerged among members of the new Lai Chi Wo community. This is the base on which the Lai Chi Wo community has reestablished its robustness and resilience.

Reviving the Agricultural Vibrancy and Ecosystem Services

Agricultural activities are the strongest manifestation of the nature-culture interplay shaping the cultural landscape of Lai Chi Wo. The farming terraces are important landscape features associated with the local Hakka settlement. The agricultural system and its associated practices serve as the basis for the community's nature-based knowledge.[37] These have been used as anchors to rehabilitate the disconnection between the natural and cultural systems. The project has rejuvenated the cultural landscape as a living agroecosystem by reviving its mosaic of land uses. It has progressively restored the farming terraces, repaired old irrigation channels and masonry walls, repaired collapsed village houses and old farm sheds, and tidied dilapidated lots and alleys to reveal the original configuration of the village landscape. More importantly, the local community has been encouraged to participate in agricultural activities to bring productivity and vibrancy back to the village.

The project's conservation and revitalization strategies have been based on an ecosystem-oriented approach that not only restores but also enhances the functionality of the rural village landscape. The agroecosystem has provided for the local community as well as served such important functions as biodiversity conservation, carbon sink, soil conservation, and water regulation.[38] The introduction of small-scale eco-agriculture and agroforestry to the Lai Chi Wo community, with the aid of low-carbon technologies such as biochar and solar-powered farming facilities, has further reduced the ecological footprint of food consumption in Hong Kong through reconnecting local eco-produce to the city's food supply chain.

All these efforts have helped build a strong sense of environmental stewardship in the community and address environmentalists' concerns about the potential damage that human impacts of the revitalization process could bring to Lai Chi Wo's valuable natural environment. These eco-friendly and climate-smart actions have not only improved production yield and facilitated agroecosystem resilience but also strengthened social capacity and solidarity and raised social awareness of the importance of rural sustainability for cities. The biodiversity data have highlighted the ecological significance of the restored agricultural landscape and, consequently, has received further support from the Hong Kong SAR government.[39]

36. William et al., *Springer Briefs*.
37. Law, Yiu, and Chick, *Vivifying Lai Chi Wo*.
38. Sonoko D. Bellingrath-Kimura, Benjamin Burkhard, Brendan Fisher, and Bettina Matzdorf, "Ecosystem Services and Biodiversity of Agricultural Systems at the Landscape Scale," *Environmental Monitoring and Assessment* 193, no. S1 (2021).
39. Environmental Protection Department, Hong Kong SAR Government, "Countryside Conservation Funding Scheme," accessed June 5, 2022, https://www.epd.gov.hk/epd/english/environmentinhk/conservation/ccfs/ccfs_main.html.

Exemplar of Rural Sustainability

The revitalization of Lai Chi Wo is a model for fostering rural sustainability in an urban context. Before the start of the project, the term "rural" was absent from mainstream local discussions of Hong Kong's development. As a result of the revitalization of the Lai Chi Wo project, the city's rural cultural landscapes are now included in Hong Kong's wider planning agendas. The project implemented revitalization strategies using nature-based solutions to tackle a slew of sustainability challenges, which are especially relevant to SDG 3—Good Health and Well-Being, by providing urban escape for Hong Kong's citizens; SDG 11—Sustainable Cities and Communities, through enhanced rural-urban symbiosis; SDG 12—Responsible Consumption and Production, by resuming agricultural productivity and localizing food production and consumption; SDG 13—Climate Action, by adopting climate smart technology; and SDG 15—Life on Earth, through measures of enhancing the biodiversity of the place.

The Lai Chi Wo revitalization model exemplifies the importance and relevance of an enhanced nature-culture relationship for the conservation of traditional agricultural landscapes and the city's positive response to sustainability challenges brought about by urbanization and globalization. The project has developed a standard-setting sustainable model of living rural heritage conservation, which is able to attain socioeconomic and environmental well-being at both local and society levels.[40]

Conclusion

A cultural landscape consists of nested and evolving nature-culture interactions at multiple levels.[41] The conceptional framework of the Lai Chi Wo revitalization project is based on the sustainability of these interactions within a specific cultural landscape. The project has emphasized the importance of rural-urban symbiosis and has been able to draw support from a variety of stakeholders, especially the local community.

After a nine-year journey of revitalization, Lai Chi Wo is now a place with more than fifty inhabitants who live and work in the village, managing six hectares of active farmland, and running diverse rural business, cultural, and environmental projects in the village. The local villagers have developed community institutions and external partnerships with government and other organizations to sustain the village services as well as its development.[42] A sustainable community, which supports the continuity of the cultural landscape, has been nurtured, and it continues to grow constantly and organically.

The Lai Chi Wo project demonstrates that cultural landscapes can generate tremendous value for society—promoting social inclusion and rural-urban interaction, fostering green economic development, and helping to enhance the overall well-being of both the local community and society at large. This revitalization model has received a "Special Recognition for Sustainable Development" in the 2020 UNESCO

40. The project was cited in the Hong Kong SAR Government's Policy Address 2017 as a successful example of rural revitalization, which has prompted the government to establish a Countryside Conservation Office with a HK$1 billion budget to expand its impact at Lai Chi Wo and other rural areas in Hong Kong. Office of the Chief Executive, Hong Kong SAR Government, *The Chief Executive's 2017 Policy Address* (Hong Kong: Hong Kong SAR Government, 2017).

41. Peter Bille Larsen and Gamini Wijesuriya, "Nature-Culture Interlinkages in World Heritage: Bridging the Gap," *World Heritage* 75 (2015): 4–15.

42. William et al., *Springer Briefs*.

Asia-Pacific Awards for Cultural Heritage Conservation. The jury applauded the project's pioneering approach to rural sustainability that "transforms notions of heritage practice from its conventional focus on material conservation to encompass living heritage in all its manifestations. . . . The project demonstrates the importance of interweaving nature and cultural heritage in setting a new urban-rural sustainability agenda for Hong Kong SAR and beyond."[43] It upholds the potential of tackling sustainability challenges by reviving the vibrancy of cultural landscapes as culture-nature interface in contemporary society.

Acknowledgments

The conservation works described in this essay were carried out under the Sustainable Lai Chi Wo Programme and the HSBC Rural Sustainability Programme initiated by the Centre for Civil Society and Governance at The University of Hong Kong. The author would like to express gratitude to The Hongkong Bank Foundation for its generous support of the revitalization of Lai Chi Wo from 2013 to 2022. Additionally, the author extends appreciation to the program partners—The Conservancy Association, the Hong Kong Countryside Foundation, and Produce Green Foundation—for their contributions during the earlier stages of the project. It is important to note that the revitalization of Lai Chi Wo would not have been possible without the endorsement and participation of the local Hakka community and the new settlers. Therefore, the author would like to express thanks to all the villagers, professionals, volunteers, and participants for their valuable time and effort in revitalizing Lai Chi Wo.

Bibliography

Agriculture, Fisheries and Conservation Department, Hong Kong SAR Government. "Plover Cove Country Park and Plover Cove (Extension) Country Park." Accessed June 5, 2022. https://www.afcd.gov.hk/english/country/cou_vis/cou_vis_cou/cou_vis_cou_pc/cou_vis_cou_pc.html.

Agriculture, Fisheries and Conservation Department, Hong Kong SAR Government. "Yan Chau Tong Marine Park." Accessed June 5, 2022. https://www.afcd.gov.hk/english/country/cou_vis/cou_vis_mar/cou_vis_mar_des/cou_vis_mar_des_yan.html.

Bellingrath-Kimura, Sonoko D., Benjamin Burkhard, Brendan Fisher, and Bettina Matzdorf. "Ecosystem Services and Biodiversity of Agricultural Systems at the Landscape Scale." *Environmental Monitoring and Assessment* 193, no. S1 (2021).

Berque, Augustin. *Thinking through Landscape*. Abingdon: Routledge, 2013.

Brockwell, Sally, Sue O'Connor, and Denis Byrne. "Introduction: Engaging Culture and Nature." In *Transcending the Culture-Nature Divide in Cultural Heritage: Views from the Asia-Pacific Region*, edited by Sally Brockwell, Sue O'Connor, and Denis Byrne, 1–11. Canberra: ANU Press, 2013.

Centre for Civil Society and Governance, The University of Hong Kong. "HSBC Rural Sustainability Programme." Accessed June 5, 2022. https://ccsg.hku.hk/ruralsd.

Chick, Hiu Lai. "The Significance, Conservation Potential and Challenges of a Traditional Farming Landscape in an Asian Metropolis: A Case Study of Lai Chi Wo, Hong Kong." *Journal of World Heritage Studies*, Special Issue (2017): 17–23.

43. UNESCO Bangkok, "2020 UNESCO Asia-Pacific Awards for Cultural Heritage Conservation—Winners Announced," December 16, 2020, https://bangkok.unesco.org/content/2020-unesco-asia-pacific-awards-cultural-heritage-conservation-winners-announced.

Du Pisani, J. A. "Sustainable Development—Historical Roots of the Concept." *Environmental Sciences* 3, no. 2 (2006): 83–96.

Environmental Protection Department, Hong Kong SAR Government. "Countryside Conservation Funding Scheme." Accessed June 5, 2022. https://www.epd.gov.hk/epd/english/environmentinhk/conservation/ccfs/ccfs_main.html.

Haila, Yrjö. "Beyond the Nature-Culture Dualism." *Biology & Philosophy* 15, no. 2 (2000): 155–75.

Hase, Patrick H. "Eastern Peace: Sha Tau Kok Market in 1925." *Journal of the Hong Kong Branch of the Royal Asiatic Society* 33 (1993): 147–202.

Hau, Billy Chi Hang, K. W. F. Lo, and K. Y. K. So. *Living Water and Community Revitalization—An Agricultural-Led Action, Engagement and Incubation Programme at Lai Chi Wo: Biodiversity Baseline and Management Plan of Freshwater and Terrestrial Habitats of Lai Chi Wo*. Hong Kong: Policy for Sustainability Lab, The University of Hong Kong, 2018.

International Council on Monuments and Sites (ICOMOS). *Québec Declaration on the Preservation of the Spirit of Place*. Quebec: ICOMOS, 2008.

Ishizawa, Maya. "Cultural Landscapes Link to Nature: Learning from Satoyama and Satoumi." *Built Heritage* 2 (2018): 7–19.

Kinsley, David R. *Ecology and Religion: Ecological Spirituality in Cross-cultural Perspective*. Englewood Cliffs, NJ: Prentice Hall, 1994.

Konsa, Kurmo. "Natural and Cultural Heritage: Framing Meanings and Practices." *International Journal of Sustainability in Economic, Social, and Cultural Context* 12, no. 4 (2016): 9–18.

Kraus, Erika. "Book Review: Gloria Pungetti, Gonzalo Oviedo, and Della Hooke (Eds.), *Sacred Species and Sites: Advances in Biocultural Conservation*." *Landscape Ecology* 29 (2014): 1461–62.

Labadi, Sophia, Francesca Giliberto, Ilaria Rosetti, Linda Shetabi, and Ege Yildirim. *Heritage and the Sustainable Development Goals: Policy Guidance for Heritage and Development Actors*. Paris: ICOMOS, International Council on Monuments and Sites, 2021. https://www.icomos.org/images/DOCUMENTS/Secretariat/2021/SDG/ICOMOS_SDGs_Policy_Guidance_2021.pdf.

Larsen, Peter Bille, and Gamini Wijesuriya. "Nature-Culture Interlinkages in World Heritage: Bridging the Gap." *World Heritage* 75 (2015: 4–15.

Law, Winnie Wai Yee, S. I. S. Yiu, and H. L. Chick. *Vivifying Lai Chi Wo: Sustainable Lai Chi Wo Programme Four Year Review and Outlook*. Hong Kong: Policy for Sustainability Lab, The University of Hong Kong, 2018.

Legislative Council Archives of Hong Kong Special Administrative Region. "Press Release. Lcq15: Conservation of Country Park Enclaves." November 18, 2015. https://www.info.gov.hk/gia/general/201511/18/P201511180710.htm.

Li, S. Y. "Community-Based Forestry and the Functions of Institutions: A Case Study of Fung Shui Forests in Hong Kong." *International Forestry Review* 20, no. 3 (2018): 362–74.

Liu, R. H. *Xinjie Jianshi* (A brief history of the New Territories). Hong Kong: Joint Publishing, 1999.

Morton, Brian. "Hong Kong's Mangrove Biodiversity and Its Conservation within the Context of a Southern Chinese Megalopolis. A Review and a Proposal for Lai Chi Wo to Be Designated as a World Heritage Site." *Regional Studies in Marine Science* 8 (2016): 382–99.

Nissim, Roger. *Land Administration and Practice in Hong Kong*. Rev. ed. Hong Kong: Hong Kong University Press, 2012.

Office of the Chief Executive, Hong Kong SAR Government. *The Chief Executive's 2017 Policy Address*. Hong Kong: Hong Kong SAR Government, 2017.

Potts, Andrew. "An Urgent Journey: Realizing the Potential of Integrated Nature-Culture Approaches to Create a Sustainable World." *George Wright Forum* 34, no. 2 (2017): 229–37.

Rössler, Mechtild. "World Heritage Cultural Landscapes: A UNESCO Flagship Programme 1992–2006." *Landscape Research* 31, no. 4 (2006): 333–53.

Rössler, Mechtild, and Roland Chih-Hung Lin. "Cultural Landscape in World Heritage Conservation and Cultural Landscape Conservation Challenges in Asia." *Built Heritage* 2 (2018): 3–26.

UNESCO. *Operational Guidelines for the Implementation of the World Heritage Convention*. Paris: UNESCO, 2021.

UNESCO Bangkok. "2020 UNESCO Asia-Pacific Awards for Cultural Heritage Conservation—Winners Announced." December 16, 2020. https://bangkok.unesco.org/index.php/content/2020-unesco-asia-pacific-awards-cultural-heritage-conservation-winners-announced.

United Nations. "Transforming Our World: The 2030 Agenda for Sustainable Development." 2015. https://sdgs.un.org/sites/default/files/publications/21252030%20Agenda%20for%20Sustainable%20Development%20web.pdf.

van Oosten, Cora J., and Wouter Leen Hijweege. "Governing Biocultural Diversity in Mosaic Landscapes." In *Forest-People Interfaces*, edited by B. Arts, S. van Bommel, M. Ros-Tonen, and G. Verschoor, 211–22. Wageningen: Wageningen Academic Publishers, 2012.

Wijesuriya, Gamani. *Living Heritage: A Summary*. Rome: ICCROM, 2015.

William, Jessica M., V. Chu, W. F. Lam, and W. W. Y. Law. *Springer Briefs on Case Studies of Sustainable Development: Revitalising Rural Communities*. Singapore: Springer, 2021.

Nizamuddin Urban Renewal Initiative: Socioeconomic Sustainability through Conservation

Sharif Shams Imon

Heritage Management and Sustainable Development Goals

The adoption of the United Nations' Sustainable Development Goals (SDGs) in 2015 and the discussions around it highlighted the critical role of culture and cultural heritage in achieving the SDGs.[1] These discussions point to two interrelated requirements for heritage management to play this role: heritage management practices must conform to the principles of sustainable development, and they must contribute toward achieving SDGs beyond a heritage site's boundaries. However, early discussions referring to the SDGs focused primarily on policies related to addressing the goals specific to heritage management only. These policy discussions were an extension of heritage bodies' deliberations on similar issues since the 1970s.[2] It soon became apparent that policies were insufficient to convert principles into practices.

The *2030 Agenda for Sustainable Development* presents an integrated framework of 5Ps: "People, Planet, Prosperity, Peace, and Partnerships."[3] These 5Ps together cover the seventeen interconnected SDGs. Among the SDGs, target 11.4 explicitly refers to heritage: "Strengthen efforts to protect and safeguard the world's cultural and natural heritage."[4] Placed under SDG 11, which aims to "make cities and human settlements inclusive, safe, resilient and sustainable," target 11.4 does not reflect the true potential of cultural heritage as "an enabler and driver of sustainable development."[5] This issue is largely addressed in UNESCO's 2019 publication *Thematic Indicators for Culture in the 2030 Agenda*. The thematic indicators offer a framework for assessing "both the role of culture as a sector of activity, as well as the transversal contribution

1. United Nations, "Transforming Our World: The 2030 Agenda for Sustainable Development," 2015, https://sdgs.un.org/sites/default/files/publications/21252030%20Agenda%20for%20Sustainable%20Development%20web.pdf; UNESCO, Policy for Integration of a Sustainable Development Perspective into the Processes of the World Heritage Convention, Resolution 20 GA 13, 2015; UNESCO, *Culture Urban Future: Global Report on Culture for Sustainable Urban Development* (Paris: UNESCO, 2016); Jyoti Hosagrahar, Jeffrey Soule, Luigi Fusco Girard, and Andrew Potts, *Cultural Heritage, the UN Sustainable Development Goals, and the New Urban Agenda* (ICOMOS Concept Note for the United Nations Post-2015 Agenda and the Third United Nations Conference on Housing and Sustainable Urban Development [HABITAT III], September 1, 2015).
2. Hosagrahar et al., *Cultural Heritage*.
3. United Nations, "Transforming Our World."
4. United Nations, "Transforming Our World."
5. UNESCO, *Thematic Indicators for Culture in the 2030 Agenda* (Paris: UNESCO, 2019), 10.

of culture across different SDGs and policy areas."[6] When implemented at a city or national level in different countries, the framework is expected to provide all parties involved in heritage and development sectors with valuable baseline data to measure progress and help decide the future courses of action. Around the same time, the International Council on Monuments and Sites (ICOMOS) took a similar approach to assist heritage practitioners "in adopting a sustainable development perspective in their heritage practices and aligning them to the SDGs."[7] However, this time, case studies, albeit brief, have been included to illustrate how various heritage projects contribute to the SDGs. The move from abstract SDGs-related policies toward anchoring policies in real projects offers much-needed clarity to the applicability of SDGs in cultural heritage practice. However, while there are examples of successful conservation projects that address one or two of the 5Ps, examples of projects or programs in which heritage is a primary enabler and driver of sustainable development and that addresses all 5Ps are scant. The Nizamuddin Urban Renewal Initiative (NURI) in Nizamuddin, Delhi, India, fills this gap well.

NURI is an excellent example of a project that demonstrates how the various components of sustainable development can come together in heritage management and contribute to the well-being of people and consequently address all the 5Ps of sustainable development. The project shows how integrating cultural heritage conservation, incorporating intangible heritage and the environment, and socioeconomic programs can improve the quality of life for people living in and around a heritage site.

Nizamuddin Urban Renewal Initiative

Led by the Aga Khan Trust for Culture (AKTC), the Nizamuddin Urban Renewal Initiative (NURI) is a cluster of projects that started in partnership among five agencies—Archaeological Survey of India (ASI), Central Public Works Department (CPWD), South Delhi Municipal Corporation (SDMC), Aga Khan Foundation, and AKTC—in 2007.[8] It built on the success of the garden restoration at Humayun's Tomb (between 1997 and 2004), a World Heritage Site in the Nizamuddin area of Delhi that drew widespread attention in India and beyond. The garden restoration, a joint effort by AKTC and ASI, was the first privately funded restoration work at a World Heritage Site in India. The scope of NURI was expanded to include the restoration of Humayun's Tomb and cultural, economic, environmental, and social programs in the area under the Historic Cities Programme of the Aga Khan Development Network and implemented through AKTC.[9] The area was chosen because of the "possibility of building on the successfully completed Garden restoration, high number of significant buildings in the area, potential of the conservation initiative to be coupled with a socio-economic development programme that would benefit a resident population, the importance of a 'living culture,' exemplary religious

6. UNESCO, *Thematic Indicators for Culture in the 2030 Agenda*, 10.
7. Sophia Labadi et al., *Heritage and the Sustainable Development Goals: Policy Guidance for Heritage and Develoment Actors* (Paris: ICOMOS, 2021), 15, https://www.icomos.org/images/DOCUMENTS/Secretariat/2021/SDG/ICOMOS_SDGs_Policy_Guidance_2021.pdf.
8. Aga Khan Development Network, *Humayun's Tomb–Nizamuddin Basti-Sundre Nursery Urban Renewal Initiative: Progress Report* (New Delhi: Aga Khan Development Network, 2008), http://annualreport2016.nizamuddinrenewal.org/docs/Annual_Report_2008.pdf.
9. "Cultural Development-Overview," accessed 18 July, 2021, https://www.akdn.org/where-we-work/south-asia/india/cultural-development/india-cultural-development-overview.

Figure 6.1: The three distinctive yet closely related components of NURI: Humayun's Tomb World Heritage Site, Nizamuddin Basti, and Sunder Nursery. (Source: Edited by Sharif Shams Imon from Google Maps.)

tolerance and easily accessible central location for the citizens of Delhi."[10] Located in the Nizamuddin area of the Southeast Delhi district, the project included three primary components: Humayun's Tomb, a World Heritage Site; Nizamuddin Basti, a dense urban settlement of a Muslim community; and Sunder Nursery, a landscaped area with numerous monuments adjacent to the World Heritage Site (Figure 6.1).

Termed a people-public-private partnership, NURI, along with environmental development, is described as a "conservation initiative to be coupled with a socio-economic development programme that would benefit a resident population" in consultation with local communities and relevant stakeholders.[11] Since 2007, NURI has completed almost three hundred subprojects of various types in the Nizamuddin area, covering a combined area of about three hundred acres.[12]

NURI: Project Components

Humayun's Tomb is one of the three UNESCO World Heritage Sites in India's capital territory, Delhi. Built under the patronage of the Mughal emperor Akbar for his father, Emperor Humayun, the mausoleum is an expansive site with a tomb building in the middle of a garden setting. The site was chosen for the emperor's mausoleum for its proximity to the shrine of Hazrat Nizamuddin Auliya. Nizamuddin Basti, an urban settlement named after the saint, has grown around the shrine over the past several centuries. Located adjacent to Humayun's Tomb and established in the early twentieth century as a horticulture nursery for the new capital development program in Delhi, the ninety-acre Sunder Nursery is a biodiversity zone and an archaeological site that includes three national monuments and several other heritage

10. Aga Khan Development Network, *Humayun's Tomb*, 9.
11. Aga Khan Development Network, *Humayun's Tomb*, 9; Aga Khan Development Network, "Cultural Development—Overview."
12. Aga Khan Development Network, *Nizamuddin Urban Renewal Initiative: Annual Report 2019* (New Delhi: Aga Khan Development Network, 2019), https://www.nizamuddinrenewal.org/assets/images/Nizamuddin-Urban-Renewal-Inititiave_Annual-Report-2019.pdf.

Figure 6.2: The three NURI components: Humayun's Tomb World Heritage Site, Nizamuddin Basti, and Sunder Nursery. (Source: Sharif Shams Imon.)

structures (Figure 6.2). There are many other heritage structures of national and local significance within the NURI area.

People and Nature-Culture Integration

NURI included several urban environment upgrading projects. One of the projects was the Sunder Nursery. This vast park is dotted with numerous heritage structures from different historical periods whose conservation was part of the initiative from the start. To date, nine heritage structures have been restored, and the landscape has been enhanced. People in Delhi and visitors to the World Heritage Site are now able to enjoy this extensive green space in the heart of a dense urban center. Street conditions have been improved. An open space of Nizamuddin Basti that used to be a rubbish dump was revitalized as a park through proper waste collection strategies (Figure 6.3). Another large open space, Outer Park, which had long been neglected, was upgraded and has become a place for holding various community events regularly. One such event is the three-day annual Apni Basti Mela (Our Own Fair). The open space is also a place for celebrating, showcasing, and expanding the market for the community's crafts-based intangible cultural heritage.

For Nizamuddin Basti, there are projects related to sanitation upgrading, cultural revival, and creating green spaces within the community. Access to proper sanitation has been a long-standing problem. Many households did not have access to proper toilet facilities, and the existing public toilets were unhygienic and lacked regular maintenance. Women in this traditionally conservative community particularly suffered the most. Toilets in many houses were not connected to a sewerage system.[13] A project to upgrade existing public toilets was taken up, and a community-led management system for these facilities was established, creating employment opportunities.[14]

The revival of cultural practices is essential for generating community pride. Several schemes to showcase the community's intangible cultural heritage, especially for the performing arts, are part of NURI. This was made possible through the conservation of monuments and the related creation of public space for such cultural activities. The community's traditional performing arts are now showcased in events and activities, attracting visitors from outside the area and contributing to the local economy (Figure 6.4).

Figure 6.3: An open space within Nizamuddin Basti, once used as a rubbish dump (left) and now revitalized as a park (right). (Source: Aga Khan Trust for Culture.)

13. Aga Khan Development Network, *Nizamuddin Urban Renewal Initiative: Annual Report—2018* (New Delhi: Aga Khan Development Network, 2018), http://annualreport2016.nizamuddinrenewal.org/docs/Annual_Report_2018.pdf.
14. Aga Khan Development Network, "Cultural Development—Overview."

While improving sanitary conditions and the urban environment have enhanced the community's everyday living experience, access to better education for youth and for healthcare, especially for women, has led to long-term positive change in the overall quality of life.

Access to good education is one of the goals of sustainable development. NURI focused on the existing school. Its physical appearance was improved as well as classroom conditions. Trained teachers have been employed so that students can have a better education. Community-managed early childhood care and development centers have been established for the holistic development of children and a better transition to the formal education system.[15]

Good healthcare is fundamental for the well-being of a community. NURI focused on improving existing healthcare services within the community by working with the concerned government departments. The existing healthcare facility within the community has now been upgraded, giving community members access to necessary healthcare services within their neighborhood.[16]

Improving Livelihood through Women Empowerment and Youth Involvement

A critical feature of the project has been the involvement of local craftspeople in the conservation work. Of particular importance, local youth have been trained and employed in many projects. About 1.5 million worker-days equivalent of employment has been created through the initiative's conservation projects.[17]

Livelihood programs based on local crafts, food, and tourism have been developed. They include women's enterprises based on local crafts, enterprises based on local gastronomy, and vocational training for local youth. Women's empowerment within the community is the most striking feature of this initiative. Traditionally conservative women of this community who used to stay indoors now can contribute to the livelihood of their families.

To ensure that future generations are aware of the area's cultural richness and to help visitors have a more holistic understanding of the cultural resources, a heritage awareness program is run by local youths. Special programs for schoolchildren are organized frequently.

Figure 6.4: The creation of spaces for ongoing cultural performances within Nizamuddin Basti is a contributing factor to the area's economic development. (Source: Aga Khan Trust for Culture.)

15. Aga Khan Development Network, *Nizamuddin Urban Renewal Initiative: Annual Report 2018.*
16. "Improving Clinical Health," accessed January 5, 2022, https://www.nizamuddinrenewal.org/health/strengthening-public.php.
17. Aga Khan Development Network, "Cultural Development—Overview."

The Role of Culture in Achieving Sociocultural Sustainability

The Nizamuddin Urban Renewal Initiative (NURI) comprises diverse project components, not all of which are conservation focused. Nevertheless, culture has played a direct or indirect role in influencing the overall outcomes of these projects. Among all the elements of NURI, the excellence of the first project of this scheme by the Aga Khan Trust for Culture (AKTC), the restoration of the Humayun's Tomb World Heritage Site, drew widespread attention locally and internationally. In addition, the conservation of almost sixty heritage structures and their continuous care has enhanced the awareness of the cultural richness of the Nizamuddin area.[18] The increased attention to the area has helped the key actors—AKTC and various government departments—forge partnerships with local and international bodies to implement numerous cultural and urban renewal projects in the area.

Economic Indicators

Regarding economic indicators, women's livelihood improved significantly. In 2008, 9 percent of women worked as domestic workers. Since then, the Insha-e-Noor program has trained over 450 women, and in 2018, 15 percent of the women in the area had their own income, the majority of them producing crafts for tourists.[19]

Livelihood generation by creating employment in conservation projects for local people is a direct economic benefit of the initiative. A renewed interest in Nizamuddin Basti's heritage outside the area also has created economic opportunities through tourism. Sair-E-Nizamuddin, a youth group trained as heritage guides, has conducted tours for over forty thousand visitors since 2010.[20] Heritage tourism in the area also has opened up a new market for local traditional crafts. The women-only Insha-e-Noor is now running a traditional crafts-based business successfully. Zaika-e-Nizamuddin, another women-only enterprise, runs a catering and home delivery service promoting "Nizamuddin Basti cuisine" within and beyond the area.

Environmental Indicators

In the environmental sector, solid waste management was almost nonexistent in the area in 2008. There are five parks, and all of them were encroached upon. Twenty-five percent of people did not have in-house toilets. In 2018, solid waste management covered 70 percent of the area through a pay-and-use system, all five parks were landscaped, and one was made for women only. Now there are two community-managed public toilets with about eighty daily users, more during festivals. In 2008, only 10 percent of the Sunder Nursery was accessible by the public; in 2018, the entire ninety acres of the park became accessible.[21]

Social Indicators

Cultural revival activities using local traditional performing arts have become possible because of the creation of cultural spaces through various conservation or renewal

---

18. Aga Khan Development Network, *Nizamuddin Urban Renewal Initiative: Annual Report 2019.*
19. Aga Khan Development Network, *Nizamuddin Urban Renewal Initiative: Annual Report 2018.*
20. Aga Khan Development Network, *Nizamuddin Urban Renewal Initiative: AKDC Annual Report 2018.*
21. Aga Khan Development Network, *Nizamuddin Urban Renewal Initiative: AKDC Annual Report 2018.*

projects. Strengthening place attachment, especially by local youth, is a direct social impact of these developments in which community members participate actively.

Several other social indicators reveal the progress made through this project. Access to education is one. In 2008, the level of enrollment at the neighborhood school was low, with only 1 percent of youth having access to primary education and vocational training. The numbers increased significantly by 2018. The enrollment at the local school is now four hundred students, and 100 percent of local youth have access to vocational training. Over 3,500 youths have been trained since 2008; of those, 60 percent have job placements.[22] Another social indicator is healthcare. Between 2008 and 2018, complete child immunization increased from 30 percent to 77 percent; the average antenatal care visits increased from less than 3 percent to almost 5 percent; home delivery of babies went from 25 percent to 5 percent; and the number of people having pathological tests in a year increased from 1,035 to more than 7,000.[23]

While all these initiatives together have improved the physical condition of the heritage sites, provided livelihood opportunities for the local community, and thus improved the quality of life for people living there, new research and the conservation of numerous heritage structures have also contributed to the expansion of the World Heritage Buffer Zone. Because of improved conservation and management measures, the World Heritage boundaries of Humayun's Tomb were expanded in 2016, increasing the World Heritage area from twenty-six to sixty-seven acres.[24]

None of this would be possible without partnerships between various organizations. AKTC has collaborated with various governmental and nongovernmental organizations to achieve NURI's goals. The conservation projects have been carried out in collaboration with the Archaeological Survey of India (ASI), the primary federal authority for heritage protection in India. Various urban improvement measures have been carried out in collaboration with the municipal authority and the Public Works Department. Outside these three government departments, the Ministry of Tourism, state and local-level government departments, local and international private organizations, and diplomatic missions in India have extended their support to NURI.

Synergy

This case study demonstrates how cultural heritage programs can contribute to sustainability. It shows how the conservation of tangible heritage and incorporating intangible heritage in the process—while improving people's quality of life—can create a sustainable heritage management program that contributes to the Sustainable Development Goals (SDGs). In 2021, in addition to receiving the Award of Excellence for heritage conservation under the UNESCO Asia-Pacific Awards for Cultural Heritage Conservation, Nizamuddin Basti also received a Special Recognition for Sustainable Development. According to the award citation, "the project embodies the exemplary approach of the Aga Khan Trust for Culture in leveraging cultural assets for the socio-economic benefit of the historic Nizamuddin Basti community in New Delhi."[25] Others have recognized the excellence of this project. For example, *Time*

22. Aga Khan Development Network, *Nizamuddin Urban Renewal Initiative: AKDC Annual Report 2018.*
23. Aga Khan Development Network, *Nizamuddin Urban Renewal Initiative: Annual Report 2019.*
24. Aga Khan Development Network, *Nizamuddin Urban Renewal Initiative: Annual Report 2019.*
25. UNESCO Bangkok, "2021 UNESCO Asia-Pacific Awards for Cultural Heritage Conservation—Winners Announced," accessed June 14, 2022, https://bangkok.unesco.org/sites/default/files/assets/

magazine in 2018 listed the Sunder Nursery as one of the world's best places to visit, and the nursery received a World Responsible Tourism Award in 2020.[26]

The Nizamuddin Urban Renewal Initiative (NURI) demonstrates how cultural revival, child education, healthcare, recreation, skills development, and women empowerment projects can contribute to the social dimension of sustainability; how job creation through conservation projects, heritage-based businesses for women, heritage tourism, skills development programs, and vocational training programs contribute to the economic dimension of sustainability; and how parks development, sanitation improvement, and solid waste management can also contribute to the environmental dimension of sustainability. All of these have been attainable because of viable partnerships with various organizations, including the community, which has always been a primary stakeholder.

By integrating conservation, socioeconomic development, and environmental and urban development objectives in one project and leveraging cultural heritage's potential to make positive changes, NURI offers a rare example of cultural heritage as an enabler and driver of sustainable development. Although the initiative is an excellent model for sustainable development in similar contexts, more real-life examples in diverse settings are needed to understand the full spectrum of cultural heritage's possible and potential contributions to sustainable development.

Bibliography

Aga Khan Development Network. "Awards Received by Akdn." Accessed May 5, 2022. https://www.akdn.org/about-us/awards-received-akdn.

Aga Khan Development Network. "Cultural Development—Overview." Accessed July 18, 2021. https://www.akdn.org/where-we-work/south-asia/india/cultural-development/india-cultural-development-overview.

Aga Khan Development Network. *Humayun's Tomb–Nizamuddin Basti–Sunder Nursery Urban Renewal Initiative: Progress Report*. New Delhi: Aga Khan Development Network, 2008. http://annualreport2016.nizamuddinrenewal.org/docs/Annual_Report_2008.pdf.

Aga Khan Development Network. *Nizamuddin Urban Renewal Initiative: Annual Report 2018*. New Delhi: Aga Khan Development Network, 2018. http://annualreport2016.nizamuddinrenewal.org/docs/Annual_Report_2018.pdf.

Aga Khan Development Network. *Nizamuddin Urban Renewal Initiative: Annual Report 2019*. New Delhi: Aga Khan Development Network, 2019. https://www.nizamuddinrenewal.org/assets/images/Nizamuddin-Urban-Renewal-Inititiave_Annual-Report-2019.pdf.

Hosagrahar, Jyoti, Jeffrey Soule, L. Fusco Girard, and Andrew Potts. *Cultural Heritage, the UN Sustainable Development Goals, and the New Urban Agenda*. ICOMOS Concept Note for the United Nations Post-2015 Agenda and the Third United Nations Conference on Housing and Sustainable Urban Development [HABITAT III], September 1, 2015.

Labadi, Sophia, Francesca Giliberto, Ilaria Rosetti, Linda Shetabi, and Ege Yildirim. *Heritage and the Sustainable Development Goals: Policy Guidance for Heritage and Development Actors*. Paris: ICOMOS, 2021. https://www.icomos.org/images/DOCUMENTS/Secretariat/2021/SDG/ICOMOS_SDGs_Policy_Guidance_2021.pdf.

Nizamuddin Renewal. "Improving Clinical Health." Accessed January 5, 2022. https://www.nizamuddinrenewal.org/health/strengthening-public.php.

---

article/Culture/files/2021-Winners-Citations.pdf.

26. "Awards Received by AKDN," accessed May 5, 2022, https://www.akdn.org/about-us/awards-received-akdn.

UNESCO. *Culture Urban Future: Global Report on Culture for Sustainable Urban Development.* Paris: UNESCO, 2016.

UNESCO. Policy for the Integration of a Sustainable Development Perspective into the Processes of the World Heritage Convention. Resolution 20 GA 13, 2015.

UNESCO. *Thematic Indicators for Culture in the 2030 Agenda.* Paris: UNESCO, 2019.

UNESCO Bangkok. "2021 UNESCO Asia-Pacific Awards for Cultural Heritage Conservation—Winners Announced." Accessed June 14, 2022. https://bangkok.unesco.org/sites/default/files/assets/article/Culture/files/2021-Winners-Citations.pdf.

United Nations. "Transforming Our World: The 2030 Agenda for Sustainable Development." 2015. https://sdgs.un.org/sites/default/files/publications/21252030%20Agenda%20for%20Sustainable%20Development%20web.pdf.

Creating Sustainable Urban Visitor Economies: Adaptive Reuse of Asian Cultural Heritage Places for Tourism

Fergus T. Maclaren

Introduction

This essay presents an overview of cultural heritage tourism in Asia and an understanding of its development in the context of sustainability initiatives, particularly the United Nations' Sustainable Development Goals (SDGs) and their relevant targets and indictors. It also delivers a simplified understanding of these sustainability frameworks with examples that show their applicability in different heritage places.

The essay reflects on the transformations occurring in cultural heritage places across Asia, including those in Macao, Mumbai, and Penang, that have been altered through tourism and driven by a number of associated factors that have shaped urban life and community development. Adaptive reuse is discussed as an outcome of these transformations, highlighting its impacts on cultural heritage and communities. The essay concludes with remarks on the future challenges and directions for leveraging tourism as a driver for sustainability of cultural heritage destinations in the Asia-Pacific region.

Tourism Growth and Standards in Asia

Robertson Collins, an American-born resident of Singapore and then-president of the International Council on Monuments and Sites (ICOMOS) Cultural Tourism Committee, asserted in 1991 in his book *A Disorderly Excursion: Notes of a Conservationist in the Asia/Pacific Region* that one of the key issues affecting travel in Asia was "the decline in the quality of quality in travel and destinations, with a loss of top-quality travellers; we have first class, but not high class."[1] This infers that while travelers can pay top dollar for flights, hotels, and services, planes can be overbooked, hotels can be overpriced, and services can be overbearing. This assertion is noteworthy on two points: it presaged the intent and formulation of the urban sustainability recommendations from the landmark United Nations Conference on Environment and Development (UNCED) or Earth Summit, convened in Rio de Janeiro, Brazil in June 1992, and it reflected the high-growth economies of the four "Asian Tigers" (Hong Kong, Singapore, South Korea, and Taiwan) that helped drive

1. Robertson Collins, *A Disorderly Excursion: Notes of a Conservationist in the Asia/Pacific Region* (Singapore: PATA Foundation, 1991).

Figure 7.1: Streams of tourists at Leal Senado Square, Macao. (Source: Hoyin Lee.)

rapid economic change in cultural heritage places in the region prior to the financial crisis of 1997–1998.

The flourishing and expansion of new economies in Asia by the 1990s helped to drive investment and urban renewal in cities that had seen little development beyond acting as colonial trading entrepôts or in cities that were slowly emerging from independence movements and regional conflicts. Such developments meant that centers with historical fabric and traditional activities were increasingly at risk. Unique places were beginning to lose their luster, or quality, from a wide range of external pressures, including rapid urbanization, depopulation, economic development, middle-class expansion coupled with social change, conservation of individual buildings rather than areas or districts, "over-emphasis on catering for the demands of tourism," and neglect of the interrelationship of the historical core and its surroundings.[2] This, in turn, helped drive tourism planners and managers, preservationists, and communities in determining how to plan for and manage these places as destinations.

The Sustainable Development Goals (SDGs) provide a comprehensive framework that can be applied to sustainable tourism. The SDGs were introduced in 2015 by the United Nations General Assembly as a collection of seventeen interlinked global goals intended to be achieved by the year 2030. As a successor to the Millennium Development Goals, which were in force from 2005 to 2015, there is an increased granularity of the goals and associated targets with the SDGs. Specifically, for the first time since the Earth Summit in 1992 and in the context of protecting and safeguarding the world's cultural and natural heritage, there are targets associated with the encouragement of sustainable tourism initiatives as seen under SDG 8—Decent Work and Economic Growth, SDG 11—Sustainable Cities and Communities, and SDG 12—Responsible Consumption and Production.

2. UNESCO, *Report of the Nara Seminar on the Development and Integrity of Historic Cities (5–7 March 1999, Nara, Japan)*, presented at the 23rd session of the World Heritage Committee, Marrakesh, Morocco, 1999.

Related SDGs and Targets, and Other Sustainability Initiatives Influencing Urban Tourism Development

The Sustainable Development Goals (SDGs) cover a number of development dimensions for World Heritage Sites (WHSs) and other cultural heritage destinations. From a tourism standpoint, targets associated with SDGs are geared toward areas where more government investment and support should be focused. In 2015, when the SDGs were launched as a call to action by the United Nations to end poverty, protect the planet, and improve the lives and prospects of everyone, everywhere, the seventeen-goal framework was established with an allocated 169 targets and 232 unique indicators to track them.

There are three specific targets where tourism is the focus or mentioned and one that deals with cultural heritage as an associated facet. These are as follows:

- SDG 8—Decent Work and Economic Growth. Target 8.9: "By 2030 devise and implement policies to promote sustainable tourism that creates jobs and promotes local culture and products."[3]
- SDG 12—Responsible Consumption and Production. Target 12.b: "Develop and implement tools to monitor sustainable development impacts for sustainable tourism that creates jobs and promotes local culture and products."[4]
- SDG 14—Life Below Water. Target 14.7: "By 2030 increase the economic benefits to Small Island developing States and least developed countries from the sustainable use of marine resources, including through sustainable management of fisheries, aquaculture and tourism."[5]
- SDG 11—Sustainable Cities and Communities. Target 11.4: "Strengthen efforts to protect and safeguard the world's cultural and natural heritage."[6]

SDG 14, target 14.7 is focused on marine environments and is not relevant to this discussion. SDG 8, target 8.9 and SDG 12, target 12.b, which appear to be the most relevant, are challenging to apply as they take a reductionist (simplistic) approach when aligned with their indicators. Specifically, these are as follows:

- *Indicator 8.9.1: Tourism direct GDP as a proportion of total GDP and in growth rate.*

  "Tourism Direct GDP [gross domestic product] (TDGDP) is defined as the sum of the part of gross value added (at basic prices) generated by all industries in response to internal tourism consumption plus the amount of net taxes on products and imports included within the value of this expenditure at purchasers' prices. . . . The value of the economic contribution of tourism captured by this indicator, and (relative) increases or decreases in it, could indicate the degree to which tourism is being successfully promoted."[7]

  The issue with this indicator is that it does not effectively measure the key premise of target 8.9: "Promoting sustainable tourism that creates jobs and promotes local culture and products." It is difficult to parse "local" from a GDP

3. United Nations, Department of Economic and Social Affairs, Sustainable Development, "The 17 Goals," accessed March 23, 2022, https://sdgs.un.org/goals.
4. United Nations, "The 17 Goals."
5. United Nations, "The 17 Goals."
6. United Nations, "The 17 Goals."
7. United Nations Statistics Division (UNSD), "SDG Indicators Metadata Repository—Indicator 8.9.1," accessed December 6, 2021, https://unstats.un.org/sdgs/metadata/?Text=&Goal=8&Target=8.9.

measurement, and heritage places are hampered in trying to discern what the actual economic benefits are for their communities using this measure.

- *Indicator 8.9.2: Proportion of jobs in sustainable tourism industries out of total tourism jobs.*

  The International Labour Organization (ILO) developed its *ILO Guidelines on Decent Work and Socially Responsible Tourism* in 2017. Its intent was to focus on "decent work in the context of promoting socially responsible tourism, and should serve as a reference tool for the ILO constituents and other tourism stakeholders in their efforts to address labour-related challenges and opportunities for the sustainable development of the tourism sector."[8] A casual search of employment platforms, such as LinkedIn and Indeed.com, would indicate that there are a number of sustainable tourism–related jobs that are open to applicants.

  As an actual job category, however, there is an apparent dissonance between the *ILO Guidelines* versus the job statements attributed to individual employment opportunities. A search for "sustainable tourism jobs" can result in descriptions that have "sustainable" and "tourism" in them but not necessarily together. There does not appear to be a formal standard being adhered to when creating these posts. Hence, from an overall visitor economy standpoint, the incongruity of the terminology and trying to demarcate "sustainable tourism industries" from the broader tourism sector can result in different, incompatible findings across jurisdictions for reporting purposes.

- *Indicator 12.b.1: Implementation of standard accounting tools to monitor the economic and environmental aspects of tourism sustainability.*

  This indicator relates to the degree of implementation in countries of the Tourism Satellite Account (TSA) and the System of Environmental and Economic Accounts (SEEA). The TSA has become the internationally recognized framework developed by the United Nations World Tourism Organization (UNWTO) and an important tool to measure tourism activity in an economy.[9] The SEEA framework integrates economic and environmental data to provide a more comprehensive and multipurpose view of the interrelationships between the economy and the environment, and changes in stocks of environmental assets as they bring benefits to humanity.[10]

  Although these frameworks are considered to be the most current, feasible means to monitor sustainability in tourism, the challenge is that not every country uses TSAs or SEEAs. Due to a disparity in resources and data measuring capabilities, this often diffuses the ability to effectively compare one country/region/city to another. The United Nations also acknowledges that the indicator does not track the target well and that the indicator is not statistically based as there is no internationally agreed statistical framework or concepts/definitions that can be applied to "sustainable tourism strategies or policies and implemented action plans."[11] There is an issue here again, as with

8. International Labour Organization, *ILO Guidelines on Decent Work and Socially Responsible Tourism* (Geneva: ILO, 2017), https://www.ilo.org/wcmsp5/groups/public/---ed_dialogue/---sector/documents/normativeinstrument/wcms_546337.pdf.
9. United Nations World Tourism Organization, "Tourism Satellite Account," accessed December 6, 2021, https://www.unwto.org/standards/on-economic-contribution-of-tourism-tsa-2008.
10. United Nations, "System of Environmental Economic Accounting," 2021, https://seea.un.org/.
11. United Nations Statistics Division, "SDG Indicators Metadata Repository—Indicator 12.b.1," accessed December 6, 2021, https://unstats.un.org/sdgs/metadata/?Text=&Goal=12&Target.

target 8.9, in trying to segregate aspects "that promote sustainable tourism that creates jobs and promotes local culture and products."

A more effective approach for assessing tourism's impacts on Asian cultural heritage places may be the indicator for target 11.4 that was part of the revision process of the *Report of the Inter-agency and Expert Group on Sustainable Development Goal Indicators* (E/CN.3/2017/2):

- *Indicator 11.4.1: Total expenditure (public and private) per capita spent on the preservation, protection and conservation of all cultural and natural heritage, by type of heritage (cultural, natural, mixed and World Heritage Centre designation), level of government (national, regional and local/municipal), type of expenditure (operating expenditure/investment) and type of private funding (donations in kind, private non-profit sector and sponsorship).*

> Cultural heritage for this indicator includes artefacts, monuments, a group of buildings and sites, museums that have a diversity of values including symbolic, historic, artistic, aesthetic, ethnological or anthropological, scientific and social significance. It includes tangible heritage (movable, immobile, and underwater), intangible heritage (ICH [intangible cultural heritage]) embedded into cultural, and natural heritage artefacts, sites or monuments. There are tourism and adaptive reuse implications, however, when assessing how to best conserve those elements. Conservation of cultural heritage refers to the measures taken to extend the life of cultural heritage while strengthening transmission of its significant heritage messages and values. In the domain of cultural property, the aim of conservation is to maintain the physical and cultural characteristics of the object to ensure that its value is not diminished and that it will outlive our limited time span.[12]

To further frame the issues around tourism development and sustainability, in 2017 the United Nations World Tourism Organization (UNWTO) coordinated and commemorated the International Year of Sustainable Tourism for Development (IYSTD), which was tied to initiatives in support of all seventeen SDGs. This designated year was intended to recognize the tremendous potential of the tourism industry to contribute to the fight against poverty and foster mutual understanding and intercultural dialogue. The IYSTD was aimed at supporting changes in policies, business practices, and consumer behavior toward a more sustainable tourism sector that can contribute effectively to the SDGs in the following five key areas:

- "Inclusive and sustainable economic growth;
- Social inclusiveness, employment and poverty reduction;
- Resource efficiency, environmental protection and climate change;
- Cultural values, diversity and heritage; and
- Mutual understanding, peace and security."[13]

Apart from a key theme focusing on cultural heritage, one of the main, tangible outcomes from the IYSTD that can be beneficial to historical places in Asia is the "Tourism4SDGs" platform by UNWTO. The website is a dynamic repository of

12. United Nations Statistics Division, "SDG Indicators Metadata Repository—Indicator 11.4.1," accessed December 6, 2021, https://unstats.un.org/sdgs/metadata/?Text=&Goal=11&Target=11.4.
13. United Nations World Tourism Organization, "Tourism and the Sustainable Development Goals," accessed December 10, 2021, https://www.e-unwto.org/doi/pdf/10.18111/9789284417254.

research, case studies, education and training programs, events, initiatives, policy papers, and company corporate social responsibility (CSR) initiatives.[14]

Ongoing Impacts of Tourism on Asian Urban Cultural Heritage

Many of the large- to medium-sized Asian cities with unique cultural heritage places are located along or at the nexus of trade routes, often with strategic, defensive, and favorable geographic purposes in mind. There are often buildings and structures related to trade and transportation infrastructure (e.g., ports, jetties, warehouses, and customs and trading houses), large government institutional buildings, districts sequestered by trade guilds and activities, ethnic groups and their services and amenities, religious and community structures, dry goods and wet markets, restaurants, and other facets that demarcate their natural and imposed geographic edges.

Layers of history and structural change (e.g., cultural, economic, physical, political, and social) have been imposed on Asia's urban cultural heritage. All three destinations included in this publication, Macao, Mumbai, and Penang, either have their foundations in or were significantly impacted by colonial planning policies giving rise to architectural styles that were directly influenced by Europe. Over time, these places developed local patinas and design elements.[15]

This uniqueness is reflected in the Outstanding Universal Values (OUVs) for the World Heritage Sites (WHSs) in all three destinations:

- Historic Centre of Macao (2005): "The site provides a unique testimony to the meeting of aesthetic, cultural, religious, architectural and technological influences from East and West. It bears witness to one of the earliest and most enduring encounters between China and the West, based on the vibrancy of international trade."[16]
- Melaka and George Town, Historic Cities of the Straits of Malacca (2008): They are considered "remarkable examples of historic colonial towns on the Straits of Malacca that demonstrate a succession of historical and cultural influences arising from their former function as trading ports linking East and West."[17]
- Chhatrapati Shivaji Terminus (Victoria Terminus) (2004) and the Victorian Gothic and Art Deco Ensembles of Mumbai (2018): Both of Mumbai's Victorian Gothic and the Art Deco ensembles around the Oval Maidan "exhibit an important exchange of European and Indian human values over a span of time," with the railway terminus reflecting British design standards and Indian architectural tradition and idioms, forging a new style unique to the city.[18]

These World Heritage designations and others in the region as well as the advent of mass, organized travel that began in the 1990s, combined with an influx of travel publications (e.g., Frommer's, Lonely Planet, Rough Guides, etc.), travel shows (e.g., National Geographic, *Parts Unknown*, Rick Steves, etc.), and films (e.g., *Crazy Rich Asians*, *The Darjeeling Limited*, *Die Another Day*, etc.) have helped to draw

14. United Nations World Tourism Organization, "Tourism4SDGs," accessed December 9, 2021. https://tourism4sdgs.org/.
15. Hilary du Cros, "Emerging Issues for Cultural Tourism in Macau," *Journal of Current Chinese Affairs* 38, no. 1 (2009): 73–99, https://journals.sagepub.com/doi/10.1177/186810260903800105.
16. UNESCO, "World Heritage List," accessed December 8, 2021, https://whc.unesco.org/en/list/.
17. UNESCO, "World Heritage List."
18. UNESCO, "World Heritage List."

visitors to these unique, urban cultural heritage destinations. The challenge is that the increased popularity of such places has resulted in physical and structural changes. This includes adaptive reuse and construction of new infrastructure, amenities, and services to accommodate increasing levels of visitation that are not always compatible with the existing historical character. Efforts to rethink sustainability and resiliency measures respective of these potential changes are needed to support their ongoing viability and critical to their survival.[19]

Adaptive Reuse Implications for Asian Urban Cultural Heritage

The European Union's Tourban project (accelerating small and medium enterprises' [SMEs'] capacity and innovation for sustainable urban tourism) acknowledges that there are conflicts in the usage of infrastructure and facilities between tourists and residents in cultural heritage places. Specifically, unwanted pressures can impact the economic, residential, and social life of these communities through the following:

- Physical overcrowding of the city, especially the historical centres and around a small number of very popular tourism hot spots. This causes conflicts in the usage of infrastructure and facilities between tourists and residents;
- Tourists' offensive behaviour, including public urination and vomiting, littering, drunkenness and noise;
- Displacement of stores and facilities for locals, replaced by souvenir shops and facilities for tourists;
- Increase of prices in the city, leading to a loss of purchasing power of residents and worsening their quality of life. This is particularly dramatic in terms of housing prices. Additionally, more and more houses are offered to tourists through platforms such as Airbnb, losing *de facto* their residential function;
- *Disneyfication* of the city, more and more perceived as a theme park and developed primarily to fit the preferences of tourists, not the needs of the residents;
- Pollution and degradation of the environment near popular tourist sites; and
- Development by residents of a negative and hostile sentiment against tourism.[20]

Communities living within and on the periphery of Asian urban cultural heritage places face a number of additional challenges when it comes to realizing the fuller benefits that may be drawn from the proximity to tourism attractions:

- Management capabilities: Limited organizational capacity and financial resources; encountering irregular and not always accountable levels of governance.
- Site sustainability: Visitor attraction and management; participation of underrepresented groups; and maintenance of traditional cultural use and activities.
- Community resiliency: Dealing with pressures to leave traditional neighborhoods, occupations, and residential areas; tourism sector's ability to respond

19. Bruce Prideaux and Dallen J. Timothy, "Themes in Cultural and Heritage Tourism in the Asia Pacific Region," in *Cultural and Heritage Tourism in Asia and the Pacific*, ed. Bruce Prideaux, Dallen J. Timothy, and Kaye Chon (London: Routledge, 2008), 1–14, https://researchonline.jcu.edu.au/27789/4/27789_Prideaux_etal_2008.pdf.
20. Tourban, *Sustainable Urban Tourism: Challenges, Best Practices and Transforming Initiatives for Cities and SME Managers* (Breda, the Netherlands: Breda University of Applied Sciences, April 2021), https://usercontent.one/wp/www.tourban.eu/wp-content/uploads/2021/04/Tourban-D1.2-eManual-Sustainable-urban-tourism-for-cities-and-SME-managers-16.04.21-def.pdf.

Figure 7.2: Tourists in front of the Gateway of India, Mumbai. (Source: Nitesh Jain.)

> to and withstand unforeseen circumstances like global pandemics, financial crises, natural disasters, and regional conflicts.[21]

This issue of managing and adapting these cultural heritage places has roots in how different stakeholders view tangible and intangible cultural heritage. Some view them as valuable for tourism foremost, some as social capital for the community, and others as a mix of both. Problematically, a few powerful stakeholders may even see them as having little value at all. Different combinations of these scenarios are possible in the Asia-Pacific region, where dissonance over the role of heritage in the transformation of historical cities and towns is commonplace.[22] In essence, local cultures develop during the dynamic process of making use of tourism to redefine their own identities.[23] Many of the changes related to adaptive reuse observed in historical centers, such as George Town (Penang) and Singapore, are driven by the explosive valuation of land, the introduction of short-term rentals, and/or the juxtaposed commodification and dying out of traditional intangible cultural heritage. The following three examples offer insight into how such changes affect the sustainability of valued cultural heritage resources.

Example 1. Since its successful World Heritage nomination in 2008, new developments and development proposals within George Town have shown a marked change in the perception of the value of old traditional environments and of remaining communities within the original urban settlement. The need for a more defined tourism product has clearly played a role in this change, as have the continued efforts of the embattled preservation community, led by the Penang Heritage Trust. To encourage the first new commercial district as a venue of economic, environmental, and social renaissance, the intent was to revive the perceived grandeur and elegance of an area that was once the domain of the island's wealthy elite, and provide for a

21. International Labour Organization, *ILO Guidelines*.
22. Ken Taylor, "Cultural Heritage Management: A Possible Role for Charters and Principles in Asia," *International Journal of Heritage Studies* 10, no. 5 (2005): 417–33.
23. Robert E. Wood, "*Tourism and Cultural Development in Asia and Oceania*, ed. Shinji Yamashita, Kadir H. Din, and J. S. Eades (Bangi, Selangor, Malaysia: Penerbit Universiti Kebangsaan Malaysia, 1997), 244 Pp. RM 30.00." *Journal of Asian Studies* 58, no. 1 (1999): 150–51.

new generation of educated, middle-class residents. As the target group is relatively small, attracting the tourist dollar through adaptive reuse and commercialization was seen as necessary for the financial viability of the planned development.[24] The concern is that this type of gentrification with an underlying thrust of revenue generation through tourism enterprises and services will drive out traditional uses and residents and drive up land prices and cost of ownership, especially after the Control of Rent Repeal in 1997 and the World Heritage nomination in 2008.[25]

Example 2. Along the east coast of the Malay peninsula, hawker food was one of the key aspects of community street life. In the 1960s, the Singaporean government began to regulate hawking for health, sanitary, and oversight purposes, moving these entrepreneurs to food stalls in designated areas (hawker centers), often near housing developments, where hawker culture flourished. The National Heritage Board calculates that there are now over 110 hawker centers across the island, vital to Singapore's identity, while also reshaping its heritage districts by commodifying and structurally integrating the intangible cultural heritage representative of these food purveyors, driving the adaptive reuse of heritage structures into new community hubs. One of the more notable examples of this transition is the Lau Pa Sat Hawker Center (Figure 7.3). A former market in the Financial District, it was transformed to a vital community culinary hub and was gazetted as a National Monument in 1973.[26]

Example 3. Short-term rentals, including Airbnb and Vrbo, were beginning to slowly gain momentum in Asia prior to the incursion of the pandemic in March 2020. The current generation of millennial travelers are prioritizing authentic experiences that allow them to live like locals in immersive settings over the standardized

Figure 7.3: Lau Pa Sat Hawker Center, Singapore. (Source: Debra Jean Ng.)

24. Gwynn Jenkins, "Interpreters of Space, Place and Cultural Practice: Processes of Change through Tourism, Conservation, and Development in George Town, Penang, Malaysia," in *Heritage Tourism in Southeast Asia*, ed. Michael Hitchcock, Victor T. King, and Mike Parnwell (Honolulu: University of Hawai'i Press, 2010).
25. "Penang State Govt Mulls Rent Control to Ensure Reasonable Rental Rates," *Sun Daily*, July 4, 2016, https://www.thesundaily.my/archive/1876130-KSARCH378560.
26. Devin Smith, "The Bells at Lau Pa Sat: A Story about Singapore's Urban Development in Six Parts," *Medium*, September 13, 2017, https://devinsmithwork.medium.com/the-bells-at-lau-pa-sat-30f5c471995e.

fare offered by hotels. The influence of the so-called Airbnb effect on local housing markets, however, has become a significant cause for concern, particularly when looking at its impacts on housing stock, prices, and communities. The Airbnb effect appears remarkably similar to the gentrification of cultural heritage districts in that it slowly increases the value of an area to the detriment of the residents, many of whom are pushed out due to financial constraints.[27]

With the intention of ameliorating these concerns, in August 2021, Airbnb announced a partnership with UNESCO (beginning in Mexico) to develop comprehensive tourism innovation and community inclusion projects to incorporate the creative sector and micro-, small-, and medium-sized cultural tourism entrepreneurs into the sustainable tourism value chain, in solidarity with the environment and cultural assets of the communities, aligned with SDG 8—Decent Work and Economic Growth, target 8.9: "By 2030, devise and implement policies to promote sustainable tourism that creates jobs and promotes local culture and products" and SDG 12—Responsible Consumption and Production, target 12.b: "Develop and implement tools to monitor sustainable development impacts for sustainable tourism that creates jobs and promotes local culture and products."[28]

Urban heritage places, particularly those that generate substantial tourism revenues, are often challenged to maintain the viability of buildings and structures within their historical fabric. Some of the negative implications include increasing land values and rents, changing use patterns from traditional activities to those that are more tourism based, new infrastructure requirements to address growing transportation and visitor flows, and so forth. However, by taking an adaptive reuse approach, whether rejuvenating buildings to maintain their historical character or finding ways to integrate intangible cultural heritage elements (seen in example 2 of Singapore's Lau Pa Sat Hawker Center), the attractiveness of such places for visitors as well as heritage qualities are maintained.

Tourism as a Driver of Change in Asia and Alignment with the SDGs

Many destinations suffer from imbalanced influxes of visitors from a seasonal, preferred day of the week or time of day, often referred to as "overtourism," while trying to maintain expectations of experience and service. It is particularly important for destinations facing threats to culture and heritage, degraded tourist experiences, overloaded infrastructure, and environmental impacts to develop tactics to "smooth" these imbalances. In some instances—that is, at World Heritage Sites (WHSs)—it makes sense simply to limit the number of visitors during periods of overtourism. For example, through a daily cap (as at China's Mount Huangshan), destinations with reservations and ticketing systems can use real-time data to prompt visitor behavior and movement around a cultural heritage place and change promotion strategies to entice visitors to experience different types of events, crafts, and traditional activities.[29] Where threats to culture and heritage have reached a critical stage, the tactics

27. Gary Barker, "The Airbnb Effect on Housing and Rent," *Forbes*, February 21, 2020, https://www.forbes.com/sites/garybarker/2020/02/21/the-airbnb-effect-on-housing-and-rent/?sh=3b2883ab2226.
28. Airbnb, "Airbnb Announces Partnership with UNESCO to Promote Cultural Tourism," Hospitalitynet, August 10, 2021, https://www.hospitalitynet.org/news/4105918.html.
29. McKinsey & Company and World Travel & Tourism Council (WTTC), *Coping with Success: Managing Overcrowding in Tourism Destinations* (New York: McKinsey and WTTC, December 2017), https://www.mckinsey.com/~/media/mckinsey/industries/travel%20transport%20and%20logistics/our%20insights/coping%20with%20success%20managing%20overcrowding%20in%20tourism%20destinations/coping-with-success-managing-overcrowding-in-tourism-destinations.pdf.

described so far may not be enough. As such, some destinations are limiting or even banning adaptive reuse of structures focused solely on tourism. As seen in the case of Amsterdam, where its efforts since 2019 have included the adoption of ordinances that prevent souvenir shops from displacing local businesses, developers from turning residential spaces into holiday lets, and new hotels from being built.[30]

More recently, the UNESCO Institute for Statistics reflected in its 2020 report *Tracking Investment to Safeguard the World's Cultural and Natural Heritage* that expenditure on heritage preservation is proportionate to the number and type of protected heritage sites. National legislation on heritage preservation also influences expenditure by defining measures, obligations, rules, and constraints in conserving historical buildings as well as sites of cultural and natural significance.[31] The report posited that management plan(s) for cultural and natural heritage and intangible cultural heritage (ICH), at the subnational, national, or international level should be elaborated on or updated every five years. These recommendations are related to the Sustainable Development Goals (SDGs) in the following manner, by incorporating the following for action and reporting purposes:

- Management plan(s) incorporating sections to manage visitors, tourism activity, and derived economic, sociocultural, and environmental impacts.
- Evidence that the benefits of tourism are shared with local communities (e.g., numbers of jobs created, heritage income for local businesses, and revenue of local council from heritage).[32]

Figure 7.4: A heritage tour in George Town, Penang. (Source: Lin Lee Loh Lim.)

30. Johannes Novy, "Amsterdam Is Laying Down a Model for What Tourism Should Look Like after COVID," *The Conversation*, June 16, 2021, https://theconversation.com/amsterdam-is-laying-down-a-model-for-what-tourism-should-look-like-after-covid-162271.
31. UNESCO Institute for Statistics, "Tracking Investment to Safeguard the World's Cultural and Natural Heritage," accessed December 7, 2021, http://uis.unesco.org/sites/default/files/documents/uis_culture_and_heritage_report_2021_web.pdf.
32. UNESCO Institute for Statistics (UIS), "Tracking Investment."

Although tangible and intangible cultural heritage aspects can be integrated into tourism strategies, this does not imply the reduction or removal of cultural activities, assets, and identities. The intent is that relevant benefits are reinvested in cultural activities.

In Malaysia, ThinkCity Sdn. Bhd. is a special project vehicle established by Khazanah Nasional Berhad, the investment holding arm of the government of Malaysia. Since 2009, ThinkCity has supported nongovernmental organizations (NGOs) and local communities in Penang through 205 projects involving building conservation, community-led shared spaces, and cultural mapping projects as well as technical assistance and capacity building programs. ThinkCity continues to support public-private partnerships, including the George Town Business Improvement District Scheme (BIDS), the Little India Joint Action Committee, Yayasan Islam Pulau Pinang, and outreach and educational programs by George Town World Heritage Incorporated.[33] Notably, during the disruptive throes to the local visitor economy caused by COVID-19 , in October 2021, ThinkCity proposed that the government allocate funds for investment in heritage conservation and urban renewal projects as a way to spur the tourism industry. The sentiment was that funding support would help to reinvigorate heritage assets and rejuvenate urban areas in keeping with targets associated with SDGs.[34]

Future Challenges and Directions for Municipal and Heritage Authorities

In 2017, the ICOMOS International Cultural Tourism Committee (ICOMOS ICTC) embarked on the renewal of its foundation doctrine, the International Cultural Tourism Charter (the Charter), which had last been updated in 1999 at the ICOMOS General Assembly convened in Mexico City. Over a twenty-one-year period, the Convention for the Safeguarding of the Intangible Cultural Heritage (2003), Convention on the Rights of Persons with Disabilities (2006), United Nations Declaration on the Rights of Indigenous Peoples (2007), along with the Sustainable Development Goals (SDGs) in 2015 and International Year of Sustainable Tourism for Development (IYSTD) in 2017, identified areas that needed to be addressed in the planning, development, and management of cultural heritage destinations.

This was particularly the case for cultural heritage places in Asia in that many were originally developed for commercial and trading purposes and not necessarily designed for the waves of visitors that would be exploring and generating interest in experiencing local sights and events, enjoying local foods, and purchasing local crafts. Simultaneously, vehicular and disabled access and the implementation of civil, digital, and information infrastructure to take on expanding resident and tourist numbers has taken time to address. This has meant different forms of adaptive reuse of heritage places to accommodate these changes, sometimes counter to the wishes of local communities who have lived in and around them.

This is why the current draft iteration of the Charter, awaiting formal ICOMOS approval, recognizes the adaptations that communities would have to make to their

33. Aga Khan Development Network, "Regeneration of Penang's George Town World Heritage Site," October 16, 2015, https://www.akdn.org/press-release/regeneration-penangs-george-town-world-heritage-site.
34. Rachael Yeoh, "Reinvesting in Heritage, Urban Renewal Can Bolster Tourism: Think City," *The Vibes*, accessed December 6, 2021, https://www.thevibes.com/articles/news/44706/reinvesting-in-heritage-urban-renewal-can-bolster-tourism-think-city.

heritage structures, traditions, and livelihoods to reasonably accommodate the growth of tourism and its cultural, economic, environmental, and social impacts, without having them completely subsumed or diluted. These adaptations are outlined in the following seven principles of the draft Charter:

> Principle 1: Place cultural heritage protection and conservation at the centre of responsible cultural tourism planning and management.
>
> Principle 2: Manage tourism at cultural heritage places through planning instruments and management plans informed by monitoring, and carrying capacity and other planning instruments.
>
> Principle 3: Enhance public awareness and visitor experience through education, sensitive interpretation and presentation of cultural heritage.
>
> Principle 4: Recognize and reinforce the rights of communities, Indigenous Peoples and traditional owners by including access and engagement in participatory governance of the cultural and natural heritage commons used in tourism.
>
> Principle 5: Raise awareness of cultural heritage and reinforce cooperation for heritage conservation among all tourism stakeholders involved in tourism.
>
> Principle 6: Increase the resilience of communities and cultural heritage sites and destinations and host communities through capacity development, risk assessment, strategic planning and adaptive management.
>
> Principle 7: Integrate climate action and sustainability measures in the management of cultural tourism and cultural heritage.[35]

For Asian cultural heritage places, Principle 7 is probably the most applicable. "Sustainability measures" infers the SDGs and that they should be a part of any decision-making when it involves cultural tourism planning, development, and management. It has been previously mentioned that the specific targets related to urban cultural heritage are targets 8.9, 11.4, and 12.b, but there can be a radiating effect into all seventeen of the SDGs (and their targets). The World Tourism Organization (UNWTO) posits that while sustainable tourism is embedded in the *2030 Agenda*, achieving the three targets, and their associated positive impacts on the other goals requires a clear implementation framework, adequate financing, and investment in technology and human resources.[36]

The emergence of more man-made and natural disasters, pandemics, conflicts, and terrorism have forced government institutions to rethink the state of conservation, especially how it is managed and used, particularly in the maintenance of local visitor economies. Of particular note is how governments should be retrenching and protecting cultural heritage that supports the local tourism sector.

For example, a recent climate change-related policy instrument has been developed to support the tourism sector becoming net zero compliant in terms of emissions requirements. Its originator, the One Planet Network, is a global community of experts, practitioners, and policymakers drawn from governments, businesses, civil society, academia, and international organizations. The policy implements the 10-Year Framework of Programmes (10YFP) on Sustainable Consumption and Production (SCP) and works toward achieving SDG 12—Ensure Sustainable Consumption and Production Patterns, which includes the sustainable tourism reporting target

35. International Council on Monuments and Sites International Cultural Tourism Committee, "Proposed Final Draft of the ICOMOS Charter on Cultural Heritage Tourism," September 27, 2021, https://www.icomosictc.org/2021/09/proposed-final-draft-of-icomos-charter.html.
36. United Nations World Tourism Organization, "Tourism and the Sustainable Development Goals," accessed December 10, 2021, https://www.e-unwto.org/doi/pdf/10.18111/9789284417254.

12.b: "Develop and implement tools to monitor sustainable development impacts for sustainable tourism that creates jobs and promotes local culture and products." The network's major contribution to the 26th session of the Conference of the Parties (COP26) in October 2021 in Glasgow, Scotland was its leadership role in the creation of the Glasgow Declaration.[37]

The declaration is a one-page pledge, which requires destinations and travel businesses around the globe, as signatories, to deliver "Climate Action Plans" within twelve months and publicly report on their progress. Climate Action Plans aligned with the Glasgow Declaration need to include five components: measuring (disclosing all travel-related emissions), decarbonization (without relying on carbon offsets), regeneration (restoring and protecting ecosystems, etc.), collaboration (sharing best practice with other travel stakeholders), and finance (ensuring they have the means to implement their plans).

The Glasgow Declaration emphasizes under "regeneration" that as much of tourism is based in regions and coastal areas (as in the case of Macao, Mumbai, and Penang) most immediately vulnerable to the impacts of climate change and rising sea levels, the proposed Climate Action Plans must ensure the sector can support affected and at-risk communities in adaptation, mitigation, resilience building, and disaster response.[38] This is reinforced by the Climate Heritage Network, which promotes the use and adaptive reuse of existing buildings and materials. Within this framework, culture and heritage institutions and tourism offerings, including heritage sites, museums, libraries, festivals, and concerts, can transform and green their own operations.[39] The Glasgow Declaration provides a state-of-the-art approach to strategizing, preparing for, and dealing with longer term, inevitable climate change impacts on cultural heritage places, among a range of destinations. This declaration's successful implementation is predicated on the level of commensurate government and community cooperation and investment.

Conclusions

Cities in Asia are places of change, whether through traditional settlement and use patterns, colonialism, postwar and postindependence economic growth, or the expansion of tourism. The modern demands, expectations, and desires to enhance local visitor economies and extract as much economic gain as possible has driven both intended and unintended change in settlement patterns and commercial purposes in cultural heritage places. This has encouraged and forced adaptive reuse to cater more to the services and amenities deemed desirable by tourists over the needs of local residents, who are often forced out due to higher rents and taxes or inconvenienced due to the changes to their social environments and available services and amenities.

The ongoing concerns in the sustainability and resiliency of the tourism sector driven by the pandemic, combined with previous issues with overtourism and loss of tangible and intangible cultural heritage, are giving governing bodies the opportunity to rethink how these unique places are being changed, while determining what restrictions are necessary to reduce loss. Instruments like the Sustainable Development Goals (SDGs) and the ICOMOS International Cultural Tourism Charter

37. One Planet Network, "The Glasgow Declaration," 2021, https://www.oneplanetnetwork.org/programmes/sustainable-tourism/glasgow-declaration.
38. One Planet Network, "The Glasgow Declaration."
39. Andrew Potts, "The Role of Culture in Climate Resilient Development," UCLG Committee on Culture Reports, nº 10, and Climate Heritage Network (Working Group 5), Barcelona, November 5, 2021.

provide the basis to rebalance the transformation and address the impacts taking place.

Bibliography

Aga Khan Development Network. "Regeneration of Penang's George Town World Heritage Site." October 16, 2015. https://www.akdn.org/press-release/regeneration-penangs-george-town-world-heritage-site.

Airbnb. "Airbnb Announces Partnership with UNESCO to Promote Cultural Tourism." Hospitalitynet, August 10, 2021. https://www.hospitalitynet.org/news/4105918.html.

Barker, Gary. "The Airbnb Effect on Housing and Rent." *Forbes*, February 21, 2020. https://www.forbes.com/sites/garybarker/2020/02/21/the-airbnb-effect-on-housing-and-rent/?sh=3b2883ab2226.

Chopra, Sonia. "Singapore's Hawker Centers Were on the Brink of Disappearing. Then the Government and the U.N. Stepped In." *Bon Appetit*, July 7, 2021. https://www.bonappetit.com/story/singapore-hawker-culture-unesco.

Collins, Robertson. *A Disorderly Excursion: Notes of a Conservationist in the Asia/Pacific Region*. Singapore: PATA Foundation, 1991.

du Cros, Hilary. "Emerging Issues for Cultural Tourism in Macau." *Journal of Current Chinese Affairs* 38, no. 1 (2009): 73–99. https://journals.sagepub.com/doi/10.1177/186810260903800105.

Euromonitor International. "Problems Facing Short-Term Rentals in Southeast Asia." August 26, 2016. https://www.euromonitor.com/video/problems-facing-short-term-rentals-southeast-asia.

Inter-Agency and Expert Group on SDG Indicators. *Revised List of Global Sustainable Development Goal Indicators*. March 2017. https://unstats.un.org/sdgs/indicators/official%20revised%20list%20of%20global%20sdg%20indicators.pdf.

International Council on Monuments and Sites International Cultural Tourism Committee. "Proposed Final Draft of the ICOMOS Charter on Cultural Heritage Tourism." September 27, 2021. https://www.icomosictc.org/2021/09/proposed-final-draft-of-icomos-charter.html.

International Labour Organization. *ILO Guidelines on Decent Work and Socially Responsible Tourism*. 2017. https://www.ilo.org/wcmsp5/groups/public/---ed_dialogue/---sector/documents/normativeinstrument/wcms_546337.pdf.

Jenkins, Gwynn. "Interpreters of Space, Place and Cultural Practice: Processes of Change through Tourism, Conservation, and Development in George Town, Penang, Malaysia." In *Heritage Tourism in Southeast Asia*, edited by Michael Hitchcock, Victor T. King, and Mike Parnwell. Honolulu: University of Hawai'i Press, 2010.

McKinsey & Company and World Travel & Tourism Council (WTTC). *Coping with Success: Managing Overcrowding in Tourism Destinations*. New York: McKinsey and WTTC, December 2017. https://www.mckinsey.com/~/media/mckinsey/industries/travel%20transport%20and%20logistics/our%20insights/coping%20with%20success%20managing%20overcrowding%20in%20tourism%20destinations/coping-with-success-managing-overcrowding-in-tourism-destinations.pdf.

Novy, Johannes. "Amsterdam Is Laying Down a Model for What Tourism Should Look Like after COVID." *The Conversation*, June 16, 2021. https://theconversation.com/amsterdam-is-laying-down-a-model-for-what-tourism-should-look-like-after-covid-162271.

One Planet Network. "The Glasgow Declaration." 2021. https://www.oneplanetnetwork.org/programmes/sustainable-tourism/glasgow-declaration.

"Penang State Govt Mulls Rent Control to Ensure Reasonable Rental Rates." *Sun Daily*, July 4, 2016. https://www.thesundaily.my/archive/1876130-KSARCH378560.

Potts, Andrew. "The Role of Culture in Climate Resilient Development." UCLG Committee on Culture Reports, nº 10, and Climate Heritage Network (Working Group 5). Barcelona, November 5, 2021.

Prideaux, Bruce, and Dallen J. Timothy. "Themes in Cultural and Heritage Tourism in the Asia Pacific Region." In *Cultural and Heritage Tourism in Asia and the Pacific*, edited by Bruce Prideaux, Dallen J. Timothy, and Kaye Chon, 1–14. London: Routledge, 2008. https://researchonline.jcu.edu.au/27789/4/27789_Prideaux_etal_2008.pdf.

Smith, Devin. "The Bells at Lau Pa Sat: A Story about Singapore's Urban Development in Six Parts." *Medium*, September 13, 2017. https://devinsmithwork.medium.com/the-bells-at-lau-pa-sat-30f5c471995e.

So, Fion Wai Ling. *Germany's Colony in China: Colonialism, Protection and Economic Development in Qingdao and Shandong, 1898–1914*. London: Routledge, 2019.

Taylor, Ken. "Cultural Heritage Management: A Possible Role for Charters and Principles in Asia." *International Journal of Heritage Studies* 10, no. 5 (2005): 417–33.

Tourban. *Sustainable Urban Tourism: Challenges, Best Practices and Transforming Initiatives for Cities and SME Managers*. Breda, the Netherlands: Breda University of Applied Sciences, April 2021. https://usercontent.one/wp/www.tourban.eu/wp-content/uploads/2021/04/Tourban-D1.2-eManual-Sustainable-urban-tourism-for-cities-and-SME-managers-16.04.21-def.pdf.

UNESCO. "Culture 2030 Indicators." Accessed December 8, 2021. http://uis.unesco.org/sites/default/files/documents/publication_culture_2020_indicators_en.pdf.

UNESCO. *Report of the Nara Seminar on the Development and Integrity of Historic Cities (5–7 March 1999, Nara, Japan)*. Presented at the 23rd session of the World Heritage Committee, Marrakesh, Morocco, 1999.

UNESCO. "UNESCO Intangible Cultural Heritage: Hawker Culture in Singapore, Community Dining and Culinary Practices in a Multicultural Urban Context." Accessed December 10, 2021. https://ich.unesco.org/en/RL/hawker-culture-in-singapore-community-dining-and-culinary-practices-in-a-multicultural-urban-context-01568.

UNESCO. "World Heritage List." 2021. https://whc.unesco.org/en/list/.

United Cities and Local Governments. "Culture in the Sustainable Development Goals: A Guide for Local Action." 2018. https://www.uclg.org/sites/default/files/culture_in_the_sdgs.pdf.

United Nations. "System of Environmental Economic Accounting." 2021. https://seea.un.org/.

United Nations, Department of Economic and Social Affairs, Sustainable Development. "The 17 Goals." Accessed March 23, 2022. https://sdgs.un.org/goals.

United Nations Statistics Division. "SDG Indicators Metadata Repository—Indicator 8.9.1." Accessed December 6, 2021. https://unstats.un.org/sdgs/metadata/?Text=&Goal=8&Target=8.9.

United Nations Statistics Division. "SDG Indicators Metadata Repository—Indicator 11.4.1." Accessed December 6, 2021. https://unstats.un.org/sdgs/metadata/?Text=&Goal=11&Target=11.4.

United Nations Statistics Division. "SDG Indicators Metadata Repository—Indicator 12.b.1." Accessed December 6, 2021. https://unstats.un.org/sdgs/metadata/?Text=&Goal=12&Target.

United Nations World Tourism Organization. "Sustainable Tourism for Development Guidebook." Accessed April 25, 2022. https://www.ilo.org/wcmsp5/groups/public/---ed_dialogue/---sector/documents/publication/wcms_216669.pdf.

United Nations World Tourism Organization. "Tourism4SDGs." Accessed December 9, 2021. https://tourism4sdgs.org/.

United Nations World Tourism Organization. "Tourism and the Sustainable Development Goals." Accessed December 10, 2021. https://www.e-unwto.org/doi/pdf/10.18111/9789284417254.

United Nations World Tourism Organization. "Tourism and the Sustainable Development Goals—Journey to 2030." Accessed November 8, 2021. https://www.e-unwto.org/doi/pdf/10.18111/9789284419401.

United Nations World Tourism Organization. "Tourism Satellite Account." Accessed December 6, 2021. https://www.unwto.org/standards/on-economic-contribution-of-tourism-tsa-2008.

Wood, Robert E. "*Tourism and Cultural Development in Asia and Oceania*. Edited by Shinji Yamashita, Kadir H. Din, and J. S. Eades. Bangi, Selangor, Malaysia: Penerbit Universiti Kebangsaan Malaysia, 1997. 244 Pp. RM 30.00." *Journal of Asian Studies* 58, no. 1 (1999): 150–51.

Yeoh, Rachael. "Reinvesting in Heritage, Urban Renewal Can Bolster Tourism: Think City." *The Vibes*. Accessed December 6, 2021. https://www.thevibes.com/articles/news/44706/reinvesting-in-heritage-urban-renewal-can-bolster-tourism-think-city.

URBAN CENTERS

Macao | Mumbai | Penang

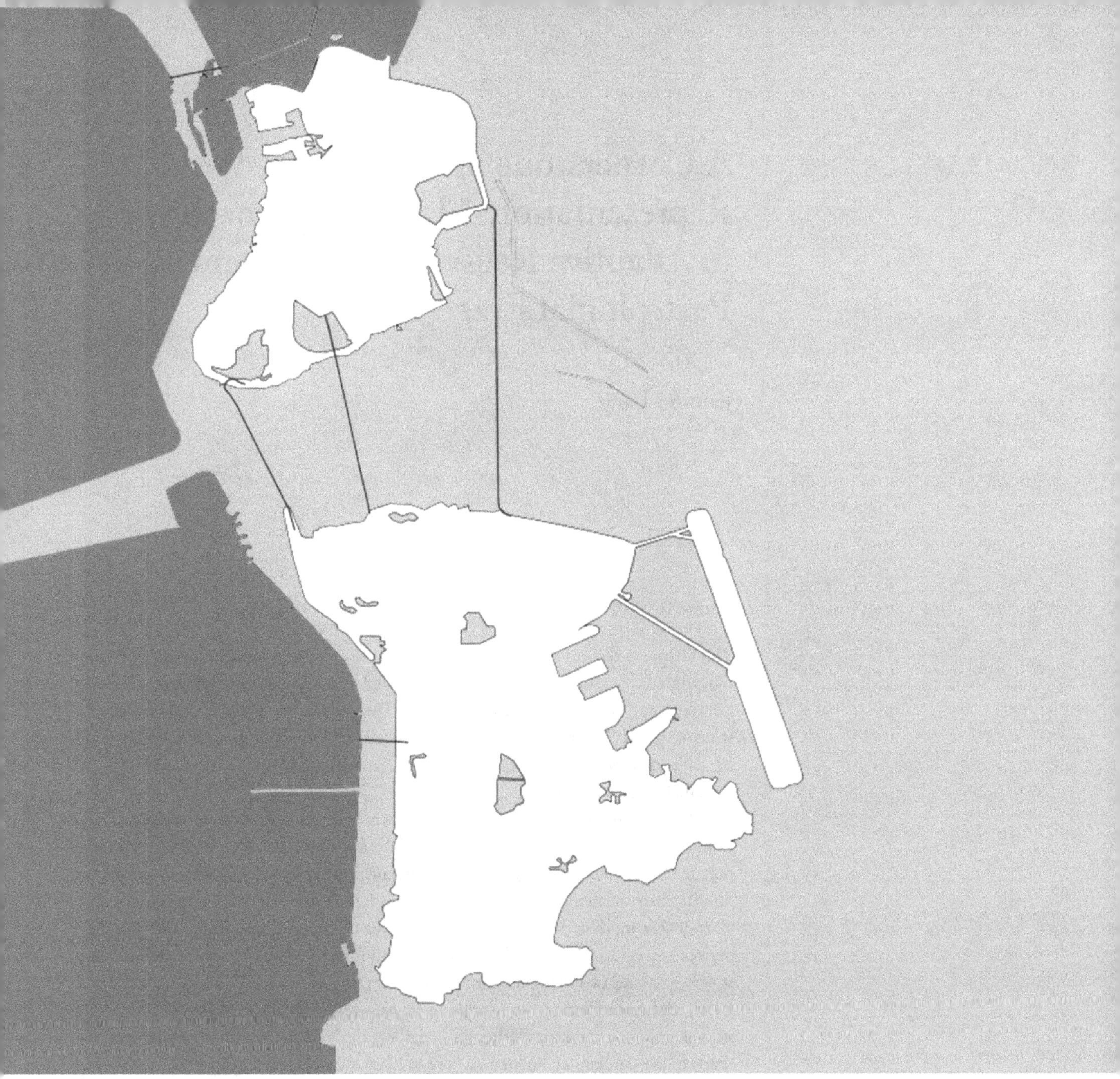

MACAO

Essay | Timeline | Case Studies

A Cornerstone in East-Meets-West Representation: Macao's Approach to Adaptive Reuse in Colonial and Postcolonial Eras

Jennifer Lang

Introduction

This chapter explores the development of adaptive reuse in Macao. A brief review of Macao's history and growth as a city is followed by a discussion of relevant conservation laws and heritage regulatory systems. The chapter includes an assessment of a selective group of adaptive reuse examples over time that indicates the evolution of Macao's conservation practice. Concluding remarks are made on adaptive reuse and sustainability in Macao.

The Portuguese began occupying Macao in the mid-sixteenth century and extended their influence in the area for nearly five centuries. As a vital international port from the sixteenth through the eighteenth centuries, Macao was an important link in trade and cultural exchange between China and the West.[1] It was the first place where modern Western architecture was introduced to China. This interface between foreign and local architectural traditions resulted in a variety of architectural styles—a blend of Portuguese architectural styles, traditional Chinese architectural styles, and Sino-Portuguese mixed styles; as a result, Macao developed into a city with a unique character. Although considerable land reclamation has altered the shape of the peninsula, the historic core of Macao developed during its occupation by the Portuguese from the seventeenth century has remained relatively intact.[2]

Macao remained a quiet enclave with little change until the outbreak of the Sino-Japanese War in 1937 and the Japanese invasion of Hong Kong in 1941. These events led to an abrupt increase in the local population as people from Guangzhou and Hong Kong took refuge in Macao, a safe wartime refuge due to Portugal's neutrality. However, the increased population had an impact on the small colony's limited building stock, and many buildings were subject to increased wear and tear. After the war, a weakened economy further accelerated the dilapidation of buildings, including those of historical value.

The situation started to change around the 1970s with the enactment of Macao's first conservation law. Additionally, the economic climate of the city was improving

1. The State Administration of the Cultural Heritage of the People's Republic of China, *The Historic Monuments of Macao (Nomination Dossier for World Heritage Inscription)* (Paris: UNESCO, 2005), 22, https://whc.unesco.org/uploads/nominations/1110.pdf.
2. Pui Yu Chan, "Community Participation in Heritage Management: A Case Study in Macau" (MS thesis, Columbia University, 2016), 38.

during the 1980s and 1990s owing to the revenue from a growing gaming industry. Together, these provided sufficient guidelines and resources for built heritage conservation. Since the late twentieth century, Macao has conserved an impressive number of buildings, and in 2005, the Historic Centre of Macao was inscribed on UNESCO's World Heritage List. With its wealth of well-conserved heritage buildings, including civic, public, and residential buildings, as well as its long experience in built heritage conservation, there is much to learn from Macao.

Relevant Laws and Regulations on the Protection of Macao's Architectural Heritage

Macao has robust heritage protection laws that have benefited from continuous updates. The development of these laws and the establishment of corresponding government and advisory bodies reflect Macao's early understanding and appreciation of its cultural heritage.

From 1953 to 1976, the Portuguese government began to identify and formulate a list of historical buildings and cultural relics of importance in Macao (further elaborated in the Macao Timeline).[3] The first law regarding the overall conservation of these "sites, buildings and objects . . . considered to be of public interest" was promulgated by the government in 1976: Macao Decree Law No. 34/76/M.[4] This first comprehensive law concerning the protection of Macao's heritage comprised a protection list of eighty-nine items, which were classified under five categories, three of which are directly related to built heritage.[5] The Committee for the Protection of Macao's Urbanistic, Natural and Cultural Heritage was set up as the statutory authority responsible for classifying these cultural heritage properties based on their heritage values, among other duties. This initial legislation focused primarily on built heritage, and as the law was promulgated by Portuguese architects and lawyers, most items included in this legislation were Portuguese-designed structures.[6]

In 1984, the government screened and reclassified the items included in the protected list with the introduction of Macao Decree Law No. 56/84/M—Protection of Architectural, Natural and Cultural Heritage, which repealed the decree of 1976. This decree includes a more comprehensive definition and classification of cultural heritage properties as "monuments, complexes, and sites"[7] and outlines a detailed protection plan for the different types of cultural heritage properties, updating the

3. Lier Mi, "Protection and Recycling of Architectural Heritage in Macau's Urban Renewal," *Advances in Social Science, Education and Humanities Research* 471 (2020): 214, https://www.researchgate.net/publication/346041963_Protection_and_Recycling_of_Architectural_Heritage_in_Macau's_Urban_Renewal.
4. "Legislation on Heritage Protection: Statutory Order No. 34/76/M August 7," Cultural Affairs Bureau, Macao SAR Government, accessed May 23, 2022, http://www.icm.gov.mo/rc/viewer/20038/1345.
5. The five categories are "1. buildings of historical interest; 2. urbanistic complexes, buildings, inscriptions and vestiges that constitute representative evidence of ancient peoples or periods in Macao's history; 3. sites of scenic or natural interest, including green zones, groups of trees or single trees whose size is especially worthy of notice; 4. sites that contain objects or vestiges of anthropological, archaeological or historical interest; 5. objects of historical or documentary interest found on the sites referred to in No. 4." See Cultural Affairs Bureau, "Statutory Order No. 34/76/M."
6. Frederick Lee and Hilary du Cros, "A Comparative Analysis of Three Heritage Management Approaches in Southern China," in *Asian Heritage Management: Contexts, Concerns, and Prospects*, ed. Kapil D. Silva and Neel Kamal Chapagain (Abingdon: Routledge, 2013), 113.
7. The decree classifies cultural heritage under seven categories; this essay focuses on categories a), b), and c) as they are directly relevant to built heritage. The full list can be found at "Legislation on Heritage Protection: Statutory Order No. 56/84/M June 30," Cultural Affairs Bureau, Macao SAR Government, accessed May 23, 2022, http://www.icm.gov.mo/rc/viewer/20038/1345.

list to include eighty-four items.[8] The Committee for the Protection of Architectural, Natural and Cultural Heritage (established under the terms of No. 2 of Article 12 of Statutory Order No. 43/92/M) replaced the Committee for the Protection of Macao's Urbanistic, Natural and Cultural Heritage. This committee is organized under the Department of Cultural Heritage of the Cultural Institute of Macao (renamed the Cultural Affairs Bureau in 1999) and plays an advisory role for matters on cultural heritage conservation in Macao.[9]

In 1992, the Portuguese government expanded the scope of cultural heritage protection with the introduction of Macao Decree Law No. 83/92/M. This law guarantees the protection of cultural heritage properties identified in Macao Decree Law No. 56/84/M and establishes an additional category of "building of architectural interest" defined as "one whose original architectural quality is representative of a significant period in the development of the territory."[10] This law stipulates that these buildings are not permitted to be demolished but are allowed to be repaired in a manner that retains their original characteristics, especially with regard to their design and the façade.[11] The updated protected list, comprising 128 items, is supplemented with maps of the city, which plot the location and classification of heritage properties. Importantly, the amended law stipulates that the Cultural Institute of Macao must be consulted before any work is carried out, including any alteration, consolidation, maintenance, and repair. The law also allows for review of both existing buildings and new buildings and includes restrictions related to building height, setback, site coverage, and roof and façade appearance in "protected zones."[12] A clear definition of such zones first appears in Decree Law No. 56/84/M: "A protected zone is the natural or man-made surroundings of designated monuments, complexes and sites, which are related to them for reasons of spatial or aesthetic integration, constituting an indispensable part of the property."[13]

China resumed jurisdiction of Macao from the Portuguese on December 20, 1999, and Macao was endowed with a new status of Special Administrative Region (SAR). To date, heritage laws and the inscription of the Historic Centre of Macao as a World Heritage Site have been promulgated by the new (Chinese) government of Macao.

World Heritage Inscription and Subsequent Heritage Laws

In 2005, the Historic Centre of Macao was inscribed on the UNESCO World Heritage List. The site includes twenty-two significant monuments with significant cultural heritage values and eight urban squares, including the streetscapes linking them, representing the historic settlement of Macao.[14] Comprised of temples and residences with unique Lingnan architectural design, and Portuguese/European churches, public buildings, residences, theaters and cemeteries, piazzas, streetscapes, and urban spaces, the Historic Centre of Macao is described as follows:

---

8. Cultural Affairs Bureau, "Statutory Order No. 56/84/M June 30."
9. Later replaced by the Cultural Heritage Committee in 2014.
10. "Legislation on Heritage Protection: Statutory Order No. 83/92/M December 31," Cultural Affairs Bureau, Macao SAR Government, accessed May 23, 2022, http://www.icm.gov.mo/rc/viewer/20038/1345.
11. Cultural Affairs Bureau, "Statutory Order No. 83/92/M December 31."
12. Cultural Affairs Bureau, "Statutory Order No. 83/92/M December 31."
13. Cultural Affairs Bureau, "Legislation on Heritage Protection: Statutory Order No. 56/84/M June 30."
14. Development Bureau, Hong Kong SAR Government, "Macao," in *Consultancy Study on the Heritage Conservation Regimes in Other Jurisdictions* (Hong Kong: Development Bureau, 2014), 112.

> The oldest, most intact and consolidated array of striking architectural heritage of predominantly European influence interwoven with Chinese settlements. . . . With Macau's strategic geographical location and historical significance as a long-standing conduit and entrepôt between China and the West. . . . [It bears] witness to the important exchange between the Portuguese and Chinese peoples.[15]

The Historic Centre of Macao was inscribed on the World Heritage List based on criteria ii, iii, iv, and vi as a living example of a settlement that represents the exchange of values between the Chinese and Portuguese in the various fields of culture, sciences, technology, art, and architecture over several centuries.[16]

The UNESCO inscription of Macao created two core protection zones of sixteen acres in total and two corresponding buffer zones of 107 acres in total.[17] Located on the western and eastern parts of the Macao peninsula, the World Heritage Site encompasses three important landscape features: Mount Hill, Barra Hill, and Guia Hill.[18] The protection of heritage properties within the World Heritage Site by buffer zones is especially important for Macao as many prominent structures, such as churches and forts, were constructed on such strategic locations as the crests of hills. Such physical and visual connections between various parts of the Historic Centre and the city are significant characteristics of Macao.[19] Related to the World Heritage inscription, in 2006 the Chief Executive's Order No. 202/2006 was issued, clearly establishing the definition and location of the Historic Centre of Macao and expanding the protection zones under the Macao Decree Law No. 83/92/M.

Macao Decree Law No. 11/2013—Cultural Heritage Protection Law was published in 2013 and continues to be enforced to date. It is a more comprehensive law, combining and repealing all previous laws related to cultural heritage protection. The law categorizes "classified immovable property" as follows:

- Monument: Monumental works of architecture, sculpture or painting, inscriptions, components, groups of elements or structures of special interest from the archaeological, historical, ethnological, artistic or scientific point of view.

---

15. Thomas Chung, "Valuing Heritage in Macau: On Contexts and Processes of Urban Conservation," *Journal of Current Chinese Affairs* 38, no. 1 (2009): 140.
16. Details of four criteria for inscription include Criterion (ii): "The strategic location of Macao on the Chinese territory, and the special relationship established between the Chinese and Portuguese authorities favored an important interchange of human values in the various fields of culture, sciences, technology, art and architecture over several centuries." Criterion (iii): "Macao bears a unique testimony to the first and longest-lasting encounter between the West and China. From the 16th to the 20th centuries, it was the focal point for traders and missionaries, and the different fields of learning. The impact of this encounter can be traced in the fusion of different cultures that characterize the historic core zone of Macao." Criterion (iv): "Macao represents an outstanding example of an architectural ensemble that illustrates the development of the encounter between the Western and Chinese civilizations over some four and half centuries, represented in the historical route, with a series of urban spaces and architectural ensembles, that links the ancient Chinese port with the Portuguese city." Criterion (vi): "Macao has been associated with the exchange of a variety of cultural, spiritual, scientific and technical influences between the Western and Chinese civilizations. These ideas directly motivated the introduction of crucial changes in China, ultimately ending the era of imperial feudal system and establishing the modern republic." See UNESCO World Heritage Centre, "The Historic Centre of Macao," accessed January 15, 2022, https://whc.unesco.org/en/list/1110/.
17. UNESCO, "Historic Centre of Macao."
18. Maps showing the boundaries of the Core and Buffer Zones of the World Heritage Site can be found at UNESCO World Heritage Centre, "Maps, The Historic Centre of Macao," accessed April 20, 2023, https://whc.unesco.org/en/list/1110/maps/.
19. Sharif Shams Imon, "Managing Change in the Historic City of Macao," *Historic Environment* 21, no. 3 (2008): 141.

- Building of architectonic [architectural] interest: [Immovable property that,] through its original architectonic quality, is representative of an important period of the evolution of the territory.
- Ensembles: Groups of constructions and areas that, by reason of their architecture, their unity, their integration in the landscape of their social homogeneity have a special value from the architectural, urbanistic, aesthetic, historic or socio-cultural point of view.
- Classified site: Combined works of man and of nature having a special value or their beauty or interest in the fields of archaeology, history, anthropology or ethnology.[20]

Key provisions of the law include the following points:

- Expansion of the definition of cultural heritage to include intangible heritage and movable heritage which are associated with the immovable heritage. Under the Cultural Heritage Protection Law, classified immovable, movable and intangible heritage are all protected by laws;
- Establishment of a Cultural Heritage Committee that is an advisory body of the Macao Government. The main responsibility of the committee is to advise on the assessment procedures, the use of immovable heritage, work in the buffer zones, work that would incur great impact on the heritage and the list of intangible heritage;
- Establishment of special guidelines to maintain the integrity and enhance the protection of the Historic Centre of Macao to satisfy the requirements of UNESCO;
- Require Cultural Affairs Bureau approval of work in buffer zones;
- Incorporate public participation in the process of establishing and implementing the policy of cultural heritage protection;
- Creation of consultation channels for public participation; and
- Clarification of rights and responsibilities for owners of cultural heritage sites, including details on compensation, tax incentives, financial support, and awards.[21]

In 2014, Administrative Regulation No. 4/2014 was issued leading to the formation of the Cultural Heritage Council to facilitate departmental and interdisciplinary collaboration in heritage protection. The council includes the Secretary for Social Affairs and Culture as well as executive officials from the Cultural Institute, Office of the Secretary for Social Affairs and Culture, Justice Affairs Services, Land, Public Works and Transport Bureau, and the Institute for Civic and Municipal Affairs.[22] In the same year, the Cultural Affairs Bureau initiated Phase 1 of a public consultation process to establish a framework for the Heritage Protection and Management Plan for the Historic Centre of Macao (澳門歷史城區保護及管理計劃). The plan, a result of Macao Decree Law No. 11/2013, aimed to protect Macao's cultural resources, increase public participation and awareness, and adhere to international standards of sustainability. Phase 2 of this public consultation process took place in 2018 and focused on mitigating or avoiding potential impact to the World Heritage due to urban development. The measures taken to mitigate impact on visual corridors were through height control of new construction projects, while those taken to avoid impact on the surrounding landscape setting were through building new transportation infrastructure underground or undersea.

---

20. Development Bureau, "Macao."
21. Development Bureau, "Macao," 117.
22. "Cultural Heritage Council, Administrative Regulation No. 4/2014," Macao SAR Government, Official Press, accessed April 20, 2023, https://bo.io.gov.mo/bo/i/2014/08/regadm04.asp.

In addition to the Cultural Heritage Protection Law, legal and planning instruments were further strengthened through the adoption of the Urban Planning Law and Land Law in March 2014.[23] These actions were taken in response to the rapid development of Macao due to gaming and tourism and the resulting changes in urban spaces. The Urban Planning Law No. 12/2013 (Urban Planning Law) is closely related to the protection of the Historic Centre of Macao and ensures that any urban planning within the protection zones and buffer zones requires that the Land, Public Works and Transport Bureau should consult with the Cultural Affairs Bureau.[24] The objective of the Urban Planning Law is to protect the cultural heritage of the city as one of the most important ways to improve the quality of life and ensure the sustainability of urban development.

In 2022, Macao released the Master Plan of the Macao Special Administrative Region (2020–2040), which outlines the city's plan to be an integral part of the Greater Bay Area and positions it as a tourist destination and a bridge between Lusophone countries and China. The Master Plan includes rezoning, land reclamation, and development and includes goals to protect cultural heritage and maintain the visual corridors and protection zones of the World Heritage Site and the entire city of Macao.[25]

Heritage Management

Macao's Cultural Affairs Bureau is under the Secretariat for Social Affairs and Culture. Formerly known as the Cultural Institute of Macao of the Macao government, it was established as a public institution on September 4, 1982, under Macao Decree Law No. 43/82/M. The key responsibilities of the Cultural Affairs Bureau related to built heritage conservation include

- the protection, maintenance and revitalization of Macao's historic, architectural and cultural heritage and to prepare guidelines ensuring their survival, growth and dissemination; and
- the promotion of research in fields connected to the understanding of Macao's cultural heritage.[26]

The Cultural Heritage Department (previously known as the Cultural Heritage Office) is the execution department for the Cultural Affairs Bureau. This department comprises the Division for Cultural Heritage Conservation and the Division for Research and Planning.[27] Consisting of professional architects, engineers, historians, and other experts and technicians, the Cultural Heritage Department is responsible for the following:

23. "Historic Centre of Macao: Conservation Issues Presented to the World Heritage Committee in 2017," UNESCO World Heritage Centre, accessed May 5, 2022, https://whc.unesco.org/en/soc/3655.
24. The State Administration of the Cultural Heritage of the People's Republic of China, *Conservation Status Report: A Descriptive Information on the Inquiry of the World Heritage Center on the State of Conservation of the Historic Centre of Macao, The Historic Centre of Macao (C1110)*, UNESCO, February 2017, 4–5.
25. The State Administration of the Cultural Heritage of the People's Republic of China State Party, *Conservation Status Report: World Cultural Heritage Historic Centre of Macao (No.: C1110) Conservation Status Report 2020*, UNESCO, November 2020.
26. Development Bureau, "Macao," 114.
27. Development Bureau, "Macao," 114; "Cultural Heritage Department," Cultural Affairs Bureau, Macao SAR Government, accessed May 5, 2022, https://www.icm.gov.mo/en/DPC.

- Classifying, restoring, renovating, and upgrading of Macao's cultural heritage.
- Advising on the limitations imposed on building works in the protected areas and preparing plans to restore historic buildings that are in a state of decay.
- Collaborating with the government to promote cultural tourism and conducting research and planning for the protection of heritage sites.[28]

Overall planning, land management, and building control in Macao fall under the Land, Public Works and Transport Bureau, which is responsible for the following:

- Providing technical support and suggestions for policy making related to Macao's physical development in land management and utilization, urban planning, infrastructure, and basic services.
- Participating in defining guidelines for the economy and society development.[29]

All proposed building works, including those for heritage buildings, are required to be submitted to the Land, Public Works and Transport Bureau for approval before being forwarded to the Cultural Affairs Bureau.[30]

Macao has had very strong laws related to built heritage from the start. The government's recognition (and subsequent conservation) of its heritage can be seen in the many examples of adaptive reuse, where most projects are protected cultural heritage properties and the adaptive reuse initiative (and support) is generally from the government. It is important to understand that in Macao, all conservation projects are initiated, carried out, and financially supported by the government.

The following three sections trace the history of adaptive reuse in Macao from early, pre-2000 examples to those from 2000 to 2010 and post-2010.

Early Examples of Adaptive Reuse in Macao: Focus on Portuguese Built Heritage

Early examples of adaptive reuse of heritage sites in Macao reveal an almost unconscious and organic reuse of heritage places. Most of these sites are prominent Portuguese buildings that were restored and adaptively reused by Portuguese architects reflecting the period during which Macao was a Portuguese colony. All of the following examples are listed in order of the date that the site opened after adaptive reuse, beginning with the earliest projects.

Originally constructed in 1784 and rebuilt in 1876, the neoclassical-style **Leal Senado Building** (163, Avenida Almeida Ribeiro), which includes a prominent municipal chamber, is located at the heart of the city center and across from Senado Square and Fountain. As a symbol of Portuguese rule in Macao and the seat of the colonial government, this civic building has been in continuous use as the city's administrative and legislative center, with its program adapting many times over the years. Through these changes, its primary façade walls, structural framework, and layout remain. Serving the public, the building's most recent use is as the headquarters for the Municipal Affairs Bureau. While some spaces continued their original

28. "Cultural Affairs Bureau," Cultural Affairs Bureau, Macao SAR Government, accessed April 4, 2022, https://www.icm.gov.mo/en/DPC; The State Administration of the Cultural Heritage of the People's Republic of China, *The Historic Monuments of Macao*, 51; UNESCO, *Asia Conserved IV: Lessons Learned from the UNESCO Asia-Pacific Awards for Cultural Heritage Conservation (2015–2019)*, ed. William Chapman (Bangkok: UNESCO, 2020), 12; Development Bureau, "Macao," 114–15.
29. Development Bureau, "Macao," 115.
30. "Brief History," Land, Public Works and Transport Bureau, Macao SAR Government, accessed May 5, 2022, https://www.dsscu.gov.mo/en/home/aboutUs/id/23.

use (such as the municipal chamber and the display area for government gazettes in the foyer), the adaptive reuse of the building also introduced spaces to accommodate new uses—library, gallery, and courtyard garden (further elaborated in the case study section of the book). The Leal Senado Building continues to serve Macao as a significant civic and symbolic presence and social anchor in the heart of the city.

Surrounded by a lush garden, the free-standing neoclassical-style mansion **Casa Garden** (13, Praça de Louís de Camões) was constructed in 1770 as a summer residence for the wealthy Portuguese merchant Manuel Pereira.[31] The Macao government took ownership of the property in 1885, and for a time, it was rented out to the East India Company as its Macao headquarters as well as housing for the company's high-ranking officials. The site was also used as the residence of Macao's governor. In the 1960s, the two-story building was transformed into the one-story Camões Museum, the first museum in Macao and the only public museum in Macao until the 1980s. The traditional museum was based on the nineteenth-century European model and displayed objects of art, history, and culture from a donated private collection, related to Macao and the South China coastal region.[32] Today, the building is the headquarters of the Orient Foundation, a private cultural institution involved in local and regional community and cultural affairs.[33] Although the building has been modified over the years, its historical character as a pleasant residence remains today, providing an interpretative glimpse into the site's heritage significance.

Prominently located on the northeastern slope of Barra Hill, facing the Inner Harbor and the mouth of the port (although the view of the Inner Harbor is now obscured by buildings), the **Moorish Barracks** (1, Calçada da Barra), also known as

Figure 8.1: Moorish Barracks (1874), 1, Calçada da Barra, Macao. Exterior view showing the building's main façades. (Source: Adelina Chan.)

31. "Headquarters Building of the Orient Foundation," Cultural Affairs Bureau, Macao SAR Government, accessed March 1, 2022, https://www.culturalheritage.mo/en/detail/hrtID95.
32. The Camões Museum closed in 1988 and the exhibits were returned to Europe. Jonathan Porter, "The Past Is Present: The Construction of Macau's Historical Legacy," *History and Memory* 21, no. 1 (2009): 63.
33. The State Administration of the Cultural Heritage of the People's Republic of China, *The Historic Monuments of Macao*, 95–96.

Quartel dos Mouros, was designed by Italian architect Cassuto and built in 1874 to accommodate a regiment from Portuguese-ruled Goa, India to reinforce Macao's police force.[34] Standing on a massive raised granite platform/wall above a narrow street, the brick-and-stone neoclassical-style building with yellow-color rendered walls and white-color rendered details shows Mughal influences (Figure 8.1). Spacious verandas with stylized ogee arches run along the two primary facades of the building with a projecting open corner tower separating them.[35] Originally housing Goan platoons, the one-story building was altered over the years, including the infilling of its two courtyards. In 1905, the building was adaptively reused for the Macao Port Authority and Marine Police Headquarters to address the issue of maritime pirates smuggling weapons and opium along the Chinese coast.[36] From 2001 to 2003, the Moorish Barracks was restored and renovated for the Macau Port Authority Offices by the architects Rui Leao and Carlotta Bruni, opening in 2005 to serve as the offices for the Macao Marine and Water Bureau. This handsome prominent landmark stands as a symbol of Macao's multiculturalism and serves as a reminder of the city's close links with Goa and other Portuguese colonies.

The **Sir Robert Ho Tung Library** (3, Santo Agostinho Square) is a three-story Macanese mansion featuring an arcaded façade with pilasters terminating in Ionic capitals, sited in a mature garden surrounded by high walls with iron gates and railings. Originally constructed in 1894 as the residence for Dona Carolina Cunha, Hong Kong businessman and comprador Sir Robert Ho Tung purchased the building in 1918 and used it as his retreat. After Ho Tung died in 1955 and in accordance with his will, the building was given to the Macao government for adaptive reuse as a public library, which opened in 1958. In 2006, a new addition, designed in stone, steel, and glass, was constructed at the site's rear garden, expanding the library with contemporary facilities (Figure 8.2).[37] Today, the building is a rare surviving example of a historical house that responds to the needs of present-day society with its new use and innovative design intervention.

Lou Lim Ieoc Garden (10, Estrada de Adolfo Loureiro) is a unique 1.78-hectare Suzhou-style garden located in the St. Lazarus District of Macao. The site was developed in 1870 as a private pleasure garden, part of the residence of the nineteenth-century merchant Lou Kau.[38] Between 1900 and 1925, Lou Kau developed the garden as a retreat space featuring narrow paths surrounded by groves of bamboo and flowering bushes, a man-made pond, a rockery, a nine-turn bridge, pagodas, and pavilions (Figure 8.3).[39] Since 1973, when the garden was purchased by the government to be used as a public garden, it has been restored, and more recently, its two pavilions—Chun Chou Tong and Iong Sam Tong—have been adaptively reused for public purposes (further elaborated in the case study section of this book). The Lou Lim Ieoc Garden serves as a harmonious green oasis for residents in the middle of

34. The State Administration of the Cultural Heritage of the People's Republic of China, *The Historic Monuments of Macao*, 13.
35. "Headquarters Building of the Marine and Water Bureau (Former Moorish Barracks)," Cultural Affairs Bureau, Macao SAR Government, accessed February 15, 2022, https://www.culturalheritage.mo/en/detail/hrtID41.
36. "Moorish Barracks: A Transcultural Landmark in Macau," *ML Macau Lifestyle*, September 18, 2019; "Moorish Barracks," Marine Government, Macao SAR Government, accessed March 1, 2022, https://www.marine.gov.mo/subpage.aspx?a_id=1432713810.
37. The State Administration of the Cultural Heritage of the People's Republic of China, *The Historic Monuments of Macao*, 35; "Sir Robert Ho Tung Library," Sir Robert Ho Tung Library, accessed March 1, 2022, https://www.library.gov.mo/en/HTlib60/building/new-building.
38. Raquel Dias, "Lou Lim Ieoc: The Garden with a Troubled History," *Macau Lifestyle*, July 18, 2019.
39. Mark O'Neil, "Macao's Secret Oasis: The Lou Lim Ieoc Garden," *Macao News*, March 30, 2021.

Figure 8.2: Sir Robert Ho Tung Library (1894), 3, Santo Agostinho Square, Macao. Exterior view showing the interface between the original building and the rear addition. (Source: Adelina Chan.)

Figure 8.3: Lou Lim Ieoc Garden (1870), 10, Estrada de Adolfo Loureiro, Macao. Exterior view showing the moon gate in the garden. (Source: Adelina Chan.)

urban Macao and is an exemplar for revitalization of an open space for community use.

Strategically located atop Mount Hill in the center of the Macao peninsula, **Mount Fortress** was built in conjunction with the Jesuits from 1617 to 1626 as the city's principal military defense. Covering an area of eight thousand square meters and designed in the shape of an irregular trapezoid with protruding corners to form bulwarks, the fort's crenelated parapets accommodated thirty-two cannons and two small watch towers. Equipped with cannons, an arsenal, military barracks, and wells, the fortress was instrumental in holding off the attempted Dutch invasion of Macao in 1622. In 1965, a weather observatory was installed on the site, and the fortress was demilitarized in 1976.[40] In 1998, the Macao Museum was moved to the site, occupying two underground levels and a purpose-built third story above the top platform.[41] Although the design, footprint, and volume of the museum respect the old military barracks prior to its decommissioning, the overall appearance and setting of the place are vastly different from the original. Owing to its new use, Mount Fortress is one of the most visited historical sites in Macao, a place where the public can learn about the city's extensive history.

Constructed in 1629 and partially rebuilt several times over the centuries, **São Tiago da Barra Fortress** (Avenida da República) is a seventeenth-century fortress advantageously located facing the Inner Harbor where all ships entering Macao once anchored. It was one of the most important fortresses in Macao due to its strategic location that ensured visibility and control of maritime activity by guarding the water entrance to the Inner Harbor. The walled site is 110 meters long and 40 meters wide, forming a platform that lies three meters above sea level. This site originally featured sixteen cannons, a warehouse for armaments and provisions, lodging for seventy soldiers, a cistern, and a small Catholic chapel.[42] In 1981, the fortress was converted into an exclusive five-star hotel (Pousada de São Tiago) with new additions within the fortress complex. The site received an Excellence Award in the Heritage Buildings Re-use Competition held by the Pacific Asia Travel Association for its adaptive reuse. However, the hotel temporarily closed for business in 2017 due to the "nuisance caused by the construction of the [nearby] Barra Transport Complex"[43] and has not reopened (at the time of writing this essay).

Located along Avenida da Praia on the island of Taipa is the **Taipa Houses-Museum** (Avenida da Praia, Taipa). The site comprises a series of five free-standing two-story buildings with covered porches constructed in 1921 as residences for local Portuguese high-ranking civil servants and their families. After the handover in 1999, the residences returned to government ownership and were restored and adaptively reused as museums to display artifacts. In 2016, the Macao SAR government revitalized the site again; today, the five buildings have been adapted as the Macanese Living Museum, Exhibitions Gallery, Creative Casa, Nostalgic House, and House for Receptions from west to east, respectively.[44] The five houses are assigned specific func-

40. "Mount Fortress," Cultural Affairs Bureau, Macao SAR Government, accessed February 15, 2022, https://www.culturalheritage.mo/en/detail/hrtID161.
41. The State Administration of the Cultural Heritage of the People's Republic of China, *The Historic Monuments of Macao*, 87.
42. "Barra Fortress," Cultural Affairs Bureau, Macao SAR Government, accessed March 1, 2022, https://www.culturalheritage.mo/en/detail/hrtID38.
43. "Sao Tiago Inn to Close Doors," *Macau Daily Times*, February 15, 2017, https://macaudailytimes.com.mo/sao-tiago-inn-close-doors.html#:~:text=The%20Pousada%20of%20S%C3%A3o%20Tiago,at%20the%20end%20of%20March.
44. "Taipa Houses," Tourism Office, Macao SAR Government, accessed March 1, 2022, https://www.macaotourism.gov.mo/en/sightseeing/museums-and-galleries/taipa-houses.

tions given their themes. The original interior layout is only retained in one house, while the others are used as gallery spaces and culture-related shops with favorable leasing terms upon approval from the Cultural Affairs Bureau. With the conservation of the elegant pastel-green stucco-façade houses, the project is a reminder of Macao's Taipa island in the early twentieth century. Unfortunately, the original view from the houses, which directly overlooked the water, has been obscured by land reclamation.

These examples of adaptive reuse in Macao predate the inscription of the Historic Centre of Macao as a UNESCO World Heritage Site. Although they suggest an unconscious reuse of heritage buildings, sometimes using a "freer" conservation approach, there is a recognition of heritage values as reflected in the decision to retain these places through adaptive reuse. During this period, the choice of new use as a museum is prevalent, with limited interpretation of the place and its conservation. However, and importantly, the projects demonstrate an almost intuitive understanding of the importance of safeguarding spirit of place.

Adaptive Reuse Projects in Macao from 2000–2010: Focus on Chinese Built Heritage

Fewer examples of adaptive reuse projects took place during the 2000–2010 period, partly due to the task of preparing the detailed dossier to support the nomination of the Historic Centre of Macao as a World Heritage Site. This was also a time of transition as Macao returned Chinese rule in 1999 and local staff filled positions formerly held by the Portuguese. Nonetheless, a small number of adaptive reuse projects were undertaken by the Cultural Affairs Bureau with considerable success.

Located within the World Heritage Site of the Historic Centre of Macao, **Lou Kau Mansion** (7, Travessa da Sé) was constructed in 1889 as a traditional Chinese residence. The two-story gray-brick symmetrical house was the home of prominent Chinese merchant Lou Kau, a gaming and opium trading tycoon at the turn of the twentieth century. The house comprises three main halls and two courtyards on the ground level, demonstrating the hierarchical spatial arrangement of Chinese residences.[45] Special features of the mansion include Chinese decorative motifs with subtle Western influence. In 2002, the Macao government began restoration work on the building, and it opened to the public in 2005 as a house museum with site interpretation. The adaptive reuse of the mansion exemplifies a cautious approach in conservation as the project safeguards the spirit of the former Chinese residence while adapting it as a spatial narrative of Macao's East-meets-West culture.

The **Tak Seng On Pawnshop** (396, Avenida Almeida Ribeiro) was established in 1917 by prominent merchant Kou Ho Ning. The art deco–style building with Chinese elements was designed with an impenetrable granite and Chinese gray brick tower structure with narrow slit windows at the back to safely house the pawned items (Figure 8.4).[46] Escaping early proposals of being converted for residential purposes (which would involve total demolition of its interiors), the front building's ground floor and its attached tower were revitalized in 2003. With much of the site's interior surviving intact, including artifacts from its pawnshop operations (e.g., log records, unopened safes, and registration tags), it was adapted as a museum focusing on the history of the pawnshop. The project was a successful partnership and

45. "Lou Kau Mansion," Cultural Affairs Bureau, Macao SAR Government, accessed April 8, 2022, https://www.wh.mo/en/site/detail/16.
46. "Tak Seng Pawnshop," Cultural Affairs Bureau, Macao SAR Government, accessed March 1, 2022, https://www.culturalheritage.mo/en/detail/hrtID68.

Figure 8.4: Tak Seng On Pawnshop (1917), 396, Avenida Almeida Ribeiro, Macao. Exterior view showing the main façades of the building. (Source: Adelina Chan.)

collaboration between the Macao government (then Cultural Institute) and a private owner in the restoration and adaptive reuse of a building. It was recognized with an Honourable Mention in the 2004 UNESCO Asia-Pacific Awards for Cultural Heritage Conservation, especially commended as "a fine example of a unique southern-China building type and has thereby protected the cultural memory associated with the region's commercial and financial history. . . . A pioneering adaptive reuse project, the restoration project has made the pawnshop one of the key landmarks on Macao's heritage trail, stimulating conservation of other commercial structures in the city."[47]

Albergue SCM (aka Albergue da Santa Casa da Misericórdia) (8, Calçada da Igreja de S. Lázaro) is located in the St. Lazarus District. The site includes a complex of four, two-story Portuguese neoclassical-style buildings placed in a U

47. UNESCO, *Asia Conserved I: Lessons Learned from the UNESCO Asia-Pacific Heritage Awards for Cultural Heritage Conservation (2000–2004)*, ed. Richard A. Engelhardt (Bangkok: UNESCO, 2007), 387.

shape facing the street and around a large, paved courtyard with mature camphor trees in the middle. The place was originally built between the 1890s and early 1900s as a leprosarium and shelter for poor elderly women by the local Catholic charity Holy House of Mercy (Santa Casa de Misericórdia). Between 2003 and 2009, the site was restored and adaptively reused as a cultural and creative venue to house an architectural firm, a gallery, a restaurant, and a retail store (further elaborated in the case study section of this book). Although the St. Lazarus District became Macao's first designated cultural heritage "site," such efforts could not counter the pressure of redevelopment as the relevant conservation law (Macao Decree Law No. 34/76/M) did not include conservation guidelines. In this context, the Albergue SCM project is an important recognition of the city's approach to area conservation, promoted by a positive public-private partnership.

Built as a residence and family home of theoretician and reformist Zheng Guanying in 1869 in São Lourenço district and part of the Historic Centre of Macao World Heritage Site, the **Mandarin's House** (10, Travessa de António da Silva) is one of the most significant conservation projects that has taken place in Macao. As the family grew, the house was expanded over time by the Zheng brothers. Occupying an area of four thousand square meters, it is one of the largest family homes in Macao. The traditional Chinese compound is divided into front and rear areas. The front area encompasses the gatehouse, servants' quarters, main garden, and a connecting building. The private family area, reached through a moon gate, includes the sedan way and the master's quarters consisting of two traditional two-/three-story, three-bay-wide, two-hall-deep Guangdong courtyard houses. The two buildings, featuring a mix of Chinese and Western design, extend along a central axis with individual house entrances facing northward. Beginning in the 1950s, the Zheng family descendants began moving out, and the houses were subdivided and rented to many tenants. Due to alterations, lack of maintenance, and fire damage, the buildings deteriorated.[48] In 2001, the Macao Cultural Affairs Bureau took over the site and, after a comprehensive study, undertook its restoration and adaptive reuse. In 2010, the Mandarin's House opened to the public as a house museum with extensive interpretation of the history of the family, site, and the conservation process (further elaborated in the case study section of this book).

This decade of adaptive reuse saw an emergence of public-private partnerships. Previously, conservation projects were solely initiated and executed by the government. However, during this period, nonprofit organizations began to take a proactive stance in the conservation and revitalization of heritage properties. After the 1999 handover, adaptive reuse projects had a stronger focus on Chinese architecture (as seen in Table 8.1) along with an increased emphasis on site interpretation and the conservation process. Heritage properties not officially listed were also recognized for their cultural heritage values and revitalization potential. This indicated an increased awareness of conservation by the public, an awareness building on the early years of governmental efforts to recognize, protect, and promote Macao's heritage resources.

48. "Mandarin's House," Cultural Affairs Bureau, Macao SAR Government, accessed March 1, 2022, https://www.wh.mo/en/site/detail/4; "Mandarin's House," Mandarin's House, accessed March 1, 2022, https://www.wh.mo/mandarinhouse/en/introduction/.

Adaptive Reuse Projects in Macao Post-2010: Ripple Effect of the World Heritage Listing

Macao's recent examples of adaptive reuse projects demonstrate a high standard of conservation practice and include extensive site-specific heritage interpretation and documentation of the conservation process. These buildings are generally more representative of traditional vernacular buildings, not monuments of the elite, and several of them are models of successful conservation partnerships between the Macao government and local nongovernmental organizations.

From 2012 to 2015, in collaboration with the Cultural Affairs Bureau, the local Tou Teo Mio Patane Mercy and Charity Association, and the Patane Mutual Aid Association, the **Patane Night Watch House** (52–54, Rua da Palmeira) was conserved and adaptively reused. The intent of the project was to revitalize Macao's only surviving example of a night watch house as a museum (honoring its original use), and through interpretation to reveal and safeguard the traditional values of mutual assistance and social service associated with the house. Its new use supports the long-term sustainability of the building and contributes to community cohesion (further elaborated in the case study section of this book).

The **Patane Library** (69–81, Rua da Ribeira do Patane) consists of a row of seven, two-story shophouses constructed in the 1930s for merchants who sold timber at the nearby shipyards. The buildings feature ground-floor arcades incorporating the sidewalk, balconies on the second floor, and balusters on the roof parapet. Macao's Cultural Affairs Bureau renovated the buildings starting in 2010, and the new library opened in 2016. The project includes the restoration of the exterior features as well as the installation of a new steel and glass façade (located behind the original heritage façade, Figure 8.5). The interiors have been entirely rebuilt to accommodate the new use as a library with modern interior design and functions, including internal connections between the seven buildings, reinforced foundations, structural enhancements to carry the increased weight loads, elevator lifts, and new fire protection services.[49]

Figure 8.5: Patane Library (1930s), 69–81, Rua da Ribeira do Patane, Macao. Exterior view of the interconnected row of seven shophouses. (Source: Adelina Chan.)

49. Mark O'Neill, "Patane Library: Retain the Old, Create the New," *Macao Magazine*, May 10, 2017.

Although the Patane Library is not located within Macao's World Heritage Site or recognized as a "classified as immovable property," this group of dilapidated buildings has been restored, repurposed, and transformed into a place for the transmission of culture and knowledge for the public of Macao.

The former **Chong Sai Pharmacy** (80, Rua das Estalagens) is a late nineteenth-century shophouse built by Dr. Sun Yat-sen in 1893 and used as one of Macao's first pharmacies and clinics offering Western medical services. The building was acquired by the Macao government in 2011 and adaptively reused as a museum and exhibition space, opening in 2016. During the conservation process, the Cultural Affairs Bureau set up focus groups and forums to engage in community consultation with stakeholders and gather research materials about the site.[50] Today, the museum features exhibits focused on archaeological artifacts discovered during the building's conservation, the restoration of the building, the history of the Lingnan-style shophouse, and Dr. Sun Yat-sen's life in Macao. The project serves as a noteworthy example of best practice that not only gives the place a suitable new use but also meticulously restores a significant traditional shophouse of Macao.[51]

Macao's Government Dockyard was first built in 1891–1898 on the Inner Harbor but is now primarily landlocked.[52] The former mechanical room of the site (Navy Yard No. 1) was revitalized as the **Macao Contemporary Arts Centre** (Rua de São Tiago da Barra) in 2016. Adaptive reuse of the former industrial building into a contemporary arts exhibition and performance space supports Macao's cultural creativity sector. The project not only broadens the understanding of cultural heritage to include industrial sites but also contributes to the cultural vibrancy of the Barra area with its new use. Unfortunately, there is little to no interpretation of the place from its former use as a component of the Navy Yard apart from a small sign at the entrance door.

Located in the remote, steeply wooded hillsides of the southeastern corner of Macao's Coloane island, is **Nossa Senhora Village** (Estrada de Nossa Senhora de Ká Hó), the former Ká Hó Leprosarium site. The village was originally constructed for female lepers by the Macao government in 1885 and comprised of two brick houses. The site was expanded in the 1930s with the addition of five one-story eclectic-style residential houses and the Chapel of Our Lady of Sorrows laid out in an arch shape along the coastline. The medical mission was suspended in 1992, and the buildings were left vacant and in a state of disrepair and damage for many years. As the only remaining leprosarium facility in Macao, the Cultural Affairs Bureau initiated the comprehensive structural reinforcement and repair of the heritage site in 2016, with partial reopening of the buildings as an exhibition space in 2019. A permanent exhibit, "Land of Hope—Historical Archives Exhibition on Leprosariums in Macao," opened in 2021. The exhibition, through archival material, documents Macao as pioneer in the field of relief, rehabilitation, and humanitarianism in the development of leprosy treatment facilities in the territory. This project showcases the government's recognition of a significant aspect of Macao's history. Although the new use of the place as an exhibition space invites some engagement from the community, there is hope to further revive the site with renewed social purpose by incorporating vocational programs for rehabilitated drug users. This is in the process of being planned.[53]

50. Development Bureau, "Macao," 120.
51. Leonor Sa Machado, "Former Chong Sai Pharmacy: A Hidden Corner of Macau History," *ML Macau Lifestyle*, July 30, 2021.
52. Jason Wordie, *Macao: People and Places, Past and Present* (Hong Kong: Angsana, 2013), 335.
53. "Leprosariums in Macao," Tourism Office, Macao SAR Government, accessed March 1, 2022, https://www.macaotourism.gov.mo/en/events/whatson/8460/.

Table 8.1: Overview of adaptive reuse projects in Macao (arranged in order of discussion in the text)

Year built	Name of site	Chinese/ Western style	Adaptive reuse project year (completion)	Current use	Current operator	Within Macao's UNESCO World Heritage Site	Classified Immovable Property under Macao's Cultural Heritage Protection Law (2014)
Early examples of adaptive reuse in Macao: Focus on Portuguese built heritage							
1876	Leal Senado	Western	1940	Cultural/ governmental	Government (Cultural Affairs Bureau)	Yes	Yes
1770	Casa Garden	Western	1960s	Cultural	Nongovernmental organization (Orient Foundation)	Yes	Yes
1874	Moorish Barracks	Western	1905	Governmental	Government (Macao Marine and Water Bureau)	Yes	Yes
1894	Sir Robert Ho Tung Library	Western	1958	Cultural	Government (Macao Public Library)	Yes	Yes
1870	Lou Lim Ieoc Garden	Chinese	1974	Cultural/ recreational	Government (Municipal Affairs Bureau)	No	Yes
1620s	Mount Fortress	Western	1998	Museum	Government (Cultural Affairs Bureau)	Yes	Yes
1629	São Tiago da Barra Fortress	Western	1981	Temporarily closed	Commercial hotel (formerly)	Buffer zone	Yes
1921	Taipa Houses-Museum	Western	2016	Cultural	Government (Cultural Affairs Bureau)	No	Yes
Adaptive reuse projects in Macao from 2000–2010: Focus on Chinese built heritage							
1889	Lou Kau Mansion	Chinese	2005	Museum	Government (Cultural Affairs Bureau)	Buffer zone	Yes
1917	Tak Seng On Pawnshop	Mixed	2003	Museum	Government (Cultural Affairs Bureau)	No	Yes
1890s–1900s	Albergue SCM	Western	2003–2009	Cultural/ creative	Nongovernmental organization (Holy House of Mercy/Santa Casa da Misericórdia)	No	Yes
1869	Mandarin's House	Chinese	2010	Museum/ cultural	Government (Cultural Affairs Bureau)	Yes	Yes

Year built	Name of site	Chinese/ Western style	Adaptive reuse project year (completion)	Current use	Current operator	Within Macao's UNESCO World Heritage Site	Classified Immovable Property under Macao's Cultural Heritage Protection Law (2014)
Adaptive reuse projects in Macao post-2010: Ripple effect of the World Heritage listing							
1940s	Patane Night Watch House	Chinese	2015	Museum	Government (Cultural Affairs Bureau) and nongovernmental organizations (Tou Teo Mio Patane Mercy and Charity Association and Patane Mutual Aid Association)	Buffer zone	Yes
1930s	Patane Library	Western	2016	Cultural	Government (Macao Public Library)	No	No
1893	Chong Sai Pharmacy	Chinese	2016	Museum	Government (Cultural Affairs Bureau)	No	Yes
1890s	Macao Contemporary Arts Centre (Navy Yard No. 1)	Western	2016	Cultural	Government (Cultural Affairs Bureau)	Buffer zone	No
1885	Nossa Senhora Village	Western	2019–2021	Cultural	Nongovernmental organization (Hold on to Hope Project)	No	Yes

These post-2010 conservation and adaptive reuse projects reflect the heightened interest in built heritage conservation in Macao after the inscription of the Historic Centre of Macao on the World Heritage List. An increasing number of nonprotected sites have been revitalized with appropriate conservation approaches. As mentioned earlier in this essay, this period also saw a wider integration of urban planning with built heritage conservation. Both conservation and urban planning efforts have played a vital role in demonstrating that Macao can be a livable city for local people as well as a sustainable tourist attraction for visitors. Balancing the two appropriately is key to safeguarding its spirit of place.

Adaptive Reuse and Sustainability in Macao

Early examples of adaptive reuse in colonial Macao helped set the foundation for later conservation development. A considerable number of buildings that were repurposed before 1999 are now part of Macao's World Heritage Site, validating that such early efforts were critical in preserving the city's heritage and facilitating its inscription. Although World Heritage inscription has dramatically boosted Macao's draw by tourists, there remain challenges that affect the city's ability to safeguard its heritage resources. The substantial increase in visitor numbers since 2005 has created significant stress and pressure on the city's heritage.[54] Accommodating gaming facilities has also had an impact. Historically, gaming facilities were located within the historic core, but with the liberalization of gaming policies in 2002, a number of casinos and related hotel and shopping services have been developed in the reclaimed inter-island Cotai area (a portmanteau of Coloane and Taipa). This has brought financial benefit to Macao, but the impact of visitors on heritage resources, within the historic core as well as Coloane and Taipa, remains a concern.[55]

In addition, there are gaps in the heritage protection system in Macao; there is no clear system for environmental review or impact assessment for developments that effect heritage sites.[56]

Concluding Remarks

This chapter has considered the history and development of adaptive reuse in Macao, highlighting many sites that demonstrate sustainable practice in conservation. These practices include engagement with the general public and specific stakeholders, partnerships between the government and nongovernmental organizations, and strengthening and supporting community knowledge through heritage education and heritage interpretation. Through these initiatives of adaptive reuse, a sense of identity and belonging in Macao is enhanced, and the safeguarding of tangible cultural heritage is demonstrated. It is hoped that such practices will be continued and expanded by the government so that the rich cultural heritage traditions in Macao will be prolonged and sustained appropriately.

54. Imon, "Managing Change in the Historic City of Macao," 19.

55. Before COVID-19, Macao had the highest gross domestic product per capita in the world. See Mirosław Michal Sadowski, "Cultural Heritage and the City: Law, Sustainable Development, Urban Heritage and the Cases of Hong Kong and Macau," *Revista română de drept comparat* 2 (2017): 235; Sharif Shams Imon, "Cultural Heritage Management under Tourism Pressure," *Worldwide Hospitality and Tourism Themes* 9, no. 3 (2017), https://doi.org/10.1108/WHATT-02-2017-0007.

56. Lee and Du Cros, "Heritage Management Approaches in Southern China," 114.

Bibliography

Chan, Pui Yu. "Community Participation in Heritage Management: A Case Study in Macau." MS thesis, Columbia University, 2016.

Chung, Thomas. "Valuing Heritage in Macau: On Contexts and Processes of Urban Conservation." *Journal of Current Chinese Affairs* 38, no. 1 (2009): 129–60.

Cultural Affairs Bureau, Macao SAR Government. "Barra Fortress." Accessed March 1, 2022. https://www.culturalheritage.mo/en/detail/hrtID38.

Cultural Affairs Bureau, Macao SAR Government. "Cultural Affairs Bureau." Accessed April 4, 2022. https://www.icm.gov.mo/en/DPC.

Cultural Affairs Bureau, Macao SAR Government. "Cultural Heritage Department." Accessed May 5, 2022. https://www.icm.gov.mo/en/DPC.

Cultural Affairs Bureau, Macao SAR Government. "Headquarters Building of the Marine and Water Bureau (Former Moorish Barracks)." Accessed February 15, 2022. https://www.culturalheritage.mo/en/detail/hrtID41.

Cultural Affairs Bureau, Macao SAR Government. "Headquarters Building of the Orient Foundation." Accessed March 1, 2022. https://www.culturalheritage.mo/en/detail/hrtID95.

Cultural Affairs Bureau, Macao SAR Government. "Legislation on Heritage Protection." Accessed May 23, 2022. http://www.icm.gov.mo/rc/viewer/20038/1345.

Cultural Affairs Bureau, Macao SAR Government. "Lou Kau Mansion." Accessed April 8, 2022. https://www.wh.mo/en/site/detail/16.

Cultural Affairs Bureau, Macao SAR Government. "Mandarin's House." Accessed March 1, 2022. https://www.wh.mo/en/site/detail/4.

Cultural Affairs Bureau, Macao SAR Government. "Mount Fortress." Accessed February 15, 2022. https://www.culturalheritage.mo/en/detail/hrtID161.

Cultural Affairs Bureau, Macao SAR Government. "Nossa Senhora Village (Former Site of the Leprosarium)." Accessed March 1, 2022. https://www.culturalheritage.mo/en/detail/2978.

Cultural Tourism Bureau, Macao SAR Government. "Tak Seng Pawnshop." Accessed March 1, 2022. https://www.culturalheritage.mo/en/detail/hrtID68.

Development Bureau, Hong Kong SAR Government. "Macao." In *Consultancy Study on the Heritage Conservation in Other Jurisdictions*, 110–29. Hong Kong: Development Bureau, 2014.

Dias, Raquel. "Lou Lim Ieoc: The Garden with a Troubles History." *Macau Lifestyle*, July 18, 2019.

Imon, Sharif Shams. "Cultural Heritage Management under Tourism Pressure." *Worldwide Hospitality and Tourism Themes* 9, no. 3 (2017). https://doi.org/10.1108/WHATT-02-2017-0007.

Imon, Shams Sharif. "Managing Change in the Historic City of Macao." *Historic Environment* 21, no. 3 (2008): 16–21.

Land, Public Works and Transport Bureau, Macao SAR Government. "Brief History." Accessed May 5, 2022. https://www.dsscu.gov.mo/en/home/aboutUs/id/23.

Lau, Joao Pedro. "A New Life." *Macao Closer Living and Arts Magazine*, January 2017.

Leao, Rui. "Opinion: Architect Rui Leao Deconstructs the Macao Urban Master Plan." *Macao News*, April 22, 2022.

Lee, Frederick, and Hilary du Cros. "A Comparative Analysis of Three Heritage Management Approaches in Southern China." In *Asian Heritage Management: Contexts, Concerns, and Prospects*, edited by Kapil D. Silva and Neel Kamal Chapagain, 112–19. Abingdon: Routledge, 2013.

Liang, Zheng, and Yile Chen. "The Protection Process and Measures of Macau's Heritage Buildings." *IOP Conference Series: Earth and Environmental Science*, 2021.

Macao SAR Government, Official Press. "Cultural Heritage Council, Administrative Regulation No. 4/2014." Accessed April 20, 2023. https://bo.io.gov.mo/bo/i/2014/08/regadm04.asp.

Mandarin's House, Cultural Affairs Bureau, Macao SAR Government. "Mandarin's House." Accessed March 1, 2022. https://www.wh.mo/mandarinhouse/en/introduction/.

Marine Government, Macao SAR Government. "Moorish Barracks." Accessed March 1, 2022. https://www.marine.gov.mo/subpage.aspx?a_id=1432713810.

Mi, Lier. "Protection and Recycling of Architectural Heritage in Macau's Urban Renewal." *Social Science, Education and Humanities Research* 471 (2020). https://www.researchgate.net/publication/346041963_Protection_and_Recycling_of_Architectural_Heritage_in_Macau's_Urban_Renewal.

"Moorish Barracks: A Transcultural Landmark in Macau." *Macau Lifestyle*, September 18, 2019.

O'Neil, Mark. "Beware of the Dark: New Museum Celebrates Forgotten Profession: The Watchman." *Macao Magazine*, July 2016.

O'Neil, Mark. "Macao's Secret Oasis: The Lou Lim Ieoc Garden." *Macao News*, March 30, 2021.

O'Neil, Mark. "Patane Library: Retain the Old, Create the New." *Macao Magazine*, May 10, 2017.

Porter, Jonathan. "The Past Is Present: The Construction of Macau's Historical Legacy." *History and Memory* 21, no. 1 (2009): 63–100.

Sa Machado, Leonor. "Former Chong Sai Pharmacy: A Hidden Corner of Macau History." *ML Macau Lifestyle*, July 30, 2021.

Sa Machado, Leonor. "Patane Night Watch House: Protecting the Community with Gongs and Lanterns." *ML Macau Lifestyle*, July 30, 2021.

Sadowski, Mirosław Michal. "Cultural Heritage and the City: Law, Sustainable Development, Urban Heritage, and the Cases of Hong Kong and Macau." *Revista română de drept comparat* 2 (2017): 208–45.

"São Tiago Inn to Close Doors." *Macau Daily Times*, February 15, 2017. https://macaudailytimes.com.mo/sao-tiago-inn-close-doors.html#:~:text=The%20Pousada%20of%20S%C3%A3o%20Tiago,at%20the%20end%20of%20March.

Sir Robert Ho Tung Library. "Sir Robert Ho Tung Library." Accessed March 1, 2022. https://www.library.gov.mo/en/HTlib60/building/new-building.

Stubbs, John H., and Robert G. Thomson. *Architectural Conservation in Asia: National Experiences and Practice*. London: Routledge, 2017.

The State Administration of the Cultural Heritage of the People's Republic of China. *Conservation Status Report: A Descriptive Information on the Inquiry of the World Heritage Center on the State of Conservation of the Historic Centre of Macao, The Historic Centre of Macao (C1110)*. Paris: UNESCO, February 2017.

The State Administration of the Cultural Heritage of the People's Republic of China. *Conservation Status Report: World Cultural Heritage Historic Centre of Macao (No.: C1110) Conservation Status Report 2020*. Paris: UNESCO, November 2020.

The State Administration of the Cultural Heritage of the People's Republic of China. *The Historic Monuments of Macao (Nomination Dossier for World Heritage Inscription)*. Paris: UNESCO, 2005. https://whc.unesco.org/uploads/nominations/1110.pdf.

Tourism Office, Macao SAR Government. "Leprosariums in Macao." Accessed March 1, 2022. https://www.macaotourism.gov.mo/en/events/whatson/8460/.

Tourism Office, Macao SAR Government. "Taipa Houses." Accessed March 1, 2022. https://www.macaotourism.gov.mo/en/sightseeing/museums-and-galleries/taipa-houses.

UNESCO. *Asia Conserved I: Lessons Learned from the UNESCO Asia-Pacific Heritage Awards for Cultural Heritage Conservation (2000–2004)*. Edited by Richard A. Engelhardt. Bangkok: UNESCO, 2007.

UNESCO. *Asia Conserved IV: Lessons Learned from the UNESCO Asia-Pacific Awards for Cultural Heritage Conservation (2015–2019)*. Edited by William Chapman. Bangkok: UNESCO, 2020.

UNESCO World Heritage Centre. "Historic Centre of Macao." Accessed January 15, 2022. https://whc.unesco.org/en/list/1110/.

UNESCO World Heritage Centre. "Historic Centre of Macao: Conservation Issues Presented to the World Heritage Committee in 2017." Accessed May 5, 2022. https://whc.unesco.org/en/soc/3655.

UNESCO World Heritage Centre. "Maps, Historic Centre of Macao." Accessed April 20, 2023. https://whc.unesco.org/en/list/1110/maps/.

Wordie, Jason. *Macao: People and Places, Past and Present.* Hong Kong: Angsana, 2013.

Zabielskis, Peter. "Challenges of Heritage Development Projects in Macau and Penang: Preservation and Anti-preservation." In *Dynamics of Community Formation*, 135–58. New York: Palgrave Macmillan, 2017.

Zhang, Queqiao. *The Story of Revitalising Heritage Buildings in Macau.* Hong Kong: Joint Publishing Hong Kong, 2020.

Macao Timeline

Adelina Chan, Jennifer Lang, and Sharif Shams Imon

This timeline summarizes key events from the essay, "A Cornerstone in East-Meets-West Representation: Macao's Approach to Adaptive Reuse in Colonial and Postcolonial Eras." It sets out Macao's major conservation-related entities, initiatives, milestones, and regulations from 1488 to 2022, including entries for the five case studies included in this publication.

1488	A-Ma Temple, after which Macao is said to be named, is built.
1557	Macao becomes a Portuguese trading post on an official lease granted by the Ming court of China.
1568	St. Lazarus District is established by Dom Belchior de Carneiro, the first bishop of the Macao Diocese. The district mainly comprises a church, leprosarium, and shelter for the poor.
1582	Cathedral of St. Paul is built by Portuguese Jesuits.
1617–1627	A two-kilometer-long city wall is constructed together with nine fortresses, which later becomes vital in defending Macao from Dutch invasion. The wall is built without authorization of the Ming government, which leads to cycles of partial destruction by the Chinese and reconstruction by the Portuguese. Eventually, it is believed that the wall falls apart over a long period when its defensive purpose gradually becomes irrelevant.[1]
1622	Battle of Macao—a war between the Dutch and the Portuguese for control over Macao as an important port for trade with the Far East. The Portuguese defeat the Dutch and solidify their stronghold in Macao.
1835	Cathedral of St. Paul is destroyed by a fire. The surviving granite façade has become a landmark/symbol of the city.
1876	Leal Senado Building is rebuilt due to damage from the 1874 typhoon.
1887 (December)	Macao is ceded to Portugal with the signing of the Sino-Portuguese Treaty of Peking, a trade treaty made between the Qing dynasty of China and the Kingdom of Portugal.

1. "An Investigation of the Construction of the City of Macao during the Ming Dynasty," Cultural Affairs Bureau, Macao SAR Government, accessed April 20, 2023, http://www.icm.gov.mo/rc/viewer/20036/1329.

1937–1945	Sino-Japanese War—a war between the Republic of China and the empire of Japan during World War II, which includes the Japanese invasion of Hong Kong in 1941. Portugal's neutrality during World War II makes Macao a safe haven for people from Guangzhou and Hong Kong.
1938–1940	Leal Senado Building undergoes renovation, repairs, and functional upgrades, including a new façade. Functional upgrades include a remodeled interior layout, installation of modern plumbing, and a new courtyard garden. (This is one of the five Macao case studies included in this book.)
1953 (December)	Governor of Macao Marques Esparteiro appoints a committee to "identify existing architectural relics" as a result of the destruction of historic buildings during World War II.[2] This is the first official acknowledgment of the need for the protection of built heritage in Macao.
1960	A working group, appointed by Governor Jaime Silvério Marques, is established to "research and to propose suitable measures to protect and value historic and buildings of architectural value."[3]
1974 (September)	Lou Lim Ieoc Garden, originally a private garden, opens as a public recreational space. (This is one of the five Macao case studies included in this book.)
1976 (August)	Macao Decree Law No. 34/76/M The city's first law regarding the conservation of "sites, buildings and objects . . . considered to be of public interest."[4]
1976	The Committee for the Protection of Macao's Urbanistic, Natural and Cultural Heritage is set up as the statutory authority responsible for classifying the cultural heritage properties under Macao Decree Law No. 34/76/M.
1982 (September)	Cultural Institute of Macao (renamed the Cultural Affairs Bureau in 1999) is founded as a public institution under the Secretariat for Social Affairs and Culture.
1984 (June)	Macao Decree Law No. 56/84/M—Protection of Architectural, Natural and Cultural Heritage The law repeals the previous law of 1976. The Committee for the Protection of Architectural, Natural and Cultural Heritage replaces the Committee for the Protection of Macao's Urbanistic, Natural and Cultural Heritage. This committee is organized under the Department of Cultural Heritage of the Cultural Institute of Macao.
1992 (December)	Macao Decree Law No. 83/92/M The law replaces earlier natural and cultural heritage legislation and establishes a new category of classified buildings: "buildings of architectural interest."
1998	Macao ratifies the UNESCO Convention concerning the Protection of the Cultural and Natural World Heritage.
1999 (December)	The handover of Macao (the return of Macao's sovereignty from the Portuguese to China) and the establishment of the Macao Special Administrative Region (SAR).
1999	Cultural Institute of Macao is renamed the Cultural Affairs Bureau.
2000	St. Lazarus District planning is complete. The existing leprosarium and shelter for elderly ladies moves to a new address.

2. "A Brief Introduction to the Protection of Macao's Cultural Heritage," Cultural Affairs Bureau, Macao SAR Government, accessed April 20, 2023, http://www.icm.gov.mo/rc/viewer/10095/2431.
3. Cultural Affairs Bureau, Macao SAR Government, "Stages of Evolution of the Legislation," accessed May 11, 2023, http://edocs.icm.gov.mo/chd/mhd10/Unhistorical1.pdf.
4. "Legislation on Heritage Protection: Statutory Order No. 34/76/M August 7," Cultural Affairs Bureau, Macao SAR Government, accessed May 23, 2022, http://www.icm.gov.mo/rc/viewer/20038/1345.

2002	Macao's gaming monopoly ends with liberalization of the gaming industry.
2005 (July)	Historic Centre of Macao is inscribed on the UNESCO World Heritage List at the Twenty-Ninth Session of the World Heritage Committee at Durban, South Africa.
2006	Chief Executive's Order No. 202/2006 is issued, clearly establishing the definition and location of the Historic Centre of Macao and expanding the protection zones under the Macao Decree Law No. 83/92/M.
2009 (January)	Albergue SCM, originally a leprosarium and shelter for elderly women (built in 1900) in St. Lazarus District, opens as a creative and cultural hub. (This is one of the five Macao case studies included in this book.)
2010	Department for the Promotion of Cultural and Creative Industries is established under the Macao SAR government's Cultural Affairs Bureau.
2010 (February)	Mandarin's House, a traditional Chinese family home (built in 1869), opens as a house museum and cultural activity venue. (This is one of the five Macao case studies included in this book.)
2013	Macao Decree Law No. 11/2013—Cultural Heritage Protection Law The law is officially gazetted to ensure protection of the Historic Centre of Macao World Heritage Site.
2014 (February)	Administrative Regulation No. 4/2014 is issued, which leads to the formation of the Cultural Heritage Council to facilitate departmental and interdisciplinary collaboration in heritage protection. The council includes the Secretary for Social Affairs and Culture as well as executive officials from the Cultural Institute, Office of the Secretary for Social Affairs and Culture, Justice Affairs Services, Land, Public Works and Transport Bureau, and the Institute for Civic and Municipal Affairs.[5] (This regulation is amended in 2019 by Administrative Regulation No. 18/2019.)
2014 (March)	Macao Decree Law No. 11/2013 The law comes into effect on the same day as the Urban Planning Law and the Land Law. The simultaneous implementation of these three laws lays a solid foundation for the protection of Macao's cultural heritage.[6]
2014 (October)	Cultural Affairs Bureau initiates phase 1 of the public consultation process to establish a framework for the Heritage Protection and Management Plan for the Historic Centre of Macao (澳門歷史城區保護及管理計劃). The plan, a result of Macao Decree Law No. 11/2013—Cultural Heritage Protection Law, aims to protect Macao's cultural resources, increase public participation and awareness, and adhere to international standards of sustainability.[7]
2015	Patane Night Watch House, a former night watch house (built in the 1940s), opens as a museum. (This is one of the five Macao case studies included in this book.)

5. "Cultural Heritage Council, Administrative Regulation No. 4/2014," Macao SAR Government, Official Press, accessed April 20, 2023, https://bo.io.gov.mo/bo/i/2014/08/regadm04.asp.
6. "A Descriptive Information on the Inquiry of the World Heritage Center on the State of Conservation of the Historic Centre of Macao," UNESCO World Heritage Center, accessed April 20, 2023, https://whc.unesco.org/document/157566.
7. Cultural Affairs Bureau, Macao SAR Government, *Ao Men li shi cheng qu bao hu ji guan li ji hua zi xun wen ben* (Public consultation on the protection of Macau's Historic Centre and management plan) (Macao: Cultural Affairs Bureau, Macao SAR Government, 2018), http://edocs.icm.gov.mo/Survey/sgchm2017/bookC.pdf.

2018 (January)	The Cultural Affairs Bureau initiates phase 2 of the public consultation process to establish a framework for the Heritage Protection and Management Plan for the Historic Centre of Macao. Phase 2 focuses on mitigating or avoiding potential impact to the World Heritage due to urban development. The measures taken to mitigate impact on visual corridors are through height control of new construction projects, while those taken to avoid impact on the surrounding landscape setting are through building transportation infrastructure underground or undersea.
2022	Master Plan of the Macao Special Administrative Region (2020–2040) is released, which includes rezoning, land reclamation, and development as well as goals to protect cultural heritage and maintain the visual corridors and protection zones of the World Heritage Site and the entire city of Macao.

Bibliography

Cultural Affairs Bureau, Macao SAR Government. "A Brief Introduction to the Protection of Macao's Cultural Heritage." Accessed April 20, 2023. http://www.icm.gov.mo/rc/viewer/10095/2431.

Cultural Affairs Bureau, Macao SAR Government. "An Investigation of the Construction of the City of Macao during the Ming Dynasty." Accessed April 20, 2023. http://www.icm.gov.mo/rc/viewer/20036/1329.

Cultural Affairs Bureau, Macao SAR Government. *Ao Men li shi cheng qu bao hu ji guan li ji hua zi xun wen ben* (Public consultation on the protection of Macau's historic center and management plan). Macao: Cultural Affairs Bureau, Macao SAR Government, 2018. http://edocs.icm.gov.mo/Survey/sgchm2017/bookC.pdf.

Cultural Affairs Bureau, Macao SAR Government. "Legislation on Heritage Protection: Statutory Order No. 34/76/M August 7." Accessed May 23, 2022. http://www.icm.gov.mo/rc/viewer/20038/1345.

Cultural Affairs Bureau, Macao SAR Government. "Stages of Evolution of the Legislation." Accessed May 11, 2023. http://edocs.icm.gov.mo/chd/mhd10/Unhistorical1.pdf.

Macao SAR Government, Official Press. "Cultural Heritage Council, Administrative Regulation No. 4/2014." Accessed April 20, 2023. https://bo.io.gov.mo/bo/i/2014/08/regadm04.asp.

UNESCO World Heritage Center. "A Descriptive Information on the Inquiry of the World Heritage Center on the State of Conservation of the Historic Centre of Macao." Accessed April 20, 2023. https://whc.unesco.org/document/157566.

Macao Case Studies

Project	Heritage Status	Nature	New Use	Original Use	Timeframe
Leal Senado Building	Monument	Government/Public	Government administrative facilities (1940)	Senate, prison, and city hall (1784)	Inaugurated in 1940
Lou Lim Ieoc Garden	Garden: Site; Chun Chou Tong: Building of architectural interest	Government/Public	Public garden; Chun Chou Tong: gallery; Iong Sam Tong: interpretation center	Private garden; Chun Chou Tong: reception hall and guest house; Iong Sam Tong: reception hall	Revitalized as a public park in 1974
Albergue SCM	Building of architectural interest	Public-private partnership	Cultural and creative venue	Shelter for the elderly	2003–2009
Mandarin's House	Building of architectural interest	Government/Public	House museum and cultural activity venue	Residential (1869–1990)	2002–2010
Patane Night Watch House	Monument	Public-private partnership	Museum	Night watch house (1940s–1970s)	2012–2015

Leal Senado Building, Macao

Adelina Chan and Hoyin Lee

The Leal Senado Building (now known as the Headquarters Building of the Municipal Affairs Bureau [IAM]) is a symbol of Portuguese rule in Macao. The modest yet dignified "Loyal Senate" and St. Paul's Ruins are the physical and social anchors of the Historic Centre of Macao World Heritage Site. While the former represents governance and the latter providence, both influence the Macanese way of life and affect urban planning in Macao, resulting in a harmonious balance of the civic and the religious. Although the current Leal Senado Building has been rebuilt, repaired, and reprogrammed for close to a century and a half, it continues to serve the people of Macao.

Figure 10.1: Leal Senado Building, now the centerpiece of Largo do Senado. (Source: Adelina Chan.)

Project Information

Address	163, Avenida Almeida Ribeiro, Macao
Original use	Senate, prison, and city hall (1784)
Previous use	Administrative office, treasury of the chamber, administrative office of the council department, and municipal public works department (1876)
New use	Municipal council chamber, library, gallery, and courtyard garden (1940)
Heritage status	Monument
Site area	638 square meters
Project cost estimate	Unknown
Funding model	Government/public (reserve fund of the Macao colonial government)*
Owner	Municipal Affairs Bureau (Instituto para os Assuntos Municipais, IAM)
Developer	NA
Architect (1939 modification)	Gastão Borges (head of the first Technical Service of the Macao government [1939])**
Contractor	Unknown
Project timeline	Inaugurated in 1940

Notes:
* R. Beltrão Coelho, *Leal Senado Macau: A Sketch of the Building* (Macao: C&C Offset Printing, 1995), 55.
** Coelho, *Leal Senado*, 55.

Project Description

Major alterations to the 1876 Leal Senado Building were carried out in 1939, and the building was inaugurated in 1940.[1] They included the addition of an opulent library and municipal chamber. The main objectives of the project were as follows:

- To repair the building for damages due to typhoons in 1936 and 1937.
- To reprogram the spaces of the building while retaining its architectural and historical character.
- To upgrade the facilities in keeping with modern hygiene standards.

The two-story Leal Senado Building may be considered small by today's standards, but the adaptability of the original 1876 building is a testament to the foresightedness of the original architect. On the ground floor, there is a foyer open to the public that serves the same purpose as it did in the past—a display area for government gazettes (Figure 10.4). There is also a gallery for art and photography exhibitions. A central stairway leads to a courtyard on the mezzanine level (between the ground and upper floors) as well as to the municipal council chamber and library on the upper floor.

The library is part of the Macao Public Library system, and it is here that valuable manuscripts are kept. Adjacent to the library is the municipal council chamber,

1. The project's completion date is based on information included on a plaque found inside the Leal Senado Building.

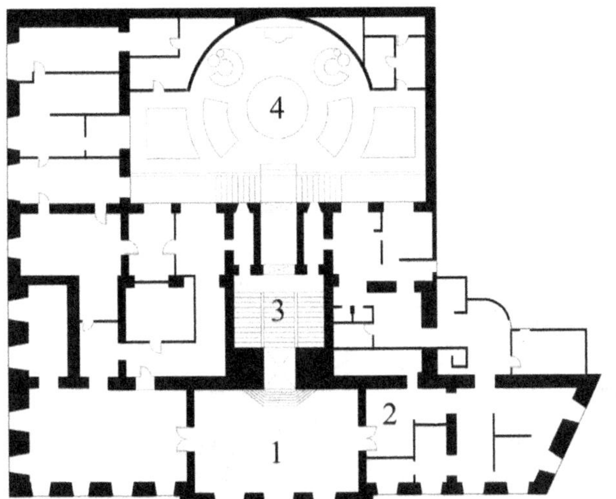

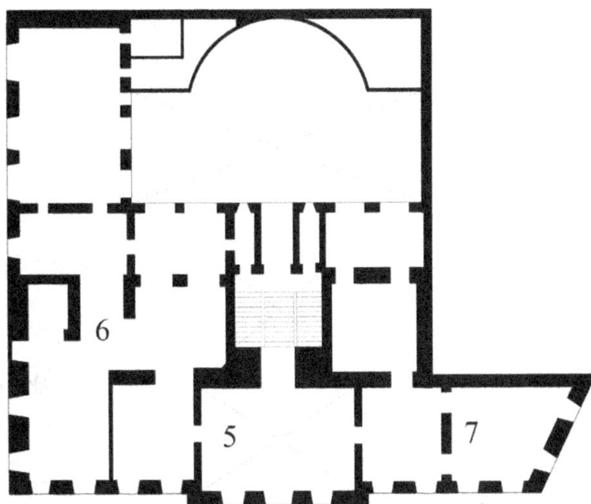

Figure 10.2: Ground- (left) and upper-floor (right) plans of Leal Senado Building, 1939—1. Foyer, 2. Gallery, 3. Staircase, 4. Courtyard, 5. Municipal Council Chamber, 6. Chapel, 7. Library. (Source: Drawn by Ng Wai Shing based on materials from Macao Archives, file number: MNL.08.39.Cart.)

where the inauguration of the governors of Macao took place and government meetings were held during the colonial period. The municipal council chamber continues to be used by the council on rare occasions, mostly for press conferences and public consultation meetings. A small chapel, accessed from the municipal council chamber, provided a place for Portuguese officials of the Catholic faith to pray before meetings.

Site History

The Leal Senado Building is located in the heart of Macao. Administration buildings (four phases) have stood on the site since the late sixteenth century. The first phase (1584–1784) included a walled compound composed of three gable-roofed buildings arranged in a U shape around a courtyard.[2] The second phase (1784–1876) appears to have been defined by a two-story building—baroque in style but lacking a central pediment—and with extensions parallel to the main block of the building.[3] The third phase, which is directly relevant to the case study, refers to the construction of the current building, which was necessitated by a devastating typhoon in 1874. The new building (1876), square-like in shape and neoclassical in style, was—at the time of construction—distinguished by a central section (frontispiece) with a triangular pediment on a high cornice and with an arched entrance and arched upper-floor windows.[4]

Project History

The 1876 Leal Senado Building served Macao well until typhoons in 1936 and 1937 led to renovations to the exterior and the interior. Changes to the exterior included lowering the roof and changing the arched entrance and arched upper-floor windows in the central section to flat-headed openings. Changes to the interior were more

2. Francisco Vizeu Pinheiro, "Using a Comparative Graphic Method in the Analysis of the Evolution of the Macao Senate," *Journal of Asian Architecture and Building Engineering* 4, no. 1 (May 2005): 72, https://www.jstage.jst.go.jp/article/jaabe/4/1/4_1_69/_pdf.
3. Pinheiro, "Using a Comparative Graphic Method," 73.
4. Pinheiro, "Using a Comparative Graphic Method," 74.

Figure 10.3: Courtyard of the 1876 Leal Senado Building. (Source: Adelina Chan.)

dramatic. As Francisco Vizeu Pinheiro notes in his study of the building, "inside modifications were deep."[5]

Given its dire state, the building had to be evacuated and an emergency fund was granted by the government of the Portuguese Republic to repair the building.[6] Necessary work was combined with reprogramming interior spaces and upgrading the facilities in keeping with modern hygiene standards.

Development Environment

The 1936 and 1937 typhoons, as well as damage caused by termites and poor construction, alerted the Macao government to the need to repair and upgrade the Leal Senado Building. There was also the impending inauguration of Governor Artur Tamagnini de Sousa Barbosa, who was popular and well respected by citizens.[7] In 1937, it was the new governor who was able to secure funds for the repair work from the Portuguese Republic. Repair works were completed in 1940.

Since 2001, after Macao's return to China, the building not only continues to serve the public but, with other monuments, also provides "a unique testimony to the meeting of aesthetic, cultural, architectural and technological influences from East and West," as stated in Macao's UNESCO World Heritage List inscription.[8] The Leal Senado Building's inclusion within the Historic Centre of Macao World Heritage Site further confirms its identity as Macao's historical administrative and legislative center.

5. Pinheiro, "Using a Comparative Graphic Method," 74.
6. R. Beltrão Coelho, *Leal Senado: Macau a Sketch of the Building* (Macao: C&C Offset Printing, 1995), 49.
7. Coelho, *Leal Senado*, 45.
8. "The Historic Centre of Macao," UNESCO World Heritage Centre, accessed January 15, 2022, https://whc.unesco.org/en/list/1110/.

Intervention

In the 1930s, the concept of adaptive reuse as we understand it today had yet to emerge. The building program was not about repurposing the building since the primary use of the building as Macao's seat of power was retained. However, the project offered an opportunity to take advantage of the need to repair substantial damage to extensively modify the building, as indicated in the title of the original 1938 building plan, *Projecto de modificação* (Modification project). It involved an aesthetic update (remodeled façade) and a functional upgrade (remodeled interior layout, installation of modern plumbing, and new courtyard garden). While it is not adaptive reuse per se, the work exemplifies the key aspects of today's adaptive reuse approach—namely, the addition of new design and functional elements in response to changing uses.

Key Challenges

- Preserving the historical building's character despite alterations and additions.
- Resisting unnecessary changes and unnecessary modern additions.

Keeping Heritage Alive

The Leal Senado Building is significant for its symbolic meaning for Macao. Through multiple changes, the building's essence remains. The spirit of the place is the spirit of the city, encapsulated in this "new" building with an old soul. The various uses over time have upheld the vision of a civic society. Historically, the Leal Senado Building was the place where decisions on governance were made, where the general public could voice their opinions, and where they could seek assistance. Although its administrative role has changed through the years, its solemn presence and open access remain a symbol of public service.

Figure 10.4. A display area for government gazettes in the foyer of the Leal Senado Building. (Source: Adelina Chan.)

On-site interpretation, primarily textual, and tourist maps provide information. In addition, the Macao World Heritage App, which provides information about buildings and structures within the World Heritage Site, can be downloaded on-site.

Long-Term Viability

As the Leal Senado Building has always been government property, whether Portuguese or the Macao SAR government, its management and maintenance rest with the government. An indication of government support is the 1939 renovation, which occurred when the world was enmeshed in World War II. At the time, the Leal Senado Building was repaired with funds from the colony's reserve.

The Leal Senado Building is managed by the Municipal Affairs Bureau (IAM), and it is under statutory protection as indicated in the World Heritage inscription. As long as Macao remains on the World Heritage List and the building continues to be managed by the government, the Leal Senado Building is likely to face few threats.

Impact

Economic: As part of Macao's World Heritage Site, the Leal Senado Building contributes to the Macao SAR's tourism economy, especially through the branding of Macao and related merchandise.

Environmental: The impact of the Leal Senado Building project cannot be fully understood without considering Senado Square (Largo do Senado), the extensive open space immediately in front of and named after the building. The Leal Senado Building can be seen as the more introverted face of Macao's city life, while the square is the extroverted face. The building and the square are one—supporting and giving context to each other. From a landscape design perspective, the Leal Senado Building is the focal point. The importance of the square has been acknowledged by the 1990s installation of the wave-patterned calçada pavement, a traditional Portuguese paving pattern. With the new pavement, the square has become a pedestrian-only zone.

Social: The Leal Senado Building and its associated Senado Square are meeting points for both local people and visitors. Locals often say, "Let's meet up at the fountain," as the fountain is a prominent feature in the square. Both the building and the square, as in the past, serve the local community by providing accessible public spaces.

> With the new plans, the services in the Leal Senado [Building] are to be better divided and more hygienic while everything of historical or architectural importance is to be preserved and re-integrated within limits that do not encroach on the main objectives.[9]
>
> —José Rodrigues Mouthinho
> (Director of Public Works, June 1938)

9. Coelho, *Leal Senado*, 55.

Bibliography

Coelho, R. Beltrão. *Leal Senado: Macau a Sketch of the Building*. Macao: C&C Offset Printing, 1995.

Cultural Affairs Bureau, Macao SAR Government. "Cultural Affairs Bureau." Accessed April 4, 2022. https://www.icm.gov.mo/en/DPC.

Pinheiro, Francisco Vizeu. "Using a Comparative Graphic Method in the Analysis of the Evolution of the Macao Senate." *Journal of Asian Architecture and Building Engineering* 4, no. 1 (May 2005): 69–76. https://www.jstage.jst.go.jp/article/jaabe/4/1/4_1_69/_pdf.

UNESCO World Heritage Centre. "The Historic Centre of Macao." Accessed January 15, 2022. https://whc.unesco.org/en/list/1110/.

Lou Lim Ieoc Garden, Macao

Adelina Chan and Hoyin Lee

Lou Lim Ieoc Garden is an early example of revitalization efforts in Macao. Originally designed as the pleasure garden for a Chinese merchant's private residence, the site, which includes such Chinese landscape features as pavilions, a moon gate, a man-made pond, and an artfully designed rock garden, forms an oasis in the St. Lazurus District. The history of the garden reveals that it has been "revitalized" several times—more by circumstance than intent. More recently, its pavilions and parts of the garden have been adapted for public use. What is left of the garden has returned to its original use as a pleasure garden, albeit for enjoyment by the general public rather than by private individuals, arguably one of the best revitalization outcomes.

Figure 11.1: View of Lou Lim Ioec Garden showing Chun Chou Tong (adapted as a gallery) and the man-made pond. (Source: Adelina Chan.)

Project Information

Address	10, Estrada de Adolfo Loureiro, Macao
Original use	Pleasure garden for a private residence Chun Chou Tong: reception hall and guesthouse Iong Sam Tong: reception hall
Previous use	Site was used by the neighboring school Chun Chou Tong: reception hall Iong Sam Tong: library, specimen room, and storage
New use	Public garden Chun Chou Tong: gallery Iong Sam Tong: interpretation center
Heritage status	Chun Chou Tong: Building of architectural interest Garden: site
Site area	10,857 square meters
Project cost estimate	Unknown
Funding model	Government/Public
Owner	Municipal Affairs Bureau (Instituto para os Assuntos Municipais, IAM)
Developer	NA
Architect	NA
Contractor	NA
Project timeline	1974: Transformation of the private garden compound to a public park, renamed after Lou Lim Ieoc

Project Description

Lou Lim Ieoc Garden, as a *private* garden, has a long history of changing use, largely due to the sale of part of the land and associated buildings. Since 1973, when the garden was purchased by the government to be used as a *public* garden, it has been restored, and more recently, its two pavilions—Chun Chou Tong and Iong Sam Tong—have been adaptively reused for public purposes. Although the project is focused on the two pavilions and their uses as a gallery and interpretation center (including an exhibition), it is the garden itself that first attracts visitors. The pavilions, as prominent features within the garden, offer the opportunity for visitors to learn more about the garden and the Lou family and to enjoy exhibitions.

Site History

The genesis of the garden began in 1870 when the prominent businessman Lou Kau purchased the land on which the garden was to be built and in 1904 entrusted his elder son Lou Lim Ieoc to realize his dream of a classical garden befitting of the family's wealth and social status. The garden project did not start in earnest until Lou Senior's suicide in 1906 at the age of fifty-nine after a series of business failures. This tragic event drove elder son Lou Lim Ieoc to commit to the garden project in memory of the family patriarch. Originally called Yu Yuen (literally, "pleasure garden"), the design drew inspiration from the famed classical gardens of Suzhou, featuring the

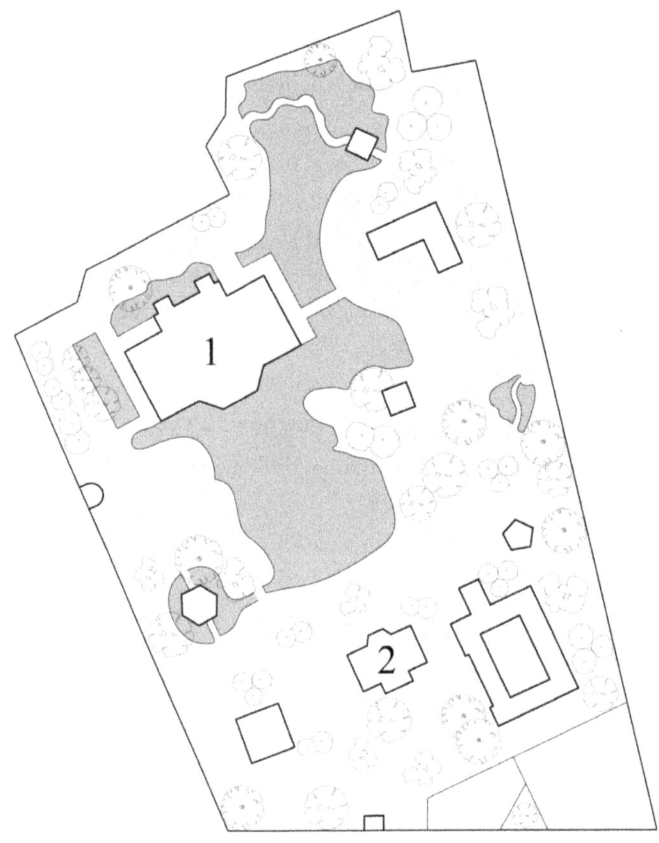

Figure 11.2: Simplified map of Lou Lim Ieoc Garden showing the extent of the current garden and its remaining attributes—1. Chun Chou Tong, 2. Iong Sam Tong. (Source: Drawn by Ng Wai Shing based on a map found in the garden directory.)

character-defining elements of stylistic architecture, artistic rockery, and poetic landscaping. In May 1912, the partially completed garden acquired historical significance when it became the place to receive the Republic of China's leading statesman Dr. Sun Yat-sen on his visit to Macao. Sun was hosted and housed in the by-then-completed Chun Chou Tong within the garden compound.

The garden was fully completed in 1925 at the height of Lou Lim Ieoc's business success. Unfortunately, his untimely death in 1927 at the age of forty-nine led to a steady decline of the family fortune to the point that the Lou family could no longer afford to keep the garden. From 1937 to 1945, a deteriorating economy brought on by the Sino-Japanese War hasten the selling off—and renting out—of the garden's land and properties. After the war, the process of parceling out the garden land for sale was hastened. In 1952, local philanthropists purchased a sizable portion of the garden and donated it to Pui Ching Middle School for its new campus development, retaining only the former Lou Lim Ioc residence as the school's administrative building. One of these philanthropists, the businessman Ho Yin, also bought the rest of the garden for his own use. In 1973, the government acquired from Ho Yin, for a reportedly low price of 2.7 million patacas, what was left of the dilapidated garden compound, which was by then less than half the size of the original Yu Yuen.[1] After undergoing extensive restoration, the garden was opened to the public in 1974 and renamed after Lou Lim Ieoc, the mastermind of this landscape masterpiece.

1. Wanyin Zhang, trans., "A Scenic Journey into the Past," *Macau Closer*, accessed April 21, 2023, https://macaucloser.com/en/magazine/scenic-journey-past.

Project History

The revitalization of Lou Lim Ieoc Garden began in 1974 when the dilapidated remains of a once-magnificent private pleasure garden were restored and adapted as a public park. The government's initiative to convert the former private garden for public use led to the adaptive reuse of a number of buildings found on the site. The two sizable buildings within the park (which are often confusingly referred to as "pavilions"), Chun Chou Tong and Iong Sam Tong, have been respectively adapted as a public art gallery and an interpretation center displaying memorabilia of the Lou family.

Iong Sam Tong is perhaps the one building that has undergone the most adaptive reuse. Its original use was similar to Chun Chou Tong, as a house for receiving and quartering valued guests, and it was adapted as a school library from 1938 to 1952 when Pui Ching Middle School rented the premises. In the 1980s, after the government acquired the garden, it was adapted as the Floral and Fauna Specimens Room of the Municipal Council of Macao. In 2010, a major restoration was carried out on the building to return it to its original appearance and adapt it to its current use as an interpretation center.

There is a third building, a residential house, that has been adapted as a museum known as the Macao Tea Culture House. It is a predominantly Portuguese-style building with minor Chinese elements that was once part of the private garden compound. It now functions as an independent museum and with a separate entrance outside the park.

Development Environment

Francisco Figueira (1934–2009), the person in charge of the Lou Lim Ieoc Garden project, was an architect from Portugal, who served in the colonial Macao government's Cultural Institute (the present-day Cultural Affairs Bureau) from 1973 to 1990, rising to the rank of deputy president. He introduced the concept of heritage

Figure 11.3: Exterior view of Iong Sam Tong (revitalized as an interpretation center). (Source: Adelina Chan.)

conservation to Macao and was instrumental in drafting the city's first built heritage conservation legislation, Macao Decree Law No. 34/76/M, dated August 7, 1976 (signed by the governor of Macao, José Eduardo Garcia Leandro, on August 4, 1976).[2]

The Macao government's acquisition of the last remaining 1.78 hectares of the original garden in 1973 was not without the significant support of private citizens, indicating that the private-turned-public Lou Lim Ieoc Garden was a public-private partnership project. Chief among the private partners was the prominent businessman Ho Yin, father of the post-handover Macao's first chief executive. Ho was the last private owner of the garden, and at the time he sold it to the government, Ho was the serving president of the powerful Macao Chamber of Commerce, which represented the interests of the local Chinese business community (the word "Chinese" appears in the official Chinese name of the organization). The unusually low price of 2.7 million patacas that the government paid for the garden indicates that there was an element of donation in the sale with the goal of relinquishing private property for the free enjoyment of the public.

Intervention

Comparing the 1967 map to the current layout (Figure 11.2), the layout of the garden is unchanged.[3] Such character-defining elements as the Bridge of Nine Curves, man-made pond, pavilions, and rock garden have been retained, helping to preserve the garden's authenticity. The main changes are those to the interiors of Chun Chou Tong and Iong Sam Tong, which have been modified for use as a gallery and interpretation center respectively. The change of use required the introduction (e.g., air-conditioning) or modification (e.g., modern lighting) of building services. Although some interior partitions have been removed to allow unobstructed spaces, the major structural elements are preserved, either exposed or covered by mechanical ductwork.

Key Challenges

As the first garden of its kind in Macao, one dedicated to public use, the biggest challenge was acquiring the site. It was only in 1973 that a considerable area was purchased by the government and revitalized for public use. Later, there were smaller challenges, such as finding the best use for the two pavilions and adapting them accordingly. Ongoing challenges include timely maintenance of the garden—and its buildings and structures—as the place is heavily used by both the community and visitors.

Keeping Heritage Alive

Lou Lim Ieoc Garden's spirit of place is protected through ongoing conservation of the garden and its attributes. In addition to improved public access to the garden and appropriate new use of the two pavilions, free, community-based activities attract a wide and appreciative audience. For example, the Municipal Affairs Bureau (Instituto para os Assuntos Municipais, IAM) organizes seasonal events, such as

2. "Legislation on Heritage Protection: Statutory Order No. 34/76/M August 7," Cultural Affairs Bureau, Macao SAR Government, accessed May 23, 2022, http://www.icm.gov.mo/rc/viewer/20038/1345.
3. The 1967 map can be found in Ana Maria Amaro, *O Jardim de Lou Lim Ieóc* (Macau: Imprensa Nacional, 1967), 27.

Figure 11.4: Interior view of Chun Chou Tong (revitalized as a gallery). (Source: Adelina Chan.)

the Mid-Autumn Lantern Festival and the Macao Lotus Flower Festival (a multisite event), to ensure that the garden is a cultural site as well as a site for leisure. Wide-ranging activities include chess playing, flower viewing, sketching and watercoloring, and tai chi or simply chatting with friends on a pond-side bench. The garden, in and of itself or as memorable backdrop, plays an important part in the daily lives of Macao people.

Long-Term Viability

Different from other cultural sites in Macao, Lou Lim Ieoc Garden is the only one where a garden is the main focus. As it is under the management of the Municipal Affairs Bureau (Instituto para os Assuntos Municipais, IAM), Lou Lim Ieoc Garden is part of a larger municipal services system that works to improve residents' quality of life. IAM, which manages Lou Lim Ieoc Garden, has a clear objective in utilizing the site's cultural richness. Chun Chou Tong is consistently used for short-term art exhibitions, while Iong Sam Tong is curated as an interpretation center with a permanent collection that shows the site's history. These two original pavilions complement each other: one focuses on Macao's current art scene, nurturing talent; the other addresses the past.

Impact

Economic: Given its location (the garden is within walking distance from Tap Seac Square and the St. Lazarus District), Lou Lim Ieoc is promoted as one of the stops in the tourism office's scheme to link heritage sites within walking distance in hopes of attracting tourists to lesser-known attractions.

Environmental: In 1992, Lou Lim Ieoc Garden was chosen as one of the eight sights of Macao that represent the colony's cultural identity long before Macao became a World Heritage Site. For years, the garden has been recognized by local Macao people as an accessible cultural site. Its garden setting makes heritage part of every life and available to all.

Social: The garden setting has changed little since its 1974 opening. Macao locals celebrate festivals, play hide-and-seek in the rock garden, practice tai chi, and sketch near the pond as in the past.

The Lou Lim Ieoc Garden is an urban oasis among the many small and green islands that dot around in densely built Macao. Over the years and through small-scale interventions, it has maintained its traditional roots and remained a place for relaxation and inspiration for locals and visitors alike.

—Sharif Shams Imon
(Professor, Department of Architecture,
North South University, Bangladesh)

Bibliography

Amaro, Ana Maria. *O Jardim de Lou Lim Ieóc*. Macau: Imprensa Nacional, 1967.

Cultural Affairs Bureau, Macao SAR Government. "Legislation on Heritage Protection." Accessed May 23, 2022. http://www.icm.gov.mo/rc/viewer/20038/1345.

Imperadori, Marco, Arturo Montanelli, and Giuliana Iannaccone. *Marreiros: An Architect between Two Cultures*. Milan: BE-MA Editrice, 2007.

Lui, Andre. "Lou Lim Ieoc Garden." Macau Memory, August 2020. https://www.macaumemory.mo/specialtopic_30564681831d4512a3fa618b2d560f13.

Zhang, Wanyin, trans. "A Scenic Journey into the Past." *Macau Closer*. Accessed April 21, 2023. https://macaucloser.com/en/magazine/scenic-journey-past.

Albergue SCM (Albergue da Santa Casa da Misericórdia), Macao

Adelina Chan and Hoyin Lee

Located in Macao's St. Lazarus District, Albergue da Santa Casa da Misericórdia was a shelter for the poor and the homeless. It is also known by its Chinese name that translates as "old ladies' home" in reference to its last use as a home for elderly women. Its location, the historic St. Lazarus District, was once an isolated area where lepers were confined and treated. In 2010, with the establishment of the Department for the Promotion of Cultural and Creative Industries under the Macao SAR government's Cultural Affairs Bureau, the district underwent official revitalization as an incubator hub for the creative industries.[1] Completed in 2009, the former "old ladies' home" was already renamed "Albergue SCM" to reflect its new creative role.

Figure 12.1: Exterior view of Albergue SCM showing three (out of four) of its buildings and a central courtyard with camphor trees. (Source: Adelina Chan.)

1. "Development of Cultural and Creative Industries (Macau)," UNESCO Diversity of Cultural Expressions, November 29, 2018, https://en.unesco.org/creativity/policy-monitoring-platform/development-cultural-creative.

Project Information

Address	8, Calçada da Igreja de S. Lázaro, Macao
Original use	Shelter for the elderly (first block built in the 1890s)
New use	Cultural and creative venue: architectural firm, gallery, multipurpose room, restaurant, and retail
Heritage status	Building of architectural interest
Site area	1,437.20 square meters
Project cost estimate	Unknown
Funding model	Public-private partnership (Cultural Development Fund of the Macao Government* and Santa Casa da Misericórdia de Mação Foundation [Holy House of Mercy])**
Owner	Holy House of Mercy, Macao (Santa Casa da Misericórdia de Mação)
Developer	NA
Architect	Carlos Marreiros (architect); Gilberto Gomes and José Silveirinha (engineers)
Contractor	Vong Kei Cheong
Project timeline	2003–2009

Notes:

* "Fundo de Desenvolvimento da Cultura (Cultural Development Fund)," Macao SAR Government, accessed March 9, 2022, https://www.fdc.gov.mo/pt/funding/normal/application-info/3.

** "List of Organizations that Were Granted Funding in the Second Quarter of 2017," Macao Foundation, Macao SAR Government, accessed May 7, 2023, https://www.fmac.org.mo/sponsorship/uploads/ueditor/file/20201103/1604369434670411.pdf.

Project Description

Albergue SCM is affectionately referred to as *por tsai uk*, a term used by Cantonese locals that means "old ladies' home," while *albergue* means "shelter" in Portuguese. As the name suggests, the place was widely known as a shelter for elderly ladies. Albergue SCM is owned and managed by the Holy House of Mercy (Santa Casa da Misericórdia), Macao's oldest charitable organization. Today, the premises are composed of four building blocks surrounding a central courtyard, where two camphor trees are the focal points. The oldest among the four blocks (Block A) was built in the 1890s and is the biggest block in the compound. It now houses an architectural firm, a gallery, and a retail store. Block B, which was built in the 1920s, now houses a restaurant. Block C, which was previously the kitchen, is now attached to Block B with the addition of a glass structure. Block D is now adapted as a multipurpose room (Figure 12.2).

The project objectives were as follows:

- To promote Macao's cultural heritage.
- To facilitate dialogue among different races.
- To promote the development of visual arts.
- To engender Macao's creativity industry.[2]

2. "Management of Albergue SCM Visits the Office of GPSAP," Macao Special Administrative Region Public Assets Supervision and Planning Office, Macao SAR Government, accessed May 7, 2023, https://www.gpsap.gov.mo/node/129#.

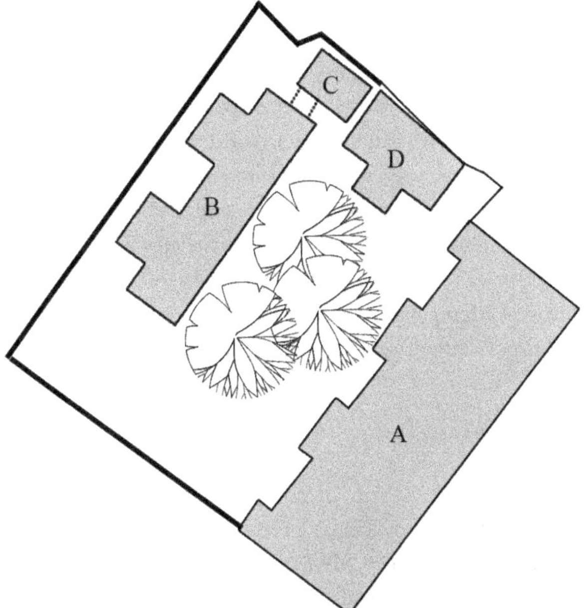

Figure 12.2: Diagram showing the layout of Albergue SCM. (Source: Drawn by Lavina Ahuja based on material from DSCC website, Macao government.)

Site History

St. Lazarus District was founded by the Catholic Diocese of Macao in 1568, shortly after the Portuguese started to settle in Macao. This district was a hinterland outside of the walled city and was chosen by the diocese to build a church-centered leprosarium and shelter. As the charity branch of the diocese, the Holy House of Mercy was established in Macao in the sixteenth century, serving both Macao locals and Portuguese Catholics. Centered around the St. Lazarus Church, a clinic, homes, and a school were built to serve the community. As the walled city expanded, the district became a residential area for middle-class Portuguese/Macanese people. Several existing buildings were razed, a grid plan was introduced, and public roads and sewers were constructed. In 1976, the Macao government formally listed St. Lazarus Church as a heritage building, and in 1984, the St. Lazarus District became Macao's first designated cultural heritage "site."[3]

In 2000, the Holy House of Mercy closed its shelter for the elderly in St. Lazarus District, marking the beginning of the district's revitalization plan spearheaded by the Macao SAR government. The goal of the district's revitalization was to utilize its cultural assets to promote the creative industry. Also, Catholic-themed annual festivals, such as St. John's Festival and the procession of São Roque (the patron saint against plague), now take place within the district. These have not only highlighted the district's Catholic past but also encouraged other community-based activities. Due to the size of its courtyard, Albergue SCM has become the anchor of these cultural activities.

3. "Legislation on Heritage Protection: Statutory Order No. 56/84/M June 30," Cultural Affairs Bureau, Macao SAR Government, accessed May 23, 2022, http://www.icm.gov.mo/rc/viewer/20038/1345.

Project History

The revitalization of Albergue SCM came shortly after Macao's return to China, when the city was adopting a broader perspective on its cultural heritage. Albergue SCM, along with other historical buildings in the district, formed a base for the development of Macao's cultural and creative industries. The adaptive reuse of Albergue SCM was a partnership between government and a charitable organization, with both committed to finding a use for the complex that would respect the historical fabric and support human ingenuity. Albergue SCM remains under the management of the Holy House of Mercy with financial support from the Cultural Affairs Bureau of the Macao SAR government (formerly known as Cultural Institute of Macao).

Development Environment

The Albergue SCM project was supported by the Cultural Affairs Bureau as well as the core project team of the Holy House of Mercy, led by architect Carlos Marreiros, who was also on the Holy House of Mercy (Santa Casa da Misericórdia) Council. As St. Lazarus District is part of the walkability scheme that includes Tap Seac Square, Albergue SCM has become an integral part of the government's attempt to weave together selected heritage sites within walking distance of one another.[4] Calçada pavement, a traditional form of Portuguese decorative paving, is used to signify the access route for heritage sites within the walkability scheme, leading people from St. Paul's Ruins and Senado Square to Tap Seac Square and St. Lazarus District.[5]

Figure 12.3: Entrance of Albergue SCM showing its gate and the calçada pavement that continues through St. Lazarus District. (Source: Adelina Chan.)

4. Launched by the Municipal Affairs Bureau, thematic routes of "Taking a Walk through the Streets of Macao—Knowing about Macao" take us on a journey along streets and alleys to rediscover the fascination of old Macao and savor the once forgotten history and tales of these areas. See "Walking Route of Conde S.," Cartography and Cadastre Bureau, Macao SAR Government, accessed May 27, 2022, https://routemap.dscc.gov.mo/en/dscc-line05.html.
5. According to Architect Carlos Marreiros, pedestrianization of the district was considered in the 1980s but was not realized (Carlos Marreiros [project architect and member of the Holy House of Mercy Council], in discussion with one of the authors, March 25, 2022).

Intervention

Initial renovation works at Albergue SCM, which began in 2000, included removing numerous layers of paint and repainting the buildings, both inside and outside, in historically accurate colors. The exterior's signature yellow color was reinstated, giving the place a distinct identity. The courtyard was paved with calçada. Its massive camphor trees were preserved, and palm trees were added in one of the corners.

The blocks of Albergue SCM were structurally upgraded with steel reinforcements, where necessary. The handsome timber roofs were repaired, including necessary waterproofing works. Water and drainage systems were concealed within the walls so as not to affect the appearance of the original architecture. The original materials of the blocks were retained and reused as much as possible, such as interior finishings, doors, and windows. The new uses did not require a lift or additional fire escape, which allowed the interior layouts of the blocks to be retained with minimal intervention.

Figure 12.4: Architect Marreiros as seen in the foyer of Block A of Albergue SCM. (Source: Adelina Chan.)

Key Challenges

- Converting the original use of an elderly home to a mixed-use cultural and creative venue.
- Securing funding from the Macao government for maintenance costs.
- Establishing community engagement with the place, as the former use was private and the complex was closed to the public.

Keeping Heritage Alive

The careful conservation of the site, now open to the public, reflects the determination of both the government and a charitable organization to respect the architectural value of the complex. Retaining "albergue" in the name of the place helps to communicate its original use. In general, Albergue SCM's significance cannot be separated from that of St. Lazarus District. When walking in the district, one senses the former, smoothly functioning small town, laid out in a grid plan with a church, clinic, and nearby cemetery. Compassion, dignity, and humility are the values that have shaped and defined Albergue SCM and, more broadly, the entire St. Lazarus District.

Owing to its thoughtful management, Albergue SCM has become a destination for community and cultural activities throughout the year, such as Macau Design Week, Dog Adoption Day, art exhibitions, St. John's Festival, lantern festival, and Christmas market. With the continuous conservation efforts from both Portuguese Macao and Macao SAR governments, the St. Lazarus District has been able to preserve its charitable legacy both in physicality and in spirit.

The two camphor trees are on the Register of Old and Valuable Trees in Macao.[6] As one of the key character-defining elements of the site, this recognition ensures their long-term protection.

Long-Term Viability

In contrast to its previous use as a shelter for the elderly, Albergue SCM opens its courtyard and doors for public enjoyment. There is a comfortable balance of private use and public use. The restaurant, Albergue 1601, and the retail store, Mercearia Portuguesa, are open to visitors, while the architectural firm and gallery remain private. Architect Carlos Marreiros, who is a member of the Holy House of Mercy (Santa Casa da Misericórdia) Council and a tenant of Albergue SCM, also curates and executes cultural events for Albergue SCM. Rents from tenants and events contribute to the financial sustainability of the place.

Since Albergue SCM is not heavily reliant on tourism for its operation, its vision in serving the public and promoting Macao culture is not dependent on changing tourism patterns. Moreover, the Holy House of Mercy, the owner and manager of the site, is a respected charitable organization for providing social services to Macao residents. In line with government policy of developing Macao's soft power, Albergue SCM and the St. Lazarus District together are an exemplary model of area conservation in Macao.

Impact

Socioenvironmental: Albergue SCM has become a base for community cultural activities, including events and exhibitions. Given the nature of the historical setting, Catholic and Portuguese themed festivals are regularly held here and also within the wider St. Lazarus District, utilizing the open space and pedestrianized zone to not only keep Portuguese heritage alive but also provide an area where locals can enjoy outdoor performances and street markets. The nearby 10 Fantasia, a creative industries incubator, is also a cultural site that connects with the pedestrianized zone.[7] The two sites, as a cluster, reinforce each other.

---

6. Macao's Register of Old and Valuable Trees. See "Despacho do Chefe do Executivo No. 168/2021," Macao SAR Government, accessed May 27, 2022, https://bo.io.gov.mo/bo/i/2021/45/despce.asp.
7. "10 Fantasia—A Creative Industries Incubator," Tourism Office, Macao SAR Government, accessed May 27, 2022, https://www.macaotourism.gov.mo/en/shows-and-entertainment/cultural-and-creative-industries-zones/10-fantasia.

Economic: Independent cafés, shops, and restaurants have started to move into the St. Lazarus District, particularly along the streets paved with calçada. The revitalization of Albergue SCM as a base for the creative industries has given direction to the area's regeneration, a role that goes much further than a partnership between government and a charitable organization. However, there remains the challenge of possible gentrification and rising rents.

> **Albergue [SCM] is a social cultural architecture, which is warm and humble, without unnecessary ornaments.**
>
> **—Architect Carlos Marreiros**

Bibliography

Cartography and Cadastre Bureau, Macao SAR Government. "Walking Route of Conde S." Accessed May 27, 2022. https://routemap.dscc.gov.mo/en/dscc-line05.html.

Cultural Affairs Bureau, Macao SAR Government. "Legislation on Heritage Protection." Accessed May 23, 2022. http://www.icm.gov.mo/rc/viewer/20038/1345.

Imperadori, Marco, Arturo Montanelli, and Giuliana Iannaccone. *Marreiros: An Architect between Two Cultures*. Milan: BE-MA Editrice, 2007.

Macao Foundation, Macao SAR Government. "List of Organizations that Were Granted Funding in the Second Quarter of 2017." Accessed May 7, 2023. https://www.fmac.org.mo/sponsorship/uploads/ueditor/file/20201103/1604369434670411.pdf.

Macao SAR Government. "Despacho do Chefe do Executivo No. 168/2021." Accessed May 27, 2022. https://bo.io.gov.mo/bo/i/2021/45/despce.asp.

Macao SAR Government. "Fundo de Desenvolvimento da Cultura (Cultural Development Fund)." Accessed March 9, 2022. https://www.fdc.gov.mo/pt/funding/normal/application-info/3.

Macao Special Administrative Region Public Assets Supervision and Planning Office, Macao SAR Government. "Management of Albergue SCM Visits the Office of GPSAP." Accessed May 7, 2023. https://www.gpsap.gov.mo/node/129#.

Tourism Office, Macao SAR Government. "10 Fantasia—A Creative Industries Incubator." Accessed May 27, 2022. https://www.macaotourism.gov.mo/en/shows-and-entertainment/cultural-and-creative-industries-zones/10-fantasia.

UNESCO Diversity of Cultural Expressions. "Development of Cultural and Creative Industries (Macau)." November 29, 2018. https://en.unesco.org/creativity/policy-monitoring-platform/development-cultural-creative.

Mandarin's House, Macao

Sharif Shams Imon

The Mandarin's House project is one of Macao's most extensive conservation projects and one that lasted for nine years. It is also the largest protected historical house in Macao.

Figure 13.1: Yuqinq Mansion and Jishan Mansion as viewed from the front courtyard. (Source: Sharif Shams Imon.)

Project Information

Address	10, Travessa de António da Silva, Macao
Original use	Residential (1869–1990)
New use	House museum and cultural activity venue
Heritage status	Building of architectural interest
Site area	Approximately 4,000 square meters
Project cost estimate	US$5.3 million
Funding model	Government/Public
Owner	Macao SAR government
Developer	NA
Architect	Cultural Affairs Bureau (Macao SAR government)
Contractor	NA
Project timeline	2002–2010

Project Description

The Mandarin's House conservation project was the largest and the longest of its kind in Macao's history, lasting for nearly a decade. Apart from conservation professionals, the project involved local residents and other members of society.

The intent of the project was to restore the mansion's original appearance and adapt it for reuse as a house museum to offer visitors a glimpse into the lifestyle of former residents and present the literary works of the most famous resident of the house, Mr. Zheng Guanying. The project's primary objectives were as follows:[1]

- To restore and reuse the place with minimum intervention.
- To offer a unique cultural experience to visitors.
- To create conservation awareness in Macao.

Site History

It is estimated that the construction of the Mandarin's House as a residence for the Zheng family started in 1869. As the family grew, the house was expanded at different times. After the family moved out of the house in the 1950s and 1960s, the house was rented out to several families who lived in subdivided rooms. At one point, there were as many as seventy-two tenants in the Mandarin's House. Long-term neglect by the house tenants caused severe damage to the house's structure. By the time the Macao SAR government bought the house in 2001, it was in an extremely dilapidated condition, covered in weeds and with fallen roofs, burnt wooden beams, and worn-out walls.[2]

The Mandarin's House was classified as "building of architectural interest" in 1992.[3] It has both traditional Chinese as well as Western architectural characteristics;

1. Cheong Cheok Kio (former head of the Cultural Heritage Department, Cultural Affairs Bureau), in discussion with the author, May 2018.
2. "Introduction: Mandarin's House," Mandarin's House, Cultural Affairs Bureau, Macao SAR Government, accessed March 1, 2022, https://www.wh.mo/mandarinhouse/en/introduction/.
3. According to Macao Decree Law No. 83/92/M.

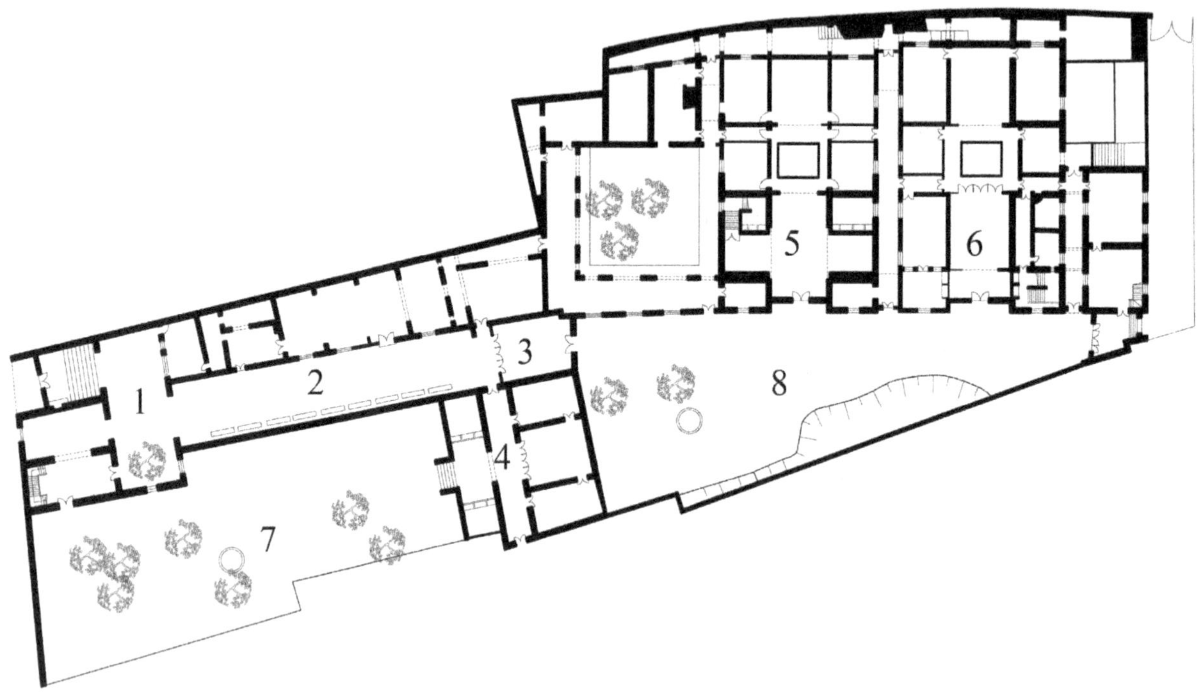

Figure 13.2: Ground-floor plan of Mandarin's House—1. Moon Gate, 2. Sedan Way, 3. Ronglu Hallway, 4. Wenchang Hall, 5. Yu-Qing-Tang (Yuqinq Mansion), 6. Ji-Shan-Tang (Jishan Mansion), 7. Main Garden, 8. Front Courtyard. (Source: Drawn by Ng Wai Shing based on materials from Cultural Affairs Bureau, "Mandarin's House.")

it is a typical Chinese-style courtyard house and features many Western architectural and decorative elements.

The house has two floors and is divided into several parts: Moon Gate, Sedan Way, Ronglu Hallway, Wenchang Hall, Inner Courtyard, Yu-Qing-Tang (Yuqinq Mansion), Ji-Shan-Tang (Jishan Mansion), Front Courtyard, and Back Gatehouse.[4] Apart from its architectural value, the Mandarin's House is also significant for its historical value. Zheng Guanying, a son of the house's original owner and a late-Qing dynasty scholar, completed the literary masterpiece *Shengshi Weiyan* (Words of wisdom in times of prosperity) here.

Project History

A local developer bought the Mandarin's House to redevelop it as an apartment complex in 1990. The last tenants of the house vacated the property around the same time. Recognizing the heritage significance of the property, the Macao government's Cultural Affairs Bureau attempted to acquire the property immediately.[5] A long negotiation process ensued. During the negotiation period, the government classified the Mandarin's House as one of Macao's cultural heritage properties under the category "buildings of architectural interest" in 1992. Eventually, through a land swap deal with the developer, the Macao government completed the acquisition in 2001 and the Cultural Affairs Bureau of the government initiated the conservation project.

4. Diagrammatic representation of the parts of Mandarin's House can be found at "Virtual Gallery: Mandarin's House," Mandarin's House, Cultural Affairs Bureau, Macao SAR Government, accessed March 1, 2022, https://www.wh.mo/mandarinhouse/en/virtual/.
5. Stephen Chan (former deputy director of the Cultural Affairs Bureau), in discussion with the author, April 2022.

Development Environment

There were no specific subsidies or incentives that helped the realization of this project. Conservation of Mandarin's House was initiated and funded entirely by the government.

Intervention

The Mandarin's House was almost uninhabitable with serious structural damage when the government acquired the property. According to a project architect, maintaining authenticity in design was the main concern since many parts of the house were either badly damaged or completely missing. The research to identify the house's former appearance revealed that the mansion was an undocumented building whose construction was not recorded. There was also no information on the construction materials used. Various analyses were carried out to determine the materials during the pre-conservation period. On-site surveys were carried out prior to that.[6]

After the government acquired the house, more in-depth study became possible. Materials and historical evidence from the site were collected, and construction materials were investigated. The direction of the conservation project was set only after the project team gained a basic grasp of the house's history gleaned through evidence and interviews with past residents.

Structures that were not a part of the original building were removed. All information collected was recorded before the demolition work.

The reconstruction of the Moon Gate at the Mandarin's House offers a good example of how the challenges of lack of historical records and missing parts were overcome. The Moon Gate at the entrance to the Sedan Way did not exist when the team first entered the house. However, research suggested the possible existence of a Moon Gate. According to the Chinese characters on a masonry piece found at the property, the opening before the Sedan Way should be round in shape. Former tenants also recalled a door similar to a Moon Gate. However, what remained unaddressed was its size and appearance, which could not be confirmed without concrete evidence. During the conservation process, some possible components of the Moon Gate, such as stone pieces or arch-shaped objects, were discovered in the garden next to the Sedan Way. Further analysis confirmed that the pieces were a part of the former Moon Gate. The discovery helped the team confirm the Moon Gate's size, which was later reconstructed (Figure 13.3).[7]

In addition to the conservation of the Mandarin's House, various spaces—both interior and exterior—were given specific functions in keeping with its new use as a house museum. These are as follows:

- A part of the entrance guardhouse has been turned into a gift shop.
- A room facing the entrance is used as a visitor information booth.
- A hall behind the visitor information booth is used as an interpretation space to present the house's history and its conservation process.
- Wenchang Hall is used as an exhibition of Zheng Guanying's work.
- The inner courtyard with its cloister is used as a temporary exhibition and activity space.

6. Cheong Cheok Kio (former head of the Cultural Heritage Department, Cultural Affairs Bureau), in discussion with the author, May 2018.
7. Cheong Cheok Kio (former head of the Cultural Heritage Department, Cultural Affairs Bureau), in discussion with the author, May 2018.

Figure 13.3: Current view of the Moon Gate. (Source: Sharif Shams Imon.)

- Yuqing and Jishan Mansions, the former living quarters of the Zheng family, are presented with a few pieces of antique furniture for the visitors to understand the traditional lifestyle.
- The Front Courtyard, a large open space in front of Yuqing and Jishan Mansions, is used as an occasional outdoor performance venue.
- A new service entrance and toilet structures have been built at the rear end of the property.
- In various parts of the house, visitors can scan a QR code with their mobile devices and experience the house's past through augmented reality.

Key Challenges

- According to a senior project architect, "We hoped that we would understand this building better step by step during the process. The early stage of our efforts laid the foundations for future conservation work. This adjustable mechanism allowed for future restoration work and expanded our knowledge of the mansion. That was why we spent a long time on the project."[8]
- Finding the exact construction materials matching the original materials was a significant challenge. Some of the materials were no longer available. The oyster-shell windows used in the house, for example, were unavailable in Macao. It is also possible that they were not available in Macao when the house was first constructed. The project team had to source farmed shells from outside Macao through contractors.
- It took the team two years to create the straw plaster that was used in the house originally. Where matching materials could not be found, modern materials were used in certain places to achieve coherence.

8. Cheong Cheok Kio (former head of the Cultural Heritage Department, Cultural Affairs Bureau), in discussion with the author, May 2018.

Figure 13.4: Group tour at the Mandarin's House. (Source: Sharif Shams Imon.)

- The team's lack of knowledge of the house's original appearance was a major challenge. Without any official records, the house's original scale and layout could not be ascertained. It was suspected that the former layout was larger than the current one and that a part of the house was either missing or removed. Thus, the team had to rely on the evidence they gathered on-site or through interviews with former tenants.

Keeping Heritage Alive

The Mandarin's House is classified as a "building of architectural interest." As such, architectural conservation was the main focus of the project. However, since significant parts of the house were missing and no records of them exist, the project aimed to maintain the condition of the building with minimum intervention while ensuring public access. The place is now primarily a house museum that contains permanent exhibitions on the conservation process as well as on the works and life of the house's most eminent former resident, Zhang Guanying. The open spaces of the house are also used as occasional cultural performance venues.

Long-Term Viability

The government provided (and continues to provide) full financial support for the conservation of the Mandarin's House and its management, operation, and maintenance. There is no entry fee. No plans for a specific use of the house were made initially; architectural conservation was the primary focus when the project started.

Impact

Economic: Given its location and limited access by public transport, the Mandarin's House attracts a fraction of visitors to Macao every year. The level of economic benefits enjoyed by businesses near more popular heritage sites in Macao are absent in the area in which the Mandarin's House is located.

Environmental: The courtyards, including the garden, of the Mandarin's House offer much needed open space to the residents of the densely built neighborhood.

Social: Although the house has the potential to be a venue for sociocultural activities for the communities living nearby, strict control of how the facilities can be used means the potential remains to be utilized.

> **We respected the principles of authenticity and truthfulness during the conservation project. We strove to restore the mansion's former appearance based on existing conditions. We think we managed to do it with its vibes recovered. We are satisfied with our efforts despite the obstacles during the process.**[9]
>
> **—Cheong Cheok Kio**
> **(former head of the Cultural Heritage Department, Cultural Affairs Bureau)**

Bibliography

Mandarin's House, Cultural Affairs Bureau, Macao SAR Government. "Mandarin's House." Accessed March 1, 2022. https://www.wh.mo/mandarinhouse/en/introduction/.

9. Cheong Cheok Kio (former head of the Cultural Heritage Department, Cultural Affairs Bureau), in discussion with the author, May 2018.

Patane Night Watch House, Macao

Jennifer Lang

As the only surviving example of a night watch house in Macao, the Patane Night Watch House serves as a significant example of heritage conservation and adaptive reuse for the city. In collaboration with the Cultural Affairs Bureau (Macao SAR government), the local Tou Teo Mio Patane Mercy and Charity Association, and Patane Mutual Aid Association, the restoration and adaptive reuse of the site as a museum not only honors the night watch tradition but also demonstrates conservation best practice through community engagement, the safeguarding of Macao's local history, and heritage interpretation. The project has had strong environmental and social impacts, supporting cohesion, identity, security, and well-being in the associated community.

Figure 14.1: Exterior view of Patane Night Watch House partially showing the courtyard of the adjacent Tou Tei Temple. (Source: Adelina Chan.)

Project Information

Address	52–54, Rua da Palmeira, Freguesia de Santo Antonio, Macao
Original use	Night watch house (1940s–1970s)
Previous use	Store and residence (including a café and sports club, 1970s–2010)*
New use	Museum
Heritage status	Monument
Site area	80 square meters
Project cost estimate	Undisclosed
Funding model	Public-private partnership (Cultural Affairs Bureau [Macao SAR government], Tou Teo Mio Patane Mercy and Charity Association, and the Patane Mutual Aid Association)**
Owner	Not registered***
Developer	Cultural Affairs Bureau, Macao SAR government
Architect	Unknown
Contractor	Unknown
Project timeline	2012–2015

Notes:

* Leonor Sa Machado, "Patane Night Watch House: Protecting the Community with Gongs and Lanterns," *Macau Lifestyle*, January 6, 2021.

** Mark O'Neil, "Beware of the Dark: New Museum Celebrates Forgotten Profession: The Watchman," *Macao Magazine*, July 2016, 82.

*** "From the Public Consultation of the 2nd Batch of Local Heritage Sites," Cultural Affairs Bureau, Macao SAR government, accessed April 8, 2022, https://www.culturalheritage.mo/pt/detail/102091.

Project Description

Located in the Patane neighborhood next to the Taoist Tou Tei Temple and at the base of the Luís de Camões Garden, the Patane Night Watch House is an example of a successful partnership between the Cultural Affairs Bureau, the Tou Tei Mio Patane Mercy and Charity Association, and the Patane Mutual Aid Association. The intent of the project was to revitalize the site as a museum honoring its original use as a night watch house. Its objectives were as follows:

- To interpret and reveal the traditional values of mutual assistance and social service within the local neighborhood.
- To safeguard folk traditions and local history.
- To restore the site to its original state.

Site History

In ancient China, the role of night watchmen was to report time and remind people to take precautions against fire and theft, forming a type of civil defense system. Following this tradition, Macao's Patane Night Watch House housed a watchman (and his family) from the 1940s until the 1970s, who provided a service for residents

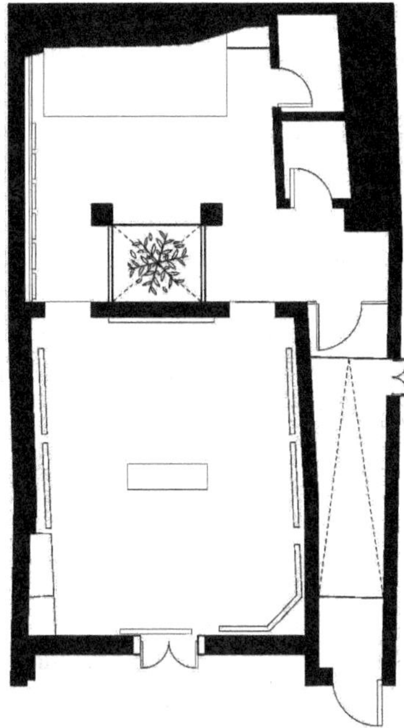

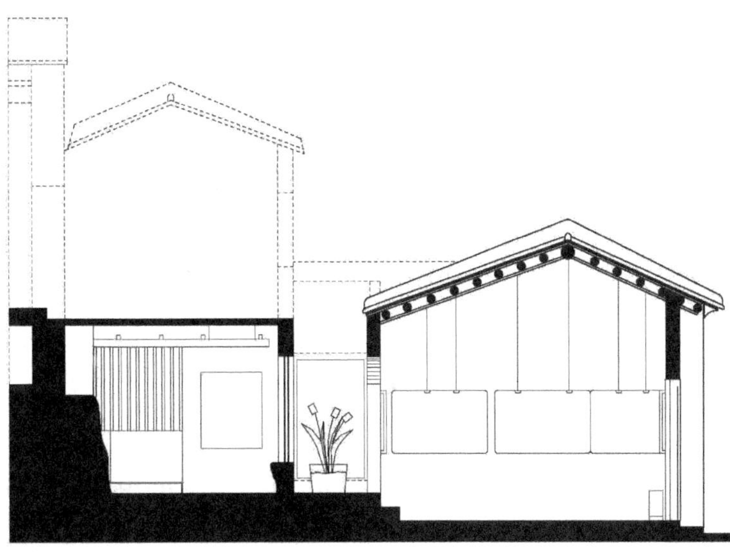

Figure 14.2: Plan and section of Patane Night Watch House. (Source: Drawn by Ng Wai Shing based on materials from Queqiao, *The Story of Revitalising Heritage Buildings in Macau*).

and merchants of the Patane neighborhood with a day and night patrol system, including holding lanterns, putting out fires, warning for typhoons and floods, looking out for burglaries and thefts, and reporting the time by striking gongs. The cost of supporting the night watchman was provided by neighborhood residents and shopkeepers as a way of protecting their lives and businesses.[1] As Macao modernized in the late twentieth century with a police system and the widespread use of timepieces, this social service was no longer needed to maintain security and ensure social order, and therefore the night watch houses were abandoned. Today, all night watch houses in Macao have been demolished, with the exception of the Patane Night Watch House.

As a reminder of Macao's past, the Patane Night Watch House is significant for its architectural, historic, and social values. Typical of vernacular southern Chinese architecture, the site comprises a one-story structure facing the street and a two-story structure at the rear, separated by a small internal courtyard. The building is accessed from the front-facing one-story structure that abuts Rua da Palmeira. The wooden entry doors feature Chinese characters reading "night watch house." Access to the upper story of the rear structure is only through the courtyard of the adjacent Tou Tei Temple as there is no internal connection between the two floors. A side entrance at the far right provides access to an open alley, which leads to the courtyard. The Patane Night Watch House museum occupies only the lower story of each structure. The gable-roofed structures are constructed with Chinese gray bricks with a lime render.

Project History

The aim of this project, a partnership between the Cultural Affairs Bureau, the local Tou Teo Mio Patane Mercy and Charity Association, and the Patane Mutual Aid Association, was to restore a local vernacular building and adapt it for use as a

1. Leonor Sa Machado, "Patane Night Watch House: Protecting the Community with Gongs and Lanterns," *ML Macau Lifestyle*, January 6, 2021, https://macaulifestyle.com/culture/heritage/patane-night-watch-house-protecting-the-community-with-gongs-lanterns/.

museum to honor the night watch tradition in Macao. In addition to researching the history and use of the site, local community members were interviewed about the night watch tradition in Macao. Given the history of the site and the input from community engagement, it was decided that the museum would focus on two themes: "Macau's Night Watch Houses" and "Image of Night Watchmen."

The museum displays include historical photographs and original artifacts, including such objects as brass gongs, fire hose nozzles, silver whistles, and wooden beaters. Interpretative videos animate the static displays. Local historians were commissioned to conduct comprehensive research on both night watch houses and the night watch tradition. They also curated the displays, work that included sourcing the photographs and artifacts as well as drafting interpretative text.[2]

Development Environment

Revitalization of the Patane Night Watch House reflects the Macao SAR government's growing interest in heritage conservation. A modest building that had outlived its purpose is given a second life through adaptive reuse. The availability of funding and the input of the local community ensures a sustainable long-term use for the place. Incidentally, the Patane Night Watch House project was completed in time for the celebration of the tenth anniversary of the Historic Centre of Macao UNESCO World Heritage inscription.[3] The Patane Night Watch House was recognized as Monument under the Macao Decree Law No. 11/2013—Cultural Heritage Protection Law.

Intervention

The key actions and interventions undertaken by the Cultural Affairs Bureau for this project included a building survey, site mapping, and structural restoration, including restoration of the façade. In addition, the original interior layout of the building was reinstated and the decorative fresco paintings on the interior walls were restored.

Key Challenges

- The project posed a challenge as the site had fallen into a state of significant disrepair as it had not been used for many years.
- The conservation process faced challenges as it was difficult to find skilled craftsmen and appropriate materials for the required work.[4]

Keeping Heritage Alive

The project reflects a sound understanding of the site's strong architectural, historical, and social values through its adaptive reuse as a museum. The new use honors the night watchmen who served to protect the community of the Patane neighborhood and highlights local history through its interpretation program. The spirit of the place is retained through its authentic setting and an appropriate restoration of the

2. Mark O'Neil, "Beware of the Dark: New Museum Celebrates Forgotten Profession: The Watchman," *Macao Magazine*, July 2016, 82.
3. O'Neil, "Beware of the Dark," 82.
4. O'Neil, "Beware of the Dark," 83.

Figure 14.3: Interior view of Patane Night Watch House looking toward the back wall of the front room. (Source: Adelina Chan.)

Figure 14.4: Interior view showing the arched entryway leading to the courtyard and inner room. (Source: Adelina Chan.)

traditional vernacular building. Importantly, the community—through interviews and oral histories, and donations of display materials—was involved in the project.

The museum is dedicated to the interpretation of the significance of the night watch tradition and the Patane Night Watch House as conveyed through the display of historical materials, as well as video interviews with local residents sharing stories about the night watch house tradition in Macao and the profession of watchmen.[5] Commissioned paintings by local artist Poon Kam Ling illustrate the daily life and work of a watchman, such as patrolling, putting out a fire, and resolving disputes among neighborhood residents.[6]

The Patane Night Watch House was a neighborhood center of assistance and information, where residents could meet to help one another. As an important part of the social fabric of Macao, the revitalized site reveals and celebrates traditional values of mutual assistance between different neighborhoods and local communities.

Long-Term Viability

The adaptive reuse of the Patane Night Watch House as a modest museum supports the long-term sustainability of the place and neighborhood. The Cultural Affairs Bureau manages and financially subsidizes the museum. There are no entry fees to visit the site. As one of only a few remaining heritage sites in the Patane neighborhood, this adaptive reuse project serves as a community model to inspire and encourage neighborhood capacity building.[7]

Impact

Economic: The restoration and adaptive reuse of the building contribute to the economic viability of the Patane neighborhood community and has the potential to be a catalyst for similar conservation projects within Macao. Additionally, the public-private partnership and funding model is an example of successful government support and collaboration with local nongovernmental organizations.

Environmental: The adaptive reuse of the Patane Night Watch House as a museum that interprets the story of a vital historical social service within the community is itself a sustainable environmental action. The conservation of the place strengthened the relationship of the site to both the surrounding community members and the surrounding landscape, including the Tou Tei Temple and Luís de Camões Garden. This project safeguards not only vernacular architecture but also the folk traditions and local history of the Patane neighborhood.

Social: "The conservation of the night watch house reveals the close relationship between the night watchmen and the community in the past, allowing visitors to understand the urban development of Macao and the promotion of traditional values of mutual assistance and the provision of community services."[8] The Patane Night Watch House is an example of a recently completed conservation project in Macao that highlights the noteworthy partnership between the Macao SAR government, the local Tou Teo Mio Patane Mercy and Charity Association, and the Patane Mutual Aid Association, thus supporting grassroots conservation initiatives and promoting

5. O'Neil, "Beware of the Dark," 85.
6. O'Neil, "Beware of the Dark," 84.
7. O'Neil, "Beware of the Dark," 83.
8. "Inauguration of the Patane Night Watch House," Cultural Affairs Bureau, Macao SAR Government, accessed April 7, 2022, https://www.culturalheritage.mo/en/detail/2276.

community engagement. This partnership can be a model for other conservation projects in the community and the city. The adaptive use of the building as a museum honoring the night watch tradition promotes the local history and traditions of the Patane community, fostering and strengthening social cohesion.

Through the opening of this museum and bringing to life this old building, more people will be able to understand the history and culture of Macao.[9]

—Ung Vai
(President of the Macao Cultural Affairs Bureau)

Bibliography

Chen, Yile, Junrui Cao, and Liang Zheng. "Research on the Building Restoration, Engineering and Materials of the Night Watch House in Macau—Taking the Patane Night Watch House in Patane as an Example." E3S Web of Conferences 284, 05004, 2021.

Cultural Affairs Bureau, Macao SAR Government. "From the Public Consultation of the 2nd Batch of Local Heritage Sites." Accessed April 8, 2022. https://www.culturalheritage.mo/Survey/cbim2018/cn/.

Cultural Affairs Bureau, Macao SAR Government. "Patane Night Watch House." Accessed March 1, 2022. https://www.icm.gov.mo/en/NightWatchHouse.

Cultural Affairs Bureau, Macao SAR Government. "Patane Night Watch House Classified Immovable Properties." Accessed March 1, 2022. https://www.icm.gov.mo/en/NightWatchHouse.

Government Portal of Macao Special Administrative Region of the People's Republic of China. "Inauguration of the Patane Night Watch House." Accessed March 1, 2022. https://www.gov.mo/en/news/58638/.

Macau Daily Times. "Heritage: Patane Night Watch House Opens Today after Renovation." *Macau Daily Times*, December 18, 2015.

O'Neil, Mark. "Beware of the Dark: New Museum Celebrates Forgotten Profession: The Watchman." *Macao Magazine*, July 2016, 80–85.

Sa Machado, Leonor. "Patane Night Watch House: Protecting the Community with Gongs and Lanterns." *ML Macau Lifestyle*, January 6, 2021. https://macaulifestyle.com/culture/heritage/patane-night-watch-house-protecting-the-community-with-gongs-lanterns/.

Zhang, Queqiao. *The Story of Revitalising Heritage Buildings in Macau*. Hong Kong: Joint Publishing Hong Kong, 2020.

9. O'Neil, "Beware of the Dark," 80.

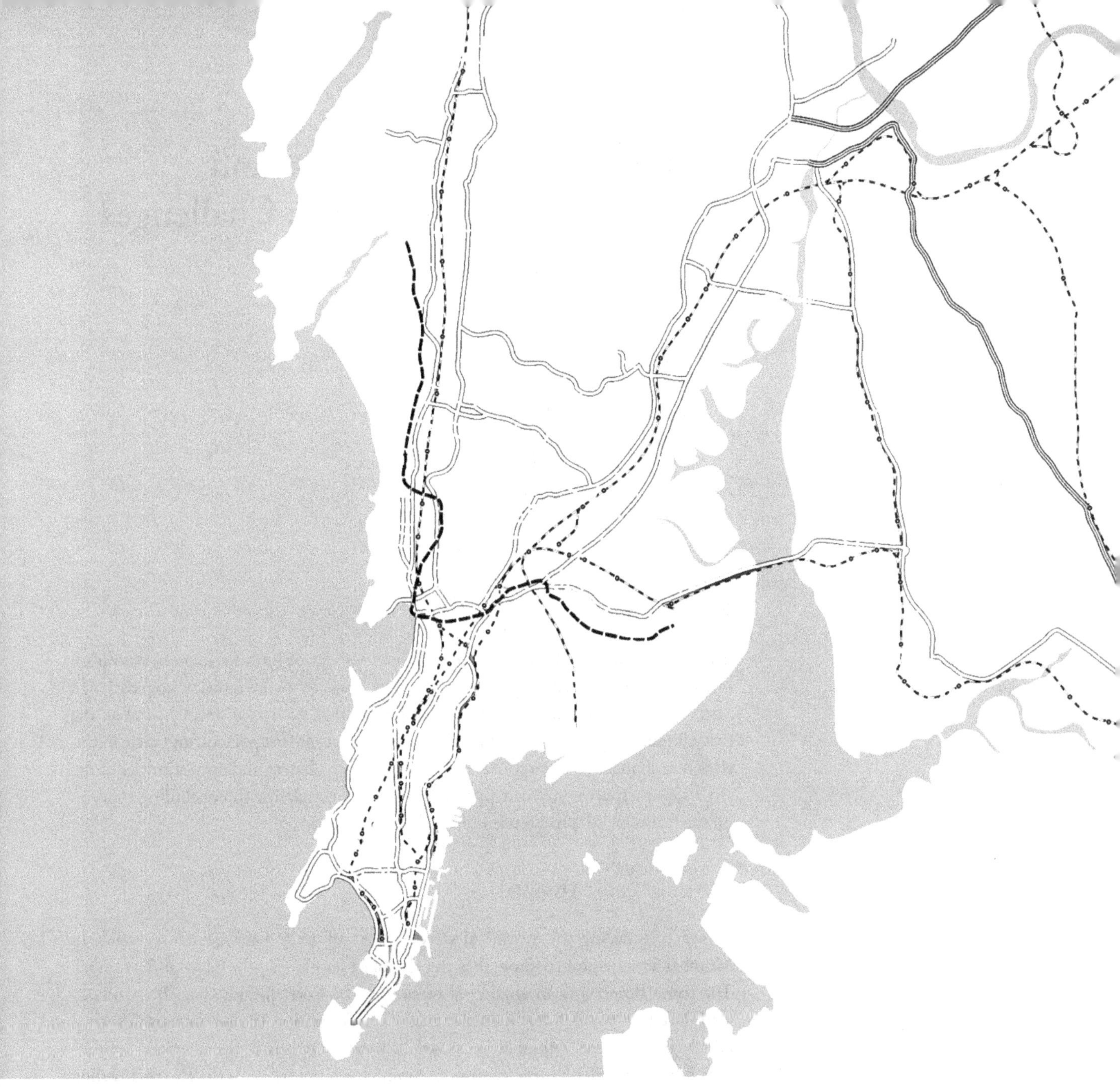

MUMBAI

Essay | Timeline | Case Studies

Built Heritage Conservation and Adaptive Reuse in Mumbai: Challenges and Opportunities

Lavina Ahuja and Lynne D. DiStefano

Introduction

This essay considers the emergence and development of built heritage conservation in Mumbai with particular focus on adaptive reuse as a conservation approach. To understand the present-day stance of built heritage conservation in Mumbai, the essay presents a background of relevant events, government policies, and civic initiatives that shaped the city's conservation practice. Challenges and opportunities of the city's approach are addressed within this context, coupled with concluding remarks on the future of adaptive reuse in Mumbai.

"Bombay" and "Mumbai"

Before considering the historical development of built heritage conservation in Mumbai, it is helpful to know that the city has two names—Bombay and Mumbai. The name Bombay is an anglicized version of the Portuguese name, "Bom-Bhaia," introduced by the British when the city was colonized in the seventeenth century. Although the name "Mumbai" was used historically by the local fisherfolk community, Bombay's official name change to Mumbai happened in 1995. The then-ruling political party saw the name "Bombay" as a legacy of British colonialism and wanted the city's name to reflect its Indigenous heritage, hence renaming it "Mumbai" to pay tribute to the goddess Mumbadevi.[1]

In this essay, the historical records of the city are presented using the name "Bombay" and the post-1995 records are presented using the name "Mumbai." With the renaming of the city, several government departments also changed their names. These changes are clarified as they occur throughout the essay.

The Beginning of Bombay

The historical account presented in this section is based largely on the research carried out by Sharada Dwivedi and Rahul Mehrotra—Bombay-based scholars whose work

1. Sridevi Nambiar, "A Brief History of How Bombay Became Mumbai," *The Culture Trip*, September 19, 2016, https://theculturetrip.com/asia/india/articles/the-history-of-how-bombay-became-mumbai-in-1-minute/.

remains an unparalleled resource for those interested in understanding the forces that made Bombay the city it is today. Among their many published works, *Bombay: The Cities Within* is an exceptional account of the city's history and sets the stage for identifying its heritage.[2]

Although Bombay's earliest origins can be traced back to the sixteenth century, when it was an archipelago of seven islands under Portuguese rule, its true development as an integrated town began only when the British acquired the islands through a marriage treaty in 1661.[3] Later, the islands were leased by the Crown to the British East India Company, and Bombay was established as a port to maintain trade links between Britain and India.

The strategic importance of Bombay became explicit when the British East India Company transferred its maritime activities from nearby Surat to Bombay in 1686. As the town rapidly grew, its main island was fortified, and several iconic buildings were constructed within the fort. Mercantile communities were encouraged to settle in the town with assurances of religious freedom as well as the liberty to trade and build homes. The walled town soon became congested and overcrowded, encouraging development to take place outside the limits of the fort walls. Diverse communities became part of the developing town, giving Bombay its cosmopolitan and inclusive spirit. By the 1850s, Bombay's seven islands were linked with reclaimed causeways, transforming the town into an integrated land mass connected to the mainland.

At this point, Bombay was already distinct from other colonial or traditional urban settlements in India as its development was never planned. The opening of the Suez Canal in 1869 and the establishment of the Bombay Port Trust in 1873 revolutionized maritime trade giving momentum to Bombay's growth as a city. Government support and private enterprise worked in tandem to create the *Urbs Prima in Indis*—the first city of India.[4]

Figure 15.1: Victorian Gothic and Art Deco Ensembles of Mumbai, World Heritage Site. (Source: Abha Narain Lambah Associates.)

2. Sharada Dwivedi, Rahul Mehrotra, and Umaima Mulla-Feroze, *Bombay: The Cities Within* (Bombay: India Book House, 1995).
3. Dwivedi et al., *Bombay*, 11.
4. Dwivedi et al., *Bombay*, 13.

With the established supremacy of the British in Bombay, the fort walls had already been considered redundant and were torn down by 1867. The cleared land underwent coordinated development creating over time ensembles of Victorian Gothic and art deco architecture—a precinct that is recognized today as a World Heritage Site (Figure 15.1).

Unconscious Adaptive Reuse

As summarized by Dwivedi, Mehrotra, and Mulla-Feroze in *Bombay: The Cities Within*:

> Bombay was built by the British expressly for maintaining trade links with India and was perhaps never expected to become a large town. The city came into being with every step of its growth being impulsive and incremental. . . . Each new development in the city thus expressed in its physical form the needs and lifestyles of the people who created or occupied these areas. And so, Bombay grew precinct by precinct, becoming a collage, not only of varying architectural styles and different urban forms, but even more importantly of the many ethnic and social groups that colonised its growing localities.[5]

During this time of rapid—and spontaneous—growth, there were purpose-built structures as well as early examples of adaptive reuse. Both building stock and open spaces were being repurposed, although without conscious cultural intentions.

One example of early adaptive reuse is that of a large palatial building that stood along the then Apollo Street (present-day Shahid Bhagat Singh Road). Serving as the governor's residence, the functions of the building changed under colonial rule—Admiralty House, residence of the commander in chief of the Indian fleet (1764–1792); a part of the building was repurposed as office and records storage for the mayor's court (1786–1788); and courthouse functioning as the court of the first recorder of Bombay (1800–1878). During these many programmatic changes to the building over more than one hundred years, the only major change to its physical appearance was the removal of the original porch when the street was widened. In 1883, the building was leased and subsequently purchased by a private owner who converted the property to the Great Western Hotel adding three annexes to the main structure. While the internal layout was modified to accommodate the new use, the street-facing façade remained almost unchanged. After India's independence in 1947, the hotel ceased operations. Its rooms were divided (and further subdivided) and mezzanine levels were inserted into rooms with generous floor heights to exploit the rental potential of the property in its conversion into a housing scheme—the Great Western Building. Former common spaces, like the banquet hall and games room, were converted—without careful planning—into residential units. Today, the property is called the Great Western Co-operative Tenants Housing Society, with its subdivided units occupied by a mix of commercial and residential uses. In a recent government assessment report, the building's planning was recorded as "very random as the entire floor is divided into office and residential premises with no clear circulation space."[6] Walking through the Great Western Co-operative Tenants Housing Society today is like going through a labyrinth of spaces that are fragmented

5. Dwivedi et al., *Bombay*, 10.
6. Mumbai Metropolitan Region Heritage Conservation Society, "Great Western Building (Old Admiralty House)," *Mumbai Metropolitan Region Heritage Conservation Society, Information System*, accessed January 13, 2022, http://www.mmrhcs.org.in/index.php/heritage-information-system/information-system.

reminders of the building's many lives. Lacking still is a formal interpretation of its rich history and heritage significance.

Another case is the revitalization of Bombay Green, a landscaped circular open space fronting the Town Hall and a well-recognized social node during the colonial period. After the removal of the fort walls, the space degenerated into an unprotected area mainly used for storage of cotton bales, opium, and other merchandise.[7] Attempts were made to revitalize the green space by removal of the storage items and repurposing it for public recreational use; however, the area remained deserted and deteriorated into a refuse heap.[8] It was only in 1863 that the then–police commissioner, Charles Forjett, initiated the idea of converting Bombay Green into a circle that acts as a marker for the most prominent east-west axial roads within the walled city. With a vision of developing the area as the business core of Bombay, the circle was seen as urban street architecture. Renamed as the Elphinstone Circle (present-day Horniman Circle), a garden was laid out in the former dusty open space and an ornamental fountain was placed at the center. Surrounded by an assembly of architecturally unified commercial buildings, the revitalization of Elphinstone Circle was an outstanding example of urban design in the renovated Fort area.[9] Today, the circle remains a shaded green space in the bustling business district, and it is a common venue for cultural and social activities.

Although adaptive reuse took place during the colonial period, there was no regulatory framework to guide the standard of these interventions. Some sites emerged with renewed programs that enriched the urban quality of Bombay, while others succumbed to well-intentioned but detrimental changes. The revitalization of Elphinstone Circle was one of the earliest urban design schemes, anchoring the city's prominent east-west axis. On the other hand, valuable buildings, like the Great Western Co-operative Tenants Housing Society, although today formally recognized as heritage buildings, suffer from poor maintenance and are in derelict states.

While Bombay's early examples of adaptive reuse cannot be regarded as indicators of heritage conservation practice, at a national level, India already had conservation policies in place. However, the scope and extent of these national policies were insufficient to address the complexities of Bombay's built heritage.

Conscious Conservation: Early Beginnings

India's earliest heritage conservation-related agency is the Archaeological Survey of India (ASI). The office was first established in 1861 under the colonial government, with an aim to formally recognize and protect the vast number of Buddhist monuments and ancient relics across the country. Since then, it has evolved as India's national agency to conserve, manage, and protect monuments and archaeological sites and propose various principles of interventions within and around them.[10]

In postindependence India, ASI is an office under the Ministry of Culture. Under the provisions of the Ancient Monuments and Archaeological Sites and Remains Act (AMASR Act) of 1958, ASI administers more than 3,650 ancient monuments,

7. Dwivedi et al., *Bombay*, 93.
8. Dwivedi et al., *Bombay*, 95.
9. Dwivedi et al., *Bombay*, 100.
10. Archaeological Survey of India, *National Policy for Conservation of the Ancient Monuments, Archaeological Sites and Remains (NPC–AMASR)* (New Delhi: Archaeological Survey of India, Ministry of Culture, 2014), https://asi.nic.in/wp-content/uploads/2018/11/national-conservation-policy-final-April-2014.pdf.

archaeological sites, and remains that are recognized as "monuments of national importance."[11] The AMASR Act does not include unprotected built heritage.

ASI has set up "Circles" to break down the administration of these monuments and sites to smaller levels of jurisdictions. Most states have an ASI Circle, usually in the state capital, and named after the city in which the Circle is located. However, larger states often have two or three Circles that look after the protection of monuments and sites. At present, there are twenty-four Circles under ASI.[12]

Apart from ASI, archaeological work and conservation of monuments in India are also carried out in some states by the Archaeological Departments. Most of these bodies were set up by the various princely states before independence. With the restructuring of India after independence, the individual Archaeological Departments have continued to function autonomously under state-appointed Directorates of Archaeology and Museums.

In the case of Mumbai, there are only a handful of ASI-recognized "monuments of national importance" that lie within the city's boundaries. There are also some historical sites recognized and protected by the Directorate of Archaeology and Museums. However, most of Mumbai's heritage is comprised of places that feature in the daily lives of people and not monuments or archaeological remains, as defined by ASI. In the words of Abha Narain Lambah, one of the city's prominent conservation experts:

> In Mumbai, . . . a person gets down at CST [railway station], which is a heritage building. If you want to get married or go to school or college here in South Mumbai, it is a heritage building. For Mumbaikars, it is an intimate thing. In Delhi, heritage is equal to dead monument where security guard is shooing away people when the building is locked down. In Mumbai, heritage buildings are living breathing structures.[13]

Distinct from other cities in India, Mumbai's heritage is not a collection of obsolete buildings and structures; instead, it is places that feature in people's everyday lives. ASI's requirement that a monument must be at least one hundred years old to qualify for protection left most of Mumbai's colonial nineteenth- and early twentieth-century heritage without protection.

Mumbai's Heritage Regulations

From the start, Mumbai was ill-prepared for growth. As one historian has observed, "To bring order into [Mumbai] from the chaos in which it has been steeped, is indeed not an easy affair."[14] The first ten years after independence were challenging for the city with thousands of refugees seeking asylum in Mumbai after India's partition. It was also a period of reassessment and consolidation for the central and state governments, when planning directions were unclear and objectives were being defined

11. The AMASR Act was amended in 2010—Ancient Monuments and Archaeological Sites and Remains (Amendment and Validation) Act, 2010.
12. Archaeological Survey of India, "History, Archaeological Survey of India," accessed January 13, 2022, https://asi.nic.in/about-us/history/.
13. Pooja Pillai, "In Mumbai, Heritage Buildings Are Living, Breathing Structures: Abha Lambah," *Indian Express*, July 8, 2018, https://indianexpress.com/article/cities/mumbai/unesco-heritage-buildings-are-living-breathing-structures-abha-lambah-5251494/.
14. Mariam Dossal, "A Master Plan for the City: Looking at the Past," *Economic and Political Weekly* 40, no. 36 (2005): 3897–900, http://www.jstor.org/stable/4417098.

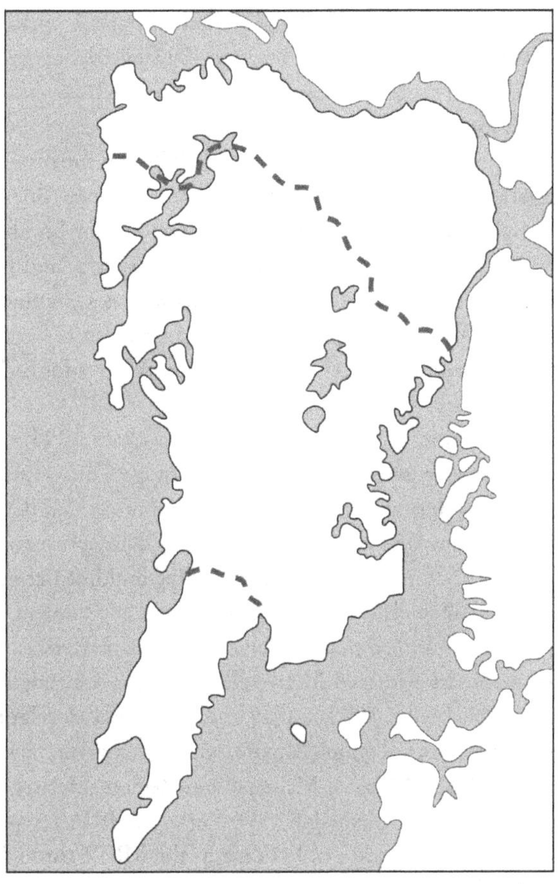

Figure 15.2: Map demarcating the boundaries of Bombay (south) and Greater Bombay (north). (Source: Drawn by Ng Wai Shing.)

and reoriented.[15] By 1950, the city's limits were extended to relieve congestion in the island city and address the needs of the fast-increasing population, thus stretching the city's boundary to what is called Greater Mumbai (formerly known as Greater Bombay) (Figure 15.2).

Housing became a key priority for Mumbai and every effort was made to tackle the problem. In the process, more and more heritage structures, including innumerable bungalows, were demolished to make way for multistoried housing. This loss reflected an unfortunate lack of awareness about the importance of conserving architecturally, historically, and socially relevant buildings and precincts.[16] Alarmed with the rapid depletion of the city's heritage, a group of concerned citizens, architects, historians, and nongovernmental organizations came together, considered the heritage significance of a number of buildings and precincts, and prepared a preliminary list (Heritage List for Greater Bombay) of those that needed to be conserved.[17]

The heritage list was reviewed by a committee of experts and presented to the minister for urban development under the state government of Maharashtra. Supporting the heritage list was a set of heritage regulations, and both were published by the state government in February 1991. At this stage, the government had not yet sanctioned the regulations or finalized the heritage list. The announcement

15. Sharada Dwivedi, "60 Years of Heritage," *Mumbai Reader, UDRI* (2010): 376–79, http://www.udri.org/portfolio-items/mumbai-reader-10/.
16. Dwivedi, "60 Years of Heritage."
17. Dwivedi, "60 Years of Heritage."

invited objections and suggestions for the proposed heritage regulations that sought to protect the city's "non-monumental" heritage. During the next four years, over nine hundred objections/suggestions were received and each one was heard.[18] After a series of modifications, in April 1995, the government sanctioned the amendment to the city's Development Control Regulations (DCR) by introducing Regulation 67, which legislated the Heritage Regulations for Greater Bombay (Heritage Regulations) as well as the updated Heritage List for Greater Bombay. The regulations recognized buildings, structures, fountains, open spaces, and precincts under three heritage categories—Grades I, II, and III—as well as separate recognition for Heritage Precincts.[19] The grading system was based on cultural heritage values and explicitly set out the appropriate interventions and procedures for each grade of heritage building and for heritage precincts.[20]

Following the sanction of the Heritage Regulations in 1995, the government laid down qualifications for membership of the Heritage Conservation Committee (present-day Mumbai Heritage Conservation Committee, MHCC) whose role was to advise the Bombay Municipal Corporation (BMC, present-day Municipal Corporation of Greater Mumbai [MCGM]) regarding building permissions for heritage buildings and precincts. BMC is the city's primary government body responsible for civic infrastructure and administration on heritage matters.

As Mumbai grew, the Mumbai Metropolitan Region Development Authority (MMRDA) was established in 1975 to plan and coordinate development activities in the Mumbai Metropolitan Region (MMR), which is governed by state administration (Figure 15.5).[21] The Mumbai Metropolitan Region–Heritage Conservation Society (MMR-HCS) was established in 1996 by the MMRDA to promote protection, preservation, and conservation of heritage in the MMR through research and demonstration-related activities.

Although Mumbai's heritage regulations were a first step for the city, they do not offer blanket protection to graded heritage buildings. Development permissions for changes to heritage within the municipal boundaries of Greater Mumbai are granted on the advice of the MHCC with the final decision resting with the municipal commissioner, while protected sites under the state's Archaeology Department are under direct control of the Directorate of Archaeology and Museums.

With its introduction of urban heritage regulations, Mumbai has become the pioneer city in India for such controls. It was also the first time that adaptive reuse was mentioned explicitly as an appropriate intervention for graded heritage buildings, both Grade II and Grade III, marking a milestone for conservation practice in Mumbai.

18. Shyam Chainani, "Heritage Legislation & Conservation: In Bombay and Elsewhere—An NGO Effort," *Mumbai Reader, UDRI* (2006): 65–67, http://www.udri.org/portfolio-items/mumbai-reader-06/.
19. Details for each category of heritage grading can be found at Town Country Planning Organization, Ministry of Urban Development, Government of India, *Model Heritage Regulations* (Mumbai: Town Country Planning Organization, 2011): 8–10, https://mmrhcs.org.in/images/documents/regulation_guidelines/Model_Heritage_Regulations.pdf.
20. The criteria for listing heritage buildings and precincts in Mumbai can be found at Town Country Planning Organization, *Model Heritage Regulations*, 6.
21. The MMR is spread over 6,328 square kilometers and consists of nine municipal corporations—Greater Mumbai, Thane, Kalyan-Dombivali, Navi Mumbai, Ulhasnagar, Bhiwandi- Nizamapur, Vasai-Virar, Mira-Bhayandar, and Panvel.

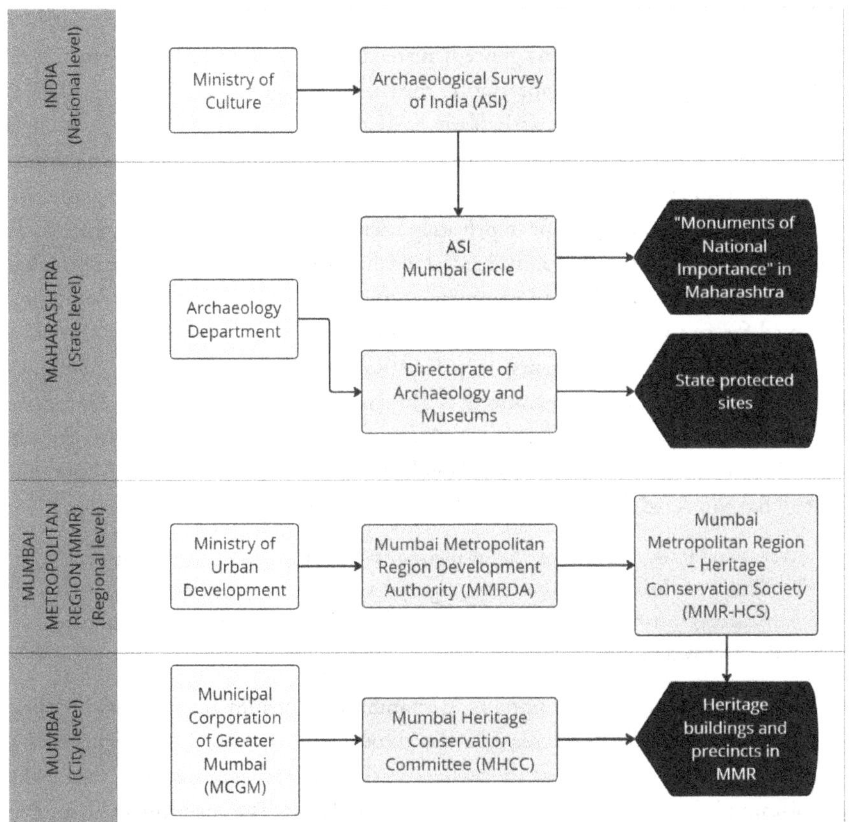

Figure 15.3: Organization of heritage management agencies in India from the national level to the city level. (Source: Drawn by Lavina Ahuja.)

The Reality of Mumbai's Heritage: Adaptive Reuse Takes the Back Seat

Mumbai's heritage conservation movement could thrive, but there are several factors limiting its potential. This section discusses some challenges and limitations that impact decision-making regarding the city's urban heritage.

Rent Control Act and Multiple Tenancies

Mumbai's historic buildings have been, and continue to be, affected by the complex conditions of multiple tenancies. The freezing of rents through the Bombay Rent, Hotel and Lodging House Rates Control Act, 1947 (Rent Control Act) have left rental rates absurdly low against market rates. This has led to disinterest among landlords to maintain their properties. As a result, building stock has deteriorated significantly. Tenants occupying these premises either do not have the capacity to maintain the buildings or are disinterested in maintaining a rental property. There is also thriving black market activity as residential units are sublet for commercial uses resulting in the unauthorized mixed use of properties. To optimize rental potential, buildings are subject to balcony enclosures, virtual stripping of exterior detail, loss of roof embellishments, and often total masking by billboards.[22]

22. William R. Chapman and Robertson E. Collins, *Urban Conservation in Bombay and Pune* (Washington, DC: International Council on Monuments and Sites and United States Information Agency, 1992), http://openarchive.icomos.org/id/eprint/1822/1/urban%20conservation%20in%20Bombay%20and%20pune.pdf.

Prime opportunities for the appropriate adaptive reuse of existing significant historical buildings have been ignored; instead, these buildings have been left to deteriorate with little or no appreciation for their heritage values. A case in point is Watson's Hotel (today known as Esplanade Mansion). Built in 1869, the building is arguably the oldest surviving prefabricated cast-iron building in India. It functioned as one of Bombay's most opulent hotels until the 1960s when it ceased operations. Falling to a similar fate as most privately owned historical buildings, the hotel's original 150 rooms were randomly subdivided and partitioned into smaller units that were let out for residential and commercial uses. The balconies were enclosed and occupied for commercial office uses. Falling under the Rent Control Act, the units were leased out for nominal rents, as little as Rs.60 per month (in 2017), encouraging tenants to remain for generations.[23] The landlord was left with little incentive to invest in the building's maintenance. A prominent Mumbai conservation expert, Abha Narain Lambah, considers Esplanade Mansion a textbook case of how rent control has impacted several historical buildings in the city:

> Watson's Hotel exemplifies the challenges faced by privately owned heritage buildings. . . . It is among the last vestiges of a specific construction period, of a particular genre of architecture, yet it is faced with the problem of under-funding and overcrowding. [24]

Today, the once glorious hotel is in shambles, its atrium scattered with debris and garbage. The property was sealed under a court order in May 2019 (Figure 15.4). Given the precarious nature of the structure, the tenants were asked to vacate the premises, and since then, the building remains abandoned. The government's Mumbai Metropolitan Region-Heritage Conservation Society (MMR-HCS), in commenting on the situation, asked two questions: "What does the state get in return? Why would it spend money on a building that is under private ownership, and even if it did, what is the assurance that the building will be looked after by the owners in later years?"[25]

Lack of Incentive through Regulation

The Maharashtra Region and Town Planning Act specifies that every municipal corporation must prepare a development plan to be implemented over twenty years. The first Development Plan (DP) of Mumbai was prepared by the Bombay Municipal Corporation (BMC) in 1964 (sanctioned in parts between 1965 and 1967). The primary focus of this DP was on (i) providing various amenities in line with a land use plan, (ii) shifting development to the near suburbs, and (iii) restricting operations of industries and trade as well as controlling population concentration in the island city. This plan met with some inevitable failures—to comply with timelines, to expand/improve the existing infrastructure, and to develop amenities proposed in the plan, among others.[26] The DP was supported by set building regulations and bylaws to implement the plan called the Development Control Regulations (DCR). However, the DCR only stipulated what was permissible; it did not provide guidelines for any

23. Suryasarathi Bhattacharya, "Esplanade Mansion: As 155-Year-Old Mumbai Landmark Faces Its End, a Look at Its Past, Present and Future," *Firstpost*, July 11, 2019, https://www.firstpost.com/long-reads/esplanade-mansion-as-155-year-old-mumbai-landmark-faces-its-end-a-look-at-its-past-present-and-future-6968751.html.
24. Bhattacharya, "Esplanade Mansion."
25. Bhattacharya, "Esplanade Mansion."
26. Rupali Ghate, "Development Plans for Mumbai," in *Urban Development Blueprint*, December 2, 2011, http://mnsblueprint.org/pdf/Development%20plans%20for%20Mumbai.pdf.

Figure 15.4: Exterior view of Watson's Hotel in its current state. (Source: Nitesh Jain.)

design controls. Owners and developers began exploiting the loopholes in the DCR resulting in increased threats to the city's heritage.

In some instances, adaptive reuse won the battle over demolition but failed to safeguard the spirit of the place. This is the case of Buckley Court located in Colaba, South Mumbai. A former hotel, the building was proposed for demolition, with the owner claiming it was ready to collapse. After negotiations with the Mumbai Heritage Conservation Committee (MHCC), the developers were given approval to construct a high-rise residential building as an addition to the small-scale heritage structure. As a "compromise," the new residential tower was designed with a huge open arch on its lower floors, intended to provide "separation" from the heritage structure (Figure 15.5). The private residential use also made the heritage building inaccessible to the public, leaving its internal attributes indeterminable. What could have been an opportunity to adapt a heritage building and convey its cultural significance turned into a project where a small-scale heritage structure was overwhelmed by an overdesigned residential tower.[27] This outcome was possible because of a loophole in the then-relevant DCR, which had no height regulations.

In 1999, an amendment to DCR Section 33(7) aimed at addressing the issue of historical buildings under the Rent Control Act. The amendment removed nearly three hundred Grade III buildings and precincts from the protective ambit of the Heritage Regulations.[28] Such buildings could now be demolished without clearance from the Mumbai Heritage Conservation Committee (MHCC), threatening the survival of historic areas of almost 41 percent of Mumbai's heritage building stock, which is under private ownership and falls within the Grade III category.[29]

This reflects the challenge of nonsupportive legislation. While Mumbai has well-structured heritage regulations, there continues to be a lack of economic incentives

27. Rahul Bhatia, "Deconstructing Hafeez Contractor," *Open*, November 5, 2009, https://openthemagazine.com/features/living/deconstructing-hafeez-contractor/.
28. Abha Narain Lambah, "Historic Preservation by Citizens," in *Cities, Cultural Policy and Governance*, ed. Helmut K. Anheier and Yudhishthir Raj Isar (London: Sage, 2017), 251–56, https://sk.sagepub.com/books/cultures-and-globalization/n25.xml.
29. Lambah, "Historic Preservation by Citizens."

Figure 15.5: Exterior view of Buckley Court, where the small-scale heritage structure is seemingly shrouded by the newly added residential tower. (Source: Nitesh Jain.)

for heritage property owners. "Heritage listing protects listed buildings from demolition, but it cannot prevent a building from ruination through sheer neglect, if not willful destruction. The Heritage Regulation acknowledges and protects the vernacular built heritage and private buildings, but there are no economic policies to support heritage, nor any fiscal incentives to help private owners restore and maintain their heritage properties."[30] This insufficiency of policy-level support leads to heritage being perceived as a burden and limitation instead of an asset and resource. The very authorities that had legislated and promoted heritage regulations developed an attitude bordering on contempt toward heritage.[31] Although Mumbai was the first city in India to implement heritage regulations, this lack of incentive has diluted the significance of heritage amid ambitious development agendas. The last development plan for Mumbai was prepared in 1981 and was adopted only thirteen years later in 1994. Development Control and Promotional Regulations (DCPR 2034), which is a new plan valid for twenty years, has been in use since 2014 and will be in force until 2034. Although this plan invited public consultation, heritage is undervalued and development is encouraged (e.g., Mumbai's World Heritage Sites and buffer zones are not defined or marked in this plan).[32]

Pressure to Provide Affordable Housing

As noted previously, in postindependence Mumbai, mass migration led to immense pressure on the city's supply of affordable housing. At the same time and for a variety

30. Lambah, "Historic Preservation by Citizens."
31. Dwivedi, "60 Years of Heritage."
32. The shortcomings of DCPR 2034 are discussed in detail at "Development Plan 2034," UDRI, accessed May 18, 2022, http://www.udri.org/projects/mumbaidp24seven/.

of reasons, the upkeep of existing building stock became difficult. To address the deteriorating condition of historical building stock, particularly those under the Rent Control Act, the government first introduced the Bombay Building Repairs and Reconstruction Act in 1969. This act proposed to collect a "repair cess" from tenants to undertake maintenance and structural repairs of historic buildings. Unfortunately, the Mumbai Building Repair and Reconstruction Board (previously known as the Bombay Building Repair and Reconstruction Board) repaired many heritage buildings without regard for their heritage attributes, thus destroying their inherent character. Eventually, this policy failed as demand outstripped the capacity of the board to repair and reconstruct. This government initiative was replaced by one that granted developers a transferable incentive Floor Space Index (FSI) of approximately 50 percent, as set out in the amended DCR Section 33(7) of Mumbai. This allowed private developers to sell the incentive FSI in the open market and enabled them to use the returns to finance the cost of repairs and reconstruction. Surplus gains from these transactions would be the developer's profit. In the case of heritage buildings, this further discouraged owners from conserving their properties as they succumbed to the builders' incentive to redevelop properties, which promised the owners/tenants handsome compensations or updated facilities and better living environments.

This strategy of urban renewal led to several piecemeal developments within Mumbai's inner-city precincts without any consideration of public amenities or infrastructural improvements, which were already inadequate. The case of Bhendi Bazaar, a historical inner-city precinct in Mumbai, illustrates well the outcome of such policies. The redevelopment project aimed to transform the historical precinct of timeworn buildings and its close-knit community into a low-cost, green-housing haven of skyscrapers.[33] However, the project has its shortcomings. Conservation expert Vikas Dilawari has commented,

> The redevelopment will disrupt the existing cultural mosaic of south Mumbai. From Crawford Market to Byculla, there is a natural fabric of the city that has already been laid out. Bhendi Bazaar is right in the middle of it. . . . The project will disrupt the long, linear stretches that make up the city, break up arterial roads and, in doing so, change everything.[34]

This reinforces the challenge to conserve the historical grain of the city and provide affordable housing in established areas with heritage building stock.

Standard of Conservation Practice

Conservation initiatives in Mumbai, especially those driven by the government and some private projects, are often "beautification driven," where the overall appearance of the main façade is given importance rather than adopting an approach that safeguards the authenticity and spirit of the place. It is common to see heritage fabric overly painted with so-called breathable paints or overlit with jarring LED lights, compromising the character-defining attributes of the place.

In the case of adaptive reuse, the common practice is to simply "reuse" existing buildings without much thought given to the impact of the new use on the place and neighborhood. Heritage buildings continue to be ruthlessly subdivided to generate maximum rental potential, even at the price of compromising their heritage values

33. Labonita Ghosh, "Oasis in the Bazaar," *Economic Times*, July 17, 2012, https://www.sbut.com/Media/Pdf/Economic%20Times%2017th%20JULY%202012.pdf.
34. Ghosh, "Oasis in the Bazaar."

and character-defining attributes. Often the choice of new use, or choice of tenant, fails to fill the gaps of societal needs and does not integrate well with the neighborhood. Such development for the "greed and not the need" is what continues to threaten the city's historical fabric.[35]

Mumbai's approach toward its heritage raises several concerns. Most of the city is under tremendous pressure due to urban transformation, with modern skyscrapers threatening to engulf, if not eradicate, entire precincts of fragile historical fabric.[36] All these challenges have resulted in a reconstruction cycle in Mumbai, where an increasing number of heritage places are being redeveloped, thus shrinking the city's already limited heritage assets (currently at 7.5 percent of the existing building stock).[37] Mumbai needs to step away from the *tabula rasa* approach and pivot toward appreciating the value of revitalizing its heritage assets.

Promise for Adaptive Reuse: Celebrating a Civic Effort

In 2003, a Vision Mumbai report prepared by McKinsey clearly outlined a set of recommendations to address Mumbai's rapidly declining economic growth and quality of life.[38] Among the recommendations, the report specifically mentioned leveraging heritage, such as restoring the Fort precinct, to improve the status of Mumbai. It also cited the need to address issues of affordable housing but highlighted that heritage should be excluded from the development process. Vision Mumbai was intended to be a ten-year plan, but as with other plans, it has yet to be implemented to any extent.

While the city's officials are focused on development plans and reports that collect dust, Mumbai has an armed force of concerned citizens who are the true drivers of change. They are taking ownership of their heritage and taking appropriate action to recognize, protect, and conserve Mumbai's urban heritage. The examples below signal a gathering momentum for protecting, conserving, and appropriately using—and reusing—Mumbai's distinctive "everyday" architecture.

The Kala Ghoda Association was formed in 1998 with the aim of maintaining and preserving the heritage of the Kala Ghoda area, South Mumbai's beloved art district. One of their most noteworthy initiatives is the annual Kala Ghoda Arts Festival. Since 1999, this arts festival allows for precinct-wide adaptive reuse of Kala Ghoda as a venue for visual arts, dance, music, theater, cinema, literature, workshops, heritage walks, and so forth. In recent years, the festival has expanded beyond the Kala Ghoda crescent, with events being held in neighboring open spaces, such as Horniman Circle. With the aim of promoting arts, crafts, and cultural heritage in the precinct, all funds raised from the festival every year are directed toward the restoration efforts undertaken by the Kala Ghoda Association in the precinct.

In 2004, a group of eminent citizens and artists formed the Friends of J. J. School of Art Trust, a civic initiative to help revive and restore the J. J. School of Arts and conserve its historical building. The project involved fundraising from both public and private sectors. This initiative provided funds for a standard-setting restoration of the school building, a task the government did not have the capacity to undertake. The project drew attention to the heritage significance of the school campus, eventually

35. Vikas Dilawari, "Conservation of the Heritage Grain of the City—Challenges and Opportunities" (talk, Museum Society of Mumbai, May 21, 2022), https://www.youtube.com/watch?v=dm8u9pd_TCM.
36. Lambah, "Historic Preservation by Citizens."
37. Dilawari, "Conservation of the Heritage Grain of the City."
38. McKinsey, *Vision Mumbai: Transforming Mumbai into a World-Class City* (Mumbai: Bombay First and McKinsey, September 2003), https://mumbaifirst.org/wp-content/uploads/2020/11/McKinsey-Report-on-Vision-Mumbai.pdf.

Figure 15.6: Exterior view of Kipling House in the Sir J. J. School of Arts. (Source: Sankraman Design Studio.)

leading to the government-initiated adaptive reuse of Kipling House (Figure 15.6), better known as the Dean's Bungalow, as an open-air cafeteria for the campus as well as an art store and exhibition and studio space for artists.[39]

The Urban Design Research Institute (UDRI), a public charitable trust dedicated to protecting the built environment and improving urban communities, was set up in 1984 by a group of concerned citizens. It is one of the key drivers for heritage matters in Mumbai, and it is actively involved in concerns of urban planning and policy as well as urban design and heritage conservation. UDRI, in collaboration with a number of nongovernmental and citizens groups, as part of the Federation of Residents Trust (FORT), was involved in the collective effort to nominate Mumbai's Victorian Gothic and Art Deco Ensembles for inscription as a UNESCO World Heritage Site (Figure 15.1). The nomination was successful, and the ensembles were inscribed on the World Heritage List in 2018. This is the first such nomination dossier from India that was drafted by citizen groups and civil society organizations.

Projects emerging from public-private partnership have proven to be immensely beneficial to the conservation movement in Mumbai. Examples include the revitalization of Mumbai's public amenities, especially its historical fountains. Scattered around Mumbai's Fort area, most of these fountains were subject to unsympathetic renovations or left in states of neglect and deterioration. Through partnerships between the government and private sector, most of these historical fountains have been restored. The conservation of Flora Fountain (further elaborated in the case study section of this book) not only restored the historical fountain to a working condition but also revitalized its surrounding area to revive it as a public meeting space. A collaboration between the Municipal Corporation of Greater Mumbai (MCGM) and the Indian National Trust for Art and Cultural Heritage (INTACH), the project was a pioneering example reinforcing the impact of thoughtful partnerships and was recognized

39. Kipling House has undergone restoration; however, operations of the new use did not commence due to management issues.

regionally for its success in "continuing [Flora Fountain's] role in the life of the community and its prominent place in the urban fabric of Mumbai."[40]

A handful of heritage places under private ownership have been conserved under the sole initiative of the owner. With generous private patronage, the Royal Opera House (further elaborated in the case study section of this book) was rescued from near collapse and revitalized from its most-recent use as a cinema to its original splendor as an opera house. The project not only revived a beloved cultural landmark of the city, but it also safeguarded the spirit of place of India's only surviving opera house.[41] Another example—and one that demonstrates economic viability of heritage through adaptive reuse—is the project of the Commissariat Building (built in 1925) located on D. N. Road, Fort, Mumbai. An architecturally prominent structure, the building was served a notice of being unsafe by the municipal corporation. As such, it could have been easily demolished and redeveloped despite being a Grade II heritage building. On the owner's initiative, the building was conserved to its original historical character. Using the conservation approach of minimal intervention, the building was structurally strengthened, and its character-defining attributes were restored. As an outcome, the narrow and dingy subdivided commercial spaces, which were also potential fire hazards, were transformed into beautiful large spaces that had potential for adaptive reuse and could attract higher market value from tenants (Figure 15.7).[42]

Although Mumbai can boast of excellent conservation projects, including those involving adaptive reuse—and largely carried out by individuals and nongovernmental groups, it is now time to join the dots. The various bottom-up efforts have garnered government attention, encouraging improved standards in heritage conservation practice. Recent governmental efforts are seen where community is put at the heart of the project (as in the case of Godhbunder Fort, further elaborated in the

Figure 15.7: The large rentable space in the Commissariat Building that is available for adaptive reuse. (Source: Vikas Dilawari.)

40. UNESCO, *Asia Conserved Volume IV: Lessons Learned from the UNESCO Asia-Pacific Awards for Cultural Heritage Conservation (2015–2019)* (Bangkok: UNESCO and SEU Press, 2020), 350–53.
41. UNESCO, *Asia Conserved Volume IV*, 184–87.
42. Dilawari, "Conservation of the Heritage Grain of the City."

case study section of this book) and technical standards of conservation works are aligning to international standards of best practice.

Future of Conservation and Adaptive Reuse

Mumbai is dynamic, distinct, and full of life, but it is not without its problems. The main one is, no one knows who is in charge of Mumbai! As summarized in a study by the Urban Design Research Institute (UDRI),

> Cities all over the world are run by elected officials, but in Mumbai the administrative power rests with the Municipal Commissioner who is appointed by the Chief Minister of the State. Thus, in effect, the State, through its Urban Development Department, governs Mumbai, when in fact, such a large and densely populated city requires bottom-up planning emerging at the ward level. Furthermore, the multiplicity of government agencies such as MMRDA, MHADA [Maharashtra Housing and Area Development], MIDC [Maharashtra Industrial Development Corporation], SRA [Slum Rehabilitation Authority] and Public Works Department responsible for managing different urban issues in the same area, without an overarching authority or a coordinated approach, is creating fractured governance.[43]

Mumbai's conservation movement faces complex challenges and countless roadblocks. Yet the city is in a position to save itself, provided it has the right means and necessary political commitment. The major concern is that the relationship between sustainability, especially economic sustainability, and conservation is inadequately recognized. Local and regional examples show that heritage places can sustain themselves, and even thrive, when revitalized with appropriate new uses. Adaptive reuse serves as a viable conservation strategy to not only safeguard heritage resources but also leverage them for sustainable development.

Today, heritage conservation practice has broadened beyond simply safeguarding physical assets but as a means to meet targets and indicators of the Sustainable Development Goals (SDGs). To keep up with this broadening scope of practice, Mumbai must invest in support and capacity building for its heritage practitioners, thereby increasing its sensitivity toward recognizing heritage as driver for sustainable development.

Bibliography

Adarkar, Neera, and Vidyadhar K. Pathak. "Recycling Mill Land: Tumultuous Experience of Mumbai." *Economic and Political Weekly* 40, no. 51 (2005): 5365–68. https://www.jstor.org/stable/4417541?seq=1#metadata_info_tab_contents.

Archaeological Survey of India. "History, Archaeological Survey of India." Accessed January 13, 2022. https://asi.nic.in/about-us/history/.

Archaeological Survey of India. *National Policy for Conservation of the Ancient Monuments, Archaeological Sites and Remains (NPC-AMASR)*. New Delhi: Archaeological Survey of India, Ministry of Culture, 2014. https://asi.nic.in/wp-content/uploads/2018/11/national-conservation-policy-final-April-2014.pdf.

Bhatia, Rahul. "Deconstructing Hafeez Contractor." *Open*, November 5, 2009. https://openthemagazine.com/features/living/deconstructing-hafeez-contractor/.

Bhattacharya, Suryasarathi. "Esplanade Mansion: As 155-Year-Old Mumbai Landmark

43. Urban Design Research Institute, *Mumbai 7 Islands Facts Myths Solutions* (Mumbai: UDRI, 2017), http://www.udri.org/wp-content/uploads/2017/11/171101-7-Islands.pdf.

Faces Its End, a Look at Its Past, Present and Future." *Firstpost*, July 11, 2019. https://www.firstpost.com/long-reads/esplanade-mansion-as-155-year-old-mumbai-landmark-faces-its-end-a-look-at-its-past-present-and-future-6968751.html.

Central Public Works Department. *Conservation of Heritage Buildings—A Guide*. New Delhi: Central Public Works Department, July 2013. http://mmrhcs.org.in/images/documents/regulation_guidelines/ConservationHertBuildings.pdf.

Chainani Shyam. "Heritage Legislation & Conservation: In Bombay and Elsewhere—An NGO Effort." *Mumbai Reader, UDRI*, no. 6 (2006): 65–67. http://www.udri.org/portfolio-items/mumbai-reader-06/.

Chapman, William R., and Robertson E. Collins. *Urban Conservation in Bombay and Pune*. Washington, DC: International Council on Monuments and Sites and United States Information Agency, 1992. http://openarchive.icomos.org/id/eprint/1822/1/urban%20conservation%20in%20Bombay%20and%20pune.pdf.

Dilawari, Vikas. "Conservation of the Heritage Grain of the City—Challenges and Opportunities." Talk, Museum Society of Mumbai, May 21, 2022. https://www.youtube.com/watch?v=dm8u9pd_TCM.

Dilawari, Vikas. *Flora Fountain (Submission Dossier for the UNESCO Asia-Pacific Awards for Cultural Heritage Conservation)*. Paris: UNESCO, 2019.

Dossal, Mariam. "A Master Plan for the City: Looking at the Past." *Economic and Political Weekly* 40, no. 36 (2005): 3897–900. http://www.jstor.org/stable/4417098.

Dwivedi, Sharada. "60 Years of Heritage." *Mumbai Reader, UDRI* (2010): 376–79. http://www.udri.org/portfolio-items/mumbai-reader-10/.

Dwivedi, Sharada, Rahul Mehrotra, and Umaima Mulla-Feroze. *Bombay: The Cities Within*. Bombay: India Book House, 1995.

Ghate, Rupali. "Development Plans for Mumbai." *Urban Development Blueprint*, December 2, 2011. http://mnsblueprint.org/pdf/Development%20plans%20for%20Mumbai.pdf.

Ghosh, Labonita. "Oasis in the Bazaar." *Economic Times*, July 17, 2012. https://www.sbut.com/Media/Pdf/Economic%20Times%2017th%20JULY%202012.pdf.

Kala Ghoda Association. "About Us." Accessed January 13, 2022. https://kalaghodaassociation.com/about-us/.

Lambah, Abha Narain. "Historic Preservation by Citizens." In *Cities, Cultural Policy and Governance*, edited by Helmut K. Anheier and Yudhishthir Raj Isar, 251–56. London: Sage, 2017. https://sk.sagepub.com/books/cultures-and-globalization/n25.xml.

McKinsey. *Vision Mumbai: Transforming Mumbai into a World-Class City*. Mumbai: Bombay First and McKinsey, September 2003. https://mumbaifirst.org/wp-content/uploads/2020/11/McKinsey-Report-on-Vision-Mumbai.pdf.

Mumbai Metropolitan Region Heritage Conservation Society. "Buckley Court." *Mumbai Metropolitan Region Heritage Conservation Society, Information System*. Accessed January 13, 2022. http://www.mmrhcs.org.in/index.php/heritage-information-system/information-system.

Mumbai Metropolitan Region Heritage Conservation Society. "Great Western Building (Old Admiralty House)." *Mumbai Metropolitan Region Heritage Conservation Society, Information System*. Accessed January 13, 2022. http://www.mmrhcs.org.in/index.php/heritage-information-system/information-system.

Nambiar, Sridevi. "A Brief History of How Bombay Became Mumbai." *Culture Trip*, September 19, 2016. Accessed January 13, 2022. https://theculturetrip.com/asia/india/articles/the-history-of-how-bombay-became-mumbai-in-1-minute/.

Pillai, Pooja. "In Mumbai, Heritage Buildings Are Living, Breathing Structures: Abha Lambah." *Indian Express*, July 8, 2018. https://indianexpress.com/article/cities/mumbai/unesco-heritage-buildings-are-living-breathing-structures-abha-lambah-5251494/.

Sunavala, Nergish. "Plea against 'Botched' Restoration at CSMT." *Times of India*, February 26, 2019. http://timesofindia.indiatimes.com/articleshow/68160887.cms?utm_source=contentofinterest&utm_medium=text&utm_campaign=cppst.

UNESCO. *Asia Conserved Volume I: Lessons Learned from the UNESCO Asia-Pacific Awards for Cultural Heritage Conservation (2000–2004)*. Edited by Montira Unakul. Bangkok: UNESCO, 2007.

UNESCO. *Asia Conserved Volume IV: Lessons Learned from the UNESCO Asia-Pacific Awards for Cultural Heritage Conservation (2015–2019)*. Edited by William Chapman. Bangkok: UNESCO and SEU Press, 2020.

UNESCO World Heritage Centre. "Chhatrapati Shivaji Terminus (formerly Victoria Terminus)." Accessed May 18, 2022. https://whc.unesco.org/en/list/945/.

Urban Design Research Institute. "Development Plan 2034." Accessed May 18, 2022. http://www.udri.org/projects/mumbaidp24seven/.

Urban Design Research Institute. *Mumbai 7 Islands Facts Myths Solutions*. Mumbai: UDRI, 2017. http://www.udri.org/wp-content/uploads/2017/11/171101-7-Islands.pdf.

Mumbai Timeline

Lavina Ahuja and Lynne D. DiStefano

This timeline summarizes key events from the essay, "Built Heritage Conservation and Adaptive Reuse in Mumbai: Challenges and Opportunities." It sets out Mumbai's major conservation-related entities, initiatives, legislations, and milestones from 1661 to 2022, including entries for the five Mumbai case studies outlined in this publication.

Dwivedi and Mehrotra's *Bombay, The Cities Within* presents a detailed historical record of the city including a comprehensive timeline. Relevant entries are extracted from this timeline to emphasize the factors influencing the adaptive reuse journey of the city.

In this timeline, the historical records of the city are presented using the name "Bombay," and the post-1995 records are presented using the name "Mumbai."

1500s–1661	Bombay is an archipelago of seven islands under Portuguese rule.
1661	Marriage treaty of Charles II of England and Catherine of Braganza of Portugal gives the Portuguese territory of "Bom Bahia" (Bombay) to the British Empire.
1668	The Crown leases Bombay to the British East India Company.
1686	British East India Company transfers its seat of governance and its maritime activities from nearby Surat to Bombay.
1715	Bombay's walled town is created.
1850s	Reclamation of causeways between Bombay's seven islands is complete, resulting in an integrated landmass connected to the mainland.
1854	Bombay's first cotton spinning mill, Bombay Spinning & Weaving Company, is established.
1857	Sir J. J. School of Art opens as an educational institution for art and architecture.
1858	British East India Company leaves, returning Bombay to direct rule under the British Crown.
1861	Archaeological Survey of India (ASI), India's earliest heritage conservation–related agency, is established.
1862	Governor Sir Bartle Frere orders demolition of fortifications.
1869	Suez Canal opens, revolutionizing maritime trade for India.

1872	Bombay Municipal Corporation (BMC) is established as the city's primary government body responsible for civic infrastructure and administration (later renamed the Municipal Corporation Greater Mumbai [MCGM]).
1873	Bombay Port Trust is established for administering the affairs of the city's port.
1898 (November)	Bombay City Improvement Trust (BIT) (later renamed City Improvement Trust [CIT]) is created in response to the Bombay's plague epidemic of 1896. The BMC hands over all vacant lands to BIT.
1933	CIT merges with the BMC.
1947 (August 15)	India gains independence from the British.
1947	Bombay Rents, Hotel and Lodging House Rates Control Act is promulgated.
1948	Master Plan for Greater Bombay is prepared by Modak and Mayer to address issues of housing and infrastructure but with no mention of heritage.
1950 (January 26)	Constitution of India comes into effect, replacing the Government of India Act (1935) as the governing document of India, turning the nation into a newly formed republic.
1950 (April)	Bombay city's limits are extended to merge the island city with the suburb, creating Greater Bombay (later renamed Greater Mumbai).
1958	Ancient Monuments and Archaeological Sites and Remains (AMASR) Act The act administers ancient monuments, archaeological sites, and remains that are recognized as "monuments of national importance."
1960 (May 1)	Bombay becomes the capital of newly formed state of Maharashtra.
1964	First Development Plan for Bombay is prepared by the BMC and is sanctioned in parts between 1965 and 1967.
1967	Mumbai Metropolitan Region (MMR) is delineated.
1969	Bombay Building Repairs and Reconstruction Act The act is promulgated to collect a repair cess (tax) from old dilapidated tenanted buildings ("cessed buildings").
1971	Under the provisions of the Bombay Building Repairs and Reconstruction Act, the Bombay Building Repairs and Reconstruction Board is formed.
1975 (March)	Mumbai Metropolitan Region Development Authority (MMRDA) is set up under the Mumbai Metropolitan Region Development Authority Act of 1974 as the primary agency for planning and coordinating development activities in the MMR.
1984	The Urban Design Research Institute (UDRI), a public charitable trust, is set up by a group of concerned citizens dedicated to the protection of the built environment and improving urban communities.
1984	The Indian National Trust for Art and Cultural Heritage (INTACH) is founded in New Delhi with the vision of spearheading heritage awareness and conservation in India.
1990 (August)	Mumbai Heritage Conservation Committee (MHCC) is constituted.
1990 (September 5)	First heritage list for Greater Bombay is submitted.
1991 (February 20)	Government of Maharashtra publishes the draft Bombay Heritage Regulations and Heritage List for Greater Bombay to invite suggestions.

1994	Development Plan for Mumbai (prepared in 1981) is adopted and is valid for twenty years.
1995	Bombay is renamed Mumbai.
1995 (April 21)	Government sanctions the Development Control Regulation No. 67—Heritage Regulations for Greater Mumbai (previously known as Heritage Regulations for Greater Bombay).
1995 (April 24)	Government sanctions the Heritage List for Greater Mumbai (previously known as Heritage List for Greater Bombay).
1996	Mumbai Metropolitan Region–Heritage Conservation Society (MMR-HCS) is established to promote protection, preservation, and conservation of heritage in the MMR through research and demonstration related activities.
1998	Kala Ghoda Association is formed with the aim of maintaining and preserving the heritage of the Kala Ghoda area, South Mumbai's beloved art district.
1999	Development Control Regulation 33(7) is amended to address the issue of historical buildings under the Rent Control Act. The amendment removes nearly 300 Grade III buildings and precincts from the protective ambit of the Heritage Regulations of Greater Mumbai.
2000	DBS House, the adaptive reuse of a former Jewish residence, opens as a coworking business center. (This is one of the five Mumbai case studies included in this book.)
2003 (September)	*Vision Mumbai: Transforming Mumbai into a World-Class City* report is prepared by McKinsey and submitted to the government of Maharashtra.
2004	Friends of J. J. School of Art Trust is formed by a group of eminent citizens and artists as a civic initiative to help revive and restore the Sir J. J. School of Art and conserve its historical building.
2004	Chhatrapati Shivaji Terminus (CST, formerly Victoria Terminus) inscribed on the World Heritage List.
2007	Maharashtra Vaibhav-State Protected Monuments Adoption Scheme (Monument Adoption Scheme) is announced.
2011	Government (MCGM) releases working papers on preparation of base map and GIS data for the Mumbai Development Plan (DP) (later known as the Development Control and Promotional Regulations 2034 [DCPR 2034]), inviting public feedback on the proposed plan.
2014	DP for 2014–2034 is in force until 2034.
2016 (March)	R and R, revitalization of a dilapidated multifunctional shed, opens as a multifunctional community space and library. (This is one of the five Mumbai case studies included in this book.)
2017	Royal Opera House, revitalization of a former cinema hall, reopens as an opera house and performance theater. (This is one of the five Mumbai case studies included in this book.)
2018	Victorian Gothic and Art Deco Ensembles of Mumbai is inscribed on the World Heritage List.
2019 (April)	Flora Fountain, revitalization of a historical fountain and its surrounding open space, opens as a public plaza. (This is one of the five Mumbai case studies included in this book.)
2022	Ghodbunder Fort (phases 1 and 2), restoration of a historical fort and revitalization of its associated open space, is complete for use by the local community. (This is one of the five Mumbai case studies included in this book.)

Bibliography

Dwivedi, Sharada. "60 Years of Heritage." *Mumbai Reader, UDRI* (2010): 376–79. http://www.udri.org/portfolio-items/mumbai-reader-10/.

Dwivedi, Sharada, Rahul Mehrotra, and Umaima Mulla-Feroze. *Bombay: The Cities Within*. Bombay: India Book House, 1995.

Lambah, Abha Narain. "Historic Preservation by Citizens." In *Cities, Cultural Policy and Governance*, edited by Helmut K. Anheier and Yudhishthir Raj Isar. London: Sage, 2017. https://sk.sagepub.com/books/cultures-and-globalization/n25.xml.

McKinsey. *Vision Mumbai: Transforming Mumbai into a World-Class City*. Mumbai: Bombay First and McKinsey, September 2003. https://mumbaifirst.org/wp-content/uploads/2020/11/McKinsey-Report-on-Vision-Mumbai.pdf.

Nambiar, Sridevi. "A Brief History of How Bombay Became Mumbai." *The Culture Trip*, September 19, 2016. https://theculturetrip.com/asia/india/articles/the-history-of-how-bombay-became-mumbai-in-1-minute/.

Urban Design Research Institute (UDRI). "Development Plan 2034." Accessed May 18, 2022. http://www.udri.org/projects/mumbaidp24seven/.

Urban Design Research Institute (UDRI). *Mumbai 7 Islands Facts Myths Solutions*. Mumbai: UDRI, 2017. http://www.udri.org/wp-content/uploads/2017/11/171101-7-Islands.pdf.

Mumbai Case Studies

Project	Heritage Status	Nature	New Use	Original Use	Timeframe
DBS House	Grade II A	Private	Co-working business center	Private residence (1895)	1998–2000
R and R	None	Private	Multifunctional community space	Multifunctional makeshift shed (2010)	January 2016–March 2016
Royal Opera House	Grade I	Private	Opera house and performance theater (2016)	Opera house and performance theater (1917)	2009–2016
Flora Fountain	Grade I	Government/Public	Ornamental fountain; Surrounding open space: public plaza	Ornamental fountain; Surrounding open space: green round-about	2016–2019
Ghodbunder Fort	Protected site	Public-private partnership	Fort and recreational space	Headquarters of the district administration for the East Indian Company (1818)	2019–2023

DBS House, Mumbai

Lavina Ahuja

DBS House (also known as DBS Heritage House) was among the first adaptive reuse projects carried out in Mumbai after the implementation of the Heritage Regulations of Greater Bombay in 1995. The project converted a former residential structure to a coworking business center with modern-day facilities, while safeguarding the heritage values of the place. It was recognized with an Award of Merit at the UNESCO Asia-Pacific Awards for Cultural Heritage Conservation in 2001, where it was seen as "a catalyst in inciting further conservation efforts in the Fort Precinct of Mumbai."[1]

Figure 17.1: Exterior view of DBS House from Prescott Road, Mumbai. (Source: Lavina Ahuja.)

1. UNESCO, "DBS House," in *Asia Conserved Volume I: Lessons Learned from the UNESCO Asia-Pacific Awards for Cultural Heritage Conservation (2000–2004)*, ed. Richard A. Engelhardt (Bangkok: UNESCO, 2007), 147.

Project Information

Address	31, Adi Murzban Road, Fort, Mumbai, India
Original use	Private residence (1895)
Previous use	Commercial (1950s)
New use	Coworking business center for DBS Financial Services*
Heritage status	Grade II A
Site area	15,000 square meters
Project cost estimate	US$400,000
Funding model	DBS Financial Services Pvt. Ltd.
Owner	DBS Financial Services Pvt. Ltd.
Developer	Unknown
Architect	Sandhya Sawant
Contractor	Sewri Construction Pvt. Ltd.
Project timeline	April 1998–September 2000

Note:

* A part of the property is used as a library and reading room used by First Church of Christ Scientist and Christian Science. This case study will only focus on the adaptive reuse by DBS Financial Services.

Project Description

The primary goal of the project was to restore the architectural significance of DBS House by revealing its character-defining attributes while enabling the building to function efficiently with an appropriate new use as a coworking business center. Its objectives were as follows:

- To repair and restore the original character of the building.
- To use reversible methodologies for repair works.
- To keep new additions to a minimum.
- To make new additions distinct yet harmoniously blended with the historical fabric.

Site History

Located in the City's Fort area, DBS House is a noteworthy example of Victorian architecture in Mumbai. Built in 1885 as the residence for a prominent Jewish family, the house was converted for commercial use during the 1950s, involving substantial alterations that diminished the character and significance of the three-story building. The exterior was marred by the installation of services, such as plumbing and air-conditioning, while the original façade of exposed red brick with white limestone ornamentation had been covered in gray cement wash. The interior was altered by the haphazard addition of mezzanine floors and a reinforced concrete staircase in the original courtyard located between the two wings of the house.[2]

2. UNESCO, "DBS House."

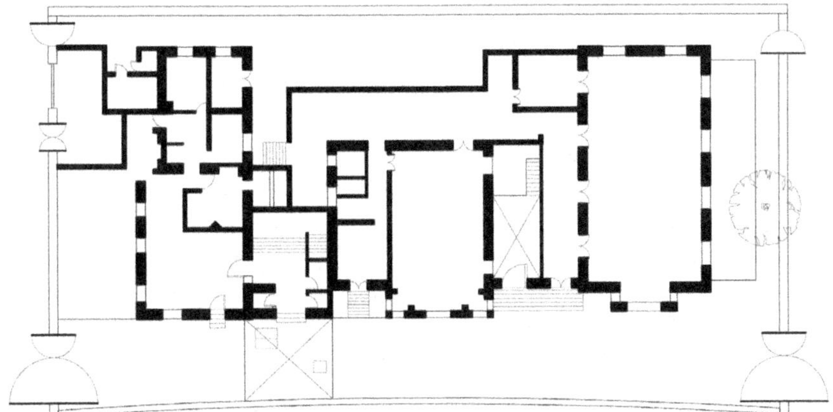

Figure 17.2: Ground-floor plan of DBS House after adaptive reuse. (Source: Drawn by Ng Wai Shing based on materials from UNESCO, *Asia Conserved I.*)

Project History

In 1988, the building was acquired by DBS Financial Services who began using it for commercial purposes. The building was recognized with a Grade III status in 1995 under the Heritage Regulations for Greater Bombay. With this renewed awareness of the heritage significance of their property, DBS Financial Services initiated a project to carry out appropriate restoration of the building as well as improve the interior layout of the building to accommodate efficiently its new use as a coworking business center. The owner funded the entire project and commissioned Sandhya Sawant, one of the city's leading conservation architects, to carry out the conservation works.

Development Environment

Although DBS House had been used as a commercial office space by DBS Financial Services since 1988, it was only seven years later that the owner decided to appropriately conserve the place and enhance its heritage significance. This reflects an increased awareness of Mumbai's "everyday" architecture, which can be seen as a positive outcome of the Heritage Regulations of Greater Bombay (further elaborated in the essay). The regulations also outlined the permitted interventions for each category of graded heritage building. In the case of DBS House, it was a Grade III heritage building prior to conservation works, which meant it "deserves intelligent conservation (though on a lesser scale than Grade II) and special protection to unique features and attributes." The regulations also allowed for adaptive reuse and building of new additions, on the final approval by the municipal commissioner. This was to ensure that heritage buildings would be conserved as opposed to being demolished.

Intervention

The main aim of the project was to restore the original character of DBS House and appropriately adapt it for its new use as a coworking business center with state-of-the-art facilities. Reversing past interventions was the first step to reveal the historical appearance of the place, which included removal of the gray cement wash from the façade and the cement from the decorative features. The original red brick façade was uncovered by using hand tools. The limestone decorative features, such as the trefoil arches, were repaired with lime putty and painted with thin layers of lime wash as protection. Extensive repairs were carried out to the roof to address the problem of water seepage, and damaged timber members were replaced using the original material. The building's character-defining attributes, such as the cornices, were restored, and missing elements were replicated using original materials. The building services visible on the exterior were relocated to improve the appearance of the façade.

For the interior, substantial repairs were undertaken to restore the structural integrity and improve the functionality of the building. The damaged wooden posts, joists, and beams on the southwestern side were repaired. New internal services were installed in such a way as to minimize their aesthetic impact while allowing for the greatest flexibility in adapting the space to suit various tenants with different spatial requirements. Electrical wiring in surface-mounted tracks at the skirting level was designed to be rerouted in minimal time. In the reconfiguration of the spatial layout, new mezzanine floors were added to maximize usable space within the existing shell. A modular partition system was also introduced to allow greater flexibility in the division of space without overloading the structure. To accommodate modern needs, the crudely constructed concrete staircase was removed and a new hydraulic lift was inserted.

Key Challenges

- The site was subject to a series of unsympathetic past interventions that masked its heritage significance.
- Substandard architectural additions presented a host of structural and technical challenges, which had to be resolved while respecting the integrity and quality of the original structure.

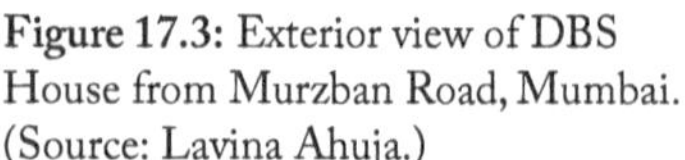

Figure 17.3: Exterior view of DBS House from Murzban Road, Mumbai. (Source: Lavina Ahuja.)

Keeping Heritage Alive

Buildings like DBS House in Mumbai are usually underappreciated for their heritage values and, in the past, were demolished to make way for redevelopment. If they manage to escape the wrecking ball, they are ruthlessly subdivided to exploit rental potential, threatening their cultural heritage values and character-defining elements. The standard-setting conservation of DBS House serves as a noteworthy example of sensitive adaptive reuse of a heritage place, while also making it economically viable.

The conservation works reveal the lost heritage significance of the place, especially by restoring its architecturally distinct façade. The choice of new use as a coworking business center responds well to the contemporary character of the Fort area as a business district. The internal layout with flexible partitions provides opportunities for various kinds and scales of uses for the building without permanent interventions that can compromise the integrity of the place. This adaptive reuse approach engages a new business community that ascribes social value to DBS House.

Long-Term Viability

DBS Financial Services, as the owner, adapted the building for use as a coworking business center. Equipped with state-of-the-art facilities, the place appeals to a variety of tenants for commercial uses. Its proximity to public transportation makes it an attractive place for commercial offices. This model ensures that the building generates sufficient returns, which can be used for upkeep and maintenance of the property in the long term.

Figure 17.4: Exterior view of DBS House showing its exposed red brick façade with white limestone ornamentation. (Source: Nitesh Jain.)

Impact

Economic: Prior to conservation works, a survey of the building revealed that it had great potential and the property would appreciate if restoration works were undertaken.[3] Today, the property can demand more competitive rents than other such buildings in the Fort area due to its striking appearance and modern-day facilities.[4] DBS House demonstrated a sustainable approach for heritage conservation at a time when Mumbai was beginning to understand the value of its heritage building stock.

Environmental: Since its restoration, the building has become a well-known landmark within the Fort area. DBS House has become a catalyst for restoration of other heritage properties along Prescott Road, which is now seen as a distinct streetscape.[5] The project demonstrates that appropriate adaptive reuse of a heritage building can inject vitality into a building as well as the surrounding area. With this renewed recognition of its significance, DBS House was upgraded to a Grade II A heritage building after conservation works.

Social: Conservation of DBS House was a large-scale project undertaken by an individual owner. Its positive outcome is testimony to the fact that major conservation works can be successfully carried out by the private sector, in this case, a corporate entity. For Mumbai, the pioneer city in India to implement heritage regulations for its "non-monumental" heritage, this project has demonstrated that adaptive reuse is a viable solution for making heritage buildings relevant in contemporary society.

> **Leading by example, the restoration of DBS House has been a catalyst in inciting further conservation efforts in the Fort Precinct of Mumbai.[6]**
>
> **—UNESCO**

Bibliography

Business Centre India. "DBS House, Prescott Road, Fort, Mumbai Central." Accessed May 19, 2022. https://www.businesscenterindia.in/office/india/maharashtra/mumbai-central/dbs-house-prescott-road-fort-97722.

Marfatia, Meher. "Here's to You, Miss Prescott!" *Mid-day*, December 10, 2017. https://www.mid-day.com/news/opinion/article/here-s-to-you--miss-prescott--18811164.

Mumbai Metropolitan Region Heritage Conservation Society. "First Church of Christ Scientist and Christian Science and DBS House." *Mumbai Metropolitan Region Heritage Conservation Society, Information System*. Accessed May 19, 2022. http://www.mmrhcs.org.in/index.php/heritage-information-system/information-system.

UNESCO. *Asia Conserved Volume I: Lessons Learned from the UNESCO Asia-Pacific Awards for Cultural Heritage Conservation (2000–2004)*. Edited by Richard A. Engelhardt. Bangkok: UNESCO, 2007.

3. UNESCO, "DBS House."
4. "DBS House, Prescott Road, Fort, Mumbai Central," Business Centre India, accessed May 19, 2022, https://www.businesscenterindia.in/office/india/maharashtra/mumbai-central/dbs-house-prescott-road-fort-97722.
5. Meher Marfatia, "Here's to You, Miss Prescott!" *Mid-day*, December 10, 2017, https://www.mid-day.com/news/opinion/article/here-s-to-you--miss-prescott--18811164.
6. UNESCO, "DBS House."

R and R, Mumbai

Rupali Gupte and Lavina Ahuja

The R and R is a small-scale, humble project that illustrates the impact of subtle revitalization initiatives. Located in one of Mumbai's high-density residential resettlement colonies, the project supports the community's initiative in reclaiming a social space and upgrades it for safe and efficient use. It was an artistic experiment in creating a social space for the public realm built in close participation with the community.

Figure 18.1: R and R, a revitalized shed in Mankhurd used as a multifunctional community space and library. (Source: Rupali Gupte.)

Project Information

Address	Lallubhai Compound, Mankhurd, Mumbai, India
Original use	Multifunctional makeshift shed (2010)
Previous use	NA
New use	Multifunctional community space including a library
Heritage status	None
Site area	46.45 square meters
Project cost estimate	US$6,500
Funding model	Private (through an art fund under project Draft)*
Owner	Sindhu Society, Lallubhai Compound, Mankhurd
Developer	NA
Architect	Khanabadosh, CAMP, Rupali Gupte, and Prasad Shetty
Contractor	Tradespersons: Sharifbhai, Ali, and Survade Society members: Lokhande and Salma
Project timeline	January 2016–March 2016

Note:
* "DRAFT | The Zurich Conference," Pro Helvetia, accessed May 30, 2022, https://prohelvetia.in/en/draft-zurich-conference/.

Project Description

The R and R project was undertaken to provide a small, multifunction, community facility in one of the city's resettlement colonies that lacked adequate social spaces in the public realm. Located in Lallubhai Compound, a resettlement colony in Mankhurd, Mumbai, one of the building societies (Sindhu Society) converted a shed, which had become dilapidated over time, for community use through self-initiated construction and without any professional help. R and R was executed as a repair-and-retrofit initiative of this dilapidated shed. The project's aims were to upgrade and revitalize the space for multiple community functions, including a library. Its objectives were as follows:

- To upgrade the shed for safe and efficient community use.
- To work closely with the local community and tradespeople during the upgrading works.
- To compensate for the lack of social spaces in the residential colony.

R and R is a pun on the term "R and R," which is used for "Rehabilitation and Resettlement" projects. In the case of the community space and library, R and R stands for "Read and Research," "Relax and Recreate," and so forth, in keeping with the open-scripted nature of the space.

Site History

Mankhurd is a site where, in the early 2000s, more than 40,000 families were resettled. This was in response to two large-scale projects initiated by the government in Mumbai: the Mumbai Urban Transformation Project (MUTP) and the Mumbai

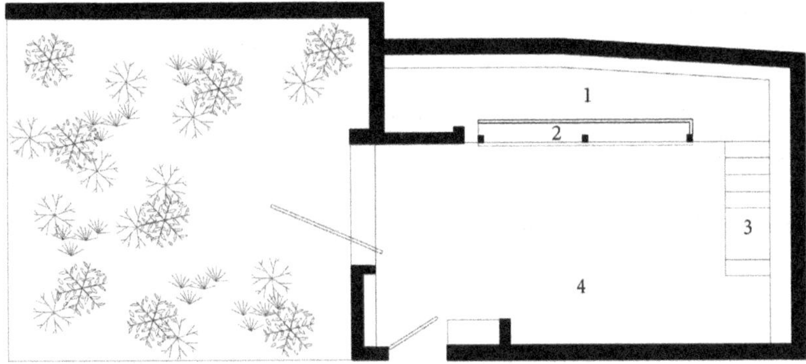

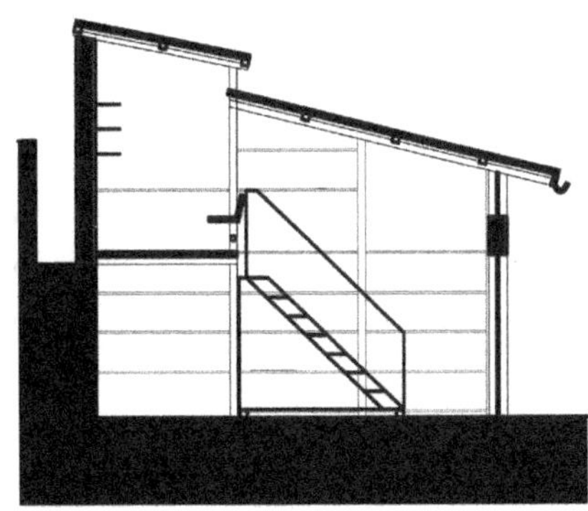

Figure 18.2: Plan and section of the R and R shed—1. Mezzanine floor with library and a small breakout balcony, 2. Mobile staircase, 3. Flexible community space. (Source: Drawn by Ng Wai Shing.)

Urban Infrastructure Project (MUIP).[1] These projects involved making new roads, widening existing roads, adding railway tracks, building bridges, and more. Most of the land needed for these projects was inhabited by people. Due to this, the local government came up with a Rehabilitation and Resettlement policy called "R and R" to acquire such land and propose mitigation measures to the "project-affected people" (PAP).

Under this new policy, any person owning land in Mumbai could develop low-cost housing and then hand it over to the government to be allotted to the PAP. In return, such a person was awarded equivalent Transferable Development Rights (TDR) to be used in other locations within the city. The rules for such development were relaxed in the city's Development Control Regulations (DCR) making it possible to construct buildings that were crammed with very small units (about twenty-five square meters) and closely packed, thus creating extremely dense neighborhoods in the city. Such neighborhoods were informally called "R and R colonies" and were often located at the periphery of Mumbai, where real estate prices were very low, economic opportunities were almost nonexistent, and social infrastructure was scarce.

Comprising seventy high-rise residential buildings, Lallubhai Compound is one of the largest R and R colonies of Mumbai. One of the building societies within the colony, Sindhu Society, constructed the R and R shed as a multifunctional space that was used as a society office, church, community space, and as a space for last rites. The shed had become severely dilapidated over time and was not used.

Project History

The R and R was a project under a wider initiative called Draft—an artist's initiative whose brief involved exploring "contemporary art that initiates, provokes and contributes to public debates."[2] The project invited (and funded) nine interdisciplinary collaboratives from nine cities (Beijing, Cairo, Cape Town, Hamburg, Hong Kong, Mexico City, Mumbai, Saint Petersburg, and Zurich) and spanned a period of one year (2015–2016). The Mumbai arm (Mumbai Collective) of this project was a collaboration between Khanabadosh (a Mumbai-based arts lab), CAMP (a Mumbai-based

1. More information on these schemes can be found at Renu Modi, "Resettlement and Rehabilitation in Urban Centres," *Economic and Political Weekly*, February 7, 2009, https://www.academia.edu/3772284/Resettlement_and_Rehabilitation_in_Urban_Centres_February_2009_Economic_and_Political_Weekly.
2. Pro Helvetia, "DRAFT | The Zurich Conference," accessed May 30, 2022, https://prohelvetia.in/en/draft-zurich-conference/.

artists' studio), and the architect/artist duo Rupali Gupte and Prasad Shetty. The Mumbai Collective began scouring the city for places to engage with. Many friendships, networks, walks, drives, and cups of tea were navigated until the team arrived at the Mankhurd, Lallubhai Compound and zeroed in on a little dilapidated shed that Sindhu Society, one of the building societies in the resettlement colony, had put together on its premises through multiple negotiations. The team decided to give this shed a second life by upgrading its structure and revitalizing its use.

Development Environment

With the displacement of communities amid Mumbai's urban plans, informal social spaces that hold cultural heritage value for their communities remained unrecognized and unprotected. This is the ugly truth of the highly urbanized metropolis of Mumbai, where the top-down agenda often focuses on monumental architecture and places of worship, and people's everyday cultural heritage slips through gaps in the system.

The R and R shed can be seen as a place where people, through their own agency, claim and create their own social space. The place features in the daily lives of the community and is an important anchor for their cultural ties. This shed was fortunate to receive funding support from the Draft initiative; otherwise, it would have probably met its inevitable fate of crumbling to the ground with little notice.

Intervention

The revitalization project of R and R aims at upgrading the structure of the place and inserting subtle interventions to make the space function efficiently for its multiple uses. The skeleton of the building is reinforced with steel members obtained from one of the largest recycling centers in Mumbai. Colored acrylic sheets and recycled plywood are fixed on the steel skeleton. At the entrance, a blue door made by a local tradesperson beckons passers-by. Inside, large swivel grille doors at the north end open the space to a backyard that is in the process of becoming a garden.

Attached to the length of the east wall is a mezzanine floor that is home to a library and a small breakout balcony. Long shelves line the south wall in a striking steplike formation that rises all the way to the roof. A mobile staircase, parallel to the long shelves, makes movement possible between the two levels. The staircase can be moved to different locations keeping the relationship between the two levels dynamic. Pieces of furniture are welded together from metal sections and are clad with recycled plywood. The railing of the mezzanine level doubles as a backrest for benches and transforms into a "viewing" parapet for the space below or for images flickering on the screen that hangs on the west wall, as if from the balcony of a cinema hall (Figure 18.4). A mason from the neighboring colony carried out masonry work and toilet retrofitting. The toilet floor is a bricolage of four different tiles in four different colors, all obtained from sample pieces in a tile shop. The toilet is connected to the main sewer line. Electric connections are pulled from the society office.

Figure 18.3: R and R shed in Lallubhai Compound. (Source: Rupali Gupte.)

Key Challenges

The R and R project was built with community participation through a process of "auto-construction"—the process of building with little or no professional help.[3] The limitations were that the process worked through porous legalities, where permissions to build were not forthcoming. However, the project demonstrated how the process of auto-construction can create spatial justice in places that are denied access to social spaces.

Keeping Heritage Alive

In Mumbai, cultural heritage is often viewed through a narrow perspective, where buildings are seen as objects to be conserved. The R and R project illustrates a shift from materials thinking to spatial thinking, which presents new ways of imagining space as a unit of social value. The project is a key example of community-initiated conservation that provides valuable social infrastructure that would otherwise be lacking by governmental agendas.

Through the support of the Mumbai Collective, the place received the much-needed funding to carry out the necessary works. The project also became a process of community empowerment, where local tradespersons gained new competences. One such example is that of Sharifbhai, a local tradesperson, who had a small workshop in a metal recycling center that made security grilles. He had never worked on a building before, but he was familiar with the craft of assembling and welding steel. He was the primary person in charge of the structural upgrade of the shed's steel framework. R and R became a place for experimentation and training, having an impact beyond the project duration.

---

3. Teresa Caldeira uses this term in her essay "Peripheral Urbanization: Autoconstruction, Transversal Logics, and Politics in Cities of the Global South," *Environment and Planning D Society and Space* 35, no. 1 (2017): 3–20, https://journals.sagepub.com/doi/pdf/10.1177/0263775816658479.

Figure 18.4: R and R shed used for community events, the railing of the mezzanine is used as a parapet. (Source: Rupali Gupte.)

Long-Term Viability

The long-term sustainability of the project requires continued financial support. In a context where resources are limited, the risk is that the community succumbs to using the place for financial gain. To maintain its social use requires steady funding for its maintenance and upkeep.

Impact

Economic: The economic impacts of this project are indirect. R and R provides a space for children to build their capacities through reading, engaging in various projects, and learning to work with computers, through which they gain confidence to become future leaders and to participate in a competitive economic environment.

Environment: The R and R project uses recycled materials and local craftsmanship that contributes to a circular economy and a sustainable form of living.

Social: R and R provides an open-scripted space that the residents use for multiple purposes, such as a library, study space, dance rehearsal room, a space for trade union meetings, a church, a food distribution center, a quarantine center, and a space for autodidacts to flourish. In a context where space in their homes is limited, the shed has become an extended home for the community, fostering social bonds in a place where resettlement has created friction and distrust over the years.

> **This project demonstrates possibilities of how new social spaces could be created using the dynamics of people's agencies.**
>
> **—Rupali Gupte**

Bibliography

Caldeira, Teresa. "Peripheral Urbanization: Autoconstruction, Transversal Logics, and Politics in Cities of the Global South." *Environment and Planning D Society and Space* 35, no. 1 (2017): 3–20. https://journals.sagepub.com/doi/pdf/10.1177/0263775816658479.

Khanabadosh. "R and R by CAMP, Khanabadosh and Rupali Gupte & Prasad Shetty." Accessed May 30, 2022. https://khanabadosh.info/projects/r-and-r/.

Modi, Renu. "Resettlement and Rehabilitation in Urban Centres." *Economic and Political Weekly*, February 7, 2009. https://www.academia.edu/3772284/Resettlement_and_Rehabilitation_in_Urban_Centres_February_2009_Economic_and_Political_Weekly.

Mumbai Metropolitan Region Development Authority. "List of R&R Colonies." Accessed May 30, 2022. https://mmrda.maharashtra.gov.in/resettlement-and-rehabilitation1.

Pro Helvetia. "DRAFT | The Zurich Conference." Accessed May 30, 2022. https://prohelvetia.in/en/draft-zurich-conference/.

Sett, Alsiha. "What Lies behind the Blue Door." *The Hindu*, June 28, 2016. https://www.thehindu.com/news/cities/mumbai/entertainment/What-lies-behind-the-blue-door/article14405595.ece.

Studio CAMP. "About (2007)." Accessed May 30, 2022. https://studio.camp/about/.

Zende, Sulbha. "The Question of Rehabilitation at Lallubhai Compound, Mumbai: Sulbha Zende." *Urban Epistemology*, December 25, 2018. https://urbanepistemologycom.wordpress.com/2018/12/25/question-of-rehabilitation-at-lallubhai-compound-sulbha-zende/.

Royal Opera House, Mumbai

Lavina Ahuja

The Royal Opera House conservation project was supported entirely by private funding. The owner's vision to conserve this culturally significant place by adhering to standards of best practice is a testimony to Mumbai's conservation movement being championed by civic effort. This meticulous restoration project reinstates the original use of the place, thus revitalizing the once-vibrant opera house and recapturing the former spirit of the place.

Figure 19.1: Exterior view of the Royal Opera House. (Source: Abha Narain Lambah Associates.)

Project Information

Address	Girgaon, Mumbai, India
Original use	Opera house and performance theater (1917)
Previous use	Cinema hall (1935)
New use	Opera house and performance theater (2016)
Heritage status	Grade I
Site area	2,400 square meters
Project cost estimate	US$2.6 million
Funding model	Private (Shri Jyotendrasinhji Jadeja)
Owner	Shri Jyotendrasinhji Jadeja
Developer	NA
Architect	Abha Narain Lambah Associates
Contractor	Savani Construction Co. Pvy. Ltd. and Skyway Infra Projects Pvt. Ltd.
Project timeline	2009–2016

Project Description

The Royal Opera House project aimed to conserve an important cultural landmark of Mumbai by reinstating its original use and restoring its physical fabric. Rescuing the place from a derelict state of disrepair, the intent of the project was to revitalize the place to its former magnificence, thus giving back to the country its only surviving opera house.[1] The objectives of the project were as follows:

- To revitalize the place not as a cinema hall but in its original function as an opera house and performance venue for live dance, music, theater, and other performing arts.
- To restore the physical fabric by upholding the spatial integrity and authenticity of form, design, and character-defining elements.
- To uphold the spirit of the place.
- To create a model for the conservation of privately owned heritage buildings in Mumbai.[2]

Site History

Inaugurated in 1911 by King George V while still under construction, the Royal Opera House was completed in 1916. The place soon became the fulcrum for cultural activities in Mumbai, playing host to some of the finest performances in the country.

1. UNESCO, "Royal Bombay Opera House," in *Asia Conserved Volume IV: Lessons Learned from the UNESCO Asia-Pacific Awards for Cultural Heritage Conservation (2015–2019)*, ed. William Chapman (Bangkok: UNESCO, 2020), 184.
2. Abha Narain Lambah, *Royal Bombay Opera House (Submission Dossier for the UNESCO Asia-Pacific Awards for Cultural Heritage Conservation)* (Paris: UNESCO, 2017).

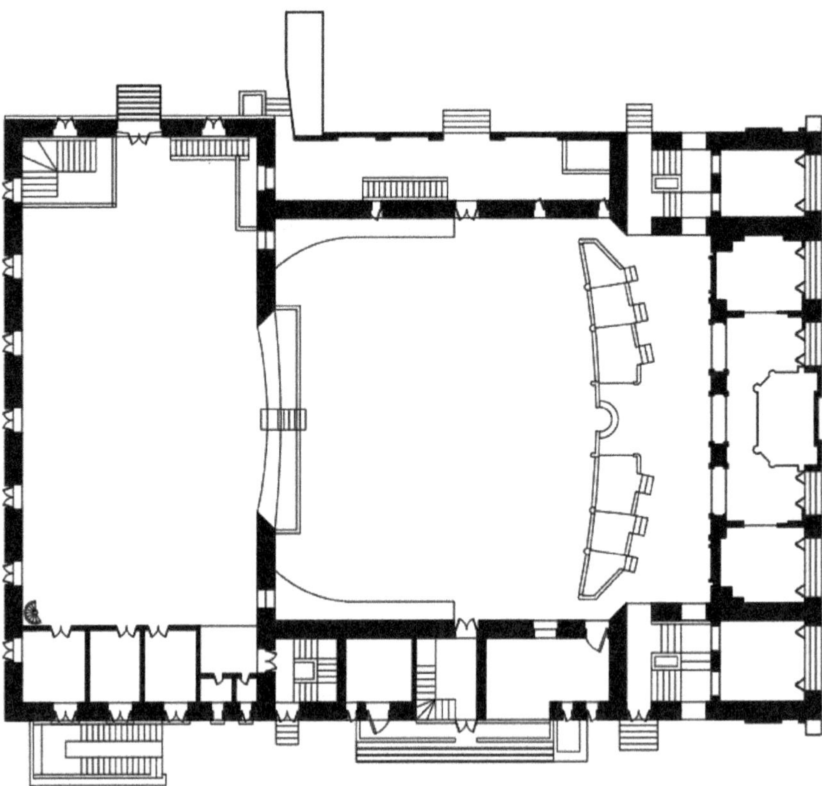

Figure 19.2: Ground-floor plan of the Royal Opera House. (Source: Drawn by Lavina Ahuja based on materials from Abha Narain Lambah Associates.)

In 1935, the place was converted into a single-screen cinema and became the chosen venue for hosting premieres of India's greatest films from the 1940s to 1970s.[3] During this change of use, the building was subjected to additions and alterations, including the addition of an exit staircase and external cladding in marble. In the 1970s, the opera house's neobaroque balconies were demolished and the interior received an "art deco" overlay.

By the 1990s, there was a decline in cinema viewership for single-screen theaters, eventually leading to the decommissioning of the Royal Opera House as a cinema in 1993. In the following years, the building was abandoned and fell into a state of neglect and disrepair. The Municipal Corporation of Greater Mumbai (MCGM) declared the place to be in a "ruinous condition likely to fall and dangerous to any person occupying, resorting to or passing by the same."[4]

Project History

After a series of ownership changes, the Royal Opera House eventually came under the custodianship of a private owner, Shri Jyotendrasinhji Jadeja. The owner appointed Abha Narain Lambah Associates to lead a team of conservation architects for the restoration and revitalization of the historical building. The project commenced in 2007 with the preparation of detailed fabric assessment reports and a conservation plan. With permission obtained from the Mumbai Heritage Conservation Committee (MHCC) in 2009, the conservation works commenced with priority on strengthening the structure of the Royal Opera House.

3. Lambah, *Royal Bombay Opera House*.
4. UNESCO, "Royal Bombay Opera House."

Figure 19.3: Exterior view of the side façade of the Royal Opera House. (Source: Abha Narain Lambah Associates.)

According to the project team, "it was a conscious decision by both the owners and the design team to reopen this project not as a cinema hall but exactly the way the building was conceived and originally designed. We all took a leap of faith and decided that [the] Opera House would re-open after 100 years as a live performance theater."[5]

Development Environment

As a privately owned heritage building in Mumbai, the Royal Opera House was not eligible for government grants or incentives to support the conservation project. In 2012, the World Monuments Fund listed the place on its list of Endangered Monuments of the World to raise awareness about its history and significance and support the effort of its owner.[6] However, as a building under private ownership, no financial aid was available under this fund.

Intervention

The interventions carried out on the Royal Opera House were divided into two phases. The first phase focused on the structural stabilization of the building and restoration of its external features. The second phase aimed at revitalizing the interior to reinstate the original layout of the place while introducing modern technical requirements for a contemporary performance theater.

Guided by archival research, the original 1917 aesthetic of the opera house was reinstated by restoring its original neobaroque elements that were shrouded under layers of unsympathetic renovations. To revitalize the place as a fully functional state-of-the-art performance theater, the project team installed modern additions to

5. "Royal Opera House," World Monuments Fund, accessed May 12, 2022, https://www.wmf.org/project/royal-opera-house#:~:text=The%20Royal%20Opera%20House%20was,Gondal%2C%20to%20preserve%20the%20building.
6. World Monuments Fund, "Royal Opera House."

Figure 19.4: Interior view of the Royal Opera House. (Source: Abha Narain Lambah Associates.)

improve the acoustics, bringing the building up to standards expected by present-day audiences. The orchestra pit was increased in size by vertically expanding it toward the adjoining basement, an intervention that created a much more usable orchestra pit without impacting views from the theater interior. Technical inputs for the interventions were provided by the team at Mumbai's National Centre of Performing Arts (NCPA). The building's safety features were also improved with the addition of fire alarms and a sprinkler system. All interventions were introduced without compromising the visual and spatial integrity of the historical interior.

Key Challenges

- The building's structural condition was a major concern and top priority to be addressed in the conservation works.
- Lack of support in the form of grants or incentives for privately owned heritage properties, which required the conservation works to be done in phases.
- Revitalizing the place for its original use while meeting the standards of a contemporary performance venue in an unobtrusive way.

Keeping Heritage Alive

"The comprehensive restoration undertaken with meticulous research and quality workmanship, successfully revived not only the magnificent neobaroque architecture but also the spirit of place of the only surviving opera house in India."[7] The cultural heritage values of the Royal Opera House are safeguarded and enhanced by revitalization of a cultural landmark of the city and a key part of Mumbai's history.

The decision to revive the original use of the place as an opera house and performance theater reinforces the spirit of the place. The original seating capacity has been maintained and attests to the building's first use. The conservation of the Royal Opera House has not only saved a cultural monument from dereliction but also given back to the city its finest cultural venue and performance theater.

Long-Term Viability

As reported by the project team, the first nine months of operation of the Royal Opera House as an opera house and performance theater reflected the commercial success of the vitalized place. Since its reopening in 2016 with the International Mumbai Film Festival, the place has become the most sought-after cultural venue in the city with a host of performances of classical music, opera, dance recitals, movie shoots, ballet, classical music, plays, Russian film festival, award functions, Chinese opera, Hindustani classical music, jazz, and theater.[8] The project not only demonstrates the successful revitalization of a historic landmark but also shows that it is possible to sustain a cultural venue if supported by a sound conservation plan and integrating this with cultural curation, sustainable management, and public outreach.[9]

Impact

Environmental: Playing host to a number of prominent cultural performers of the country (and internationally), the Royal Opera House became the cultural epicenter of the neighborhood. Since its inauguration, it has contributed in such great measure to the growth of the neighborhood that the precinct has acquired the name "Opera House"; and in 1995, Opera House was listed as a Heritage Precinct under the Heritage Regulations for Greater Bombay.[10] Since its reopening in 2016, the Royal Opera House has infused new life into South Mumbai, creating a cultural landmark that seamlessly integrates with the heritage character of the Opera House precinct. With its renewed significance and contribution to the city, the Royal Opera House was upgraded to Grade I heritage building in 2016.

Socioeconomic: Revitalization of Royal Opera House to its original use has received an outstanding positive response from citizens of Mumbai. This can be seen in the curation and patronage of the various events held at the venue, the inclusion of the site in heritage walks of Opera House, and its extensive coverage by local media. This project, which for years suffered due to an absence of funding or support for privately owned heritage, has shown today that restoration of historical buildings helps save a city's collective cultural memory.

7. UNESCO, "Royal Bombay Opera House."
8. Lambah, *Royal Bombay Opera House*.
9. Lambah, *Royal Bombay Opera House*.
10. Mumbai Metropolitan Region–Heritage Conservation Society (MMR-HCS), *Conservation Guidelines for Opera House Precinct* (Mumbai: MHR-HCS, 2002), http://mmrhcs.org.in/images/documents/projects/precinct-studies/Study_of_Opera_House_Precinct/Study_of_Opera_House_Precinct_w0Tjm0.pdf.

> **This project has demonstrated that the conservation of privately-owned buildings is both possible and viable, and is in the public interest.**[11]
>
> **—UNESCO**

Bibliography

Baig, Amita. "A 21st-Century Overture." *World Monuments Watch Blog*, December 8, 2016. https://www.wmf.org/blog/21st-century-overture.

Lambah, Abha Narain. "How We Restored Mumbai's 100-Year-Old Opera House." *NDTV Blog*, October 17, 2016. https://www.ndtv.com/blog/how-we-restored-mumbais-100-year-old-opera-house-1475238.

Lambah, Abha Narain. *Royal Bombay Opera House (Submission Dossier for the UNESCO Asia-Pacific Awards for Cultural Heritage Conservation)*. Paris: UNESCO, 2017.

Mumbai Metropolitan Region–Heritage Conservation Society (MMR-HCS). *Conservation Guidelines for Opera House Precinct*. Mumbai: MHR-HCS, 2002. http://mmrhcs.org.in/images/documents/projects/precinct-studies/Study_of_Opera_House_Precinct/Study_of_Opera_House_Precinct_w0Tjm0.pdf.

UNESCO. *Asia Conserved Volume IV: Lessons Learned from the UNESCO Asia-Pacific Awards for Cultural Heritage Conservation (2015–2019)*. Edited by William Chapman. Bangkok: UNESCO, 2020.

World Monuments Fund. "Royal Opera House." Accessed May 12, 2022. https://www.wmf.org/project/royal-opera-house#:~:text=The%20Royal%20Opera%20House%20was,Gondal%2C%20to%20preserve%20the%20building.

11. UNESCO, "Royal Bombay Opera House."

Flora Fountain, Mumbai

Lavina Ahuja

The Flora Fountain project conserved one of Mumbai's most prominent fountains and revitalized its surrounding area for enhanced public use. The project exemplifies the role of conservation—to not only restore historical built fabric but also revitalize open spaces that can serve the community. It leverages heritage to give back to the city a much-needed public space, serving as an exemplar for other such sites in Mumbai and beyond.

Figure 20.1: Flora Fountain and its surrounding public plaza. (Source: Vikas Dilawari.)

Project Information

Address	Fort, Mumbai, India
Original use	Ornamental fountain Surrounding open space: green roundabout
Previous use	Surrounding open space: transportation hub (1940s), parking space (1960s), traffic island with pedestrian thoroughfare (1980s)
New use	Ornamental fountain Surrounding open space: public plaza
Heritage status	Grade I
Site area	Approximately 215 square meters
Project cost estimate	US$530,000 (fountain and surrounding open space)
Funding model	Municipal Corporation of Greater Mumbai (MCGM)
Owner	Municipal Corporation of Greater Mumbai (MCGM)
Developer	NA
Architect	Vikas Dilawari
Contractor	Phase I: INTACH Greater Mumbai Chapter with conservators from INTACH Conservation Institutes (ICI, New Delhi) Phase II: Hi-tech Engineers Pvt. Ltd.
Project timeline	Phase I (Fountain restoration): September 2016–January 2019 Phase II (Surrounding open space revitalization): April 2018–April 2019

Project Description

The Flora Fountain site comprises a historical ornamental fountain and its surrounding open area. The project aimed to restore the fountain by adhering to international standards of best practice in conservation and to revitalize its surrounding open space for improved public use. The objectives of the project were as follows:

- To restore the fountain in a scientific manner and make it functional.
- To revitalize the surrounding open area into a usable public space rather than being an inaccessible ornamental green patch.
- To set a high benchmark in the conservation field, especially for other government-led projects.[1]

Site History

Mumbai's (then Bombay) Fort area saw the building of several fountains in the mid-nineteenth century. Some were installed to provide clean drinking water to commuters, while others were purely ornamental in nature. These fountains shaped the

1. Vikas Dilawari, *Flora Fountain (Submission Dossier for the UNESCO Asia-Pacific Awards for Cultural Heritage Conservation)* (Paris: UNESCO, 2019).

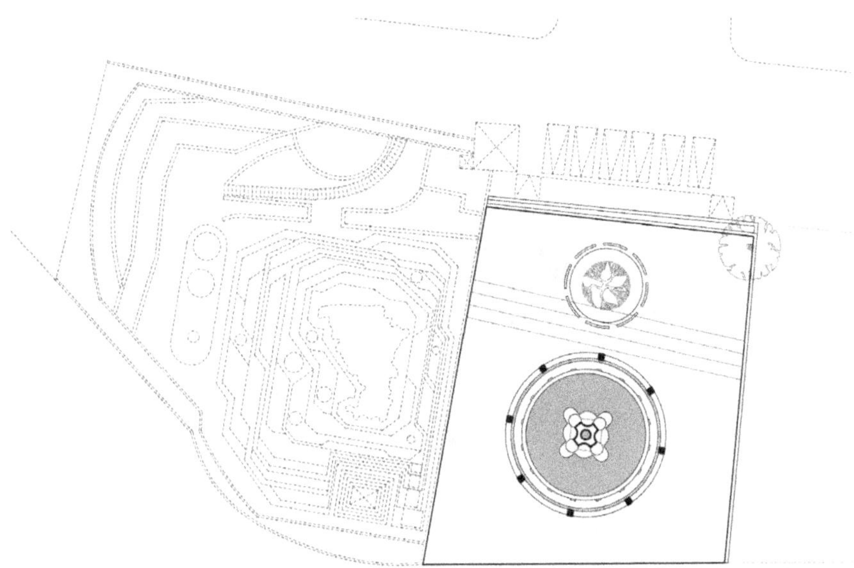

Figure 20.2: Site plan showing Flora Fountain and its surrounding open space. (Source: Drawn by Ng Wai Shing.)

cityscape of Mumbai, serving as the focal points of roundabouts at the intersections of main roads.

Flora Fountain is located at the intersection of three major roads in Mumbai's historical Fort area: Veer Nariman Road, Mahatma Gandhi Road, and Dr. Dadabhai Naoroji Road. The site was initially planned as a green roundabout with an ornamental fountain. In the 1940s, it became an important transportation hub for the city, used as a tram stop and taxi parking area. As the city underwent rapid transformation, so did the fountain and its setting. With the discontinuation of the tram service, the site's main use became that of a parking area. In the mid-1980s, the site was divided into two entities. The northern section became an inaccessible landscaped green area with memorials and the southern section remained a parking area. This reduced Flora Fountain to a traffic island within an elliptical raised landscaped area surrounded by fencing. The site lost its city square–like character, and the surviving public open space became an east-west pedestrian thoroughfare that eventually was paved (Figure 20.3).

Flora Fountain, once a visual and social pause point for locals as well as visitors, faded amid the fast-paced development of the city, making it difficult for people to appreciate the monument and its open space. The fountain was used sparingly on selected occasions and was painted regularly as part of its, supposedly, maintenance and upkeep.[2] The site was subjected to encroachment, graffiti, and vandalism, posing a threat to its heritage values and character-defining elements.

Project History

Flora Fountain was recognized with a Grade I heritage status in 1995 according to the Heritage Regulations for Greater Bombay and is under government ownership. In 2016, the Municipal Corporation of Greater Mumbai (MCGM) decided to restore the fountain to its original state. The corporation chose not to have an open tender for the restoration of the fountain and instead invited collaboration from

2. In the 1990s, maintenance of the fountain and its surrounding area were handed over to a corporate entity.

Figure 20.3: Flora Fountain before revitalization showing the inaccessible landscaping around the fountain. (Source: Vikas Dilawari.)

professional institutions and experts. The project was carried out with the assistance of the Indian National Trust for Art and Cultural Heritage (INTACH) through its Greater Mumbai chapter, which is the country's premier nongovernmental organization in heritage conservation.

MCGM appointed Vikas Dilawari as the conservation architect and expert for the project. The initial scope of work was limited to restoration of the fountain. The conservation architect proposed to expand this scope to include the revitalization of the surrounding open area of the site, emphasizing that the setting is inextricably linked to the significance of the place.

Development Environment

Mumbai was the first city in India to have heritage legislation (introduced in 1995). In 2004, it became the first city in the country to have a site that is not protected by the Archaeological Survey of India (ASI)—namely, Chhatrapati Shivaji Maharaj Terminus (CSMT) or erstwhile Victoria Terminus railway station, listed as a World Heritage Site.

When Victorian Gothic and Art Deco Ensembles of Mumbai was listed as a World Heritage Site in 2018, it was encouraging to note that the focus widened from an individual building (e.g., CSMT) to a larger precinct. Despite this, the city still lacks sufficient legislation for its protection. Flora Fountain is a Grade I site per Mumbai's Heritage Regulations; however, it is not located within the boundary of the World Heritage Site and is vulnerable to the impact of insensitive developments. Prior to conservation works, its maintenance was commissioned to a corporate entity that had limited understanding of maintaining heritage structures. As a result, the site was subject to unsympathetic interventions under the pretext of "maintenance and upkeep."

Intervention

The project had two phases: the first phase focused on the restoration and repair of the engineering mechanisms and sculptures of the fountain in order to revive its original use as a fully functioning water fountain; the second phase involved improving the immediate surroundings of the fountain to encourage public engagement and to enhance the visitor experience.[3]

A detailed account of the restoration works carried out in the first phase can be found in *Asia Conserved Volume IV: Lessons Learned from the UNESCO Asia-Pacific Awards for Cultural Heritage Conservation (2014–2019)*.[4] This section will focus on the second phase of the project, revitalization of the surrounding open area of the fountain.

The second part of the project focused on the revitalization of the immediate surrounding of the fountain. During this phase, all insensitive past additions were removed, including the elliptical raised landscape area and railing. The site was leveled and covered with basalt stone paving to demarcate the public plaza around the fountain. This was a conscious decision to reinstall the basalt paving as it gave a local distinctiveness to the site and was the historical stone used for Mumbai's pavements in the past. A *champa* (temple) tree was planted on the site and stainless-steel benches, designed especially for the place, were installed to encircle the small green area.[5]

During the conservation works, old tram tracks were revealed. These were retained as a reminder of the site's history. The tram tracks were excavated and relaid after the site was leveled.

Figure 20.4: The site was paved with traditional basalt instead of concrete pavers. These were laid in alignment with the tracks of tram as discovered on site. (Source: Vikas Dilawari.)

3. UNESCO, "Flora Fountain," in *Asia Conserved Volume IV: Lessons Learned from the UNESCO Asia-Pacific Awards for Cultural Heritage Conservation (2014–2019)*, ed. William Chapman (Bangkok: UNESCO, 2020), 351.
4. UNESCO, "Flora Fountain."
5. UNESCO, "Flora Fountain."

Key Challenges

- Previous interventions carried out to the place had significantly damaged some key attributes of the fountain structure and compromised public accessibility to the site.
- In the revitalization of the surrounding open area, the site had to be leveled without sufficient records of potential underground services and water pipes, hence hiring an experienced structural engineer was instrumental to navigate this challenge.[6]
- During the planning stage, the conservation architect proposed a larger master plan for the area that linked Flora Fountain's public plaza to other nearby open areas in order to create an integrated series of public spaces. The long-term vision was to pedestrianize the connecting streets on weekends and give the city free and accessible spaces that could be used for a wide range of public activities. Unfortunately, this plan was not sanctioned by the authorities.[7]

Keeping Heritage Alive

As one of the finest Renaissance Revival style sculptures in the city, Flora Fountain is a major landmark for Mumbai, especially with its prominent location in the heart of the city.[8] Its inclusion in Mumbai's World Heritage Site boundary further confirms its significance as a part of the city's heritage assets. Restoration of the fountain to its former state, and, more important, to a fully functioning condition revives the heritage significance of this urban ornament. Revitalization of the surrounding open space reinstated civic accessibility to the place. What was a walking corridor has now acquired a public plaza–like quality, making it a social node for people to gather and use freely.

The project was recognized with an Award of Merit in the 2019 UNESCO Awards for Cultural Heritage Conservation. The jury commended the project for "[transforming] the space, giving it a renewed lease on life as a public meeting place. The project has not only recovered the fountain's artistic beauty, but has also validated the site's continuing role in the life of the community and its prominent place in the urban fabric of Mumbai."[9]

Long-Term Viability

Following the standard-setting conservation of Flora Fountain, the Municipal Corporation of Greater Mumbai (MCGM) has shown keen interest in continuing the maintenance of the place. A maintenance contract has been tendered to a specialized agency by the MCGM, and the contract stipulates that a conservator advise on upkeep measures. Recently, the maintenance of the site was awarded to a professional maintenance agency.

6. Vikas Dilawari (project conservation architect), in discussion with the author, May 19, 2022.
7. Vikas Dilawari (project conservation architect), in discussion with the author, May 19, 2022.
8. UNESCO, "Flora Fountain."
9. UNESCO, "Flora Fountain."

Impact

Environmental: Since its revitalization, Flora Fountain has regained its fame as a landmark in the city. The public plaza provides accessibility to the fountain, making it an inviting open space. Local users are often seen gathering on the plaza or using it as recreational area. The reinstated function of the fountain supplements the vitality of the surrounding open space.

To the south side of Flora Fountain is a site occupied by the metro railway authority, which is undergoing construction works. It is hoped that the positive outcome of revitalizing Flora Fountain by using traditional basalt pavers and creatively designed urban furniture will be echoed in the adjacent site. Together, they could create a cohesive public plaza that the city greatly needs.

Socioeconomic: The revitalization of Flora Fountain has encouraged more engagement with the place by the local community as well as increased tourist visits. Tour operators now use the fountain as a starting destination for tours of the historic Fort District, and since its opening, people are often seen photographing the place. It is an excellent example of positive transformation of a place and space. The project has increased public awareness of the city's fountains and open spaces, pushing the envelope of conservation beyond buildings.

> **[Flora Fountain] now goes beyond just being an individual entity but forms a cohesive public environment around it.**[10]
>
> —Vikas Dilawari

Bibliography

Bhalerao, Sanjana. "Flora Fountain Mumbai: Landscaping at Final Stage, Fountain Plaza to Be Fully Open in a Month." *Indian Express*, May 2, 2019. https://indianexpress.com/article/cities/mumbai/flora-fountain-mumbai-landscaping-at-final-stage-fountain-plaza-to-be-fully-open-in-a-month-5705727/.

Dilawari, Vikas. *Flora Fountain (Submission Dossier for the UNESCO Asia-Pacific Awards for Cultural Heritage Conservation)*. Paris: UNESCO, 2019.

Tahseen, Ismat. "Mumbai's Flora Fountain to Look Like London's Trafalgar Square." *Times of India*, September 21, 2018. http://timesofindia.indiatimes.com/articleshow/65887837.cms?utm_source=contentofinterest&utm_medium=text&utm_campaign=cppst.

Thevar, Steffy. "Mumbai's 155-Year-Old Iconic Flora Fountain Unveiled after Renovation." *Hindustan Times*, January 25, 2019. https://www.hindustantimes.com/mumbai-news/mumbai-s-155-year-old-iconic-flora-fountain-unveiled-after-renovation/story-0AwcDVEF8fhcKzm89QPPsM.html.

UNESCO. *Asia Conserved Volume IV: Lessons Learned from the UNESCO Asia-Pacific Awards for Cultural Heritage Conservation (2014–2019)*. Edited by William Chapman. Bangkok: UNESCO, 2020.

10. Dilawari, *Flora Fountain*.

Ghodbunder Fort, Mumbai Metropolitan Region

Lavina Ahuja

Figure 21.1: Aerial view of Ghodbunder Fort and its surrounding village. (Source: Sohaib Iliyas, Studio Recall.)

The Ghodbunder Fort conservation project includes the historical fort as well as its associated open area. Initiated by the municipal corporation, the project highlights a pivotal shift in the local government's approach, where conservation is seen as a means not only to restore the tangible fabric of the fort but also to recognize and enhance the site's community values.

Project Information

Address	Ghodbunder Road, Ghodbunder Village, Thane, Mumbai Metropolitan Region, Maharashtra
Original use	Fort used for trading horses and storing weaponry (1550s)
Previous use	Headquarters of the district administration for the East Indian Company (1818)
New use	Fort and recreational space
Heritage status	Protected site, Archaeology Department of Maharashtra
Site area	9 acres
Project cost estimate	US$2 million (INR 15.5 crores)*
Funding model	Government (Mira Bhayandar Municipal Corporation)
Owner	Government (Mira Bhayandar Municipal Corporation)
Developer	None
Architect	Sankraman Design Studio (Sapna Lakhe and Shwetambari Shinde)
Contractor	M. Devang Construction Co.
Project timeline	Phases 1 and 2: 2019–2022 Phase 3: 2022–2023

Note:
* The conversion rate is taken at US$1=INR77.82.

Project Description

The conservation of the Ghodbunder Fort site was initiated with the intention to restore only the historical fort. As the social value of the place was revealed during the site study, the scope of work was extended to revitalize its associated open space as a landscaped recreational area for the nearby village community. The objectives of the revitalization of the open space were as follows:

- To interweave the conservation of the fort and the open space to reflect the heritage significance of the site as a whole.
- To regenerate community associations of the villagers with the fort.
- To provide a space for enhanced public use.

Site History

Ghodbunder Fort is located in the Ghodbunder village, which lies on the fringe of the Mumbai Metropolitan Region (in the state of Maharashtra) and falls under the jurisdiction of the Mira Bhayandar Municipal Corporation (MBMC). Built in the 1550s by the Portuguese, the fort was initially named Cache de Tanna. The site was used by the Portuguese to trade horses, and hence it came to be called Ghodbunder Fort (*ghode* [horses] and *bunde* [port]).[1] It also served as storage for weaponry during wars in precolonial India. In 1818, the British East India Company took over the fort and made it the headquarters of its district administrative office.

1. Sankraman Design Studio, *Heritage Conservation of Ghodbunder Fort (Heritage Walk Pamphlet)* (Mumbai, April 2022).

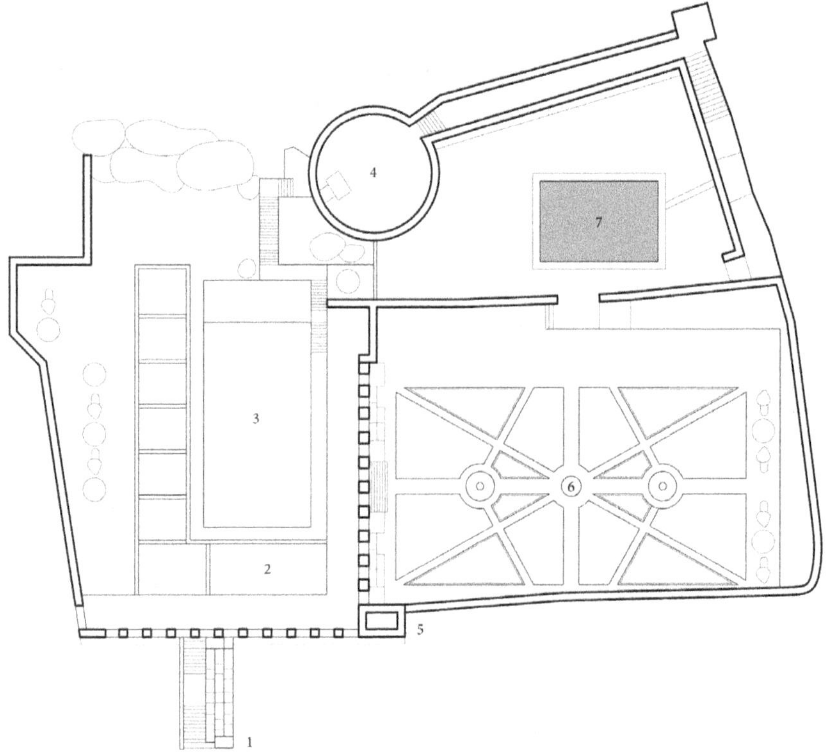

Figure 21.2: Site plan of Ghodbunder Fort—1. Entrance, 2. Granaries, 3. Small courtyard, 4. Bastion, 5. Southeast Garden room, 6. Large courtyard, 7. Water tank. (Source: Drawn by Ng Wai Shing based on materials from Sankraman Design Studio.)

Ghodbunder Fort is a coastal fort site consisting of fort walls and a bastion, which has a storage room under it. Within the fort there are multiple small rooms that were used as residences and granaries in the past and that enclose a small courtyard. The site has a larger open space in its southeast corner and a water tank in the northeast section.

After the decolonization of India in 1947, sites occupied by the British were left largely without a purpose. During this time, the site was unofficially reclaimed by the community of Ghodbunder village, where its open space was used for festivals, sports, and other recreational activities. Today, the fort is a place of belonging for the community of nearby Ghodbunder village, who see it as their own and have taken ownership of the site's open space.

Although the Ghodbunder Fort is a protected site under the state's Archaeology Department (headed by the Directorate of State Archaeology and Museums, Maharashtra), it remained in a neglected condition with no regular maintenance. The site was shrouded under layers of vegetation, and there was structural fragility in the arches and granaries. The access steps to the bastion were in a degraded state and unfit for use.

Project History

Ghodbunder Fort was listed under the state's Maharashtra Vaibhav-State Protected Monuments Adoption Scheme (Monument Adoption Scheme), which was announced in 2007.[2] Under this scheme, protected sites under the state's Archaeology

2. Dhaval Kulkarni, "Govt to Allow Private Donors to Fund Conservation of Monuments," *Hindustan Times*, February 7, 2022, https://www.hindustantimes.com/cities/mumbai-news/govt-to-allow-private-donors-to-fund-conservation-of-monuments-101644254894280.html.

Department can be "adopted" by public entities or private organizations for conservation, development, and maintenance for a stipulated period. The scheme creates "a mechanism that works parallel to the existing government system for conservation and protection. It will bring in private funding for the upkeep of monuments, involve local communities in conservation and ensure that the financial gains from these projects are utilised for heritage conservation itself."[3]

The Ghodbunder Fort site was adopted by the Mira Bhayandar Municipal Corporation (MBMC), a civic administration body that looks after local infrastructure and public amenities of the Mira Bhayandar area. The conservation project of the fort site was initiated by MBMC with advisory support from the Directorate of State Archaeology and Museums, Maharashtra. As an officially empaneled firm of the state's Archaeology Department, Sankraman Design Studio was commissioned by MBMC to carry out conservation and revitalization of the site.

Development Environment

Since the Ghodbunder Fort project was under the state government's Monuments Adoption Scheme, this ensured that the interventions carried out were respectful of the heritage significance of the place. The scheme's agreement outlined the nature of works permitted as well as the expected outcomes from this partnership. It also required the inclusion of community participation in conservation works. This arrangement put forth a framework for the conservation of the site that was helpful to curb any proposals that would be detrimental to heritage value or would sideline the interest of the local community.[4]

Intervention

The approach to conserving Ghodbunder Fort was two pronged: first to restore the physical fabric of the fort and second to revitalize the open space for enhanced use by the villagers. As the project was funded by the Mira Bhayandar Municipal corporation (MBMC), which has a fixed annual budget, the work was phased.

Following an initial site assessment, the initial project task was to clear unwanted vegetation on the site. The first phase focused on restoring the built fabric of the fort by reversing unsympathetic changes of the past. Layers of cement plaster were removed from the brick walls of the bastion and granaries. Plaster and grouting were reapplied using lime plaster that was prepared on-site. This phase undertook the major landscaping works of the open area, including leveling the ground and installation of stone pavers for improved access (Figure 21.3). The choice of using hardscape for this intervention (as opposed to softscape, e.g., grass cover) was governed by concerns regarding the long-term maintenance of the open space.

In the second phase, access to the bastion was rebuilt by leveling the ground and rebuilding its steps in local basalt stone. The bastion wall and arches were also repaired during this phase. The objective of these repairs was to stabilize the structure and maintain the life of the built fabric by reversing insensitive past interventions. The overarching aim was to restore the place minimally while revitalizing the open space for the village community and eventually tourists.

3. Kulkarni, "Govt to Allow Private Donors."
4. Sapna Lakhe and Shwetambri Shinde (principal architects, Sankraman Design Studio), in discussion with the author, May 2022.

Figure 21.3: Landscaping interventions carried out in the open area during phase 1. (Source: Sankraman Design Studio.)

The final phase of the project, which is ongoing at the time of writing, includes reconstruction of retaining walls on the south and north sides. This phase also considers the provision of urban furniture, security, and services for the site that can provide a comfortable user experience.

Key Challenges

Monument Adoption Scheme:

- The scheme is beneficial for historical sites under government ownership that are in neglected conditions due to lack of sufficient funding. However, the "adoption" agreement has broad definitions of the project scope, leaving room for loopholes that can be detrimental to the heritage significance of the place.[5]
- With the "adoption" of a site, often the host organization has an expectation of economic benefit from the partnership. In some cases, this can lead to proposals that are in the interest of profit making but do not protect the core values and community of the place.

Ghodbunder Fort site condition:

- As with most government projects, the statutory approvals come before work can begin on-site. Due to the uncontrolled growth of natural vegetation on-site, it was challenging to gauge the degree of damage to the existing fort walls. This resulted in changes in the project budget.

Ghodbunder Fort site setting:

- Ghodbunder Fort is a part of Ghodbunder village, where village houses are organically laid out on-site with some houses abutting the fort walls. The village houses that sit at the edge of the fort site restrict access to the fort. Additionally,

---

5. Sapna Lakhe and Shwetambri Shinde (principal architects, Sankraman Design Studio), in discussion with the author, May 2022.

the targeted works for phase 3, which include reconstruction of the retaining walls, could be damaging to these village houses. It remains a challenge to strike a balance between achieving the project goals while causing minimal displacement to the village community.

Keeping Heritage Alive

Historically, the fort remained detached from the public domain given its authoritative and governmental role. The conservation project of Ghodbunder Fort not only conserves the tangible historical fabric through necessary maintenance interventions but also rejuvenates the open space for use by the villagers. As a place linked with the Ghodbunder village, the project formally recognizes the community's association with the fort, thus safeguarding a place of special meaning to the local community. The revitalization of the open space aims at promoting the social value of the fort, with a secondary focus on architectural interventions that are limited by budget constraints.

The architectural team responsible for the project, Sankraman Design Studio, has been actively promoting the heritage significance of the site. One such initiative is their guided heritage walk that includes stories about the history of the fort and its community values as well as sharing information about the conservation project's objectives and processes (Figure 21.4). This initiative has led to further awareness of the place, as the Ghodbunder Fort site is increasingly featured in local media and social media channels.[6]

Long-Term Viability

The maintenance of Ghodbunder Fort is managed by the Mira Bhayandar Municipal Corporation (MBMC). The MBMC plans to partner with a third-party agency to

Figure 21.4: A heritage walk at Ghodbunder Fort. (Source: Sankraman Design Studio.)

6. "Mumbai's Lesser-Known Iconic Forts: A Trip Down the History Lane," *Financial Express Online*, May 25, 2021, https://www.financialexpress.com/lifestyle/travel-tourism/mumbais-lesser-known-iconic-forts-a-trip-down-the-history-lane/2258440/.

plan, manage, and promote activities for the site, including guided heritage walks and small-scale events. It also intends to introduce ticketing to the site for special organized events. These plans could be helpful to facilitate controlled visitation and establish a model for commercial sustainability of the place. In the development of these plans, the MBMC aims to keep the site free and accessible for the local community, protecting their interests and associations with the place.

Impact

Economic: The preliminary vision for the project is creating a place for cultural tourism. The aspiration showcases a balanced approach where the community can continue to use the site freely and tourists are welcomed within certain limitations. With the establishment of this model, there is potential for the site to be economically sustainable. Also, local villagers have shown interest in leveraging the increased visitation to Ghodbunder Fort by setting up food and beverage stalls for visitors.

Socioenvironmental: The conservation works have improved the accessibility to and safety for Ghodbunder Fort, enabling enhanced use of the place while extending its physical life. The revitalization of the open space provides villagers a platform to carry out communal celebrations and other recreational activities. The fort stands as a backdrop to a local school to the south of the site. Students at the school are now encouraged to participate in the community's festive celebrations, especially taking part in performances and plays. The schoolchildren are also using the ancillary rooms of the fort for smaller activities, such as art classes and dance rehearsals. This revitalization not only strengthens the social values of the place but also integrates the village community with the school community, forming a larger sphere of cultural influence.

> **The effort towards the conservation aims to give back to the community not only a piece of history but a space that engages them.**
>
> **—Sapna Lakhe and Shwetambri Shinde (Sankraman Design Studio)**

Bibliography

Christopher, Aaron. "Ghodbunder Fort Restoration to Begin Next Month, Deadline 2020." *Indian Express*, July 11, 2019. https://indianexpress.com/article/india/ghodbunder-fort-restoration-to-begin-next-month-deadline-2020-5824313/.

Kulkarni, Dhaval. "Ghodbunder Fort & Home to Savarkar Made Eternal." *DNA*, July 8, 2019. https://www.dnaindia.com/mumbai/report-dna-special-ghodbunder-fort-home-to-savarkar-made-eternal-2769568.

Kulkarni, Dhaval. "Govt to Allow Private Donors to Fund Conservation of Monuments." *Hindustan Times*, February 7, 2022. https://www.hindustantimes.com/cities/mumbai-news/govt-to-allow-private-donors-to-fund-conservation-of-monuments-101644254894280.html.

Maharashtra Tourism. "Ghodbunder Fort, Mumbai." Accessed May 12, 2022. https://www.maharashtratourism.gov.in/-/ghodbunder-fort.

"Mumbai's Lesser-Known Iconic Forts: A Trip Down the History Lane." *Financial Express Online*, May 25, 2021. https://www.financialexpress.com/lifestyle/travel-tourism/mumbais-lesser-known-iconic-forts-a-trip-down-the-history-lane/2258440/.

Sankraman Design Studio. *Heritage Conservation of Ghodbunder Fort (Heritage Walk Pamphlet)*. Mumbai, April 2022.

PENANG

Essay | Timeline | Case Studies

Adaptive Reuse within the Context of Penang's Bottom-Up Conservation Movement: Creating a Sustainable Future for Heritage

Laurence Loh and Lin Lee Loh-Lim

Introduction

Located on the northeastern cape of Penang Island, George Town is the capital city of the state of Penang in Malaysia. It was founded by Captain Francis Light, a British trader, and became a trading port in the Straits of Malacca in the 1800s. He was responsible for laying out the original grid of streets in George Town; however, the city's development during the nineteenth century can be attributed to the early migrant communities who found in George Town a place to make a living and begin a new life.[1]

George Town is set against the backdrop of Malaysia's culturally complex society and political and cultural policies. In addition to the Malays, it is home to a relatively large proportion of minority cultures and races (such as the Acehnese, Chinese, Indians, and Nyonya Babas). The architecture of George Town reflects its cultural diversity, with architectural styles reflecting an eclectic mix of colonial and Asian attributes.

George Town is Malaysia's sole UNESCO World Heritage Site, jointly inscribed with Malacca (listed as Melaka and George Town, Historic Cities of the Straits of Malacca). It has the largest intact collection of pre–World War II buildings in Southeast Asia, with over five thousand within the World Heritage Site. This is due primarily to Malaysia's Rent Control Act that controlled the rentals of buildings built before January 31, 1948.[2] The provisions of this act contributed to inadvertent conservation of a number of prewar buildings in the inner city of George Town.

This essay discusses the evolution of Penang's conservation practice, which has been largely a bottom-up movement. It covers key milestones of every decade, starting

---

1. State Government of Penang, *Heritage Management Plan, State Government of Penang* (Kuala Lumpur: State Government of Penang and Badan Warisan Heritage Services Sdn. Bhd., February 2008), https://whc.unesco.org/en/documents/103167.
2. Rent control in Malaysia existed even before World War II. The Control of Rent Ordinance 1948 repealed the following ordinances: Control and Charged Land (Restriction) Enactment 1940; Rent and Charged Land (Restriction) Ordinance 1947; Increase of Rent (Restriction) Ordinance 1939; Increase of Rent (Restriction) Enactment (Johore) 1939; and Rent and Charged Land (Restriction) Enactment (Kedah) 1360 Hijra/1941. See Mohammad Abdul Mohit and Mohd Bashir Sulaiman, "Repeal of the Rent Control Act and Its Impacts on the Pre-war Shophouses in Georgetown, Malaysia," *Journal of the Malaysian Branch of the Royal Asiatic Society* 79, no. 1 (2006): 107–21, http://www.jstor.org/stable/41493817.

from the 1980s when conservation was first officially mentioned by federal and state governments. With particular focus on the emergence of adaptive reuse as a conservation strategy, the essay also touches on examples that illustrate the challenges faced by heritage practitioners in Penang. Projects that have emerged as success stories in the face of these challenges and become exemplars for the city (and beyond) are also discussed. Concluding remarks are made on the lessons learned from the adaptive reuse journey of George Town and Penang.

Genesis of a Bottom-Up Conservation Movement

In Malaysia, there is a three-tier governmental system of managing built heritage—federal government, state government, and local authorities. Conservation issues are controlled at the federal level by the Ministry of Tourism and Culture and partially by the Ministry of Housing and Local Government. In Penang, the state government, the Penang State Executive Council (EXCO), is responsible for general policy with respect to the planning, use, and development of all land and buildings within the jurisdiction of local authorities. The State Planning Committee (SPC), chaired by the chief minister, makes decisions on planning policies relating to the conservation, use, and development of land in the state and may give directions to the local authority to adopt and implement decisions of the SPC. The Municipal Council of Penang Island (Majlis Perbandaran Pulau Pinang [MPPP]) is the local authority, and its statutory functions are provided in accordance the Town and Country Planning Act (1976).[3] The federal-level Town and Country Planning Act introduced a two-tier system of development planning—the State Structure Plan, which provides general policy, and the Local Plan, which sets out specific policies. In addition, there is provision for a Special Area Plan, which comprises detailed projects and programs. MPPP adopts a general statutory framework of a number of laws, among which is the Antiquities Act, 1976 (superseded by the National Heritage Act, 2005).[4]

This section sets out the conservation and revitalization journey in Penang starting from the 1970s. It presents the genesis of a bottom-up conservation movement that changed Penang's approach from renewal to revitalization.

1970s–1990s: Building Conservation Consciousness

The story of conservation in Penang cannot be separated from that of ideological contestation and the pivotal role of civic society in raising awareness of the need to conserve built heritage. In his article "Conservation on the Move—A Penang Perspective," Laurence Loh wrote,

> The concept of conservation in Penang had humble beginnings . . . as with all things that have great potential and promise. . . . Its first official appearance came in the form of a conservation plan for the City of George Town prepared by the Central Area Planning Unit [CAPU] of the City Council.[5]

CAPU was formed by the Penang government in the late 1960s. In the early 1970s, CAPU introduced a policy on conservation areas in George Town. A Conservation

3. Majlis Perbandaran Pulau Pinang (MPPP) was renamed as Majlis Bandaraya Pulau Pinang (MBPP) in 2014. This essay uses the name MPPP for the historical account of Penang. State Government of Penang, *Heritage Management Plan.*
4. State Government of Penang, *Heritage Management Plan.*
5. Laurence Loh, "Conservation on the Move—A Penang Perspective," *Majalah Arkitek* 3, no. 1 (January/February 1999): 60.

Figure 22.1: View of George Town showing the high-rise KOMTAR. (Source: Hoyin Lee.)

Plan for George Town was prepared by the unit as support material for the town plan, known as the Interim Zoning Plan 1/73. The Singapore model of "conservation areas" and "comprehensive development areas" (CDAs) was parachuted into this plan, which was approved by the state government in 1973 and gazetted in 1974.[6]

After World War II, George Town experienced a prolonged period of almost zero growth with reports that there was no construction activity for nearly seven years.[7] During the early 1970s, the state government pushed hard to revitalize the economy of Penang through industrialization and real estate development. Among the first proposals for urban renewal to be implemented was the establishment of the Penang New Urban Centre, a project that aimed to develop three CDAs within George Town as identified in the Interim Zoning Plan 1/73. The perceived highlight of this proposal was the first inner-city high-rise building known as KOMTAR—a sixty-five-story multipurpose complex comprising commercial units, retail outlets, and a transportation hub (Figure 22.1). The development of this center resulted in the dislocation of several blocks of rent-controlled tenants and displacement of a number of local businesses and trades. The move was seen by conservationists as an excuse to justify wholesale destruction of large neighborhoods within the inner city. This was made possible under Local Government Act 1976, where provisions of the law granted the local authorities power to carry out urban planning, including administration of the planning systems and development control, among other things.[8]

6. Lik Meng Lee, Yoke Mui Lim, and Yusuf Nor'Aini, "Strategies for Urban Conservation: A Case Example of George Town, Penang," *Habitat International* 32 (2008): 293–304, https://www.researchgate.net/publication/236900064_Strategies_for_Urban_Conservation_A_case_example_of_George_Town_Penang.
7. Lee, Lim, and Aini, "Strategies for Urban Conservation."
8. Nik Hashim Ibrahim and Mohd. Yahya Nordin, "Local Government System in Malaysia" (Ministry of Internal Affairs and Communications), accessed April 19, 2023, https://www.soumu.go.jp/main_content/000336349.pdf.

From a legal standpoint, the concept of conservation had been recognized officially as a legitimate planning consideration under CAPU's policy and Conservation Plan for George Town. The explanatory notes of the policy and plan stated,

> The intention of this policy is to encourage greater environmental sensitivity in renewal or rehabilitation work; this will give scope for the greater appreciation of the historical and social environment of the locality.[9]

However, the tone of these notes was tentative with no mention of a framework or procedures. The promotion of conservation by the state government over the next decade was negligible. In the 1980s, there was a massive drive to redevelop George Town and Penang. Buildings were demolished, familiar sites were cleared, and memories were erased.

In the mid-1980s, the famed College General, the only Roman Catholic training institute for the brotherhood in Asia, was demolished for a shopping mall. People in Penang were appalled and outraged, and the first surge of social activism occurred. Street protests were held and flyers and T-shirts were printed and distributed but to no avail. This incident revealed the need for public awareness of heritage conservation. In 1986, a small group of conservation advocates, with conservation architect and expert Laurence Loh at the helm of the Pertubuhan Akitek Malaysia (Malaysian Institute of Architects) Northern Chapter and in conjunction with the Municipal Council of Penang Island (Majlis Perbandaran Pulau Pinang [MPPP]), organized the International Conference on Urban Conservation Planning. The first of its kind in Malaysia, the aim of the conference then was to introduce the fairly unknown concept of conservation to public and professional bodies. It is purported to have left a lasting impression on local architects and planners.

Gathering momentum from the conference, the MPPP prepared a draft Structure Plan in 1987, which proposed that "areas and buildings of historical, cultural and architectural significance or with other attractive and pleasant features worth preserving" should be identified and appropriate steps should be taken "to conserve or preserve in the planning for growth."[10] Along with the plan, a document titled *Design Guidelines for Conservation Areas in the Inner City Area of George Town, Penang* was produced by the MPPP. It was prepared with internal advice from expert planners and supported by the German technical agency GTZ. The guidelines formed the basis and the rationale for many "zones" proposed in the Structure Plan, which included identifying the inner city of George Town as a conservation area. Two years later, the state government approved the 1987 Municipal Council of Penang Island Structure Plan, which demarcated five conservation areas guided by concepts, objectives, and design requirements, which was subsequently extended to six areas. While the structure plan identified conservation areas, there was no specific legislation for the protection of heritage properties. The first inventory and survey of heritage buildings of George Town was published in 1994 and was undertaken by Alexander Koenig of GTZ during his time as heritage conservation consultant to the MPPP (1990–1993).

In the late 1980s, Penangites came together once again in an attempt to save Penang Hill, a cultural landscape of great importance—the first hill station in the then–British Empire with a functioning early twentieth-century funicular railway. The state government had envisioned "Disneyland type" projects for this site, but fortunately, the proposal was declined by the Penang electorate, removing the chief

9. State Government of Penang, *Heritage Management Plan*, 42.
10. Majlis Perbandaran Pulau Pinang (MPPP), *Draft Structure Plan* (Penang: MPPP, 1987), 98.

minister from office (1990). The new chief minister was forced to gazette a Local Plan for Penang Hill that had protection measures, such as the conservation of designated buildings, percentage of footprint allowed for increase in building areas, and recommended carrying capacity of the hill station.

Nongovernmental organizations and key individuals in Penang led the way in the move to "save" important buildings. In 1985, Penang Heritage Trust was formed to promote "the conservation and permanent preservation for the benefit and education of the people of Penang all those buildings, trees, books, manuscripts, writings, scrolls, documents, antiques, paintings, reproductions or other artistic or similar objects which because of their historical association, architectural features, aesthetic value or for other reasons are considered by the Council of the Society to form part of the heritage of Penang."[11]

In 1989, Cheong Fatt Tze Mansion (Blue Mansion) was purchased by a private company with an initial aim to save a dilapidated mansion of great heritage significance. The purchase was criticized and questioned with naysayers asking, "What can you do with it?" The conservation of Cheong Fatt Tze Mansion was driven and supported by a Penang-based couple with a convincing vision along with some help from family and friends. Eventually revealing its potential for adaptive reuse as a heritage boutique homestay, the project remains an exceptional achievement for the conservation movement in George Town (further elaborated in the case study section of the book).

The 1980s were more about "building awareness," as it was termed then. It began with an emphasis on built heritage and material culture. The idea of adaptive reuse was referred to only vaguely. Priority was placed on saving buildings from total loss, not on what to do usefully with them.

1990s: The Tipping Point

In 1991, there was the first gathering of conservation-minded individuals and organizations from around the region in Penang at a seminar funded by the United Nations High Commissioner for Refugees (UNHCR). As an outcome, the Asia and West Pacific Network for Urban Conservation (AWPNUC) was formed. The network sought to facilitate exchange of cultural information and technical expertise in urban conservation within the region. Over the next few years, an annual symposium of AWPNUC was held in various cities, and heritage practitioners and organizations shared their experience and knowledge.[12] The internet was in its infancy, and these symposia were important in building a supportive heritage network.

Around the same time, a major rescue project was negotiated successfully with the state government. A large enclave of government housing quarters built by the British was saved from demolition and redevelopment as the government had been persuaded to set an example for owners of heritage buildings (Figure 22.2). The conservation works were minimal; the buildings were simple and did not require extensive work. Adaptive reuse emerged as a viable option. The entire enclave was retained and restored; spaces were rented for various uses, including eateries and shops and a heritage hotel.

11. Penang Heritage Trust, *Constitution of Penang Heritage Trust* (Penang: PHT, 1986).
12. In all, six international symposia were held allowing important regional exchanges of information and learning: Penang (1991), Adelaide (1992), Hanoi (1993), Nara (1994), Yogyakarta (1995), and Taipei (1997).

Figure 22.2: View of the British housing quarters that were rescued from demolition. (Source: Lin Lee Loh Lim.)

In 1993, the conservation movement in Penang reached a turning point. The Metropole Hotel, an important building on a prominent road, was surreptitiously and illegally demolished on Christmas Day behind hastily erected hoarding. The building had many important historical connections with Thailand, and unfortunately for the perpetrators, it also had political associations. The 1994 general elections for Penang was imminent, the local population was appalled at the lawlessness displayed, and the press gave unrelenting negative coverage. The local authorities were forced to set up an independent council to address concerns. The Building Conservation Advisory Council (BCAC) was established and comprised sixteen professional and civil society groups. The BCAC proposed a list of recommendations and guidelines that were adopted almost in entirety by the local authority in 1995. The *Guidelines for Conservation Areas and Heritage Buildings in George Town* replaced the 1987 guidelines. The new ones included a full statement of the state government's policy for the identification and protection of heritage buildings, conservation areas, and other elements of the historical built environment.

In 1996, another momentous event for conservation took place. The recently restored and still-unoccupied Cheong Fatt Tze Mansion was extensively damaged by piling works for a new multistory car park in an adjoining site. The owners of the mansion took legal action with an injunction to stop works, an action never undertaken before in "the historical building versus new development" scenario. Public opposition to the new development was expressed through daily news coverage, street protests, and legal battles all the way to the federal court of appeal. Eventually, the local authority issued a total ban on hammer piling in the inner city of George Town (later defined by the boundary of George Town's World Heritage Site) and extended the law recently to include any development project next to a heritage building in Penang. This was a major achievement for conservation. Clearly, Cheong Fatt Tze Mansion has had "enormous impact and influence on the preservation movement in Penang by prompting the Local Government to enact strong preservation measures."[13]

13. UNESCO, "Cheong Fatt Tze Mansion," in *Asia Conserved: Lessons Learned from the UNESCO*

Late 1990s–Early 2000s: Toward World Heritage Listing

In 1997, the first UNESCO Conservation Conference for George Town and Malacca took place. It focused on the Outstanding Universal Value (OUV) of the two historical port cities and was designed to draw the attention of the respective state governments and local authorities. Strategic conversations ignited community aspirations for global recognition. Thus started the bid for World Heritage status. However, as a preliminary step, built heritage needed to be protected and conservation management plans were required.

In the early 2000s, after rounds of lobbying the federal government, George Town was placed on the Tentative List of World Heritage Sites in a joint nomination with Malacca. The preparation of the World Heritage Site boundary of George Town, particularly the Core Zone (Property) and Buffer Zone, can best be described as a "bloody battle." Developers fought to ensure that the site boundary was as small as possible. Advocates of listing were castigated in the press and negative scenarios proliferated. What was demarcated as the original Core Zone eventually became the Core and Buffer Zones. Boundaries of the proposed World Heritage Site followed no discernable logic, arching and curving based on the success of lobbying by groups and individuals. Finally, in 2008, "Melaka and George Town, Historic Cities on the Straits of Malacca" was inscribed on the list of World Heritage Sites.

With the World Heritage listing came the need to identify and protect cultural heritage assets within George Town as a World Heritage Site. In response, buildings (within the World Heritage Site boundary) are categorized under four categories, which are nested under the wider categories of "Conservation" and "Compatible Development."[14] Conservation Category 1 includes eighty-two important buildings, cemeteries, gateways, and sites. Some of these (buildings and monuments, in particular) were gazetted under the Antiquities Act 1976 and are now part of the National Heritage Act 2005, which includes additional buildings and monuments. Conservation Category 2 includes heritage places of special interest, primarily shophouses, as well as a wide range of small-scale items and objects. The Compatible Development categories are technically planning tools as one category addresses Infill, while the other considers Replacement. Infill refers to vacant sites or sites with temporary buildings, and only those sites where compatible redevelopment is permitted. Replacement, on the other hand, refers to the replacement of buildings without significant cultural heritage value, and only where "sensitive" redevelopment is permitted.[15]

In 2010, George Town World Heritage Incorporated (GTWHI) was established as a state heritage agency by the Penang state government. Its objective was to spearhead efforts in safeguarding the OUV of the World Heritage Site of George Town.

Asia-Pacific Awards for Cultural Heritage Conservation (2000–2004), ed. Richard A. Engelhardt (Bangkok: UNESCO, 2007).

14. George Town World Heritage Incorporated, "Buildings," May 6, 2021, https://gtwhi.com.my/our-work/buildings/.
15. State Government of Penang, *Heritage Management Plan*.

Challenges and Opportunities of Heritage Management

Repeal of the Control of Rent Act and the Emergence of Adaptive Reuse as a Conservation Strategy

The year 2000 could be called the year of adaptive reuse strategies for Penang, the year of the Repeal of the Control of Rent Act (the Act), which was imposed on the entire country after the end of World War II. The Act controlled the rent arrangement of all prewar properties and left Penang with the largest number of rent control premises in the country. Landlords gained little, houses were neglected, main tenants subleased to numerous subtenants. With the repeal of the Act, landlords, who had been receiving close to prewar rentals (less than one-tenth of market rates), could now force eviction of their tenants, but they could not demolish their properties. Coupled with the 1997 Asian economic recession, which had cooled development, Penang was left with many vacant and abandoned properties. This raised the questions of "What do you do with them?" and "How do you reuse them?"

In George Town, the ownership of more than five thousand premises within the World Heritage Site was concentrated in the hands of a few. Concerns regarding the future of these places were addressed through a community engagement exercise organized by Penang's heritage groups (led by the Penang Heritage Trust), the local authority, and the state government. Questions revolved around "What can I do with my heritage house?" and "Is the government going to help me repair my house?"

The questions concerning reuse were overwhelmingly answered with World Heritage inscription. From 2009 until 2019, the adaptive reuse of shophouses in the World Heritage Site escalated, especially for hospitality and tourism purposes, resulting in "an increase in the number of hotels by 190% (+116), especially smaller guesthouses and boutique hotels, and an increase in the number of hotel rooms by 140% (+3,325)."[16]

Figure 22.3: A street of shophouses in George Town before revitalization. (Source: Lin Lee Loh Lim.)

16. ThinkCity, *George Town World Heritage Site, Population and Land Use Census, 2009–2019, A City in Transition* (George Town: ThinkCity Sdn. Bhd., September 2021), https://thinkcityinstitute.org/wp-content/uploads/2021/11/George-Town-A-City-in-Transition.pdf.

Before World Heritage listing, initial attempts at adaptive reuse, such as small antique shops, crafts shops, and teahouses, were unsuccessful. There was not enough volume or enough interest, and business plans were unrealistic. The word went around that "just because you are in a heritage building does not guarantee you will do well." With World Heritage inscription in 2008, the speed and volume of George Town's growth as a "successful" site has been overwhelming. The value of land per square meter is among the highest in the entire country. The prices of heritage houses have spiraled, and businesses have expanded exponentially, at least until the COVID-19 pandemic. However, not all adaptive reuse projects have proven to be sustainable, especially those involving "outsider incursions." For example, well-heeled non-Penangites purchased large swaths of buildings, evicted all tenants, conducted sterile restorations, painted the buildings in uniform colors, and attempted reuse strategies that do not seem to be working. Perhaps such initiatives are not the Penang style, where a combination of unique built heritage with distinctive intangible cultural heritage has created a George Town success story. The people of Penang are invested in this story; they feel they have fought for it and that it belongs to them. It is because of this that adaptive reuse strategies are locally bound.

Loss of Living Communities

In 1997, a disheartened Malay urban community around the Lebuh Aceh Mosque (Figure 22.4) approached the Penang Heritage Trust (PHT) for help saving their historic homes from demolition and their community from disbandment. The community could neither articulate adequately their concerns and fears to the authorities nor conduct the historical research and prepare the presentation necessary to persuade the powerful landowner, the Muslim Religious Council of Penang, to drop their proposals. The community, together with PHT and Badan Warisan Malaysia (Heritage of Malaysia Trust in Kuala Lumpur), managed to "shame" the council into respecting the wishes of the descendants of the original donors of the land, and the development proposals were scuttled. A small revitalization project was carried out using UNESCO-LEAP (Local Effort and Preservation) funds, with some repairing and repainting of the community's timber houses.

In the mid-2000s, PHT was approached for help by a century-old jetty-dwelling community, the Koays, the last remaining intact Hui Chinese community with Muslim origins. A state highway planner from Kuala Lumpur, the nation's capital, had drawn a line through this coastal community with little to no understanding of the place and the consequences of building the proposed road. The state awarded a tender, which was accepted, and eviction orders were given to the residents. It was at this point that the community became aware of the highway. In opposition, there were campaigns, demonstrations, high-ranking interventions, historical presentations, and press conferences but all too late. The financial and legal implications were massive. Eventually, the community was disbanded, the jetty and homes were demolished, and nesting grounds for protected night herons were destroyed. The state government lambasted the nongovernmental organizations: "Why didn't you tell us earlier about this important cultural asset?" Conservation advocates lamented the absence of transparency and stressed the critical need for cultural mapping before planning decisions. Indeed, because of the strength of civil society in Penang and the problems faced by governments in imposing nonconsultative actions, most (if not all) development proposals are now usually well investigated and promoted prior to implementation. It might be said that the government now employs all methods, including media marketing, in order to promote proposals.

Figure 22.4: View of the Lebuh Aceh Mosque and its immediate context. (Source: Ka Sing Yu.)

Saving Sia Boey

In 2014, the Penang Transport Master Plan, which includes rapid transport systems and highways, was drawn up. It proposed that the Prangin Canal area (also known as Sia Boey), situated at the border of George Town's World Heritage Site, be transformed into the Integrated Exchange Hub servicing two monorail lines and a Light Rail Transit (LRT) line. The plan was criticized by heritage groups who believed "no thought or foresight has been given to the streetscape, pedestrian accessibility, tangible and intangible heritage, and other values associated with the land. Age-old trees will have to make way for the monorail lines, buildings will have to be torn down to facilitate the construction of stations, and livelihood of traditional fisherfolk and our natural resources will be compromised."[17] UNESCO was informed of the potential negative impact of the planned transport hub on the Outstanding Universal Value of George Town's World Heritage Site. In 2015, the granite basin for Sia Boey was discovered and political decisions were made to develop the site into Malaysia's first urban archaeological park. Site adjustments to the transport hub and LRT lines were made to reduce potential negative impact on George Town's World Heritage Site. In 2019, the Sia Boey Urban Archeological Park opened. Its aims are to support

17. Penang Heritage Trust, "Prangin Market and the Penang Transport Master Plan," accessed May 31, 2023, https://pht.org.my/prangin-market-and-the-penang-transport-master-plan/.

the UNESCO World Heritage Site of George Town by providing programming and space for local residents, as well as repairing shophouses and bringing together cultural heritage education, heritage conservation, sustainable development, and urban greenery.

Building Heritage Awareness

Attempts to spread awareness on the importance of heritage conservation started as early as 2000 with the launch of monthly heritage site visits by Penang Heritage Trust (PHT) members. These visits included the opportunity to meet people and communities associated with specific places, leading to an increased interest in conservation as well as an increased membership for PHT.[18]

Building heritage awareness has also included the recognition and conservation of living heritage. It is part of the Outstanding Universal Value of George Town's World Heritage Site and it informs adaptive reuse projects. It conveys the spirit of place and connects the city's built heritage with its intangible values. By 2000, one of the essay's coauthors, Loh-Lim, decided to focus on Intangible Cultural Heritage (ICH). In 2001, a study was conducted on the location of traditional trades throughout the inner city through PHT. To establish pathways for conserving ICH, Loh-Lim launched the Living Heritage Treasures of Penang Awards in 2005 to acknowledge and recognize Penangites who exemplified local skills and trades from artisan carving, Chinese calligraphy, and paper cutting to rattan weaving, shoemaking, and traditional cooking. Many of these people had never been acknowledged or acclaimed, and their skills needed to be documented and transmitted to others—a matter of sustaining a critical part of Penang's cultural heritage. The awards continue to this day. A logical offshoot from the Living Heritage Treasures was the Penang Apprenticeship Programme for Artisans (PAPA) that was established in 2007. The program was designed originally to pair apprentices with acknowledged artisans, both receiving funding. It has since evolved into short-term learning to promote traditional skills.

In 2007, blue historic streets plaques appeared on every major inner-city street corner (Figure 22.5). George Town is unique in its multicultural origins and the contributions of all its communities toward the early growth of the port settlement. While the colonial administrators honored their own people and interests through street signage, local communities ignored the official street names, preferring those in local dialects that helped them find their way or locate traders or craftspeople. Wayfinding was through references to activities, areas, contributions of outstanding community members, local personalities, occupations, physical aspects of an area, prominent buildings, and trades. Loh-Lim, through PHT and with funding from local authorities, documented the local names for all streets and arranged for plaques to be installed at all street corners. They continue to be a fascinating source of knowledge for community history and local trades.

Urban Regeneration

When George Town was listed as a World Heritage Site, there was an urgent need to protect and conserve the city's unique heritage. ThinkCity, a nonprofit organization, was created to launch the George Town Grants Programme (GTGP), designed to spearhead urban regeneration with the goal of promoting community engagement

18. The initiative was led by local conservation expert Loh-Lim, a coauthor of this essay.

Figure 22.5: An example of a blue plaque as seen at Love Lane, George Town. (Source: Lin Lee Loh Lim.)

Figure 22.6: A shophouse in George Town after conservation and revitalization. (Source: Lin Lee Loh Lim.)

and to preserve and celebrate heritage through financial and technical support. GTGP was responsible for activating close to three hundred catalytic projects within the World Heritage Site in the first five years following inscription.

At the beginning, a model of clustering individual building conservation projects in strategic locations to stimulate area revitalization and to give visibility to the idea of renewal was used. This resulted in an "explosion" of conservation and cultural place-making activities that rejuvenated the face of George Town (Figure 22.6).

Since 2012, in partnership with the Aga Khan Trust for Culture (AKTC), ThinkCity has completed several key public realm projects focused on area conservation and rejuvenation, climate action, and historic landscapes (parks and streetscapes) within the city. The projects both employ and promote the Sustainable Development Goals as a set of metrics for deliverables locally, nationally, and internationally. Using AKTC's Historic Cities Programme workbook, the partnership focused on the North and East Seafronts of the World Heritage Site's Core Zone where major monuments and landmarks stand within the maritime hub and where Captain Francis Light, acting for the East India Company, established the trading port of George Town.[19] There was a need to restore and rejuvenate a major precinct that had lost its integrity and cohesive history through uncoordinated development interventions over time, resulting in the blurring of significant layers of history. It was seen as an important undertaking by the state government to complement and enhance individual efforts by the private sector, catalyzed in part by the GTGP and spurred on by World Heritage inscription.

In 2015, the George Town Conservation and Development Corporation (GTCDC) was established as a joint partnership between the Penang state government, AKTC, and ThinkCity. To build support and attract investment in public realm upgrading, GTCDC started its mandate with a pilot project called Armenian Park, which converted an open space once usurped by an informal thieves' market into a green space within the heart of a vibrant heritage enclave. Capitalizing on the momentum, GTCDC moved to "the jewel in the crown," the nexus of the harbor front and its godowns, Fort Cornwallis (the first major building erected by the British), the Esplanade and Town Parade Ground, the original courthouses (now the State Assembly building), a historical clock commemorating the coronation of Queen Victoria of Great Britain, the neoclassical Town Hall and City Hall, and numerous nineteenth-century commercial buildings that used to house banks, European trading houses, and shipping companies.

Restoration of Fort Cornwallis is ongoing at the time of writing. The historical stone seawall fronting the Esplanade has just been completed. The fountain garden next to the Town Hall (now under restoration) has been restored in accordance with the Florence Charter. Landscaping and connecting roadside pavements and pathways continue to be upgraded to improve pedestrian access. With each intervention, George Town's Outstanding Universal Value and the attributes embedded in it are respected.

Application of area conservation planning principles suggest how sustainable transformation can take place. Ten years of engagement are starting to show how investment in public realm projects contribute significantly to cultural sustainability, making George Town inclusive, resilient, safe, and sustainable through efforts that safeguard Penang's cultural and natural heritage.

Toward Sustainability

In 2022, UNESCO Bangkok launched the Sustainable Heritage Management Masterclass series that uses regional success stories to reveal the various competences that ensure the vibrancy of heritage sites. This online education initiative invites participants to learn from standard-setting cases in heritage management through direct contact with project teams and solve challenges by applying newly acquired knowledge and skills.[20]

From UNESCO Bangkok's standpoint, Cheong Fatt Tze Mansion, recognized as the "Most Excellent Project" in the 2000 UNESCO Asia-Pacific Awards for Cultural Heritage Conservation, remains an exemplar of heritage conservation

19. The Aga Khan Historic Cities Programme (AKHCP) works on regeneration projects in historic areas in ways that spur social, economic, and cultural development. Its central objective is to improve the lives of the inhabitants of these historical areas while promoting models that will sustain these improvements. AKHCP has shown how the creation of parks and gardens, conservation of landmark buildings, improvements to the urban fabric and the revitalization of cultural heritage, in many cases the only assets at the disposal of the community, can provide a springboard for social development.
20. ThinkCity Institute, "Sustainable Heritage Management, Masterclass 1: Building a Legacy," accessed June 29, 2022, https://thinkcityinstitute.org/sustainable-heritage-masterclass/legacy/.

management twenty-three years on. The mansion was chosen as the site for the first Masterclass series. It was identified as a project that has sustained the owner's choice of use as a heritage hotel over a long period, having gone through three reiterations to stay relevant.

Conclusion: Lessons Learned

The term "adaptive reuse" came late in the heritage conservation timeline of Penang. While the advocacy of the 1980s and watershed events of the 1990s moved the conservation needle, the confluence of private and public initiatives in the 2000s kick-started the practice of building conservation, with adaptive reuse at the heart of projects. In time, a critical mass has brought attention and visibility to the heritage movement.

However, there is more to be done. The Antiquities Act 1976 was promulgated in the 1970s with its inadequacies purportedly addressed in the National Heritage Act 2005. The act grants the preservation and conservation of National Heritage, which is defined as "natural heritage, tangible and intangible cultural heritage, underwater cultural heritage, treasure trove and other manifestations such as heritage food and heritage persons."[21] The act is enforced and administered by a newly created role of a commissioner of heritage appointed by the Ministry of Tourism and Culture Malaysia. The act provides for the establishment of a National Heritage Register that can be inspected by members of the public, implying the importance of public participation in the field of heritage conservation. Even with this law, to date, there are no regulations in the act that define, classify, and guide the conservation of entire urban heritage sites, such as George Town and Malacca, despite their joint inscription as a World Heritage Site.

While 2008 signified the saving of a heritage city with far-reaching effects, Penang should now take the lead in partnering with UN-Habitat to be an integral part of a comprehensive sustainability plan at the national level.[22] It is imperative that the state government review and evaluate its plans and public realm proposals within the context of the Sustainable Development Goals (SDGs), including the associated targets and indicators. It should insist that project partners justify their proposals against the SDGs to independent reviewers and the people of Penang and be prepared to modify them if they are not compatible or worse, if they are directly contradictory to the sustainability goals that Penang is promoting.

With the almost fifty-year-long conservation journey of George Town and Penang, one of the primary lessons learned is that the most sustainable adaptive reuse of a building or structure is one that is closest to the original intention or use. This is exemplified through the successful case of Cheong Fatt Tze Mansion, where the project architect (and coauthor of this essay), Laurence Loh, recalls,

> In the early years, whilst we were restoring the building as close to its original fabric as possible, one message kept coming back to haunt me. It said: "The cycle of life must be reintroduced into the place." I used this intuitively to guide decision-making. The end product speaks for itself.

21. The Commissioner of Law Revision, *Malaysia, Laws of Malaysia, Act 645, National Heritage Act* (Kuala Lumpur: The Commissioner of Law Revision and Percetakan Nasional Malaysia Berhad, 2006), https://gtwhi.com.my/wp-content/uploads/2020/12/National-Heritage-Act-2005.pdf.
22. In 2018, the Penang state government signed a partnership with UN-Habitat under the leadership of the new director general (from Penang) to promote the United Nations' SDGs in its development goals.

> We believe we have created a place with a sense of spirit to which people want to return to again and again, all by highlighting the essence of the place through a thoughtful adaptive reuse strategy. The strategy recognizes the touchable and intangible cultural values that are unique but never attempts to overwork them.[23]

And most important, "the appropriate use of a heritage site is often the key to revealing the cultural values embedded within its original design and purpose, which is, in turn, the first step towards enshrining the spirit of place."[24]

Bibliography

George Town World Heritage Incorporated. "Buildings." May 6, 2021. https://gtwhi.com.my/our-work/buildings/.

Ibrahim, Nik Hashim, and Mohd. Yahya Nordin. "Local Government System in Malaysia." Ministry of Internal Affairs and Communications. Accessed April 19, 2023. https://www.soumu.go.jp/main_content/000336349.pdf.

Lee, Lik Meng, Yoke Mui Lim, and Yusuf Nor'Aini. "Strategies for Urban Conservation: A Case Example of George Town, Penang." *Habitat International* 32 (2008): 293–304. https://www.researchgate.net/publication/236900064_Strategies_for_Urban_Conservation_A_case_example_of_George_Town_Penang.

Loh, Laurence. "Conservation on the Move—A Penang Perspective." *Majalah Arkitek* 3, no. 1 (January/February 1999).

Loh, Laurence. "New Use—Old Fit." Paper presented at the Conservation of Urban Heritage: Macao Vision International Conference, September 2002.

Majlis Perbandaran Pulau Pinang (MPPP). *Draft Structure Plan*. Penang: MPPP, 1987.

Mohit, Mohammad Abdul, and Mohd Bashir Sulaiman. "Repeal of the Rent Control Act and Its Impacts on the Pre-war Shophouses in Georgetown, Malaysia." *Journal of the Malaysian Branch of the Royal Asiatic Society* 79, no. 1 (2006): 107–21. http://www.jstor.org/stable/41493817.

Penang Heritage Trust (PHT). *Constitution of Penang Heritage Trust*. Penang: PHT, 1986.

Penang Heritage Trust (PHT). "Prangin Market and the Penang Transport Master Plan." Accessed May 31, 2023. https://pht.org.my/prangin-market-and-the-penang-transport-master-plan/.

State Government of Penang. *Heritage Management Plan, State Government of Penang*. Kuala Lumpur: State Government of Penang and Badan Warisan Heritage Services Sdn. Bhd., February 2008. https://whc.unesco.org/en/documents/103167.

The Commissioner of Law Revision. *Malaysia, Laws of Malaysia, Act 645, National Heritage Act*. Kuala Lumpur: The Commissioner of Law Revision and Percetakan Nasional Malaysia Berhad, 2006. https://gtwhi.com.my/wpcontent/uploads/2020/12/National-Heritage-Act-2005.pdf.

ThinkCity. *George Town World Heritage Site, Population and Land Use Census, 2009–2019, a City in Transition*. George Town: ThinkCity Sdn. Bhd., September 2021. https://thinkcityinstitute.org/wp-content/uploads/2021/11/George-Town-A-City-in-Transition.pdf.

ThinkCity Institute. "Sustainable Heritage Management, Masterclass 1: Building a Legacy." Accessed June 29, 2022. https://thinkcityinstitute.org/sustainable-heritage-masterclass/legacy/.

UNESCO. *Asia Conserved: Lessons Learned from the UNESCO Asia-Pacific Awards for Cultural Heritage Conservation (2000–2004)*. Edited by Richard A. Engelhardt. Bangkok: UNESCO, 2007.

23. Laurence Loh, "New Use—Old Fit" (paper presented at the Conservation of Urban Heritage: Macao Vision International Conference, September 2002), 142.
24. Loh, "New Use—Old Fit," 143.

Penang Timeline

Laurence Loh and Lin Lee Loh-Lim

This timeline summarizes key events from the essay "Adaptive Reuse within the Context of Penang's Bottom-Up Conservation Movement: Creating a Sustainable Future for Heritage." It sets out Penang's major conservation-related entities, initiatives, milestones, and regulations from 1786 to 2022, including entries for the five case studies included in this publication.

1786	George Town is founded by Captain Francis Light, who issues orders to lay out the streets in a gridiron pattern for this new settlement on the northeastern cape of Penang Island.[1]
1957 (January 1)	George Town is given a city status per a royal charter issued by Queen Elizabeth II.
1957 (August 31)	Malaysia (then Malaya) gains independence from the British.
1962	Penang New Urban Centre development is first proposed with the high-rise KOMTAR as the focal point of the project.[2] (The project starts in the mid-1970s.)
1967	Control of Rent Act 1966 (Act 56) A federal government act that contributes to the protection of a number of prewar buildings within the inner city of George Town.[3]
Late 1960s	Central Area Planning Unit (CAPU) is formed by the Penang State government.

1. Lik Meng Lee, Yoke Mui Lim, and Yusuf Nor'Aini, "Strategies for Urban Conservation: A Case Example of George Town, Penang," *Habitat International* 32 (2008): 293–304, https://www.researchgate.net/publication/236900064_Strategies_for_Urban_Conservation_A_case_example_of_George_Town_Penang.
2. Soon-Tzu Speechley, "Komtar: Malaysia's Monument to Failed Modernism," Failed Architecture, June 6, 2016, https://failedarchitecture.com/komtar-malaysias-monument-to-failed-modernism/.
3. Rent control in Malaysia existed even before World War II. The Control of Rent Ordinance 1948 repealed the following ordinances: The Control and Charged Land (Restriction) Enactment 1940, the Rent and Charged Land (Restriction) Ordinance 1947, the Increase of Rent (Restriction) Ordinance 1939, the Increase of Rent (Restriction) Enactment (Johore) 1939, and the Rent and Charged Land (Restriction) Enactment (Kedah) 1360 Hijra/1941. (See Mohammad Abdul Mohit and Mohd Bashir Sulaiman, "Repeal of the Rent Control Act and Its Impacts on the Pre-war Shophouses in Georgetown, Malaysia," *Journal of the Malaysian Branch of the Royal Asiatic Society* 79, no. 1 [2006]: 107–21, http://www.jstor.org/stable/41493817.)

1973 and 1974	CAPU introduces a policy on conservation areas in George Town. A Conservation Plan for George Town is prepared by the unit as support material for the town plan, known as the Interim Zoning Plan 1/73. "Conservation areas" and "comprehensive development areas" (CDAs) are introduced. The plan is approved by the state government in 1973 and gazetted in 1974.[4]
1974 (January 1)	Prime Minister Tun Abdul Razak drives the first pile for KOMTAR—a sixty-five-story, polygonal office tower with a four-story podium. (The project was developed over eleven years, between 1974 and 1985.)[5]
1974	The two local governments on Penang Island, the George Town City Council and the Penang Island Rural District Council, are merged to form the Municipal Council of Penang Island (Majlis Perbandaran Pulau Pinang [MPPP]).[6]
1976	Antiquities Act 1976 "The act provides for the control and preservation of, and research into, ancient and historical monuments, archaeological sites and remains, antiquities and historical objects and to regulate dealings in and export of antiquities and historical objects and for matters connected therewith."[7]
1976	Local Government Act 1976 (Act 171) The act formalizes the 1974 merger of local governments with the establishment of a district council and municipal council. Provisions of the law grant the local authority power to perform urban planning and management functions (among other things).[8] Gazetted on March 25, 1976.[9]
1976	Town and Country Planning Act 1976 This act is closely related to built heritage by means of development plans and development control. It introduces a two-tier system of development planning—the State Structure Plan, which provides general policy, and the Local Plan, which sets out specific policies. In addition, there is provision for a Special Area Plan, which comprises detailed projects and programs. Gazetted on March 25, 1976.[10] (The Town and Country Planning Act was amended four times over 1993–2007.)[11]
Mid-1980s	College General, the only Roman Catholic training institute for the brotherhood in Asia, was demolished for redevelopment. This event sparked social activism in Penang.
1985	Penang Heritage Trust (PHT), a nongovernmental organization, is established to promote conservation.

4. Lee, Lim, and Aini, "Strategies for Urban Conservation," 302.
5. Speechley, "Komtar."
6. Majlis Perbandaran Pulau Pinang (MPPP) was renamed as Majlis Bandaraya Pulau Pinang (MBPP) in 2014. This essay uses the name MPPP for the historical account of Penang.
7. UNESCO Cultural Heritage Laws Database, *Laws of Malaysia, Act 168, Antiquities Act 1976*, https://en.unesco.org/sites/default/files/malaysia_law_act168_1976_engl_orof.pdf.
8. Ainul Jaria Maidin and Bashiran Begum Mobarak Ali, "Powers of the Local Authority in Regulating Land Planning and Development Control: Whither Control," *Journal of the Malaysian Institute of Planners* 7 (2009): 133–47, https://www.planningmalaysia.org/index.php/pmj/article/download/75/73.
9. "Laws of Malaysia—DOA," Department of Agriculture Malaysia, accessed June 2, 2023, http://www.doa.gov.my/index/resources/info_doa/akta171_kerajaan_tempatan_1976.pdf.
10. "Town Planning and Country Act, Act 172," Laws of Malaysia, accessed June 2, 2023, https://tcclaw.com.my/wp-content/uploads/2020/12/Town-and-Country-Planning-Act-1976.pdf.
11. Nur Farhana Azmi, Faizah Ahmad, and Azlan Shah Ali, "Mechanisms for Protecting the Identity of Small Towns in Malaysia," *MATEC Web of Conferences* 66, no. 00113 (2016), https://www.matec-conferences.org/articles/matecconf/pdf/2016/29/matecconf_ibcc2016_00113.pdf.

1986	International Conference on Conservation and Urban Planning is organized by a small group of conservation advocates, including conservation architect and expert Laurence Loh at the helm of the Pertubuhan Akitek Malaysia (Malaysian Institute of Architects) Northern Chapter, and in conjunction with the Municipal Council of Penang Island (Majlis Perbandaran Pulau Pinang [MPPP]).
1987	*Design Guidelines for Conservation Areas in the Inner City Area of George Town, Penang* is produced by MPPP and introduces the concept of conservation areas.
1987	Penang Island Structure Plan is approved by the Penang State government. It proposes that "areas and buildings of historical, cultural and architectural significance or with other attractive and pleasant features worth preserving" should be identified and appropriate steps should be taken "to conserve or preserve in the planning for growth."[12]
1988	Inventory and Survey of Heritage Buildings of George Town is prepared under the German Technical Cooperation Scheme (GTZ, a German Government Agency). (The inventory is published in 1994.)
Late 1980s	Penang Hill is proposed to be redeveloped, provoking civil protests (Save Penang Hill campaign).
1990	Koh Tsu Koon is elected the new chief minister of Penang and is perceived to be more sympathetic to conservation appeals.
1990	CAPU is dissolved with the replacement of state leaders in 1990.
1991	Asia and West Pacific Network for Urban Conservation (AWPNUC) is formed as an outcome of a seminar funded by the United Nations High Commissioner for Refugees (UNHCR). (In 2007, the activities of AWPNUC are taken over by Lestari Heritage Network, Penang.)
1993 (December)	Metropole Hotel is illegally demolished.
1994	Building Conservation Advisory Council (BCAC) is established and comprises sixteen professional and civil society groups.
1995	*Guidelines for Conservation Areas and Heritage Buildings in George Town* are produced and incorporate BCAC's recommendations. These guidelines replace the 1987 guidelines.
1995	Cheong Fatt Tze Mansion, adaptive reuse of a former extended-family home as a heritage boutique hotel, is completed. The place opens to the public in 2001. (This is one of the five Penang case studies included in this book.)
1996	Legal injunction against hammer piling at neighboring Cheong Fatt Tze Mansion leads to an eventual ban on hammer piling in the inner city of George Town.
1997	UNESCO Conservation Conference for George Town and Malacca takes place, starting the bid for World Heritage status.
1997	Lebuh Aceh Mosque community, with the help of the PHT, save their historic homes from demolition and their community from being disbanded. A small revitalization project is conducted using UNESCO LEAP (Local Effort and Preservation) funds, with some repairs and repainting of the timber houses.
1997	Rent Control Act is repealed (coming into force on January 1, 2000).

12. Majlis Perbandaran Pulau Pinang (MPPP), *Draft Structure Plan* (Penang: MPPP, 1987), 98.

2000	Cheong Fatt Tze Mansion is recognized as the "Most Excellent" project at the UNESCO Asia-Pacific Awards for Cultural Heritage Conservation.
2005	National Heritage Act 2005 is gazetted. The act provides for the preservation and conservation of National Heritage, which is defined as "natural heritage, tangible and intangible cultural heritage, underwater cultural heritage, treasure trove and other manifestations such as heritage food and heritage persons."[13] It is enforced and administered by the Commissioner of Heritage appointed by the Ministry of Tourism and Culture Malaysia and provides for the establishment of a National Heritage Register.
2005	PHT's "Living Heritage Treasures of Penang" Awards is inaugurated—a celebration of intangible cultural heritage. People who define Penang cultural heritage are selected and honored. This program continues to date.
2007	Suffolk House, restoration and adaptive reuse of a former government house as an events space and restaurant, is completed. (This is one of the five Penang case studies included in this book.)
2007	Traditional Street Names Plaques project is initiated and administered through the PHT and funded by the local authority.
2008	Suffolk House is recognized with an "Award of Distinction" at the UNESCO Asia-Pacific Awards for Cultural Heritage Conservation.
2008	The Historic Cities of the Straits of Malacca, comprising George Town and Melaka, are jointly listed as a World Heritage Site.
2008	Commencement of the Penang Apprenticeship Programme for Artisans (PAPA), a training program associated with the Living Heritage Treasures Awards of the PHT.
2009	ThinkCity (arm of Khazanah, Malaysia's sovereign fund) is formed as a nonprofit organization.
2010	George Town World Heritage Incorporated (GTWHI) is established as a state heritage agency by the Penang State government to spearhead efforts in safeguarding the Outstanding Universal Value (OUV) of the World Heritage Site of George Town.
2011	Conservation Management Plan and Draft Special Area Plan are drawn up, incorporating a historic urban landscape approach (HUL).
2014	MPPP is renamed Majlis Bandaraya Pulau Pinang (MBPP).
2015	George Town Conservation and Development Corporation (GTDC) is established as a joint partnership between the Penang State government, the Aga Khan Trust for Culture, and ThinkCity.
2016	Penang State government moved to gazette George Town World Heritage Special Area Plans.
2016	United Asian Bank (UAB) Building, restoration and adaptive reuse of a former godown as offices for Khazanah Nasional (an investment arm of the federal government) and ThinkCity (a consultancy and project delivery think tank), is completed. (This is one of the five Penang case studies included in this book.)
2018	Penang State government signed a partnership with UN-Habitat under the leadership of the new director general (from Penang) to promote the UN Sustainable Development Goals (SDGs) in its development goals.

13. The Commissioner of Law Revision, *Malaysia, Laws of Malaysia, Act 645, National Heritage Act* (Kuala Lumpur: The Commissioner of Law Revision and Percetakan Nasional Malaysia Berhad, 2006), https://gtwhi.com.my/wp-content/uploads/2020/12/National-Heritage-Act-2005.pdf.

2019 (November)	Penang Harmony Centre, adaptive reuse of a heritage bungalow as an interfaith community space for Penang, is completed. (This is one of the five Penang case studies in this book.)
2019 (November 9)	Sia Boey Urban Archeological Park opens. Its aims are to support the UNESCO World Heritage Site of George Town by providing programming and space for local residents, as well as repairing shophouses and bringing together cultural heritage education, heritage conservation, sustainable development, and urban greenery.
2022	UNESCO Bangkok launches the Sustainable Heritage Management Masterclass with Cheong Fatt Tze Mansion as the study site for the first masterclass series.
2022	Hin Bus Depot, adaptive reuse of a run-down former bus depot and maintenance compound as an arts space, is completed and opens to the public. (This is one of the five Penang case studies included in this book.)

Bibliography

Azmi, Nur Farhana, Faizah Ahmad, and Azlan Shah Ali. "Mechanisms for Protecting the Identity of Small Towns in Malaysia." *MATEC Web of Conferences* 66, no. 00113 (2016). https://www.matec-conferences.org/articles/matecconf/pdf/2016/29/matecconf_ibcc2016_00113.pdf.

Department of Agriculture Malaysia. "Laws of Malaysia—DOA." Accessed June 2, 2023. http://www.doa.gov.my/index/resources/info_doa/akta171_kerajaan_tempatan_1976.pdf.

Laws of Malaysia. "Town Planning and Country Act, Act 172." Accessed June 2, 2023. https://tcclaw.com.my/wp-content/uploads/2020/12/Town-and-Country-Planning-Act-1976.pdf.

Lee, Lik Meng, Yoke Mui Lim, and Yusuf Nor'Aini. "Strategies for Urban Conservation: A Case Example of George Town, Penang." *Habitat International* 32 (2008): 293–304. https://www.researchgate.net/publication/236900064_Strategies_for_Urban_Conservation_A_case_example_of_George_Town_Penang.

Maidin, Ainul Jaria, and Bashiran Begum Mobarak Ali. "Powers of the Local Authority in Regulating Land Planning and Development Control: Whither Control." *Journal of the Malaysian Institute of Planners* 7 (2009): 133–47. https://www.planningmalaysia.org/index.php/pmj/article/download/75/73.

Majlis Perbandaran Pulau Pinang (MPPP). *Draft Structure Plan*. Penang: MPPP, 1987.

Mohit, Mohammad Abdul, and Mohd Bashir Sulaiman. "Repeal of the Rent Control Act and Its Impacts on the Pre-war Shophouses in Georgetown, Malaysia." *Journal of the Malaysian Branch of the Royal Asiatic Society* 79, no. 1 (2006): 107–21. http://www.jstor.org/stable/41493817.

Speechley, Soon-Tzu. "Komtar: Malaysia's Monument to Failed Modernism." Failed Architecture, June 6, 2016. https://failedarchitecture.com/komtar-malaysias-monument-to-failed-modernism/.

The Commissioner of Law Revision. *Malaysia, Laws of Malaysia, Act 645, National Heritage Act*. Kuala Lumpur: The Commissioner of Law Revision and Percetakan Nasional Malaysia Berhad, 2006. https://gtwhi.com.my/wp-content/uploads/2020/12/National-Heritage-Act-2005.pdf.

UNESCO Cultural Heritage Laws Database. *Laws of Malaysia, Act 168, Antiquities Act 1976*. https://en.unesco.org/sites/default/files/malaysia_law_act168_1976_engl_orof.pdf.

Penang Case Studies

Project	Heritage Status	Nature	New Use	Original Use	Timeframe
Cheong Fatt Tze Mansion	Grade 1	Private	Heritage boutique homestay	Extended-family home (late nineteenth century)	1990–2001
Suffolk House	Grade 1	Public-private partnership	Events venue / Restaurant	Home of the Governor of Penang (1808)	2000–2007
United Asian Bank (UAB) Building	Grade 2	Public-private partnership	Offices	Port godown, banks, and offices	2014–2016
Penang Harmony Centre	Category 2	Government/Public	Interfaith community space	Private residence (1880)	July 2018–July 2019
Hin Bus Depot	Category 2	Private	Arts space	Bus depot (1818)	2013–2022

Cheong Fatt Tze Mansion (Blue Mansion), Penang

Lin Lee Loh-Lim

Cheong Fatt Tze Mansion (Blue Mansion) is arguably the earliest exemplar of revitalization and conservation best practice in the state of Penang. To quote from the citation for the Most Excellent Project in the 2000 UNESCO Asia-Pacific Awards for Cultural Heritage Conservation, "the restoration of the Cheong Fatt Tze Mansion is an exceptional achievement for the conservation movement in Penang. It served as a model for restoration projects in the George Town community and its impact prompted stronger heritage measures in the city and, indeed, the broader region."[1]

Figure 24.1: Exterior view of Cheong Fatt Tze Mansion, Penang. (Source: Arkitek LLA.)

1. UNESCO, "Cheong Fatt Tze Mansion," in *Asia Conserved: Lessons Learned from the UNESCO Asia-Pacific Awards for Cultural Heritage Conservation (2000–2004)*, ed. Richard A. Engelhardt (Bangkok: UNESCO, 2007).

Project Information

Address	14 Leith Street, 10200, George Town, Penang, Malaysia
Original use	Extended-family home (dating from the late nineteenth century)
New use	Heritage boutique homestay
Heritage status	Grade 1
Site area	Site area: 5,200 square meters Built-up area: 3,250 square meters
Project cost estimate	US$2 million
Funding model	Private
Owner	Cheong Fatt Tze Mansion Pt. Ltd.
Developer	NA
Architect	Laurence Loh and Lin Lee Loh-Lim
Contractor	NA
Project timeline	1990–1995: Restoration of the mansion 1999–2000: Electrical and plumbing fit out 2001: Open to public 2016–2021: Continuous upgrades

Project Description

The project started with the perceived need to save an exceptional building from ruin and collapse. It then evolved into the necessity of undertaking an exemplar to demonstrate quality conservation with authenticity and integrity as driving principles. Its objectives were as follows:

- To demonstrate the possibility of retaining "spirit of place" with minimal loss of honesty and accuracy.
- To achieve a use that would be faithful to the past yet truly answering present needs.
- To keep abreast of current needs and to validate their incorporation into the conservation.

The adaptive reuse of Cheong Fatt Tze Mansion (Blue Mansion) attempted to introduce a use that would be in keeping with the original owner's intent. The precepts of the large, extended-family home belonging to the Cheong family would have allowed those with even minimal connections to the family a shelter over their heads. The current use as a heritage boutique homestay allows an echo of various events and celebrations that would have featured in the lives of the Cheong family. Current users of the homestay are now eating, sleeping, celebrating, mingling, and relaxing as users of the mansion would have done in the past.

In the transformation of the original extended-family home of thirty-eight rooms with five granite-paved courtyards to a heritage boutique homestay with eighteen bedrooms, two restaurants (indoor and outdoor), lounge and bar, museums, and gift shop, the specific project objectives were to be historically accurate, technically competent, sustainable, and ready to "build back better." The project brief also covered readiness to explain the conservation approach to a skeptical audience, along with a mindset to teach and learn from the conservation process.

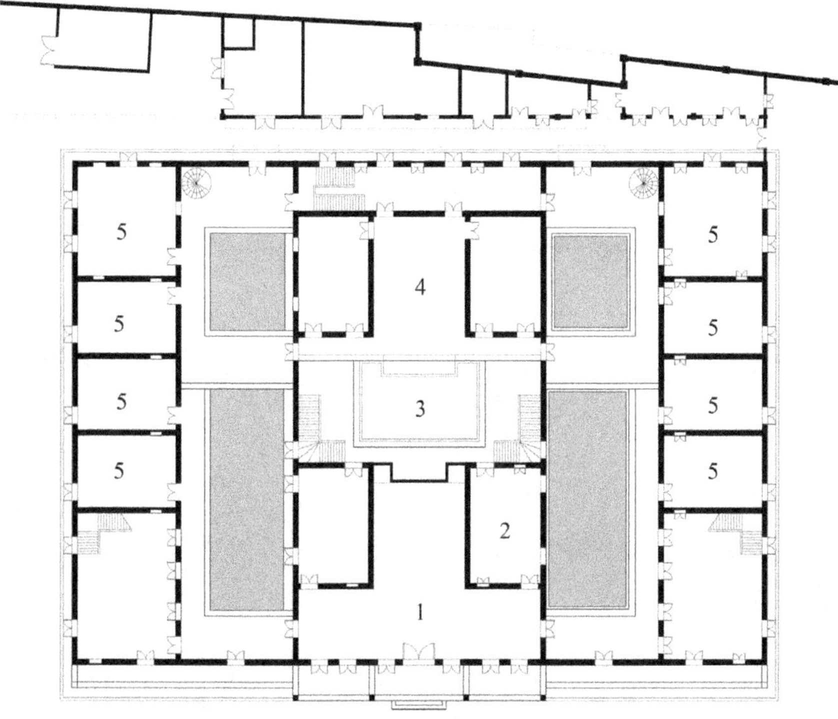

Figure 24.2: Ground-floor plan of Cheong Fatt Tze Mansion—1. Entrance, 2. Gift shop, 3. Courtyard, 4. Restaurant, 5. Guest rooms. (Source: Drawn by Ng Wai Shing based on materials from Arkitek LLA.)

Site History

Cheong Fatt Tze Mansion sits in all its splendor in the World Heritage Site of Melaka and George Town, Historic Cities of the Straits of Malacca, highlighting the important contributions of the early impoverished Chinese migrants to Penang. The site is located on one of the most significant streets in George Town. Referred to as "Hakka Millionaires Row," Leith Street housed several vice consuls for the Manchu government of China in the late-nineteenth century and was named after one of the early governors of Penang. It also stood amid the four earliest educational institutions of the island and exemplified the modern outlook of its early settlers. Cheong Fatt Tze Mansion is a reminder of the early successful entrepreneurs who made their fortunes elsewhere in the region but built their mansions in George Town.

Cheong Fatt Tze Mansion is a Chinese courtyard house, which uses southern Chinese building typology and materials, and reflects national and regional influences. It has a distinctive sense of scale, proportion, and space. Although a late nineteenth-century building, its form dates back three thousand years to the Chow dynasty. "It is an edifice of impressive delicacy with an exceptional quality of design and craftsmanship . . . an architecture of great assurance and maturity . . . a cultural statement in its Chinese-ness while articulating an openness to the incorporation of imported ideas and forms from other lands."[2]

Prior to the conservation works, the mansion was structurally stable but in disrepair and dilapidation from misuse. While the Cheong family still resided in the main house, there were thirty-four illegal squatter families occupying wings and outbuildings. Delicate timber carvings and filigree works were abused, termites were a major threat, and historical floor tiles were ripped off or cemented over. Glaswegian

2. Lin Lee Loh-Lim, *The Blue Mansion: The Story of Mandarin Splendour Reborn* (Penang: L'Plan Sdn. Bhd., January 2002).

Figure 24.3: Interior courtyard of Cheong Fatt Tze Mansion. (Source: Laurence Loh and Lin Lee Loh-Lim.)

ironworks were rusted or removed, art nouveau stained glass panels and gothic windows were immeasurably damaged, and the flooring and large timber columns and capitals were all compromised.

Project History

The conditions of Cheong Fatt Tze's will stated that the mansion could only be sold upon the death of his last son. This took place in 1989, and the mansion was then put on the market. Conservation of the place had to be done given the prominence of both the architecture and the man. At that time, conservation laws were nonexistent in Penang, and restoration standards and expertise were abysmal. It is often said that the senior Cheong chose the right people at the right time and made sure they did it right.[3]

The conservation of Cheong Fatt Tze Mansion was supported solely by private funding and driven by a Penang-based couple with a convincing vision along with

3. Lin Lee Loh-Lim, *The Blue Mansion: The Story of Mandarin Splendour Reborn*, rev. ed. (Penang: L'Plan Sdn. Bhd., 2012).

some help from family and friends. Initially, a company was set up to purchase and hold the property (Cheong Fatt Tze Mansion Pt. Ltd.). Later, a second company called Straits Indigo Pt. Ltd. was formed to manage the operations of the heritage homestay.

Development Environment

The adaptive reuse of Cheong Fatt Tze Mansion is an early example of George Town's journey to conservation consciousness. At that time, local authorities had no awareness and no specific policies to aid conservation efforts. Certain materials that were required to be imported to conduct authentic restoration were subject to taxation. Foreign artisans could not be brought in to carry out specialized work. For example, the colored porcelain rice bowls required for *chien nien*, the mosaic style of ornamentation where the bowls are carefully clipped with pliers into shards, were subjected to a "foreign crockery" tax despite the assurance that the bowls were to be broken for restoration works. Specialized artisans required for this craft, which is practiced exclusively by the Fujianese and Teochew, had to be brought in on visitor visas, showing the insufficient governmental support for authentic conservation works at the time.

Intervention

The intervention required for achieving the vision of this project went beyond that of an ordinary conservation project as it was an attempt to set benchmark standards in a completely new field. The interventions/actions were more philosophical and social in nature. There was much that was not known, and therefore an approach of great humility and willingness to learn was adopted. With this careful approach, the Cheong Fatt Tze Mansion, a place of great complexity and encompassing many values and philosophies, slowly revealed itself.

Geomancers deduced the feng shui, and Chinese historians and philosophers construed the original approach. The local community was encouraged to share oral histories and "grandmothers' stories." Considerable help was sourced from "experts" involved in similar projects, and the entire exercise was one of ascertaining, discovering, understanding, and sharing.

Key Challenges

- In the early 1990s, challenges lay in creating awareness, obtaining political support, and in convincing local workmen that modern building techniques were not always suitable and could not replace the skills and materials of the past.
- The lengthy restoration of the property from acquisition to fit out and utilities as well as ongoing maintenance had one major setback. Piling works at a neighboring site damaged the property, requiring additional restoration and leading to a pivotal legal battle.

Keeping Heritage Alive

As the project advanced, the cultural heritage significance of the place had a growing impact on the conservators. They were only vaguely aware of the mansion's significance at the beginning, and the entire process was one of learning. The architectural, historical, and social significance of the place began to unfold with increasing research and input.

Cheong Fatt Tze was an important figure beyond Penang. Flags were flown at half-mast upon his death, and the modern Chinese government printed first day cover stamps in his honor as recently as 2016, one hundred years after his death. The man's political and social standing during his lifetime was marked with acclaim and honors from all quarters. His home in Penang, which was his favorite, exemplified his standing. The people of Penang feel a sense of ownership of this magnificent Cheong family home.

The architectural marvels of the mansion were unraveled as the project progressed, with their remarkable combinations of East and West attributes, reflecting the cultural exchanges during the late nineteenth and early twentieth centuries. The intricacies of almost perfect geomancy and spirit of place were carefully discerned in the conservation process. The local community took great pride in the restoration and showed their appreciation by donating furniture and other memorabilia from the nineteenth and early twentieth centuries.

The entire approach was one of retention of authenticity. "Expressed through the tangible built heritage, these intangible values give the place its distinctive character, an aura that draws people to the place, that speaks to them, engages in their emotions and, often, gives them a sublime experience of their surroundings."[4] The spirit of Cheong Fatt Tze Mansion was always in its use as a large home for a large extended family, where people enjoyed companionship, ate, slept, and celebrated life's events. Today, in its use as a heritage boutique homestay, the place is being used in exactly that spirit.

A great deal of effort was put into the interpretation of the site to ensure that all visitors, both local and foreign, appreciate the values of the place. Large banners with the history of the man and the house as well as the conservation process are prominently displayed outside. Two in-house museums are set up with displays of historical artefacts from the mansion—audiovisual displays, architectural plans and elevations, as well as family photographs, clothes, memorabilia, and so forth.

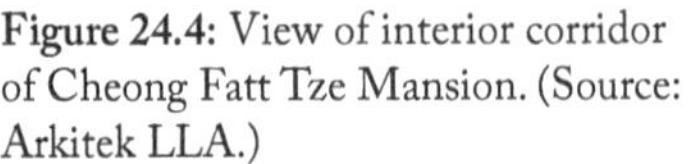

Figure 24.4: View of interior corridor of Cheong Fatt Tze Mansion. (Source: Arkitek LLA.)

4. UNESCO, "Cheong Fatt Tze Mansion."

Restoration materials of traditional plasters, dyes, organic timber finishes, tiles, and traditional porcelain works are also displayed with engaging interpretation of the materials and techniques. Guided tours in different languages are offered several times a day to in-house guests as well as visitors.

Long-Term Viability

The low-impact use of the Cheong Fatt Tze Mansion as a heritage boutique homestay demonstrates sustainability. The considerable economic return helps ensure that its fragility is not compromised. The public spaces of the mansion are also used for events, including their controlled use as a filming location (*Indochine* and *Crazy Rich Asians*). Nothing that could threaten the integrity of the place is allowed.

The long-term sustainability of the place is seen in its strategic planning, inclusive approach to marketing, and working with young and dynamic local staff. There is also a persistent and continuous rekindling and renewal of social awareness of the significance of the site. This approach has been tested in the recent restrictions necessitated by the COVID-19 pandemic. Instead of closing or folding the homestay, a decision was made to initiate fresh and exciting outlets—Mangga, an outdoor food and beverage outlet, was set up under a historical mango tree on the site. By installing timber platforms and greenery, local community activity has been rekindled through gatherings under the tree, sitting on mats and cushions, and celebrating life and greenery.

Impact

Economic: Through its adaptive reuse as a heritage boutique homestay, Cheong Fatt Tze Mansion has opened employment opportunities for a number of locals, especially for its food and beverage operations and housekeeping requirements. The mansion also serves as a training premise for students in the food and beverage industry as well as for tour guides.

Environmental: To date, this is the most exceptional conservation project in George Town. It was the earliest one, and it was conducted on an uncompromising, global best-practice platform. Its award-winning efforts and its international exposure have led to fundamental changes in existing—and inappropriate—laws and regulations.[5] The legal battle against hammer percussion piling in the historic city led to the local authorities placing a blanket ban on all hammer piling in George Town as well as near heritage buildings outside of the city limits. This forthright approach has ensured that glitches in conservation work are fully exposed, and it has led to the enactment of more protective and encompassing laws and regulations.

Social: The Penang public "took ownership" of the mansion. Their pride in acknowledging the restoration was demonstrated by their donations of furniture and so on. Besides the homestay, the daily tours and the restaurants ensure that the mansion is always accessible. Tours for schoolchildren and people with special needs are conducted regularly. Arrangements for events and celebrations are weekly affairs and an open house is conducted on a regular basis. "The restoration of the Cheong

5. Cheong Fatt Tze Mansion has been recognized with the following awards: 1995, Conservation Excellence Award—PAM Malaysian National Architectural Award; 2000, Most Excellent Project—UNESCO Asia-Pacific Awards for Cultural Heritage Conservation; 2004, Best ASEAN Cultural Preservation Effort—ASEANTA Excellence Awards; 2011, 10 Greatest Mansions & Grand Houses in the World—Lonely Planet.

Fatt Tze Mansion is an exceptional achievement for the conservation movement in Penang. It served as a model for restoration projects in the George Town community and its impact prompted stronger heritage measures in the city and, indeed, the broader region. A meticulous application of research coupled with scientific analysis, traditional artisan skills, and when necessary, imported materials and workmanship, ensured the authenticity and methodology of its reconstruction."[6]

Cheong Fatt Tze, the Blue Mansion, requires no advertising; it is its own best promoter and is testimony to the brilliance of its original owner and its original builder and designer. The [restorers and] current owners consider themselves merely as sustaining the vision and [are] honoured to be caretakers.[7]

—Lin Lee Loh-Lim

Bibliography

Loh-Lim, Lin Lee. *The Blue Mansion: The Story of Mandarin Splendour Reborn*. Penang: L'Plan Sdn. Bhd., January 2002.

Loh-Lim, Lin Lee. *The Blue Mansion: The Story of Mandarin Splendour Reborn*. Rev. ed. Penang: L'Plan Sdn. Bhd., 2012.

UNESCO. *Asia Conserved: Lessons Learned from the UNESCO Asia-Pacific Awards for Cultural Heritage Conservation (2000–2004)*. Edited by Richard A. Engelhardt. Bangkok: UNESCO, 2007.

6. UNESCO, "Cheong Fatt Tze Mansion."
7. Loh-Lim, *The Blue Mansion* (2012).

Suffolk House, Penang

Lin Lee Loh-Lim

Suffolk House represents the finest of Georgian architecture in Penang, a style that was transformed in its passage through India into the Malay Peninsula. The mansion was home to several early governors of the East India Company and remains a romantic icon representing a high moment in the genesis of a historical island port settlement. It is also a symbol of the resolution of the people of Penang, who strove for more than fifty-two years to "conserve an iconic ruin that once teetered on the brink of oblivion," finally achieving the restoration and adaptive reuse of the place.[1]

Figure 25.1: Exterior view of Suffolk House. (Source: Arkitek LLA.)

1. Laurence Loh, *Suffolk House* (Penang: HSBC Printers RP Printers S/B, 2007).

Project Information

Address	Ayer Itam Road, Penang, Malaysia
Original use	Home of the governor of Penang (1808)
Previous use	Private home/Canteen and classrooms for neighboring school (Methodist Boys School)
New use	Events venue/Restaurant
Heritage status	Grade 1
Site area	Site area: 6,051.71 square meters Built up area: 1,404.95 square meters
Project cost estimate	US$2 million
Funding model	Tripartite funding: Public (state), private (HSBC), and private (community donors)
Owner	Penang state government
Developer	NA
Architect	Laurence Loh (Arkitek LLA Sdn. Bhd.)
Contractor	NAJCOM Sdn. Bhd.
Project timeline	2000–2007 (Save Suffolk House campaign, 1956–2007)

Project Description

The immediate goal of the project was to save Suffolk House from total collapse. The importance of the mansion was never in question. The estate on which the mansion stood was originally the property of the founder of modern Penang, Captain Francis Light. The conservation of Suffolk House took into consideration the entire estate, including the double-story mansion, its expansive gardens, as well as the Ayer Itam River and original historical bridge. The house was intended to be reused as a venue for events, such as weddings and celebrations as well as concerts and plays.

The criteria for the UNESCO Asia-Pacific Awards for Cultural Heritage Conservation formed the guidelines for the project. As such, the objectives of the project were as follows:

- To save the mansion and demonstrate the manner in which the process and the final product can contribute to the surrounding environment and the local community's cultural and historical continuum.
- To articulate the structure's heritage values in order to convey the spirit of the place through the conservation work.
- To demonstrate appropriate use or adaptation of the structure.
- To demonstrate sensitive interpretation of the cultural, social, historical, and architectural significance of the place in the conservation work.
- To demonstrate an understanding of the technical issues of conservation/restoration in interpreting the place's significance.
- To demonstrate the use and quality control of appropriate building, artisan, and conservation techniques.
- To demonstrate the use of appropriate materials.

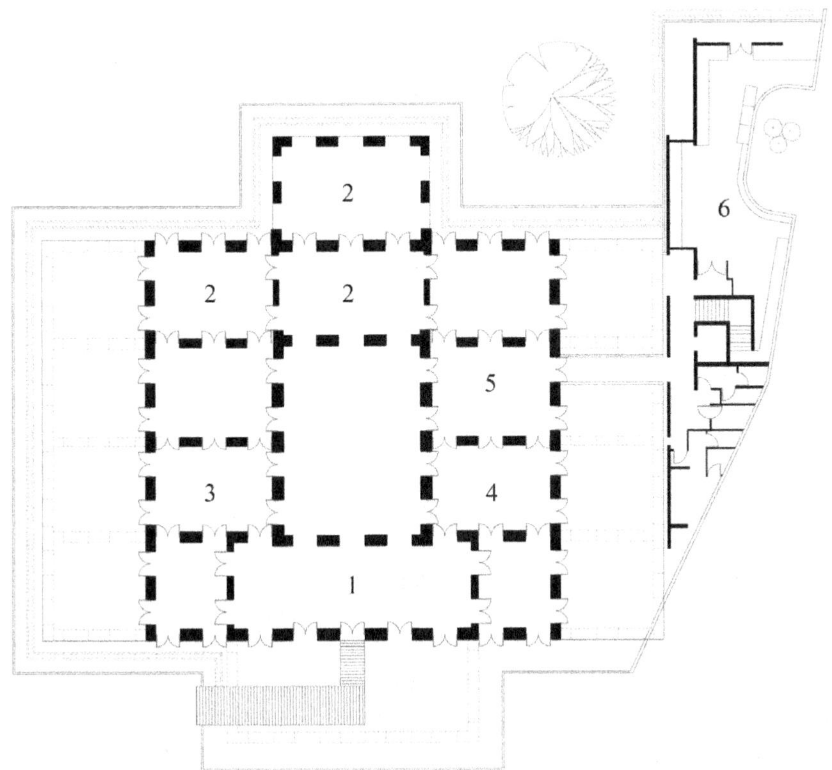

Figure 25.2: Ground-floor plan of Suffolk House—1. Reception hall, 2. Café, 3. Rooms, 4. Office, 5. Shop, 6. Pantry. (Source: Drawn by Ng Wai Shing based on materials from Arkitek LLA.)

- To demonstrate how well any added elements or creative technical solutions respect the character and inherent spatial quality of the place.
- To demonstrate the influence of the project on conservation practice and policy locally, nationally, regionally, and internationally.
- To demonstrate the ongoing socioeconomic viability and relevance of the project and provision for its future use and maintenance.
- To showcase technical consistency, complexity, and sensitivity in the project methodology.[2]

Site History

Suffolk House stands as one of the most controversial conservation projects in Malaysia. Even identifying its original builder is controversial as studies by historians, architects, and sociologists have cited either Captain Francis Light, the founder of modern Penang, or W. E. Phillips, one of the governors of Penang. Whether it was built by Light or Phillips, based on William Daniels's painting, *View of Suffolk House, Prince of Wales Island* (1818), it was a magnificent building, a pure example of Anglo-Indian form (outside India) and based primarily on Georgian architecture. It is unique of its kind in Penang and in Malaysia.

The historical significance of the mansion dates to when it served as the governor's residence and Government House from 1805 to the 1820s. Critical political issues, such as the establishment of Singapore, were most likely first discussed by

2. UNESCO, "Regulations: UNESCO Asia-Pacific Awards for Cultural Heritage Conservation," in *Asia Conserved II: Lessons Learned from the UNESCO Asia-Pacific Awards for Cultural Heritage Conservation (2005–2009)*, ed. Montira Unakul (Bangkok: UNESCO and iGroup Press, 2014), 423.

Sir Stamford Raffles in Suffolk House when he visited Governor Bannerman. Due to the change of ownerships at the turn of the twentieth century, many alterations and changes were made to the house. Before it was abandoned in the 1970s due to its dilapidated condition, it was used as a canteen and classrooms by the neighboring Methodist Boys School.

Suffolk House is an inspiring example of how an important historical building in Malaysia survived numerous attempts to demolish it by many parties. Public interest in saving Suffolk House started in 1956 with the launch of the Save Suffolk House campaign. The continuing deterioration of Suffolk House over the years and the truly remarkable efforts to save it are well documented in *Saving Suffolk House*.[3] The Penang Heritage Trust (PHT), in particular, was responsible for several attempts to publicize the mansion's condition, raise money, and to stabilize and protect it.

Prior to the start of the conservation project in 2000, the condition of Suffolk House was considered to be "crumbling and shameful," and the place could only be aptly described as "a pile of bricks" (Figure 25.3). A 1990s attempt by the PHT to slow down deterioration and damage from the tropical weather was the erection of scaffolding around the mansion to support a temporary protective metal deck roof. This attempt proved futile. The famed Marble Hall on the ground floor had a gaping cobra's nest in the center. The teak timber staircase had a full-grown tropical tree reaching through the first landing to the roof. None of the bedrooms could be accessed as all the timber floors had collapsed. Arches (interior and exterior) had buckled, columns had disintegrated, and any existing timber elements were held together by "armies of termites linking hands." The PHT also convinced the government of Adelaide, South Australia (founded by William Light, the son of Francis Light) to send a team of experts to conduct a full dilapidation study of Suffolk House. The report of this study was sent to the state government in yet another attempt to kick-start the restoration.

Figure 25.3: As-found condition of the ballroom on the upper floor of Suffolk House. (Source: Laurence Loh, *Suffolk House* [Penang: HSBC Printers RP Printers S/B, 2007].)

3. Loh, *Suffolk House*.

Project History

The prominence of Suffolk House and its ongoing shameful deterioration was of such consequence that its conservation became a political as well as a social issue for the Penang community. As stated by Professor Northcote Parkinson for the Municipal Council of Penang Island (MPPP) in 1960, "Suffolk House is emphatically worth saving. To neglect it any longer would be a blunder. To destroy it now would be a crime."[4]

However, "the advocates of conservation from the private sector actually had no control of the process, no ownership rights and no legitimate, legal or statutory responsibility or need."[5] Nonetheless, after five long years of needless bureaucracy, ownership reverted to the state in 1999, and the Methodist Church exchanged Suffolk House and the surrounding land for a piece of state land already being used by the Methodist School as a football field.

The project was supported by a committed and resolute conservation nongovernmental organization, an indomitable conservation architect, an enthralled and beguiled CEO of a major international bank, and a supportive chief minister. Suffolk House brought them together with its magic and kept them captivated till the conservation was complete. It was the first, and to date most successful, tripartite effort comprising the community, a corporate body, and the government.[6]

Development Environment

As the property was owned by the Penang state government and the initial financier was the Hong Kong and Shanghai Banking Corporation (HSBC), doors for funding support were open. Many private companies and individuals, including the ordinary Penangite, wanted to share a small part of the story of Suffolk House. Even contractors, suppliers, and utility companies bent over backward to accommodate novel requests.

The funding model evolved in a very organic fashion. The state funded Phase 1 (repairing the central portion of the mansion and the jack roof), while the state and HSBC funded Phase 2 (outstanding restoration works). When the restoration was completed, there was little funding left for the fit out, and it was then that the public—both corporate and private—stepped in to help.

Intervention

The entire conservation process of eight years involved continuous political intervention and balancing various parties, where mediations were weekly tasks. A noncompromising insistence on meeting the standards of best practice in conservation (as outlined in the project objectives) required maintaining an equilibrium between civil servants, financiers, historians, individuals, local interest groups, and politicians. Classes, discussions, process and materials demonstrations, tours, and site visits became weekly rituals.

Once a period of significance had been decided on, which was based on discussions with architects, conservationists, historians, and researchers, all additions and

---

4. Northcote Parkinson, *Study on Suffolk House* (Penang: MPPP, 1960).
5. Loh, *Suffolk House*.
6. The success of this partnership is validated through its recognition with an Award of Distinction at the 2008 UNESCO Asia-Pacific Awards for Cultural Heritage Conservation.

changes were reversed as far as possible. Examination of early paintings and sketches of the house as well as findings from excavation works were used as points of reference. The most obvious changes in terms of the building's external appearance were the substitution of a pitched roof for the original flat roof and a single-story lean-to addition on the western side. In relation to the floor plan, the east and west colonnades had structurally detached from the building after the flat roofs had failed in terms of watertightness. This resulted in their being demolished and led to a thirteen-bay building becoming a nine-bay building. However, this change is not apparent when the building is viewed from the western side, where the present entrance is located. In the main house itself, only air-conditioning, fans, lighting, and security systems were added. Appropriate furnishings, such as Victorian mirrors and lamps were sourced from India. An early brick bridge on the site, which was depicted in oil paintings, was carefully reconstructed. All utilitarian needs, such as kitchens and elevators for people with disabilities, were sited externally and designed to be clearly distinguishable from the original structure.

Key Challenges

- The biggest challenge of the Suffolk House project was the politics of conservation. After decades of struggles and eight years (2000–2007) of restoration and fit out, it was imperative that the team needed to secure the ongoing socioeconomic viability, sustainability, and cultural relevance of the project, as well as provide for its future use and maintenance. A shocking political change took place in early 2008, when an entirely new state government won control in Penang. (Suffolk House is owned by the state government of Penang.) The new government had no understanding of the cultural heritage significance of the place and its history.
- Suffolk House had been leased to and managed by Badan Warisan Malaysia (BWM), a nongovernmental organization. It had set up an interpretation center together with an events venue. However, the rent that the new government wanted to levy was beyond the capacity of BWM, which gave up the lease. The new lessee has transformed the house into a fine-dining restaurant. Some interpretation panels remain.

Keeping Heritage Alive

The prominence of Suffolk House and the politics surrounding it, amplified by continuous media coverage, have ensured that its significance is well known and appreciated. The conservation project has been continuously open to evaluation and study by many parties, locally as well as internationally. This has augured well for retaining the authenticity and integrity of the place in all aspects.

The site's history, stories that have been told, myths, and memories and the continuing tales, use, and emotions all contribute to its current identity and spirit of place. The conservation project was a successful effort to restore, with sensitivity and intuition, an early nineteenth-century Anglo-Indian garden house, the first great house of Penang.[7]

7. Frank Campbell in a South Australian Conservation Unit (SACON) report commissioned by the PHT in 1993, describes the Anglo-Indian garden house as "an arid zone house of two or three storeys of masonry with a terracotta-tiled parapetted flat roof." Additionally, Ian Nairne Morson in *A Short Account of Francis Light, 18thC Merchant Adventurer, Resident of Phuket, and Founder of Penang* describes Light's garden house as "a Malay pavilion owned by Francis Light with a thatched roof and surrounded by a fence interwoven with boughs of greenery."

Given the substantive importance of the building as well as the prolonged efforts to save it, every stage of the conservation process was documented. Each room/space has interpretation plaques as well as before-and-after images. Historical tours are provided upon arrangement, and a visit to Suffolk House remains one of the highlights of visiting Penang. All essential paintings of Suffolk House have been reproduced and can be viewed in various rooms on-site.

Long-Term Viability

Use of Suffolk House as an events space and a fine-dining venue supports the economic sustainability of the place. Cultural heritage guides are trained to ensure that visitors are presented with riveting tales spreading awareness of the historical significance of the house.

Suffolk House sits on the banks of the Ayer Itam River on the island. Flooding of the river would present a future problem. Accordingly, arrangements have been made with the Department of Rivers and Water Channels (Jabatan Parit dan Salur) to ensure sufficient netting, ponding areas, and trash traps to protect the house.

Attempts have also been made to secure long-term tenancy agreements with the owner, the Penang state government. Maintenance and repairs are part of the agreement to ensure protection and continuation of the place.

Impact

Economic: The adaptive reuse of Suffolk House has set a higher standard of quality tourism in Penang as well as Malaysia.

Figure 25.4: Architect Laurence Loh giving a presentation at Suffolk House. (Copyright: UNESCO and ThinkCity; Credit: Pilloworks.)

Environmental: The immediate goal of preventing the total collapse of the crumbling Suffolk House was achieved. The house was restored to 1818, the height of its significance. The citation in the Award of Distinction in the 2008 UNESCO Asia-Pacific Awards for Cultural Heritage Conservation sums up the impact of the project: "The restoration of Suffolk House has returned one of the most important colonial heritage landmarks in Penang to its former state of grandeur after years of neglect. . . . The restoration works were carried out to a high level of technical competence and demonstrate standard-setting excellence in craftsmanship. The public-private partnership in undertaking the project has renewed the building's historic role and serves as a worthy model for future restoration initiatives in the Penang World Heritage site."[8]

In addition to the careful restoration and appropriate adaptive reuse of Suffolk House, the entire green zone around the building has been conserved. To maintain the idyllic setting, the river has not been canalized, and all the mature trees have been retained. Area conservation at this point is not recognized as a planning policy in Penang, but the wholistic approach to conservation seen at Suffolk House is a superb exemplar as such policy is developed.

Social: The restoration and adaptive reuse of Suffolk House has brought conservation to the doorstep of ordinary Penang folk. Through the public's involvement and ongoing accessibility to the place, there is a sense of shared ownership. As "one of the most memorable and immortal buildings in Penang," all of Malaysia knew about the ongoing conservation of Suffolk House.[9] Donors came from around the country and wanted to be part of this recapture of a magnificent edifice. Its magnificence has assured its impact and ultimately its survival.

It was a journey of patience in which I gathered knowledge about her [Suffolk House's] past and the heritage values ingrained within her walls as I revisited ideas and decisions over and over again, all in the search for authenticity. The people who worked with me within the layers of time and space that all converged into the single site are very special people, all of them. Together we created a space that will inherit new meanings, even as we take home a part of our past.[10]

—Laurence Loh

Bibliography

Loh, Laurence. *Suffolk House*. Penang: HSBC Printers RP Printers S/B, 2007.

Parkinson, Northcote. *Study on Suffolk House*. Penang: MPPP, 1960.

UNESCO. *Asia Conserved II: Lessons Learned from the UNESCO Asia-Pacific Awards for Cultural Heritage Conservation (2005–2009)*. Edited by Montira Unakul. Bangkok: UNESCO and iGroup Press, 2014.

8. UNESCO, "Suffolk House," in *Asia Conserved II: Lessons Learned from the UNESCO Asia-Pacific Awards for Cultural Heritage Conservation (2005–2009)*, ed. Montira Unakul (Bangkok: UNESCO and iGroup Press, 2014), 279.
9. Loh, *Suffolk House*.
10. Loh, *Suffolk House*.

United Asian Bank (UAB) Building, Penang

Lin Lee Loh-Lim

The restoration and adaptive reuse of the United Asian Bank (UAB) Building, a former godown, as offices for Khazanah Nasional (an investment arm of the federal government) and ThinkCity (a consultancy and project delivery think tank) embody the principles of sustainability. In 2018, the project won the PAM (Malaysian Institute of Architects) Building of the Year award as well as the PAM Gold Award for Excellence in the Adaptive Reuse Category. It is also the first Malaysian conservation project to attain the US-based LEED (Leadership in Energy and Environmental Design) Gold Certification, which recognizes a "design framework that seeks to create quality, healthy, highly efficient and cost-saving green buildings."[1] The UAB Building now stands as a globally recognized project of sustainability achievement bringing heritage works in the country to a new level of international recognition.

Figure 26.1: Exterior view of the UAB Building. (Source: Arkitek LLA.)

1. US Green Building Council, "LEED," accessed May 30, 2022, https://leed.usgbc.org/.

Project Information

Address	21–35, China Street Ghaut, 10300 George Town, Penang, Malaysia
Original use	Godown (1926)
Previous use	Port godown, banks, offices of the British Authorities (Resident Commissioner's Office), and later, Chief Minister's Office
New use	Offices for Khazanah Nasional and ThinkCity (digital library, exhibition spaces, meeting rooms, multipurpose spaces, and research center for urban regeneration projects)
Heritage status	Grade 2
Site area	3,700 square meters (36,000 square feet)
Project cost estimate	US$2.5 million (RM11.6 million)
Funding model	Private (50 percent), semiprivate (20 percent), public (Khazanah Nasional, 30 percent)
Owner	Tetuan Malihome Sdn. Bhd.
Developer	NA
Architect	Arkitek LLA Sdn. Bhd.
Contractor	Protech Heritage Services Sdn. Bhd.
Project timeline	End 2014–mid-2016

Project Description

The United Asian Bank (UAB) Building project aimed to set new benchmarks in conservation and adaptive reuse. These benchmarks included the integration of twenty-first-century spaces in a historical building within the context of the World Heritage Site of George Town. The project sought to promote environmental sustainability and compatibility with standards of heritage conservation in Malaysia. Its objectives were as follows:

- To respond innovatively to the historical context.
- To reveal the qualities and cultural heritage significance of the place.
- To conserve the place with high standards and with appropriate use and reuse of materials.
- To incorporate biophilic design features that seek to connect our inherent need to affiliate with nature in the modern built environment.
- To promote continuity.
- To have a wide-ranging social influence.

The adaptive reuse of the UAB Building combines a programmatic response that increases the resilience of the site using innovative design features with broad ecological considerations. The project transforms the former godown into an office space comprising workspaces and meeting rooms as well as large community spaces for exhibitions, presentations, talks, and so forth. By understanding the existing building, spaces are rearranged to adapt to contemporary functions that are in line with traditional patterns of use. The project responds to the requirements for flexible,

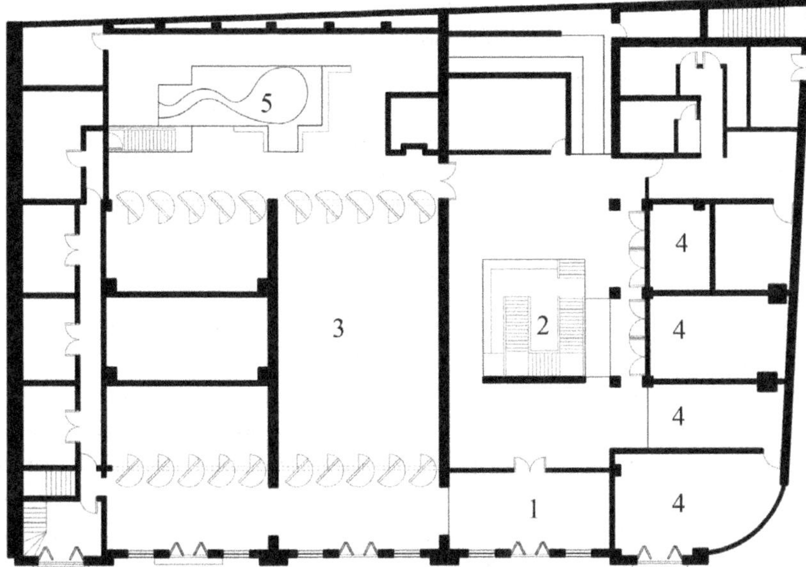

Figure 26.2: Ground-floor plan of the UAB Building—1. Entrance, 2. Staircase, 3. Multipurpose room, 4. Meeting rooms, 5. Courtyard. (Source: Drawn by Ng Wai Shing based on material from Arkitek LLA.)

collaborative workspaces that go hand in hand with activated spaces that engage the community. This spatial planning was shaped by contextual considerations and the integration of Outstanding Universal Value recognized in George Town's World Heritage Site, all while incorporating current sustainability considerations.

Site History

Built in 1926, the United Asian Bank (UAB) Building is located on China Street Ghaut on reclaimed land along the eastern coastline of George Town, where trading of tin and rubber burgeoned and dominated the commercial realm of the harbor front. When the building was commissioned by Yeap Chor Ee in the early 1920s, he was one of the most prominent merchants occupying Weld Quay (a location near the original port of Penang). Dominating the sugar trade in Penang for over three decades, he later became (and remained) the only individual in the country to single-handedly establish a bank, Ban Hin Lee Bank. His mercantile operations and amenities (e.g., financial institutions, godowns, offices, oil mills, and trading houses) and his determination and faith in the booming trading industries in Malaya led to a significant transformation of Weld Quay as part of an entrepôt city.

Over the past century, the UAB Building has gone through significant change of use, from a godown to banks and to offices of the British Authorities (Resident Commissioner's Office and, later, Chief Minister's Office), accommodating the city's ever-changing social and economic needs. Eventually left abandoned for several years, the owner, Tetuan Malihome Sdn. Bhd., sought long-term tenants for the building that could help revitalize the building and the vicinity.

From an innovation perspective, the UAB Building has landmark architectural and engineering value. It was the first building in Penang to be built with ferro concrete (reinforced concrete). The neoclassical building was equipped with a thick building envelope to provide fire protection and to ensure goods stored were kept under constant temperature and, more important, kept dry from the humid tropical climate. Large windows and oversized loading doors provided ample light and air circulation. On the upper floor, air vents above the window sills and teak lanterns on the rooftop were ingenious solutions for additional ventilation and natural light.

The building remains among the finest examples of a post–World War I two-story mercantile office-cum-godown in the port settlement in Penang.

Due to the somewhat awkward and inelegant reuse of original storage spaces as commercial offices over the years and the introduction of poor materials (such as plywood and acrylic-based paints), the condition of the entire structure was compromised—termite infested, damp, and unattractive.

Project History

The United Asian Bank (UAB) Building is located in one of the most significant parts of George Town's World Heritage Site, the waterfront. The owner, who had several other major properties to manage, was keen to find willing tenants who had the means to conduct a worthy restoration. Khazanah Nasional is an investment arm of the federal government, while ThinkCity, a subsidiary of Khazanah, is an urban regeneration think tank and project delivery partner. The two organizations came together as partners and initiated the adaptive reuse project to give a new lease on life to an underutilized historically significant building.

Development Environment

There were no specific incentives or subsidies that helped the realization of this project. Adaptive reuse of the United Asian Bank (UAB) Building was anchored by an excellence-driven client with a sufficient budget, which was key to achieving new sustainability standards in heritage conservation.

Intervention

When confronted with a historical port-side godown that had been clumsily converted into office and commercial banking spaces, the evolving design approach grew to become more than restoration and adaptive reuse. It sought to be an example of international conservation and sustainability standards.

First, the godown typology with an inner courtyard and high ceilings was retained. Setting an example for surrounding conservation works, original building materials were retained as much as possible. Where design or regulatory considerations made this impossible, materials were salvaged and repurposed for furnishing and other items. Efficient use of spaces and the interconnectedness of public and private realms were achieved through carefully planned circulation and flow, both horizontally and vertically. The first floor was punctured to allow the insertion of a now-celebrated staircase. Despite the opportunity cost of lost floor space, the gain from the liberated flow between the floors has transformed the relationship of spaces.

Second, restoration and adaptive reuse of the building went beyond conserving physical and cultural heritage. The project applied the principles of biophilic design, which recognizes the human need to affiliate with nature and other forms of life. This perspective became the driving force and key consideration in developing workspaces as well as public spaces.

Key Challenges

- The project focused on design innovation with respect to energy and water efficiency, creating excellent indoor quality in terms of natural light and ventilation,

Figure 26.3: View of the interior courtyard of the UAB Building. (Source: Arkitek LLA.)

and recycling materials and resources (such as water). The challenge lay in convincing the client and contractor to adhere to these standards of sustainable design.

- The project also sought to have a positive impact on both the neighborhood and the World Heritage Site of George Town. The subsequent street landscaping and upgrading of China Street Ghaut is one such outcome.

Keeping Heritage Alive

The conservation and adaptive reuse of the United Asian Bank (UAB) Building not only embodies standards in conservation practice but also extends the place's physical life with contemporary options for community use. It also demonstrates twenty-first-century ecological options for adaptive reuse projects.

The project has kept heritage alive by revealing the significance of the place through design and usage of spaces, choosing appropriate materials and reusing discarded materials, adopting an innovative response to historical context using a biophilic approach, implementing programs and usage compatible with context, and promoting community continuity.

Long-Term Viability

The conservation process has enhanced rather than altered the character of the building. It has kept the historical structure intact. The choice of materials has been appropriate, and there is continuity of an appropriate use as a flagship and benchmark building for the company (70 percent) and an attractive, accessible community space (30 percent).

Figure 26.4: A community event held in the multipurpose space of the UAB Building. (Source: ThinkCity.)

Due to Malaysia's rapid political changes and the building's connections to the Ministry of Finance, ThinkCity was forced to take over the tenancy of the entire building from Khazanah Nasional. At the time of writing, ThinkCity has managed to secure tenancies that are able to sustain the building. It has evolved into a vibrant digital creative hub servicing the city of George Town. The long-term sustainability of the building remains at the forefront of planning, and innovative responses are continuously sought.

Impact

Economic: The United Asian Bank (UAB) Building is now viewed as a desirable address to operate from. This renewed recognition of the significance of the place has allowed ThinkCity to secure tenancies, which contribute toward sustaining the maintenance of the building.

Environmental: Standard-setting adaptive reuse of the UAB Building has raised the bar for the latest preferred conservation approach in Malaysia. As mentioned in the citation of the 2018 PAM (Malaysian Institute of Architects) Building of the Year award and Gold Medal Award of Excellence in Adaptive Reuse Category, the "exemplary edifice . . . not only honors its rich architectural lineage but also resolutely demonstrates the innate connection to nature and natural processes to enhance health and wellbeing of spaces to work, play, and live in." For example, occupants' comfort, well-being, and productivity are ensured through improved indoor air quality, and existing natural areas and restored damaged areas now provide habitat and promote biodiversity.

In addition, the project has achieved a high degree of water efficiency by equipping the building with water-saving equipment ranging from low-flow taps and dual flush systems to a water-harvesting and automated irrigation system for the courtyard landscaping. Different zones of the courtyard are watered at different times depending on solar heat distribution to prevent excessive loss of water through evaporation. Since there was insufficient space for landscaping to meet the LEED specifications, a vertical garden and a naturalized courtyard were introduced as solutions.

The UAB Building has become an accelerator for the critical urban rejuvenation of the neglected precinct between the busy downtown and the waterfront of George Town. Beyond George Town, this approach to adaptive reuse in the context of a UNESCO World Heritage Site is encouraging building owners, practitioners, and decision-makers in urban planning and policymaking to pursue higher standards in conservation practice.

Social: Since its revitalization, the UAB Building has become a part of the vibrancy of the George Town social and cultural scene. A generous 30 percent of the building's floor space has been intentionally conserved, upgraded, equipped, and activated for utilization by the inner-city community. The George Town Festival 2017 successfully utilized designated spaces in the building for various exhibitions and talks, while state events and bookings for a vast array of academic, cultural, and social events continue to pour in. The project demonstrates an exemplary understanding of cultural significance, community aspirations, and effective branding/promotion.

> **An exemplary edifice which not only honors its rich architectural lineage but also resolutely demonstrates the innate connection to nature and natural processes to enhance health and well-being of spaces to work, play, and live in.**
>
> **—Arkitek LLA**

Bibliography

US Green Building Council. "LEED." Accessed May 30, 2022. https://leed.usgbc.org/.

Penang Harmony Centre, Penang

Laurence Loh and Tan Bee Eu

Penang Harmony Centre is an example of the successful adaptive reuse, with a contemporary touch, of a heritage bungalow as a community building. It has been highly acclaimed and accorded the PAM Award 2020 Gold, a national award, for design excellence in adaptive reuse. The building is also a winner of the Edge-PAM Green Excellence Award 2021 and Silver Award for Interior Design excellence in Adaptive Reuse category of REKA Awards 2022.

Figure 27.1: View of the heritage lodge (right) and the new community hall addition (left) of Penang Harmony Centre. (Source: Tan Bee Eu.)

Project Information

Address	15, Scotland Road, Penang, Malaysia
Original use	Residential, known as Wickham Lodge (1880)
Previous use	Administrative office for Penang Integrity Institute (Institut Integriti Pulau Pinang)
New use	Interfaith community space providing public amenities, such as community hall, function room, meeting rooms, and discussion area for community-held cultural/religious celebrations
Heritage status	Category 2
Site area	4,589 square meters
Project cost estimate	US$569,476 (RM2.5 million)*
Funding model	Penang state government
Owner	Penang state government
Building Operator	Penang Harmony Corporation Sdn. Bhd.—Harmonico
Developer	Chief Minister Incorporated of Penang
Architect	BEu Tan Architect (BETA)
Contractor	CLK Builders PLT.
Project timeline	July 2018–July 2019 (six months design period and six months construction period) Official launch: November 2019

Note:
* Conversion is taken at US$1=RM4.39.

Project Description

Penang Harmony Centre was envisioned to be an interfaith community space for Penang. The core objective was to promote harmony and foster interaction among Penang's diverse multiracial community by creating a central hub for religious activities and one-point events node. The intent of the state was twofold: to encourage awareness and understanding of the community's cultural celebrations and religious festivities and to foster religious tolerance.

To achieve this objective, an independent administrator and operator was needed to ensure smooth running of the space-sharing facility. Hence, the state government set up "Harmonico"—Penang Harmony Corporation Sdn. Bhd. as a subsidiary under the Penang Chief Minister's Corporation (CMI) to oversee day-to-day operations of the center.

Harmonico's mandate is as follows:

- To implement the policies formulated by the state government.
- To nurture and apply values of unity among the local community as well as promote harmony among them.
- To organize religious festivals for religions other than Islam at the state government level.
- To act as a cultural hub for all non-Muslim associations/organizations.

- To promote Penang as a diverse multireligion tourism destination.
- To manage the Harmony Centre.

To respond to the programmatic requirements of the proposed center, the site's traditional Malay-style residence, referred to as the lodge in this case study, was conserved and repurposed as a multipurpose hall. Complementing the heritage residence, a community hall was constructed next to the lodge. All public amenities, such as the community hall, function room, meeting rooms, and discussion area for community-held cultural/religious celebrations, are programmed into the existing 4,300 square-foot lodge. The new 2,800 square-foot community hall, complete with annex toilets, caters to larger events.

Site History

Wickham Lodge (completed 1880) is a single-story, elevated Malay-styled residence nestled in lush lawn. It was commissioned by Sir Henry Alexander Wickham, an adventurer best remembered for his role in procuring a large number of viable *Hevea brasiliensis* seeds, a rubber tree species, from Brazil in 1876. The seeds were shipped to England, where they were planted, nourished, and distributed to Southeast Asia, including British Malaya. The seedlings thrived, propelling Asia to the forefront in rubber production. For his contribution, Wickham was knighted by King George V in the 1920 Birthday Honours for services in connection with the rubber plantation industry in the Far East.

As an adventurer with a passion for the Far East, Wickham decided to build an authentic Malay-style wooden lodge as his holiday retreat in Penang's Ayer Itam area, which was scarcely inhabited at the time. He stayed at the lodge as part of his numerous visits to the Federated Malay States, such as Perak and Pahang, to inspect and monitor the quality of rubber trees. In his diary, he recorded evenings when he would often relax in the living room of the lodge, looking at the lush greenery of Penang with a glass of port or sherry in one hand and a cigar in the other.

Following Wickham's death in 1928, the lodge was soon left abandoned and fell into disrepair. With the establishment of the Penang Public Library next door, the lodge was refurbished and used as administrative offices for the Penang Integrity Institute (Institut Integriti Pulau Pinang). It was only with the establishment of the Penang Harmony Centre that Wickham Lodge was conserved, returning the site to its former glory, which includes a carefully designed and serene setting.[1]

At the start of the conservation project, it was determined that the building was structurally sound, but there were signs of dilapidation in the roof, rotten timber steps and column bases, and walls were damaged by rising damp. Existing timber paneled windows were covered by metal grilles in the interior, an addition for security reasons.

The layout of the house was altered over the years with additional partitions, glass windows, and an external staircase to suit the office function. Natural ventilation was minimal with most rooms converted to air-conditioned office spaces. The air was stagnant, the interior claustrophobic, and there was little or no visual connection to the outdoors.

The interior was dark and relied heavily on artificial lighting. The central zone of the house was windowless due to the extensive interior partitioning for various meeting rooms as well as a discussion area and store/filing room. Existing timber

1. The research contributing to the content in this section is credited to Enzo Sim.

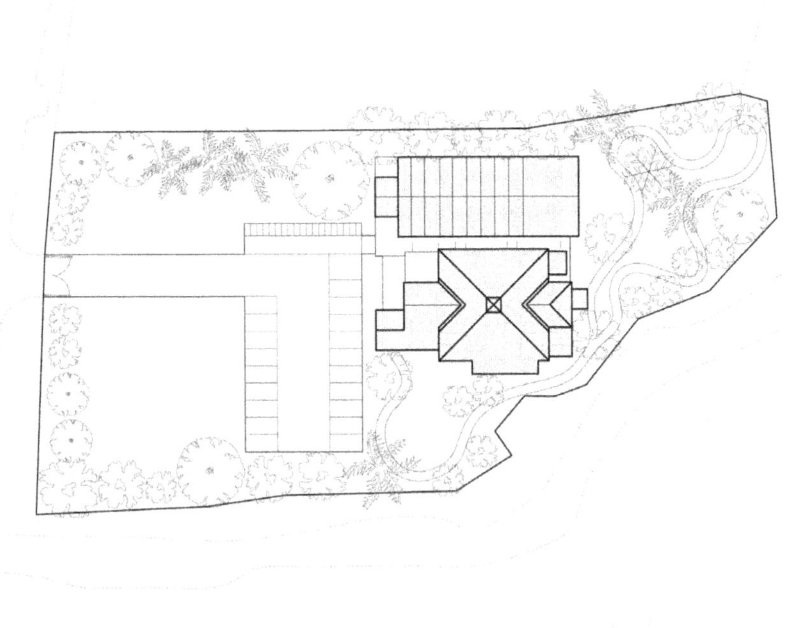

Figure 27.2: Site plan of Penang Harmony Centre. (Drawn by Ng Wai Shing based on materials from BEu Tan Architect.)

floorboards were covered with carpet. The numerous changes and modifications undermined the original character of the Malay-style lodge.

Project History

The Penang Harmony Centre project was an initiative by the Penang State government in 2018 under the former chief minister of Penang, Y. B. Lim Guan Eng. Its purpose is to provide a space for non-Islamic religious affairs and a community hall to accommodate religious events, cultural celebrations, community festivities, and functions of nongovernmental organizations.

The state of Penang has a rich legacy of temples and churches as well as clan and cultural associations. The state received numerous funding applications from various groups to build community halls for their respective places of worship and events. Instead of building multiple community halls (which would not be fully utilized due to seasonal celebrations), the approach used is one of space sharing, transforming an existing place into Penang Harmony Centre, a "one-stop" events hub for all cultural and religious groups.

The project uses the Penang state government's partnership model of 4Ps (public, private, people, and professional) to bring together the government implementing agency of the Penang Chief Minister's Corporation (CMI), religious communities, such as Malaysian Consultative Council of Buddhism, Christianity, Hinduism, Sikhism and Taoism (MCCBCHST), and professional consultants to create a first-of-its kind interfaith community building.

Development Environment

Due to its unique objective—a "space-sharing" concept of a cultural event hall—it received RM2.5 million in state funding.

Intervention

The design of Penang Harmony Centre was inspired by the notion of "going back to basics," employing rudimentary ventilation and daylighting strategies throughout the spaces. Aimed to be energy efficient, the repurposed timber lodge was redesigned to be cross-ventilated naturally along the longitudinal spine from the front to the back of the house by eliminating interior walls. The central jack roof was modified to allow passive stack ventilation, a vertical escape for hot air. As the interior spaces of the existing building were dark, the original interior timber stud walls were removed to bring in sunlight from the sides. In the middle zone of the lodge (the central foyer), a skylight feature was created by removing the existing ceiling panels and adding simple, clear roofing sheets to bring in natural lighting and ventilation. The roof structure remains exposed to celebrate the heritage character of the building.

The heritage lodge is complemented by a new 2,800 square-foot community hall with facilities that can cater events for up to two hundred persons. The roof line of the new community hall was borrowed from that of the existing lodge to ensure that the old and the new buildings would blend in a harmonious way. The building height of the new community hall was controlled to avoid overpowering the existing lodge in terms of scale and proportion. The roof form of the existing lodge was deliberately celebrated and kept intact. The community hall is distinguished by "accordion walls"—alternating rhythms of solid walls and clear glass windows—used on both sides of the hall. This has created soothing and uplifting indirect natural lighting. Strips of skylights, running from side to side, enhance the lighting quality. The extensive use of controlled natural lighting minimizes the need for artificial lighting during the day.

New landscaping has provided a kampung-like sense of place. Footpaths meander through garden shrubs, palm trees shade hidden pockets of gardens, and benches and swings act as focal points. To add some playfulness, a large-scale version of "snakes and ladders" using rustic concrete pavers is found beside the lodge.

Key Challenges

The ultimate challenge in this project was time and budget. The construction was fast-tracked to meet the stipulated completion date given by the client. The project was completed on time within six months. To meet the schedule, construction work had to run concurrently for both the lodge and the community hall. A small gap between the buildings made this possible. Given the existing site conditions (existing structure and mature trees), frequent inspections and site visits to solve unexpected problems were required.

Keeping Heritage Alive

The community hall was positioned carefully to avoid overpowering the lodge, a heritage building of importance. With a spacious front lawn, the new building could have been placed in front of the existing building. Yet the architect made the conscious decision to retain the central focus on the lodge. All existing trees on-site were retained to capture the sense of place.

Figure 27.3: Interior view of the lodge showing the newly inserted skylight, which brings in natural light. (Source: Tan Bee Eu.)

Figure 27.4: View of the lodge and the community hall showing the harmonious roof lines and scales of the structures. (Source: Tan Bee Eu.)

Long-Term Viability

The state government established a new government-linked entity named "Harmonico" as the operator of the facility. This is the key strategy that ensures the sustainability of the operation. (The vision of Harmonico is to instill universal values and spiritual understanding among different faiths as a foundation for an inclusive and harmonious society.)

Impact

Socio-environmental: The completed buildings are a hub and gathering place for a multiracial community. The project has also activated the streetscape of an otherwise abandoned site. Upon its successful completion, neighboring owners initiated upgrading of their respective compounds, seemingly inspired and motivated by Penang Harmony Centre.

Communities from various religious backgrounds can now hold large cultural/religious celebration events at a state-owned property with a heritage context. The center has been well received by these communities and highly acclaimed with several design accolades.

This humble project would not have been a success without the commitment from state government, consultants, and contractor, all working together to fast-track the project.

—Tan Bee Eu

Hin Bus Depot, Penang

Laurence Loh and Tan Shih Thoe

Hin Bus Depot is a game-changer project for Penang that represents architecture without architects. The project was undertaken and sustained by the private sector without any government funding. It demonstrates a clear understanding of heritage values and an intuitive ability for conservation through immersion, observation, and critical thinking.

Figure 28.1: Main street entrance of the original Hin Company Ltd. building. (Source: Thum Chia Chieh.)

Project Information

Address	31A, Jalan Gurdwara (formerly Brick Kiln Road), 10300 George Town, Penang, Malaysia
Original use	Bus depot for the Hin Company Ltd., Penang
Previous use	Informal car repair workshop and recycling yard
New use	Arts space
Heritage status	Category 2
Site area	Over 5,574 square meters
Project cost estimate	US$358,912 (RM1.5 million)*
Funding model	Private (Paradigm Realty Sdn. Bhd.)
Owner	Paradigm Realty Sdn. Bhd.
Developer	NA
Architect	None
Contractor	Owner
Project timeline	2013–2022

Note:
* The conversion rate is taken at US$1 = RM4.39.

Project Description

Hin Bus Depot consists of several stand-alone buildings and open social spaces within a single compound. The project goal was to revitalize this run-down former bus depot and maintenance compound by conserving and repurposing it as an arts space. Its objectives were as follows:

- To create an artist-led venue that supports independent artists and provides a space for unconventional art shows;
- To build a sustainable community that promotes and supports creative and social enterprises in a space that is accessible, inclusive, and affordable; and
- To connect to the general public and encourage stakeholder engagement with businesses and residents in the area.

The project introduced a completely new use for the former bus depot and maintenance compound, transforming it into a vibrant arts collective supported by multiple users. Presently, the space offers a variety of uses, such as galleries and open-air exhibition spaces, a performance deck, food and beverage outlets, and a well-received Sunday market.

Site History

Hin Company Ltd. was one of several private companies awarded motorbus licenses to operate on Penang Island in the aftermath of World War II. To house and maintain their then-famous Blue Buses, the Hin Company built the bus depot along Brick Kiln Road (now known as Jalan Gurdwara) in 1947. Constructed in an art deco style, a somewhat rare style of architecture amid George Town's Georgian and Victorian houses, the depot had its heyday in the 1970s and at that time was believed to be the most stylish bus depot in Penang. The depot withstood both time and change, but once left vacant, it soon suffered from the brutal tropical weather.[1]

After the bus service was terminated in the 1970s, the bus depot site was rented out as an informal car repair workshop and recycling yard. As there was little to no building maintenance during this period, the site gradually fell into serious disrepair and overall neglect. The terra-cotta roofs of several outbuildings had collapsed and the hard standing, where buses once stood, was littered with debris and rubbish.

In 2010, the Hin Bus Depot site came into the possession of its current owner, Paradigm Realty Sdn. Bhd., a holding company comprising of a board of directors and managing director at the helm. The owner adapted the site as an arts space. The revival of the bus depot and maintenance compound, which includes and celebrates the architecturally significant art deco façade of the main building that faces a prominent thoroughfare, serves as a reminder of the colonial government's efforts to restore George Town by reactivating essential public services after World War II. The Hin Bus Depot project is a testament to the love and loyalty displayed by business doyens after the war who contributed to the rebuilding efforts in George Town.

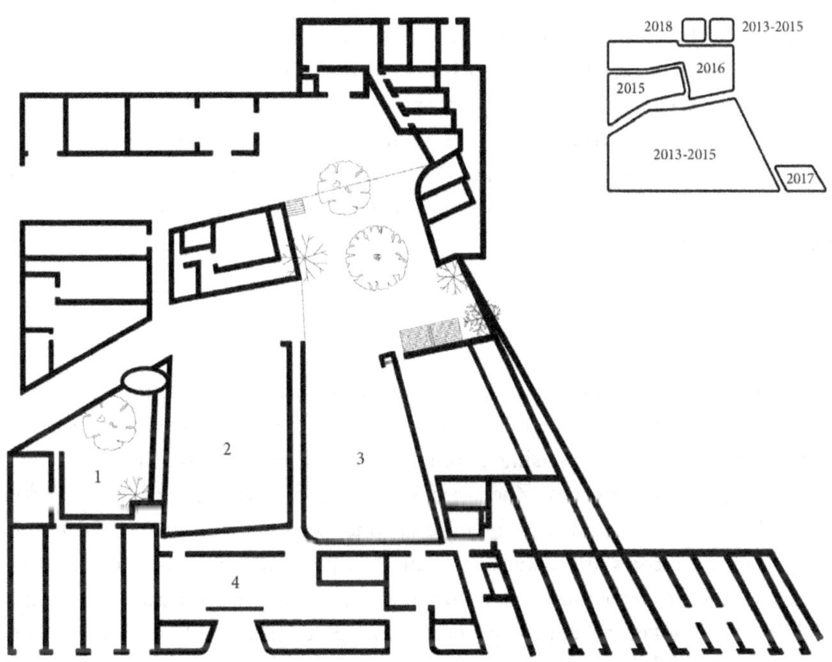

Figure 28.2: Site plan of Hin Bus Depot—1. Lawn (B), 2. Deck, 3. Lawn (A), 4. Gallery. Key plan showing the timeline of site revitalization. (Source: Drawn by Ng Wai Shing based on materials from Hin Bus Depot website.)

Project History

Hin Bus Depot's latest adaptive reuse story began with one artist's search for an exhibition location. Known as the man who introduced interactive street art murals to Penang, Ernest Zacharevic, a young Lithuanian artist, was searching for a space for his first solo exhibition. Numerous sites were dismissed until the shabby, abandoned Hin Company Bus Depot came to mind. It was a perfect match. His exhibition titled "Art Is Rubbish Is Art" opened its doors to the public on January 17, 2014, featuring works of art made from once-loved junk, discarded treasures, and overlooked street items. The venue itself seemed an integral part of the exhibition's theme—the

1. Hin Bus Depot, "Our Story," accessed May 23, 2022, https://hinbusdepot.com/story.html.

original structures of the once-abandoned depot had been retained, with only necessary repairs and additions made for operational purposes.[2]

The owner, in parallel, saw the exhibition as an incentive to kick-start a revival of the site. In the first phase of the project, RM350,000 was invested to repair the existing toilet blocks, build a raised timber deck under the maintenance shed (the Deck), and demolish the concrete slabs in the open area to create a parklike environment with trees and grass (the Lawn). Subsequently, the owner continued to progressively repair other stand-alone buildings on the site as existing tenants voluntarily moved out. Renewal works continue periodically as spaces are upgraded for new tenants.

Development Environment

The development and growth of the arts space at Hin Bus Depot was organic. The project did not receive direct subsidies or any incentives. There were no major renovation works involved, and only plans for minor works had to be submitted for approval to the local authority. Most of the funds required to sustain the site through difficult times were injected by the owner, who is the main sponsor of the project. The potential of the place as a creative community hub became evident after the staging of the art exhibition by Ernest Zacharevic. The owner chose to fund the exercise exclusively, including the running costs, until such time as the place became self-sufficient. The project was not viewed as a commercial enterprise per se. The growing popularity of Hin Bus Depot as an arts space vindicated the owner's decision, and it was on a good revenue trajectory until it had to shut down temporarily because of the COVID-19 pandemic. Today, Hin Bus Depot has quickly regained its position as a premier place for art activities in Penang.

Intervention

The adaptive reuse of Hin Bus Depot applied the principles of place making. From a heritage conservation perspective, the approach was to practice maximum retention and minimum intervention, using materials as found (whenever possible).

Taking a cue from Ernest Zacharevic's approach of celebrating shabby abandonment, the original structures of the once-abandoned bus depot were retained, with only necessary repairs and additions made for operational purposes. Users of the spaces were left to offer their interpretations of "minimum intervention." It could be said that the low-key bohemian approach with no design controls was instrumental in enticing the "right" type of artistic tenants to the place. Surprisingly, the freedom of interpretation did not create inappropriate interventions as they were often guided by precedents on site. Many of these were set by the owner's initial interventions to the place.

Other than essential roof work and repairing the toilets, only minimal refurbishment was done to preserve the heritage significance and original design of the bus depot. Even the paint on the walls was kept intact to reflect the layers of stories related to the building complex over the years, documenting its transformation from a bus depot to an informal car repair workshop and a recycling yard, and now an arts space.

Today, the building complex offers a variety of spaces (Figure 28.2). The Gallery, where most of the art exhibitions are accommodated, occupies the Art Deco Building

2. Hin Bus Depot, "Our Story."

Figure 28.3: View of the deck that is used as a performance stage, a festive marketplace, and a multipurpose space for events. (Source: Tan Shih Thoe.)

facing Jalan Gurdwara. The Deck—a covered, raised space behind the Gallery—is where most performances, festivals, and events take place (Figure 28.3). Between the Gallery and the Deck, the existing blacktop bus driveway has been turfed and planted with trees to provide a green refuge (the Lawns) for visitors to experience some "peace and quiet" away from the busy main road. The Hin Bus Depot project adopted two rain trees from a nearby development site in 2018, which provide ample shade and serve as a popular space for visitors.

The arts space's longest running program is the Hin Market, a Sunday market for artists, crafters, designers, and makers to showcase and sell their products. Designed for accessibility, Hin Market is open to small businesses for a low fee and provides free entrance to the public. Starting with six stalls at the end of 2015, it now hosts seventy stalls each weekend, with a visitor count of more than 1,200. Over the years, Hin Market has produced successful entrepreneurs who have set up their own cafés, restaurants, shops, and studios both within the site as well as in other parts of Penang.

The interventions introduced in the project were derived from studies of best-practice exemplars in Penang—for example, Cheong Fatt Tze (Blue Mansion)—coupled with the owner's immersion and observational skills in the heritage milieu from a very early age. The project did not employ architects or designers, but the design responded intuitively to the needs of the site.

Key Challenge

- The biggest revitalization challenge was the programming of the spaces to ensure that vibrancy was kept at a high-energy level. The nonstop event creation and communication process proved to be a never-ending exercise. It took the owner-cum-promoter five years of intensive management to arrive at a commercially self-sustaining level and to see Hin Bus Depot grow as a destination.

Keeping Heritage Alive

The architectural and historical values of Hin Bus Depot have been conserved through retention of the plan and most of the permanent structures within the site.

The spirit of the place was recaptured when the site was activated with a contemporary use that imbued the place with qualities that encouraged creative responses and rejuvenated the neighborhood. Nothing in a city exists in isolation except when it is disconnected from its urban ecology. The intention of the project was to reverse this condition. The approach used was incremental renewal that ensured controlled gentrification with local characteristics.

The adaptive reuse concept of Hin Bus Depot, which includes the subtle transformation of the original spaces through art installations, food and beverage outlets, and a performance deck under a double-volume, steel-frame structure (constructed originally as a maintenance shed)—and all coming off a green open space—represents an intuitive interpretation of the site and its potential. By creating unique touchpoints that turned a derelict site built for utilitarian purposes into a place with spirit that would draw people to it from all walks of life, the project demonstrated a clear understanding of the cultural heritage values of the bus depot site and its sense of place.

The Hin Bus Depot experience has left an indelible impression on the owner, especially the managing director, who has been the driving force behind the art space concept. The project has given him a sense of purpose, of serving a worthwhile cause focused on nurturing a younger generation of artists full of idealism and unfettered ideas, untainted by economic imperatives and the call of commercial gallery owners. The vision of harnessing raw talent, positioning the property in a larger landscape, and being a catalyst for change had inexplicable appeal that morphed into conviction. He is committed to expanding the initiative, while maintaining the original objectives.

Long-Term Viability

The hidden development potential of the site, its strategic location, and its heritage design were what attracted the present owner to purchase the property. All the shareholders of the holding company (Paradigm Realty Sdn. Bhd.) of Hin Bus Depot grew up in the historic core of George Town. They appreciate its beauty, understand the rhythms of the city, the organic pace of evolution and growth, and the potential for the property to increase significantly in value over the long term. In this sense, survival of Hin Bus Depot in its present form for several decades is ensured.

With this approach, the owner adapted the former bus depot site as an arts space, leasing out spaces in the medium term to tenants, who would add value to the property in its present form and make it an attractive place while also enhancing the surrounding area. Funding support was extended by the owner, where necessary, to upgrade the premises to a respectable standard commensurate with the agreed use.

Hin Bus Depot also rents out some of its larger spaces—especially the Gallery, Deck, and Lawns—for corporate events to generate revenue. Preferential rates are often given to social enterprises whose goals align with those of creating a sustainable community and providing a platform for artistic execution. Hin Bus Depot works with tenants first to support the needs of these events, including audiovisual support and catering, before sourcing for external vendors, where necessary.

Hin Bus Depot as an arts space extraordinaire has developed into a viable and socially inclusive, alternative creativity center and visitor attraction that recognizes the development potential of artists, makers, and performers. It offers space for freedom of expression and space to those needing to experiment without regulation and constraints. It is a physical asset and management model that actively contributes to the talent pool in the creative sector in Penang. This ensures that it continues to be socially sustainable and relevant for as long as there is belief and commitment.

Impact

Economic: As a social enterprise, Hin Bus Depot is not driven by balance sheets and rates of return. Its indirect economic impact is manifested in the number of start-ups that have grown into established businesses, especially in the cultural creative industry locally. Several of the small weekend stall holders have opened permanent shops of their own in Penang and artists their own galleries and studios. A restaurant that took up a double-story building in Hin Bus Depot is now one of the top twenty restaurants in Malaysia.[3]

Environmental: Environmentally, the public realm in its vicinity has improved with tree planting on the street and upgrading works. The adaptive reuse of Hin Bus Depot has potential to be a catalyst for rejuvenating the surrounding area. The heritage values and attributes embedded in the place reinforce the outstanding universal values of the George Town World Heritage Site. It is an integral part of the historical city's planning morphology.

Social: The social impact is of the highest order in relation to the neighborhood and the arts and creative community and Penang as a whole. Hin Bus Depot serves a need that is not met well by established state institutions with their cumbersome legal and regulated frameworks. As a high-profile destination, local businesses see the advantage of association with the project or locating themselves in the neighborhood. It has an organic, gradual uplifting effect and has given the area a sense of identity. With the influx of visitors, especially on weekends, its fame and leadership status has been enhanced, especially through its exposure on social media platforms.

To create a broader impact, the Hin Bus Depot management aspires to be more aggressive and ambitious in its programming by reaching out to other similar art spaces in the region, to partake in exchanges and partnerships on a larger platform, to internationalize content and activities in order to connect with a larger audience. In the long run, the aim is to enlarge the Hin Bus Depot company's social enterprise

Figure 28.4: Sunday market at the revitalized Hin Bus Depot. (Source: Hin Bus Depot.)

3. Samantha Lim, "The Top 20 Restaurants in Malaysia in 2021," *Tatler Asia Group*, January 21, 2021, https://www.tatlerasia.com/dining/awards/the-top-20-restaurants-in-malaysia-this-2021.

portfolio to include other functions and enterprises as well as reach out to funding sources to help activate and finance initiatives and projects that sustain its primary vision.

> **It is fortunate that such an exciting site was bought by a Penang family who believes in Penang, its legacies and its histories, its special DNA, and is prepared to contribute to its long-term future by using the power of art to engage with the younger generations and to continue to be part of the change.**
>
> **—Tan Shih Thoe**

Bibliography

Hin Bus Depot. "Hin Bus Depot." Accessed May 23, 2022. https://hinbusdepot.com/index.html.

Lim, Samantha. "The Top 20 Restaurants in Malaysia in 2021." *Tatler Asia Group*, January 21, 2021. https://www.tatlerasia.com/dining/awards/the-top-20-restaurants-in-malaysia-this-2021.

Khoo, Suet Leng. "Creative Transmission and Industrialization of Traditional Crafts: Lessons from the Creative City of Kanazawa, Japan." *International Journal of Crafts and Folk Art* 2 (2021): 88–115.

Conclusion

Lavina Ahuja and Lynne D. DiStefano

Introduction

Asia is unique—the way we built, inhabit, and conserve are all different from the rest of the world. During the early days of "formal" conservation practice, most documents with guidelines on best practice had Eurocentric views. This has changed and continues to change, as we now see a number of Asia-based conservation guidelines (or Asian adaptations of existing guidelines). One of the purposes of the two books—*Asian Revitalization* and *Revitalization in Aisa*—is to highlight the specific challenges faced in Asian urban centers when it comes to conserving and revitalizing built heritage. These challenges can range from economic factors, such as resource availability, environmental factors, such as Asia's diverse climate and its related impacts, to social factors, such as poverty and population explosion. Yet within such unique contexts, noteworthy and standard-setting examples of adaptive reuse have emerged. Something is being done right in these places and the impact is unfolding. Capturing these Asian stories is the primary aim of the two books.

Revitalization in Asia considers conservation, specifically adaptive reuse, in three urban centers—Macao (SAR, China), Mumbai (India), and Penang (Malaysia). The book is a continuation and expansion of *Asian Revitalization*, which looks at adaptive reuse in Hong Kong (SAR, China), Shanghai (China), and Singapore. The main objectives of this book are twofold: establishing a broader understanding of adaptive reuse against the background of a sustainability framework (in this case, the Sustainable Development Goals [SDGs]) and providing examples of adaptive reuse in three Asian urban centers. The examples are set within the context of the conservation initiatives of each place, thus allowing a holistic understanding and (possibly) appreciation for the projects. In this concluding chapter, the theme of sustainability is summarized by revisiting the SDGs as a framework that can be applied in conservation practice, and the conservation efforts of three urban centers (Macao, Mumbai, and Penang) are compared. Key takeaways on the broadened scope of the term "adaptive reuse" are suggested. The way forward is reflected on with thought-provoking questions and deliberations.

Sustainability in Adaptive Reuse Practice

As mentioned in the "Introduction" of this book, "heritage is increasingly seen as an integral pillar for sustainable development in all its dimensions, and therefore deeply relevant to everyone. Indeed, the 2030 Agenda for Sustainable Development recognizes heritage, both cultural and natural, as a fundamental part of the global development agenda."[1] This book aligns itself with the Sustainable Development Goals (SDGs) as a theoretical basis for sustainability. The SDGs form an international framework, which practitioners across a number of sectors are aiming to meet through plans and actions. As important as the SDGs are, they are complicated, lying in a realm that seems distant from conservation practice. It is often seen as a challenge to understand and distill the SDGs into practical action plans that have cultural heritage as their primary focus. The opening essays of this book draw reference to specific SDGs to emphasize the applicability of certain goals/targets. However, the case studies chalk out a broader sustainability approach. As tempting as it may seem, using and promoting the SDGs as a checklist of seventeen goals and 169 targets is not the intention of this framework or this book.

However, the SDGs can broaden our understanding of the three dimensions (pillars) of sustainability—economic, environmental, and social (it would be helpful to refer to Figure 1.1 in the Introduction). In regard to the economic dimension, the SDGs push the envelope of this dimension to include how cultural heritage can promote new forms of productivity and socioeconomic development. In some cases, cultural heritage can contribute to enhancing the identity of a place and eventually branding it. The example of Nizamuddin Urban Renewal Initiative (elaborated in the essay "Nizamuddin Urban Renewal Initiative: Socioeconomic Sustainability through Conservation") is a standard-setting example of how cultural heritage programs can contribute to sustainability. The case study demonstrates that "conservation of tangible heritage and incorporating intangible heritage in the process—while improving people's quality of life—can create a sustainable heritage management program that contributes to the SDGs."[2] On the other hand, Fergus T. Maclaren's essay, "Creating Sustainable Urban Visitor Economies: Adaptive Reuse of Asian Cultural Heritage Places for Tourism," is a candid assessment of the impact of tourism on heritage assets. The essay reminds us that catering to tourists may be seen as an "easy win," but there is a real risk that such actions can destroy the very thing it showcases. Although heritage can be (and should be) leveraged for economic sustainability, the approach needs to be thoughtful and responsive to the intrinsic character of each heritage place.

Positioning the environmental dimension within the framework of the SDGs suggests, among other things, strengthening the nature-culture link of cultural heritage places, including building resilience in the face of climate change, natural disasters, and so forth, by reducing vulnerabilities. The Lai Chi Wo project, discussed in the essay "Transforming a Dilapidated Rural Village into a Nature-Culture Interface for Social-Ecological Sustainability: Lai Chi Wo, Hong Kong," focuses on the importance of recognizing and reinforcing the nature-culture relationship that involves a number of actors, especially the local community. "The Lai Chi Wo project demonstrates that cultural landscapes can generate tremendous value for society—promoting social inclusion and rural-urban interaction, fostering green economic

1. UNESCO, *Asia Conserved Volume III: Lessons Learned from the UNESCO Asia-Pacific Awards for Cultural Heritage Conservation (2010–2014)*, ed. William Chapman (Bangkok: UNESCO, 2019), 324.
2. Quoted by Sharif Shams Imon in the essay "Nizamuddin Urban Renewal Initiative: Socioeconomic Sustainability through Conservation," which is included in this book.

development, and helping to enhance the overall well-being of both the local community and society at large."[3] Other aspects of the environmental dimension are those of embodied energy and operational energy. Most projects discussed in this book demonstrate how adaptive reuse, when compared with demolition and rebuilding, retains the embodied energy of a place. However, there are often challenges with long-term performance of adaptive reuse projects with regard to operational energy. In *Asian Revitalization*, Donovan Rypkema's essay titled "Measuring the Impacts: Making a Case for the Adaptive Reuse of Heritage Buildings" discusses environmental internal metrics for adapting heritage buildings. This sheds light on a quantitative approach to adaptive reuse using embodied energy as a unit of measurement. The application of this approach can be instructive in long-term planning and management of heritage places. Eventually, the way forward is to build resilience against environmental factors, which can be done if all actors involved in a city's mechanics work alongside each other with a sustainability mindset.

As for the social dimension, the SDGs encourage wider understanding of the concept by questioning how future generations can be engaged in maintaining the continuity of cultural heritage and how it can become a response to the needs of local communities (including marginalized minority communities). The "R and R, Mumbai" case study shows that the seemingly simple intervention of reclaiming social space can build a community's resilience and contribute to its cultural continuum.

In this book, although specific SDGs are mentioned in several of the essays, the case studies address sustainability broadly, using the more familiar terms of economic, environmental, and social sustainability. It is worth mentioning once again, the SDGs are not meant to be used as a checklist. In fact, in some cases the SDGs were introduced well after the project completion dates. The approach of this book is to demonstrate how sustainable actions—whether they are implied or articulated—are integral to each successful project, reflecting a sustainability approach rather than the application of specific SDGs. This approach reinforces the growing awareness that culture has a role to play in all seventeen SDGs (as illustrated in the ICOMOS publication *Heritage and the Sustainable Development Goals: Policy Guidance for Heritage and Development Actors*) and not only SDG 11—Sustainable Cities and Communities and, more specifically, target 11.4: "Strengthen efforts to protect and safeguard the world's cultural and natural heritage." This approach not only acknowledges the importance of the SDGs but also seeks to make their intent more accessible and better understood through sustainability clusters under the three dimensions of sustainability.

Macao, Mumbai, and Penang

Looking at the three centers chosen for this book, each has its own significance, stories, and complexities. In terms of adaptive reuse, each center has its own trajectory, but there are commonalities as well as differences between them. All places focus on identifying—or reinforcing—appropriate uses for existing places of community, regional, or national importance. Some of the projects have become standard-setting examples, others have contributed more quietly to the vitality of communities. In all cases, the objective has been to conserve as much of the building and structural fabric as possible or to revive spaces for public enjoyment.

3. Quoted by Hiu Lai Chick, Katie in the essay "Transforming a Dilapidated Rural Village into a Nature-Culture Interface for Social-Ecological Sustainability: Lai Chi Wo, Hong Kong," which is included in this book.

Differences are seen in the level of community involvement (from bottom up to top down), the funding model (from privately or publicly funded to public-private partnerships), the management structure (from governmental departments to privately owned and operated enterprises), and the scale (from small-scale projects to community-wide initiatives). For Macao, the conservation initiative is largely government led. The World Heritage listing of the Historic Centre of Macao has been a contributing factor to the recognition and conservation, often through adaptive reuse, of the heritage grain of the city. In Mumbai and Penang, the conservation movement gained momentum with the power of civic voices, and sometimes these voices were loud. Key actors have contributed to the survival of heritage in both of these urban centers. A notable difference is that in Penang, the drive to inscribe George Town on the World Heritage list was spearheaded by the government and supported by heritage practitioners and thinkers. In Mumbai, the nomination dossier for the World Heritage listing of the Victorian Gothic and Art Deco Ensembles of Mumbai was drafted by citizen groups and civil society organizations.

Adaptive reuse is not articulated as a distinct government policy in many of the places (although Mumbai's Heritage Regulations mention it), but it is embedded in how each urban center has found—and continues to find—new (and sometimes continuing) uses for a broad cross-section of officially or unofficially valued buildings, structures, and spaces. Heritage preservation and revitalization are the primary push for almost all of the cases featured in this book. An important and sometimes unintentional outcome is a project's contribution to all three dimensions of sustainability.

Looking at the three urban centers of this book in terms of sustainable conservation practice, Penang shows structured and clear long-term visions for most of its projects. In Mumbai, the urgency to save heritage from disappearing often supersedes the amount of thought and time that could go into planning long-term sustainability actions and leveraging the maximum impact of projects. However, many projects have emerged with noteworthy sustainable impact, some intentional and some happy coincidences. In Macao, the adaptive reuse of heritage as museums is still a popular choice. Their long-term sustainability and relevance to societal needs can be debated.

There is much to learn from the three centers and much they can learn from each other. The common thread that emerges is that the recognition of culture—and cultural heritage by extension—can indeed be a driver for sustainable development, not only within site boundaries but also beyond.

Revitalization: More than Adaptive Reuse

In *Asian Revitalization*, the "Introduction" mentions that "the term 'adaptive reuse' generally implies both change of use and change to the fabric of the place."[4] Through the research and writing of this book, a certain elasticity in the use of the term "adaptive reuse" has emerged, suggesting that "revitalization" can be viewed as an umbrella term, with adaptive reuse as one of its implementation instruments. Places, as seen in the case study examples chosen for this book, can be revitalized with little change of use or change to the fabric of the place. The long-term goal is to promote a conservation practice that conforms to principles of sustainable development and is not limited by textbook definitions of approaches and interventions.

---

4. Katie Cummer and Lynne D. DiStefano, eds., *Asian Revitalization: Adaptive Reuse in Hong Kong, Shanghai, and Singapore* (Hong Kong: Hong Kong University Press, 2021).

Closing Thoughts

Although different perspectives have shaped this book, there is more that can be said. It is often championed that "the greenest building is one that is already built," yet one of the conundrums of adaptive reuse, especially in urban areas facing development, is how best to conserve—and reuse—existing heritage resources that escape demolition. The adverse impact of tall buildings in historical areas is suggested through the essays of this book, but there are inevitable consequences of a low-height approach, too. In *Asian Revitalization*, Michael Turner's essay "Adaptive Reuse within Urban Areas" discusses the considerations of adaptive reuse in urban contexts. While the essay concludes with insightful observations, there is more to be explored on the topic, particularly about the impact of urban heritage conservation on the existing infrastructure of a city.

Another challenging aspect of urban conservation is when heritage places are destined to become part of a new building or building complex. How much of the original fabric needs to be retained? Is an exterior wall or two enough? Can the interior space be reconfigured? What is an acceptable use? Ultimately, when there are so many changes, the original buildings and structures are unrecognizable. They have become stage sets, possibly providing human scale but ultimately adding little to environmental and social sustainability. Economic sustainability is another matter as the partially integrated buildings and structures can contribute—on a superficial level—to the financial success of a development.

What is the answer? There is no one-size-fits-all answer; each jurisdiction needs to tailor its response to such challenges, which requires concentrated thought, just as Geddes recommended 150 years ago. Here is where the notion of a "values-based approach" in heritage management is crucial. This approach suggests that heritage management should be based on understanding the place and incorporating a wider range of values into the decision-making process (Figure 29.1).

A values-based approach promotes thoughtful management of change rather than freezing heritage in its time. For urban centers, an incremental approach is recommended, where cities evolve over time rather than transform rapidly (although there are some situations that demand a transformative approach in response to pressing needs, particularly in the wake of natural disasters). The case studies covered in this book showcase a values-based approach; however, more needs be said about the long-term management and planning of heritage that is adaptively reused.

Figure 29.1: Model for a values-based approach to heritage management. (Drawn by Lavina Ahuja based on Kate Clark's original diagram.)

Adaptive reuse as a mainstream approach has increasingly gained traction. At the time of writing, the Museum of Modern Art (MOMA) is featuring an exhibition called "Reuse, Renew, Recycle: Recent Architecture from China." As described on MOMA's website, the exhibit offers "bold visions for social and environmental sustainability" as shared by a new generation of Chinese architects.[5] In 2021, Anne Lacaton and Jean-Philippe Vassal received the Pritzker Architecture Prize for their "reverence for pre-existing buildings," among other accomplishments.[6]

It is now clear that adaptive reuse—in all its manifestations—is a matter of importance, if not urgency. It is also a matter of building resilience to devastating worldwide events—from floods and forest fires to pandemics and wars (unfortunately, all these events were witnessed during the time of writing this book). Heritage and adaptive reuse in particular can be, and should be, leveraged to build a sustainable future that contributes to the economic, environmental, and social well-being of all.

Bibliography

Clark, Kate. "The Shift Toward Values in UK Heritage Practice." Values in Heritage Management: Emerging Approaches and Research Directions, September 9, 2019. https://www.getty.edu/publications/heritagemanagement/part-two/5/.

Cummer, Katie, and Lynne D. DiStefano, eds. *Asian Revitalization: Adaptive Reuse in Hong Kong, Shanghai, and Singapore*. Hong Kong: Hong Kong University Press, 2021.

Labadi, Sophia, Francesca Giliberto, Ilaria Rosetti, Linda Shetabi, and Ege Yildirim. *Heritage and the Sustainable Development Goals: Policy Guidance for Heritage and Development Actors*. Paris: ICOMOS, 2021. https://www.icomos.org/images/DOCUMENTS/Secretariat/2021/SDG/ICOMOS_SDGs_Policy_Guidance_2021.pdf.

Pritzker Architecture Prize. "Anne Lacaton and Jean-Philippe Vassal." Accessed June 5, 2023. https://www.pritzkerprize.com/laureates/anne-lacaton-and-jean-philippe-vassal#laureate-page-2286.

Museum of Modern Art. "Reuse, Renew, Recycle: Recent Architecture from China: MOMA." Accessed June 5, 2023. https://www.moma.org/calendar/exhibitions/5342.

UNESCO. *Asia Conserved Volume III: Lessons Learned from the UNESCO Asia-Pacific Awards for Cultural Heritage Conservation (2010–2014)*. Edited by William Chapman. Bangkok: UNESCO, 2019.

5. Museum of Modern Art, "Reuse, Renew, Recycle: Recent Architecture from China: MOMA," accessed June 5, 2023, https://www.moma.org/calendar/exhibitions/5342.
6. Pritzker Architecture Prize, "Anne Lacaton and Jean-Philippe Vassal," accessed June 5, 2023, https://www.pritzkerprize.com/laureates/anne-lacaton-and-jean-philippe-vassal#laureate-page-2286.

Index